What a marvelous author Chris Wright is! Here you get the distilled insight of someone who knows mission and knows the Scriptures—and because he is an Old Testament specialist, he gives that major part of the Scriptures the prominence it deserves, even (especially?) when we are thinking about a subject such as mission that might seem to belong to the New Testament. And he doesn't confine himself to scriptural themes but enables us to get inside lots of particular Scriptures, all in easily manageable chunks. What do theology and mission have to do with each other? This book powerfully answers the question.

—JOHN GOLDINGAY, David Allan Hubbard Professor of Old Testament, Fuller Theological Seminary

This is the first volume in a new series on biblical theology. It is extraordinarily readable, written by a preacher who knows how to communicate simply, clearly, and fascinatingly. It is refreshingly adventurous, as it explores the theme of mission in biblical passages where you might not have expected to find it. It is excitingly controversial in discussing such matters as the relation of care for the planet to evangelism, but always in an irenic manner. It is also remarkably practical, being concerned with the theological underpinning for the church's action in the world. It is surprisingly relevant, concerned as it is with the central story of God's mission to the world as the template that must shape the work of the church. It is outstandingly down-to-earth in showing how our daily lives must be outworkings of our missionary calling. It is thus eminently commendable both for its own sake and also as setting a high standard for the other volumes to follow in this series.

—I. HOWARD MARSHALL, Emeritus Professor of New Testament, University of Aberdeen

The Mission of God's People is more than a biblical theology. It is a journey through the call God has given to his people to impact the world in the way God desires. Lausanne made famous the dictum, *The whole church is to take the whole gospel to the whole world*. Wright gives us the whole Bible with a whole theology for the whole task of mission tied to creation, redemption, and new creation. The point: we should know where we are going and why. This book brings us there very nicely, fully using both Testaments, and even gives us questions to reflect upon in order to move us to action. Well done.

—DARRELL L. BOCK, Research Professor of New Testament Studies, Dallas Theological Seminary

If Chris Wright's *Mission of God's People* is a harbinger of things to come in Zondervan's new series, Biblical Theology for Life, we are in for a treat. As the first in this series, this volume not only serves as a delightful sequel and complement to his highly acclaimed *The Mission of God*, but it has also put his holistic interpretation of the Scriptures into the hands of laypeople. This is biblical theology at its best. For too long biblical scholars, theologians, and pastors have driven a wedge between the Hebrew Bible and the Christian New Testament by focusing on the discontinuities. Wright has shown us another way. Through his comprehensive reading of the whole Bible, he offers a robust portrayal of Israel's mission and our own. Just as Israel was called and sent out into the world to give witness to the grace of "the LORD" (Yahweh), so we are "the people whom God has loved, chosen, redeemed, shaped and sent into the world in the name of Christ" (p. 433). Thank you, Chris, for showing us that God's election is not about us; it is about the world. May this work inspire his church to greater faithfulness in giving verbal witness to God's redemptive grace for the cosmos, but also to greater ethical faithfulness as we embody his grace in the microcosms in which we live.

—DANIEL I. BLOCK, Gunther H. Knoedler Professor of Old Testament, Wheaton College Graduate School

How do we help the Christian community stand up for the faith in daily conversation and promote the gospel with the whole of life? The most popular method, though the least effective, is simply to "command" our people to speak more boldly and live more zealously. Chris Wright shows another way, and I think it's the only way to enthuse our people to give their all to God's mission. He tells us the story, from Genesis to Revelation, of God's passion to fill the earth and to bless the nations, and he tells it in such a way that none of us, whether Christian leader or new believer, could fail to sense the excitement, gravity, and privilege of being involved in the mission of God's people.

—JOHN DICKSON, Director, Centre for Public Christianity; Senior Research Fellow, Department of Ancient History, Macquarie University

Following his landmark book, *The Mission of God*, Christopher Wright shows in *The Mission of God's People* that grounding missions practice in the prior action and plan of God does not render the church static or passive. In this masterful survey, Wright demonstrates decisively what happens when the whole church starts reading the whole Bible and reflecting the full scope of God's good news in all our life and witness in the world. This is the long-awaited road map that moves missions from the practice of a few elite professionals to the faithful witness of all of God's children. If want to help your church become a missional church, I cannot think of a better place to begin that journey than this book. I assure you, you will discover afresh who you are in Christ and what you are here for!

—TIMOTHY C. TENNENT, President and Professor of World Christianity, Asbury Theological Seminary

A wonderfully kaleidoscopic biblical overview of the privileged role afforded to all of God's people in fulfilling the Missio Dei in the world. Chris Wright demonstrates that the theme of the mission of God and his people is a prominent and unmistakable thread running through the elaborate tapestry of the whole of Scripture. In so doing, he provides a ringing affirmation that it is the responsibility of the whole church to bear witness to Christ and his kingdom in every area of the world geographically, as well as in every sphere of society.

—LINDSAY BROWN, International Director, Lausanne Movement for World Evangelization

BIBLICAL THEOLOGY FOR LIFE

THE **MISSION** OF **GOD'S PEOPLE**

*A Biblical Theology of
the Church's Mission*

CHRISTOPHER J. H. WRIGHT

general editor JONATHAN LUNDE

ZONDERVAN®

ZONDERVAN.com/
AUTHORTRACKER
follow your favorite authors

ZONDERVAN

The Mission of God's People
Copyright © 2010 by Langham Partnership International

This title is also available as a Zondervan ebook. Visit www.zondervan.com/ebooks.

This title is also available in a Zondervan audio edition. Visit www.zondervan.fm.

Requests for information should be addressed to:

Zondervan, *Grand Rapids, Michigan 49530*

Library of Congress Cataloging-in-Publication Data

Wright, Christopher J. H.
    The mission of God's people : a biblical theology of the church's mission / Christopher J. H. Wright.
      p. cm.
    Includes bibliographical references and index.
    ISBN 978-0-310-29112-1 (softcover)
    1. Mission of the church. 2. Missions. 3. Church work. I. Title.
  BV601.58.W75 2010
  262'.7—dc22
                                               2010004714

Cover design: Rob Monacelli
Cover photography: David Sacks/Getty Images
Interior design: Matthew Van Zomeren

Printed in the United States of America

11 12 13 14 15 15 16 17 18 19 /DCI/ 29 28 27 26 25 24 23 22 21 20 19 18 17 16 15 14 13 12 11 10 9 8 7

For
Suzy and Ed

All the royalties from this book have been irrevocably assigned to Langham Literature (formerly the Evangelical Literature Trust).

Langham Literature is a programme of the Langham Partnership International, founded by John Stott. Chris Wright is the International Director.

Langham Literature distributes evangelical books to pastors, theological students and seminary libraries in the Majority World, and fosters the writing and publishing of Christian literature in many regional languages.

For further information on Langham Literature, and the other programmes of LPI, visit the website at **www.langhampartnership.org**

In the USA, the national member of the Langham Partnership International is John Stott Ministries. Visit the JSM website at: **www.johnstott.org**

langham partnership international
EQUIPPING A NEW GENERATION OF BIBLE TEACHERS

CONTENTS

DETAILED TABLE OF CONTENTS

REFLECTING ON RELEVANCE

SERIES PREFACE

The question "What does the Bible have to say about that?" is, in essence, what the Biblical Theology for Life series is all about. Not unlike other biblical explorations of various topics, the volumes in this series articulate various themes in biblical theology, but they always do so with the "So what?" question rumbling about and demanding to be answered. Too often, books on biblical theology have focused mainly on *description*—simply discerning the teachings of the biblical literature on a particular topic. But contributors to this series seek to straddle both the world of the text and the world in which we live.

This means that their descriptions of biblical theology will always be understood as the important *first* step in their task, which will not be completed until they draw out that theology's practical implications for the contemporary context. Contributors therefore engage both in the *description* of biblical theology and in its contemporary *contextualization*, accosting the reader's perspective and fostering application, transformation, and growth. It is our hope that these informed insights of evangelical biblical scholarship will increasingly become enfleshed in the sermons and discussions that transpire each week in places of worship, in living rooms where Bible studies gather, and in classrooms around the world. We hope that this series will lead to personal transformation and practical application in real life.

Every volume in this series has the same basic structure. In the first section, entitled "Queuing the Questions," authors introduce the main questions they seek to address in their books. Raising these questions enables you to see clearly from the outset what each book will be pursuing, inviting you to participate in the process of discovery along the way. In the second section, "Arriving at Answers," authors develop the biblical theology of the topic they address, focusing their attention on specific biblical texts and constructing answers to the questions introduced in section one. In the concluding "Reflecting on Relevance" section, authors contextualize their biblical theological insights, discussing specific ways in which the theology presented in their books addresses contemporary situations and issues, giving you opportunities to consider how you might live out that theology in the world today.

Long before you make it to the "Reflecting on Relevance" section, however, we encourage you to wrestle with the implications of the biblical theology being described by considering the "Relevant Questions" that conclude each chapter. Frequent sidebars spice up your experience, supplementing the main discussion with significant quotations, illustrative historical or contemporary data, and fuller explanations of the content.

In sum, the goal of the Biblical Theology for Life series is communicated by its title. On the one hand, its books mine the Bible for theology that addresses a wide range of topics, so that you may know "the only true God, and Jesus Christ, whom [he] sent" (John 17:3). On the other hand, contributing authors contextualize this theology in ways that allow the *life*-giving Word (John 1:4; 20:31) to speak into and transform contemporary *life*.

Series Editor
Jonathan Lunde

PREFACE

"So this is the simplified version of *The Mission of God,* then?" is a comment I have heard quite often while working on this book, and have needed to correct, and do so again here. It is true that a few years ago I published *The Mission of God: Unlocking the Bible's Grand Narrative*[1] and, true, that is a rather big book. The difference between it and this one, however, is much more than just their relative size.

In *The Mission of God* I was arguing for a missional hermeneutic of the whole Bible. My concern was to ask if it is possible and right for Christians to read their whole Bible from the perspective of the mission of God and what happens when they do. The argument of that book is that all the great sections of the canon of Scripture, all the great episodes of the Bible story, all the great doctrines of the biblical faith, cohere around the Bible's central character—the living God and his grand plan and purpose for the whole of creation. The mission of God is what unifies the Bible from creation to new creation. That book lays the foundation for this one.

In this book, I am asking the "so what?" question on behalf of those of us whom this God of the Bible has called into saving and covenant relationship with himself—the church, the people of God from Abraham to the population of the city of God in Revelation. Who are we and what are we here for? If the Bible renders to us the grand mission of God through all generations of history, what does it tell us about the mission of God's *people* in each generation, including our own? What is *our* mission?

This specific focus on the mission of the church means that we will not be surveying every biblical doctrine that could be said to be relevant to mission in general. There are many of those. For example, the nature of the incarnation, the doctrine of the atonement, the great truth of the resurrection, the doctrine of judgment, the doctrine of God's sovereign providence, the Trinity—all these have huge implications in a broader theology of mission. And they will also doubtless be topics for other books in this series on Biblical Theology for Life. I have not tried to address them all, except as they emerge naturally in discussion of the texts we will survey in our exercise in biblical theology.

In this volume, our prime concern is simply to ask the question: "What does the Bible as a whole in both testaments have to tell us about why the people of God exist and what it is they are supposed to be and do in the world?" What *is* the mission of God's people?

So we will be exploring the Bible, as you'd expect in a book of biblical theology. For reasons of space, it is not possible to print out in full every passage of Scripture

---

1. Christopher J. H. Wright, *The Mission of God: Unlocking the Bible's Grand Narrative* (Downers Grove, IL: IVP, and Nottingham: IVP, 2007).

that is referred to in the chapters to follow, though key ones that come in for extended study will be. So this is the kind of book that, really, you just have to read with an open Bible ready to hand. I would urge you to pause regularly to check out the references and read them. Imitate the Bereans, if you like, who even when they had the apostle Paul teaching them, "examined the Scriptures every day to see if what Paul said was true" (Acts 17:11).

A small note on the name of God: most of the time I have followed the English translation tradition and used "the Lord" or "the LORD" for the divine name in the Old Testament. But when it seemed important to emphasize that this God had a personal, revealed name, which distinguished him as the one true living God from all other so-called gods, I have used the four Hebrew letters–YHWH. Nobody seems quite sure exactly how it was pronounced, though "Yahweh" has become common.

I am grateful to Jonathan Lunde (the Series Editor) and Katya Covrett (Senior Acquisitions Editor at Zondervan) for inviting me to contribute to this exciting new series, Biblical Theology for Life (what other kind of biblical theology should there be?). It is particularly pleasing to be "paired" with Jonathan in the first two volumes in the series, since perhaps no title could go better with this book on the mission of God's people than his on the biblical theology of discipleship. For disciples we are and disciples we are to make more of, said Jesus.

I am grateful too to InterVarsity Press, which published my book *The Mission of God*, for the permission granted me to quote significant portions of that book.

It may become apparent as you read what follows that many of the texts we will look at are ones I have preached on. Thus, often that sermonic atmosphere survives in the exposition and application of the text. I have not tried to conceal that. After all, it is hoped that this series will be of help to pastors and preachers, and it is certainly one of the passions of my own ministry to preach on mission as often as I can–from the Old Testament especially.

And that explains the dedication too. Our youngest daughter, Suzannah, probably heard more of my sermons on mission than any other living soul, by accompanying my wife, Liz, and me on many occasions to churches of all shapes and sizes for "mission weekends". Some of those sermons she heard so often she would mimic them mercilessly later. I trust that this book will do more than recall that nostalgic mimicry, but also foster the missional commitment to Christ that she now shares with her husband, Edmund. The book, finished just a few weeks too late to serve as a wedding present, is dedicated to them both with love and prayer.

Christopher J. H. Wright
October 2009

INTRODUCTION

Think of a doctrine—any doctrine between 200 and 2000 (AD). Multiply it by historic confessions. Divide by denominational variations. Add a suspicion of heresy. Subtract the doctrine you first thought of. And what are you left with? Probably just about the sum of what theology and mission have in common in the mind of your average Christian—not much.

Theology, after all, is all in the head—reflection, argument, teachings, creeds and confessions of faith. We think of a theological *library* where ideas get stored. Mission, or missions, is *doing*—practical, dynamic, achieving results. We think of the mission *field* where people go and do exciting stuff. Not only do theology and mission not seem to have much in common in themselves, it is easy to get the impression that most of those interested in the one have little interest in the other.

I am the son of missionary parents and I studied theology at Cambridge. But the two seemed to have little connection in my youthful zeal as a Christian. They certainly had no connection in my Cambridge theology studies, where (as far as I remember) "missiology" was not even a word at the time. Most of my Christian friends who were interested in supporting and praying for missionary work were not interested in theology, beyond weekly Bible studies. And the theology department certainly wasn't interested in mission.

Theology, it seems, is all about God. It rummages around in what (mostly dead) people have thought and written about God, God's character and actions, God's relationship to the world, to human society, God's involvement in the past, present and future, and the like. Mission, in happy contrast, is all about us the living, and what we (or some of us at least) believe we are supposed to be doing in the world to help God along a bit. Mission seems to be about helping God to get over those barriers of strange cultures and faraway places that he seems to have such difficulty crossing.

So, in mutual suspicion, theologians may not relish their theories being muddied by facts on the ground and the challenging questions thrown up by the messiness of practical mission. Practitioners of mission, in quick riposte, may not wish to see their urgent commitment to getting on with the job Christ entrusted to us delayed by indulgent navel-gazing about obscure long words ending in—ology.

And so the dangerous result is that theology proceeds without missional input or output, while mission proceeds without theological guidance or evaluation.

My hope is that this book will at least help to answer that broad question, *"What do theology and mission have to do with each other?"* And of course, this series is called "Biblical Theology for Life", so we are thinking especially of that branch of theology known as "biblical theology"—with its attempt to embrace the broad and unifying theological themes that span the whole of the Bible, though articulated in different ways within the great variety of the canon.

Now, I don't know which of the phrases on the cover of this book most moved you to buy it (or at least to be reading it) – *The Mission of God's People*, or *A Biblical Theology of the Church's Mission*. That is, I don't know whether you are primarily excited by mission (and perhaps wondering how it connects with theology, if at all), or whether you are primarily interested in biblical theology (and perhaps mildly puzzled at the thought that mission would be included in its scope: isn't mission what comes *after* the Bible? Doesn't mission come in the *practical* theology box, along with homiletics, pastoralia, evangelism, etc.?). Either way, I hope that one major result of reading this book is that you will gain a satisfactory answer to those questions and understand that biblical theology and mission are integrally related to each other.

There should be no theology that does not relate to the mission of the church – either by being generated out of the church's mission or by inspiring and shaping it. And there should be no mission of the church carried on without deep theological roots in the soil of the Bible.

No theology without missional impact; no mission without theological foundations.

That is the vision that inspires this modest essay.

PART ONE

QUEUING
THE QUESTIONS

CHAPTER 1

WHO ARE WE
AND WHAT ARE
WE HERE FOR?

MISSION OR MISSIONS?

The title of the book, *The Mission of God's People*, immediately sends a question to the top of the queue. It is a question of definition: What pops into our mind when we see or hear the word "mission"? Perhaps we are more familiar with it in the form "missions", which usually brings to mind all the cross-cultural missionary work of the churches we are familiar with. We think of missionary societies, of evangelistic and church-planting missions, of long-term career missionaries or short-term missions, and of global networks of such agencies and individuals, like the Lausanne Movement.

God's Sending

All of these images have in common the notion of sending and being sent. That sense, of course, lies at the Latin root of the word *mission* itself, and is very appropriate. And very biblical too. There is no doubt that the Bible shows God sending many people "on a mission from God", and the missionary movement in the book of Acts begins with a church responding to that divine impulse by sending Paul and Barnabas out on their first missionary journey.

But recognizing that mission has at its heart a sense of sending and being sent only raises another question: sent to do what? The Bible tells us that God did send many people. But the range of things for which people were sent is staggeringly broad. "Sending" language is used in all the following stories. Joseph was sent (unwittingly at first) to be in a position to save lives in a famine (Gen. 45:7). Moses was sent (unwillingly at first) to deliver people from oppression and exploitation (Ex. 3:10). Elijah was sent to influence the course of international politics (1 Kings 19:15–18). Jeremiah was sent to proclaim God's Word (e.g., Jer. 1:7). Jesus claimed the words of Isaiah that he was sent to preach good news, to proclaim freedom, to give sight for the blind, and to offer release from oppression (Lk 4:16–19; cf. Isa. 61:1).

The disciples were sent to preach and demonstrate the delivering and healing power of the reign of God (Matt. 10:5–8). As apostles they were sent to make disciples, baptize and teach (Matt. 28:18–20). Jesus sent them into the world in the same way that the Father had sent him, which raises a lot of interesting questions and challenges (John 17:18; 20:21). Paul and Barnabas were sent with famine relief (Acts 11:27–30). Later they were sent for evangelism and church planting (Acts 13:1–3). Titus was sent to ensure trustworthy and transparent financial administration (2 Cor. 8:16–24). Later he was sent for competent church administration (Titus 1:5). Apollos was sent as a skilled Bible teacher for church nurture (Acts 18:27–28). Many unnamed brothers and sisters were sent out as itinerant teachers for the sake of the truth of the gospel (3 John 5–8).

So, even if we agree that the concept of sending and being sent lies at the heart of mission, there is a broad range of biblically sanctioned activities that people may be sent by God to do, including famine relief, action for justice, preaching, evangelism, teaching, healing and administration. Yet when we use the words "missions" and "missionaries", we tend to think mainly of evangelistic activity. What will our biblical theology have to say to that? We will think about this more in chapter 12.

God's Purpose

Another common usage of the word "mission", however, is a sense of purpose or goal-orientation. Even in the secular world we talk about organizations having a "corporate mission", which may well be summed up in a pithy "mission statement". So to ask the question, "What is the mission of God's people?" is really to ask, "For what purpose do those who call themselves the people of God actually exist? What are we here on earth for?"

> It is not so much the case that God has a mission for his church in the world, as that God has a church for his mission in the world. Mission was not made for the church; the church was made for mission—God's mission.
>
> *Chris Wright*[2]

But to answer that we have to go one step further back and ask, Whose mission is it anyway? And of course, the answer to that has to be—it is the mission of God. God himself has a mission. God has a purpose and goal for his whole creation. Paul called this the "whole will [plan] of God" (Acts 20:27; cf. Eph. 1:9–10). And as part of that divine mission, God has called into existence a people to participate with God in the accomplishment of that mission. All *our* mission flows from the prior mission of God. And that, as we will see, is broad indeed. "Mission arises from the heart of God himself, and is communicated from his heart to ours. Mission is the global outreach of the global people of a global God."[1]

1. John Stott, *The Contemporary Christian: An Urgent Plea for Double Listening* (Leicester: IVP, 1992), 335.
2. Wright, *The Mission of God*, 62.

Singular and Plural

That broad definition allows us to include many different *missions* within the category of *mission*. Perhaps the easiest way I can explain the difference that I perceive between talking about mission (singular) and missions (plural) is to use analogies from other human activities.

We can speak about *science* (singular), and we have a generic concept in mind. It speaks of the challenge of discovery, experimentation and explanation. It speaks of a method, an ethos, a system of values, certain paradigms that govern scientific enquiry, a certain kind of faith and a strong kind of commitment. Science is a dimension of human life and civilization.

But then there are *sciences*. When we use the word in the plural, we are speaking of a whole vast range of activities which have scientific aims, methods, criteria and controls. There are physical sciences, with many subdivisions in the exploration of the natural world and our universe. There are social sciences, life sciences, and the like. And then there's the science of economics. And statistics. But let's not stray into science fiction.

My point is, science is a generic word for a whole array of human endeavour that can be characterized as sciences. There is a multitude of activities that can be justly characterized as science, and from time to time scientists themselves argue over whether this or that particular activity is "really science" at all. But (rather like the parts in Paul's description of the body), one legitimate science cannot say to another, "because you are not physics, you are not real science." Nor can one legitimate science say about itself, "because I am not physics, I don't belong to the world of science." There is a universal concept, broadly understood, and there is a multiplicity of embodiments of it in practical life.

One could build the same analogy with regard to *art* and *the arts,* or to *sport* and *sports.* There are all kinds of artistic and sporting activities, but we know what we mean when we use a generic concept like art or sport to include that variety and multiplicity.

So when I speak of *mission*, I am thinking of all that God is doing in his great purpose for the whole of creation and all that he calls us to do in cooperation with that purpose. Mission, like science, has a conceptual, generic breadth, and a word like "missional" can be as broad in significance as "scientific". And I would suggest that the word "missionary" should have the same kind of breadth of possibility as the word "scientist". Like the latter, it is a word you have to fill with specific meaning rather than assume or imagine what the said person actually does.

But when I speak of *missions*, I am thinking of the multitude of activities that God's people can engage in, by means of which they participate in God's mission. And it seems to me there are as many kinds of missions as there are kinds of sciences – probably far more in fact. And in the same way, in the variety of missions

God has entrusted to his church as a whole, it is unseemly for one kind of mission to dismiss another out of a superiority complex, or to undervalue itself as "not real mission" out of an inferiority complex. The body image has powerful resonance here too.

That is why I also dislike the old knock-down line that sought to ring-fence the word "mission" for specifically cross-cultural sending of missionaries for evangelism: "If everything is mission, then nothing is mission." It would seem more biblical to say, "If everything is mission … everything is mission." Clearly, not everything is *cross-cultural evangelistic* mission, but everything a Christian and a Christian church is, says and does should be missional in its conscious participation in the mission of God in God's world.

Perhaps you have heard of this definition of mission? *"World evangelization requires the whole church to take the whole Gospel to the whole world."* It comes from the Lausanne Covenant.[3] It is a fine ringing slogan, which actually has even earlier roots.[4] But each of its three phrases leads us into a cluster of questions. It provides a convenient framework to set out some of the issues that our biblical theology of mission will address—though not necessarily in this particular order.

THE WHOLE WORLD
The Whole World as the Goal of God's Mission

"What's the world coming to?" we sometimes ask when things seem just too much beyond our understanding or control. But it's a good question to ask when we are thinking about the mission of God's people too, for it points us towards a future that ultimately lies in God's hands. As we said above, our mission flows from God's mission, and God's mission is for the sake of his whole world—indeed his whole creation.

So we have to start by seeing ourselves within the great flow of God's mission, and we must make sure that our own missional goals—long term and more immediate—are in line with God's. For that purpose, we need to know the story we are part of, the great story that the Bible tells that encompasses the past and the future.

But how many churches that are keen on mission, or how many mission agencies that pursue their agendas with urgency and zeal pause to think about that great story—where it has come from so far, what shape it has from the *whole* Bible (not just a few missionary verses), and where it is going? And yet if our mission efforts lose touch with that story or set off on all kinds of tangents from it, we have to ask: Whose mission are we on? Whose agenda are we pursuing?

---

3. The Lausanne Covenant was the product of the first Lausanne Congress on World Evangelization, convened by Billy Graham in 1974. The Covenant was drafted by a group led by John Stott. It can be read in full at: http://www.lausanne.org/covenant. The phrase quoted above comes from Paragraph 6.

4. It was used by the World Council of Churches in its New Delhi report in 1961, and even before that in the Lambeth Conference report of 1958.

So our first task in Part 2 will be to gain some necessary orientation by giving attention to the story we are part of if we consider ourselves to be God's people on God's mission. That will be our focus in chapter 2.

The Whole World and the Scope of Our Mission

God's mission, we will find from the Bible, includes the whole of creation. But where does that truth lead us in terms of our mission on earth? Especially, what does it imply for our treatment of that part of creation entrusted to us—planet Earth? It is generally accepted among Christians (and more widely) that we ought to be good stewards of the earth's resources. But do we have a *missional* responsibility beyond that level of moderately responsible living? We are all conscious of the ecological challenges that face the human race. We may rightly feel confused in the welter of alleged facts and scary projections, not knowing how much is objective reality and how much is the result of media frenzy or political machination. Nobody can seriously doubt that we face enormous global problems, but we may well differ widely over the best way forward from where we seem to have reached.

But is this a matter that should be on the agenda of Christian mission? How does our biblical theology help us address that question? At the very least, one might say, if the goal of God's mission is the new creation that we anticipate from the climax of the Bible's story, then mission in the midst of the story ought to have some place for our response to creation as it is now. Traditionally, however, the concept of mission in Christian circles has been confined to the needs of human beings. So, is ecological concern and action a biblically legitimate missional concern, or merely a contemporary obsession driven by the world's agenda? We will think about that question in chapter 3.

The Whole World as the Arena of Our Mission

Where does "missionary" work begin and end? We so easily fall into compartmentalized thinking, splitting up our world into different zones. The very word "mission" often comes along with the notion of "the mission field", which normally means "foreign countries out there, but not here at home." This has been a Western way of looking at the world, but it is also found in other parts of the world that now have strong missionary-sending churches. The reality is, of course, as soon as you think seriously about it, that the mission field is everywhere, including your own street—wherever there is ignorance or rejection of the gospel of Jesus Christ.

But another equally damaging false dichotomy is between the so-called sacred and secular realms, and "mission" is located firmly in the first. So mission is something either that specially commissioned Christians manage to do full-time, if they can get enough "support" to do so, or something that other Christians (the vast majority) do in odd moments of time they have to spare from the necessity of having to work for a living. Maybe they can fit "a mission trip" into a vacation, or go on a "church mission" over the weekend.

But what about the rest of life? What about the rest of the "world" – the world of work, the public arena, the world of business, education, politics, medicine, sports, and the like? In what sense is that world the arena of the mission of God's people, and what does such mission consist of? Is it only the moments of evangelistic opportunity in that world, or can our work itself participate in God's mission?

> The Church must be seen as the company of pilgrims on the way to the end of the world and the ends of the earth.
>
> Lesslie Newbigin[5]

To push the question further, do the people of God have any responsibility to the rest of human society in general beyond the imperative of evangelism? What content do we put into biblical phrases like being a blessing to the nations, or seeking the welfare of the city, or being the salt of the earth or the light of the world, or doing good (one of the commonest expressions used by Paul and Peter)? Do these concepts figure in our biblical theology of mission?

Perhaps this sounds like the hoary and familiar debate about the relationship between evangelism and social action, but I hope that our study of biblical theology in the following chapters will take us beyond the traditional polarizing and prioritizing that, in my opinion, so distorts and pulls apart what God intended to be held together.

So even a simple expression like "the whole world", then, raises all kinds of issues for us. It is geographical (all the earth), but it is also ecological, economic, social and political. And we remember too that the Bible speaks about the "end of the world" – though it is not so much an end as a new beginning. So "the whole world" includes time as well as space. The church needs to relate to both. We are sent to the ends of the earth, and we keep going till the end of the world.

THE WHOLE CHURCH
Who Are the People of God?

"The Mission of God's People", announces our title page. Could I not have just used the book's subtitle, "The Church's Mission"? Well, yes perhaps, but only if we have got our biblical theology of the church straight, and that is probably an optimistic assumption. For many Christians, the word "church" takes them back only to the supposed birthday of the church in the book of Acts on the day of Pentecost. But is that a valid perception? When and where did the people of God come into existence, and for what reason? How does the existence and mission of this people relate to the mission of God in and for his world? When did their mission begin, and how and when will it end?

5. Lesslie Newbigin, *The Household of God: Lectures on the Nature of the Church* (London, SCM, 1953), xi.

Or to put this question another way, how does the mission of the church in the New Testament (that most of us can relate to, since if nothing else we are familiar with the so-called Great Commission and vaguely recall that it comes at the end of a gospel) relate to the identity and history of Old Testament Israel? Did Israel have a "mission", and if so, what was it? Indeed, does the Old Testament have any relevance to Christian mission at all—other than a few popular "call-stories" like Moses, Isaiah and Jeremiah (so useful for missionary sermons), and the object lesson of a single reluctant missionary who was embarrassed and angry at his own success (Jonah)?

How many sermons have you heard on a missionary Sunday preached from the Old Testament? How many times have you preached a missionary sermon from the Old Testament yourself, if you are a pastor? If the answer is "lots and lots", I'd love to hear from you to compare notes, since I try to do it wherever I go. But if the answer is "very few" or "hardly ever", then the point of my question is clear. Where and when do we start in constructing a *biblical* theology of the mission of God's people, and what happens if we include the Old Testament?

So we need to think carefully about what the Bible as a whole has to say about who exactly are "God's people", and in what sense they are (and always have been) a people with a mission. That is why I make no apology for including so much exposition of Old Testament texts in the chapters that follow. After all, the New Testament church did not actually have a New Testament when they set out on the task of world mission. It was the Scriptures of the Old Testament that provided the motivation and justification for their missional practice, as well as the underlying theological assumptions and expectations that reassured them that what they were doing was "biblical" (as we would say).

What Kind of People Are We?

What kind of person is your postman? The question hardly seems to matter at a functional level. Whoever delivers mail to your address has a job to do, and the point is to make sure that the job gets done, not to worry about the morals of the person who does it. The man may have been cheating on his wife the night before, but so long as you get the mail next morning, so long as the message gets delivered to you, that doesn't matter (to you).

Unfortunately, there is a danger that the expression "the whole church *taking* the whole gospel to the whole world" turns the church into nothing more than a delivery mechanism for the message. All that matters is "getting the job done"—preferably as soon as possible. And sadly there are some forms of missionary strategy and rhetoric that strongly give that impression.

The Bible, in stark contrast, is passionately concerned about what kind of people they are who claim to be the people of God. If our mission is to share good news, we need to be good news people. If we preach a gospel of transformation, we need to show some evidence of what transformation looks like. So there is a range of questions we need to ask about "the whole church" that have to do with things like integrity, justice, unity and inclusion, and Christlikeness. The biblical word is "holiness", and it is as much a part of our missional identity as of our personal sanctification.

But should we include *ethics* in our understanding of *mission* in this way? Does it not lead to "works righteousness" and legalism? Surely we should concentrate exclusively on calling people to *faith*? Well, we may struggle with seeing a tension there, but the apostle Paul saw only integration when he described his own life's mission as calling all the nations to "faith's obedience". The gospel is something to be obeyed (according to Paul), not just believed. That will lead us to some interesting texts and reflections. Chapters 5 – 8 will explore a variety of biblical texts that stress the ethical dimensions of the mission of God's people.

What Are the Priorities and Limits of Our Mission?

A postman delivers the mail to your home. That is his prime function in life. His job description requires him to do that. Now of course, he may come in and help you fix a blocked drain, if he has time. Or he may offer to carry out the garbage. Or feed the cats while you are away. He may enjoy serving the social needs of the community in lots of little ways, like Postman Pat in the children's books. But that's not what his "real job" is. And some people may even accuse him of wasting his employer's time on "secondary" things. He should stick to what he's sent to do and get the job done as quickly and efficiently as possible.

A medical missionary couple I knew had been running a rural hospital in Africa for years when they received a communication from their church in Australia that they had been reclassified as "secondary missionaries", because they were not directly engaged in evangelism and church planting (even though fruitful evangelistic work was actually happening among staff and patients at the hospital). Needless to say, this brought them little encouragement. But was such "classification" biblically legitimate?

So another question arises in relation to the church's mission: What exactly is it? Is there something that is primary that makes everything else secondary – however desirable and helpful those other things may be? Once again, the perceived division between evangelism and social action surfaces.

Is the church's mission *primarily* the delivery of the message of the gospel – in which case the verbal element is all that really matters? Or does the church's mission include the embodiment of the message in life and action? Sometimes this question is raised as the tension between *proclamation* and *presence*. Or between *words* and *works*. In some of the chapters below we will explore the integration of what the church is meant to *be* as well as what the church is meant to *say*.

THE WHOLE GOSPEL

How Big Is Your Gospel?

This question is clearly linked to those above. What exactly is the gospel that lies at the core of our mission? It is the good news of what God has done through Jesus Christ for the redemption of the world. But what is the scale and scope of God's redemption? The Bible describes God as "Redeemer" from very early on.[6] What content does the word hold for those who spoke of God in that way, and what does it then imply for those who are among the redeemed? What kind of experience is redemption, and what kind of life is then expected of the redeemed? This is something we shall explore in chapter 6.

One of the dangers with a word like "gospel" is that we all love it so much (rightly), and want to share it so passionately (rightly again), that we don't take time to explore its full biblical content. Who invented the word, for example? What did Jesus and Paul mean when they used it—particularly since, as I've already said, they had no New Testament to read to tell them. Did they find "the gospel" in the Old Testament?

And if it does go back to the Old Testament (as we will see), what does that do to our understanding of what the good news actually is? Once again, we will find that the Bible itself will correct our tendency to reduce the gospel to a solution to our individual sin problem and a swipe card for heaven's door, and replace that reductionist impression with a message that has to do with the cosmic reign of God in Christ that will ultimately eradicate evil from God's universe (and solve our individual sin problem too, of course).

No Other Name

But at the end of the day, mission is a matter of loyalty. The ambassador must have complete loyalty to the government he or she represents. A trusted messenger will faithfully deliver what his sender said, not his own opinions.

So the mission of *God's* people has to start and finish with commitment to the *God* whose mission we are called to share. But that in turn depends on *knowing* our God—knowing God in depth, from experience of his revelation and his salvation. So what exactly is it, then, that we are to *know* and to remain loyal to? In both testaments, God's people are called to nonnegotiable, uncompromising loyalty to the uniqueness of God—revealed as YHWH in the Old Testament, and walking among us in the incarnate life of Jesus of Nazareth in the New.

The mission of God's people flows from the uniqueness of the God of the Bible, supremely revealed to us in the uniqueness of Christ. That is both the *source* of our

---

6. It first occurs in Gen. 48:16 (NRSV), but then explodes into prominence in Exodus (6:8; 15:13).

mission (for this is the one who sends us into the world in his name), and also the *content* of our mission (for all that we say and do is to bear witness to the truth that the Lord is God and there is no other, that Jesus has been given the Name that is above all names, and that there is "no other name given under heaven by which we must be saved", Acts 4:12).

As we turn, then, in part 2 to our journey through some of the great texts and themes of a biblical theology of the mission of God's people, this is a sampling of the questions and issues we will face. As I've said, we will not necessarily follow the same order as the framework I have just used to survey those questions. For this is biblical, not systematic, theology, and my hope is that as we expose ourselves to the rich array of biblical texts from both testaments and spend time in the task of exegesis and exposition, we will find broad answers to those broad questions—or even that some of the questions melt away in the wider perspectives of the Bible itself.

PART TWO

ARRIVING AT ANSWERS

CHAPTER 2

PEOPLE WHO KNOW THE STORY THEY ARE PART OF

WORLD MISSION AND THE BIBLE STORY

So where shall we start? A great number of books (and sermons) on the topic of Christian mission start with the Great Commission—the final words of Jesus to his disciples before his ascension, sending them out into the world to make disciples of all nations. It's a natural instinct to start there because it chimes in with so much else that the New Testament has to say about Jesus and his followers, and about Paul and the early Christians. Mission confronts you whichever gospel you read to find Jesus, and it only intensifies after that in Acts and the epistles.

> Matthew's Jesus instructs his disciples to make disciples and baptize in all the world. Luke's Jesus commissions his followers to go to Jerusalem, Judaea and the ends of the earth, and John's Jesus says "as the Father sent me, so I send you". The story of Acts *is* the story, or rather a story, of early Christian mission. And ... the letters [of Paul] confirm that not only he but a good many other Christians ... believed it their business to travel around the known world telling people that there was "another king, this Jesus".
>
> World mission is thus the first and most obvious feature of early Christian praxis.[1]

And we have to ask, Why? What was it that made Christianity a missionary faith from the very start? What made the first followers of Jesus so passionately, courageously and unstoppably committed to telling the world about him?

Well, you might respond, because Jesus told them to. They had the Great Commission. It was a matter of obedience. And that would be true, given the endings

---

1. N. T. Wright, *The New Testament and the People of God* (Christian Origins and the Question of God 1; London: SPCK; Minneapolis: Fortress, 1992), 361.

of Matthew, Luke and John that we have just noted—though we should remember that the Gospels were not written until well after the church's mission had been going for many years, so the written record of Jesus' words was not in their hands, as it were.

But if this simple obedience to the Great Commission were the major reason *in the consciousness* of the early Christians, it is surprising that it is never mentioned anywhere else in the New Testament. Don't misunderstand me here. I am not suggesting for a moment that the Great Commission never happened, only that it is not referred to as an explicit driver for the missionary expansion of the church in the New Testament after Acts 1.

> Christianity did not spread by magic. It is sometimes suggested that the world was, so to speak, ready for Christianity: Stoicism was too lofty and dry, popular paganism metaphysically incredible and morally bankrupt, mystery-religions dark and forbidding, Judaism law-bound and introverted, and Christianity burst on the scene as the great answer to the questions everyone was asking. There is a grain of truth in this picture, but it hardly does justice to historical reality. Christianity summoned proud pagans to face torture and death out of loyalty to a Jewish villager who had been executed by Rome. Christianity advocated a love which cut across racial boundaries. It sternly forbade sexual immorality, the exposure of children, and a great many other things which the pagan world took for granted. Choosing to become a Christian was not an easy or natural thing for the average pagan.
>
> *N. T. Wright*[2]

Or some people have argued that the world was simply ready for the Christian gospel, such that the message just spread like wildfire, filling the vacuum, as it were, of the failure of other philosophies and worldviews. But this is an inadequate explanation, even if there is some truth in it. The Christian message may indeed have answered questions that other religions and philosophies could not, but that did not mean that joining the despised Christian sect was instantly attractive. Calling people to conversion was to confront them with serious and costly demands.

So what compelled the first followers of Jesus, Jews as they were, to make the world their mission field?

Knowing the Story

"Jews as they were"—I slipped that in because it is the key to the answer. That is, those first believers *knew the story they were in*. And they knew the story because they knew their Scriptures. They were Jews. They knew the story so far, they understood that the story had just reached a decisive moment in Jesus of Nazareth, and they knew what the rest of the story demanded.

In fact, when the first missionary journeys produced a sudden influx of "pagan" converts (let's call them Gentiles, or people from the non-Jewish nations from here on), and when that in turn produced a big theological problem for the Jewish Christians, how was the problem resolved? They met in Jerusalem in the first council of the Christian faith, and the event is recorded in Acts 15. As an aside, it is worth noting that the first Christian council was called because of the problems caused by highly successful Christian mission. It would be wonderful if all church committees, councils, conferences and congresses had the same cause!

The problem was solved *not* by referring to the command of Jesus. One could easily imagine Peter standing up to say to the critics, "Listen, friends, *Jesus told us* to go and make disciples of all nations and that is what Paul and Barnabas are doing. So back off!" But instead, James settles the matter by reference to the prophetic Scriptures. He quotes from Amos 9 and affirms that what the prophet foresaw is now happening: the house of David is being restored and the Gentile nations are being brought in to bear the name of the Lord. That's where the story pointed, and that's what was now happening.

Or come with Paul to Pisidian Antioch in Acts 13. It was a Gentile city, but Paul went to the Jewish synagogue on the Sabbath, as he usually did. What did he do? He told them their own story (the Old Testament narrative) as a prelude to telling them about Jesus and then adding "the good news: What God promised our ancestors he has fulfilled for us, their children, by raising up Jesus" (Acts 13:32–33). The story led to Jesus, Messiah, crucified but risen.

But the story went further. For when some of the Jews rejected the message while Gentile "God-fearers" (converts to Jewish faith) accepted it, Paul had an Old Testament passage for them too, to justify his missionary appeal to them. He quotes Isaiah 49:6 and applies it to himself and his missionary colleagues:

"For this is what the Lord has commanded *us*:

"'I have made you a light for the Gentiles,
    that you may bring salvation to the ends of the earth.'"

When the Gentiles heard this, they were glad and honored the word of the Lord; and all who were appointed for eternal life believed. (Acts 13:47–48; italics added)

Once again, Paul could easily have said, "*Jesus* commanded us to bring this good news to you Gentiles." He could even have referred to the specific missional command that he, Paul, had personally received in his conversion-commissioning encounter with the risen Christ on the way to Damascus. But instead, Paul points to the Scriptures and the story they tell—the story that leads inevitably to the gospel going to the nations. And he took that "story-yet-to-come" aspect of the words of the prophet and heard in them a command from the Lord himself.

In fact, even for Jesus himself this was the foundation of the Great Commission. Luke gives us the fullest account of how Jesus commissioned the disciples after his resurrection, and what is striking is the emphasis that Luke (and Jesus, of course) placed upon the understanding of the (Old Testament) Scriptures. Luke 24 describes the first day in the life of the risen Jesus. And how did he spend it? Teaching the

Scriptures. Another aside: As an Old Testament teacher most of my life I find this a rather reassuring thought that Jesus spent the afternoon and evening of his resurrection day systematically teaching the Old Testament.

What we would give for the notes of those two lectures! For there were in fact two "Resurrection Lectures", and they were subtly different.

Messiah and Mission

The first was on the road to Emmaus to the two disciples whose big problem was their disappointment that the redemption of Israel, which they had hoped Jesus was going to accomplish, did not seem to have happened. Jesus went through the whole canon of the Old Testament ("Moses and all the Prophets") to explain how it all led up to him, the Messiah, and how his death and resurrection were in fact the way God had kept his promise to Israel (Luke 24:13–27). So that first lecture went through the Old Testament *in order to make sense of the story so far* – the story that led up to Jesus himself, the whole point, purpose and destination of the story.

But then, in the evening, with the rest of the disciples in Jerusalem, Jesus went through the Old Testament for the second time – not because they didn't know it (they probably knew huge sections of the Old Testament by memory), but to help them *understand* where it led.

> He said to them, "This is what I told you while I was still with you: Everything must be fulfilled that is written about me in the Law of Moses, the Prophets and the Psalms."
>
> Then he opened their minds so they could understand the Scriptures. He told them, "This is what is written: The Messiah will suffer and rise from the dead on the third day, *and repentance for the forgiveness of sins will be preached in his name to all nations, beginning at Jerusalem. You are witnesses of these things.*" (Lk. 24:44–48; italics added)

This time, you notice, he surveys the Old Testament *in order to make sense of the story from there on* – that part of the story they were about to embark on, of bearing witness to the saving power of the death and resurrection Jesus to all nations. In other words, for Jesus, "This is what is written" governed not only the *messianic* meaning of the Scriptures, but also their *missional* significance. The Old Testament tells the story that not only leads up to Jesus but one that also leads on to mission to the nations.

Jesus often spoke about how the course of his own life – his suffering, death and resurrection – was governed by the Scriptures. Here he is extending that to the ongoing mission of the church as well. It is all part of the same great story that the Scriptures mapped out. This means that the Great Commission was not something

Jesus thought up as an afterthought—something for the disciples to be getting on with while he went back to heaven. It was not just something that rested solely on his own authority as the risen Lord (though, of course, it is fully warranted by that, as Matthew's version makes clear). It was the inevitable outcome of the story as the Scriptures told it—leading *up to* the Messiah and leading *on to* mission to the nations.

You could say about the church's worldwide mission that Jesus commanded it because the Scriptures demanded it. Jesus knew the story too. You could say, in another sense, that's because he wrote it.

TAKING THE STORY AS A WHOLE

So we are seeking, in this book, for a "Biblical Theology of the Church's Mission". What better examples could we follow than Jesus and Paul? We need to pay attention to the whole story of the Bible and see our mission in the light of all of it.

Indeed, we need to ask ourselves right up front: How well do you actually know the biblical story? If Jesus and Paul saw fit repeatedly to go over it with those who knew their Old Testament Scriptures inside out, how much more do we need to make sure we are familiar with the content of the Bible as a whole? Tragically, even among Christians with great enthusiasm for world mission, there is often not only profound ignorance of great vistas of biblical revelation, but even impatience with the prolonged effort that is needed to soak ourselves in these texts until our whole thinking and behaviour are shaped by the story they tell, the worldview that story generates, the demands it lays upon us and the hope it sets before us. The attitude of some is that all you need is the Great Commission and the power of the Holy Spirit. Bible teaching or biblical theology will only serve to delay you in the urgent task. Presumably I can take comfort in the fact that you are reading this book, which means that this is an attitude you don't share.

"Just do it" seems to have spilled over from Nike to being the slogan of some forms of Christian mission. I was at a large mission mobilization congress where the slogan was "Just go!" My first reaction was to say, "Just hold on." Even Jesus spent three years training his disciples before he told them to "Go", and even that time was scarcely enough to radically reshape their scriptural understanding in the light of his own identity, to understand where the biblical story was leading in relation to himself and the future of Israel and of the world. How much more is such training needed when we hear that Bible reading and knowledge among evangelical Christians is at a shamefully low ebb.

I find it helpful to visualize the biblical story as an actual line on which one can plot key points. The four major sections of the biblical story line are—Creation, Fall, Redemption in History, and New Creation. Within the Redemption in History section, of course, falls by far the largest portion of the biblical story, and it needs further subdivision.

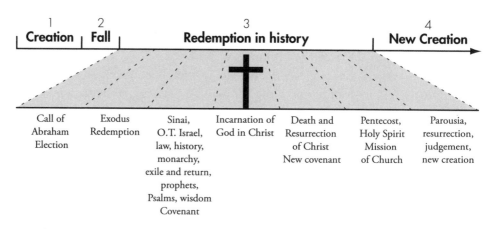

1 Creation	2 Fall	3 Redemption in history			4 New Creation
Call of Abraham Election	Exodus Redemption	Sinai, O.T. Israel, law, history, monarchy, exile and return, prophets, Psalms, wisdom Covenant	Incarnation of God in Christ	Death and Resurrection of Christ New covenant	Pentecost, Holy Spirit Mission of Church	Parousia, resurrection, judgement, new creation

1. Creation

The Bible does not begin at Genesis 3 (or end at Revelation 20). You might think so when you listen to some presentations of the Bible's message and mission. That is to say, the Bible is not just about the solution to our sin problem and how to survive the day of judgment. It begins with creation and ends with new creation. So our biblical theology of mission needs to take this great beginning and ending seriously.

The creation narrative provides two of the fundamental planks for the foundational Christian worldview, for it answers two of the most fundamental questions that all philosophies and religions answer in different ways: *Where* are we? and *Who* are we? That is to say, first, what is this universe in which we find ourselves? Where did it come from and why does it exist and is it even real? And then, second, What does it mean to be human? Are we gods, or merely animals that have evolved a bit further than the rest? Does human life have any value, meaning and purpose?

The distinctive answers that the Bible gives to these questions have profound implications for our understanding of mission in God's world in the midst of human beings like ourselves, made in the image of God.

2. Fall

Human disobedience and rebellion against the Creator God brought disastrous results (Gen. 3 – 11). Evil and sin weave their way into every aspect of God's creation and every dimension of human personhood and life on earth. *Physically*, we are subject to decay and death, living within a physical environment that is itself under the curse of God. *Intellectually*, we use our incredible powers of rationality to explain, excuse and "normalize" our own evil. *Socially*, every human relationship is fractured and disrupted – sexual, parental, familial, societal, ethnic, international – and the effect is consolidated horizontally through the permeation of all human cultures, and vertically by accumulation through the generations of history. And *spiritually*, we are alienated from God, rejecting his goodness and authority. Romans 1:18 – 32 outlines all of these dimensions in its analysis of the fruit of Genesis 3.

If there is good news for such dire realities, it needs to be pretty big. The glorious truth is that the Bible gives us a gospel that addresses every dimension of the problem that sin has created. God's mission is the final destruction of all that is evil from his whole creation. Our mission therefore has to be as comprehensive in scope as the gospel the whole Bible gives us.

3. Redemption

God chose not to abandon or destroy his creation, but to redeem it. And he chose to do so within history through persons and events that run from the call of Abraham to the return of Christ. While every part of this great story has its particular contribution to the whole, we do need to see this whole section of the line as a fundamental unity – the single great saving act of God. I think the unity between the Old and New Testament sections of this part of the biblical story of redemption is why Revelation pictures the redeemed humanity in the new creation singing the song of Moses and the song of the Lamb (Rev. 15:3). This will save us from the common misunderstanding that the Old Testament is Salvation Plan A (failed), and the New Testament is Salvation Plan B (success). That is a severe distortion of the story. But without falling into that trap, we can still trace the two main parts of the story in Old and New Testaments.

Old Testament

By the time the story has reached Genesis 11, the human race faced two huge problems: the sinfulness of every human heart, and the fracturing and confusion of the nations of humanity. God's plan of redemption addressed both. In the call of Abraham God set in motion a historical dynamic that would ultimately not only deal with the problem of human sin but also heal the dividedness of the nations.

The election of Abraham was explicitly for the blessing of all nations on earth. God's command and promise to Abraham can legitimately, therefore, be called the first Great Commission – "Go … [and] be a blessing … and all peoples on earth will be blessed through you" (Gen. 12:1 – 3). God's plan, then, was to deal with the problem of humanity – sin and division – through Israel, the people of Abraham.

The exodus provides the prime Old Testament model of God acting as Redeemer. This is what redemption looks like when God does it. It is an act that simultaneously demonstrates God's faithfulness, justice and love. And the people who know themselves to be the redeemed people of this God, now revealed as YHWH, are called upon to model before the nations what it means to be redeemed and to live redemptively in their own society.

At Sinai, God entered into covenant with Israel, still with the rest of the nations in view, calling them to be his representatives (priestly) and to be distinctive (holy). He gave them his law as a gift of grace – not so that they could earn his salvation, for they had already been redeemed, but to shape them as his model people, to be a light to the nations.

As the history of Israel moved forward, however, through the era of the settlement in the land, the judges, and the monarchy, it became increasingly clear that Israel not only could not and would not live by the standards of God's law in response to his saving grace, but actually proved themselves to be no different from the nations. The law itself, as Paul saw so clearly, exposed the fact that Israel was as much in need of God's salvation as the rest of the nations. There is no difference, all have sinned. Israel, the servant of the Lord, called to be a light to the nations, turned out to be a failed servant, blind to God's works and deaf to his Word. They too needed God's salvation.

Nevertheless, the Old Testament continues though the prophets to point forward and to insist that God would keep his promise to bring blessing to the nations and salvation to the whole world, and that he would do so through Israel. In other words, the failure of historical Israel was anticipated by God and did not represent a failure of *God's* plan. In the mystery of his sovereign purpose it would lead to salvation going to the ends of the earth as God always intended. But if Old Testament Israel proved to be unfaithful, how could it then happen?

New Testament

The New Testament presents to us the answer that the prophets point towards: the One who would embody Israel as their Messiah, who would be faithful where they had been rebellious, who would be obedient unto death, and through his death and resurrection would bring about not only the restoration of Israel but also the promised salvation to the ends of the earth.

So the story line of the Bible moves on until "when the set time had fully come, God sent his Son, born of a woman ..." (Gal. 4:4). The incarnation of God in Christ brings two new factors into our theology of mission: the inaugurated presence of the kingdom of God and the incarnational model and principle itself.

In Jesus, the reign of God entered human history in a way not previously experienced—though the expectation of it and the ethical implications of it are thoroughly rooted in the Old Testament. The dynamic action of the kingdom of God in the words and deeds of Jesus and the mission of his disciples changed lives, values and priorities, and presented a radical challenge to the fallen structures of power in society. To say "Jesus is Lord", and not Caesar or any of his successors, is a major missional mandate in itself. Luke can find no more missional way to end his second volume than by leaving Paul in Rome where he *"proclaimed the kingdom of God* and taught about the Lord Jesus Christ—with all boldness and without hindrance" (Acts 28:31; italics added).

But, as the parables of Jesus emphasized, God inaugurated his reign in hidden, humble ways—choosing to enter the world himself, coping with all its limitations and frustrations. It is a pattern that Jesus then laid on his followers for their own costly engagement with the world and all its issues, as he prayed to his Father—"As you sent me into the world, I have sent them into the world" (John 17:18; cf. 20:21).

The cross and resurrection of Jesus bring us to the central point of the whole line of redemption in history. Here is God's answer to every dimension of sin and evil in the cosmos and all their destructive effects. The gospel presents us with an accomplished victory that will ultimately be universally visible and vindicated. If we have been as radical as we ought in our analysis of the effects of the fall, then we must be equally radical and comprehensive here in our understanding of all the ways in which the cross and resurrection reverse and ultimately destroy those effects. The cross must be central to every dimension of the mission of God's people—from personal evangelism among individual friends to ecological care for creation, and everything in between.

Just as the exodus redemption led to the creation of the covenant people of Old Testament Israel, so the Easter redemption led to the eschatological gift of the Holy Spirit at Pentecost and the birth of the church. But while the church as the community of followers of Jesus was birthed at Pentecost, its roots go back, of course, to the people of God since Abraham. For the church is nothing less than the multinational fulfillment of the hope of Israel, that all nations will be blessed through the people of Abraham. The *expansion* of Israel to include the Gentiles (note carefully: not the *abandonment* of Israel in favour of the Gentiles), in and through Christ, fulfilled the promise to Abraham and accomplished God's purpose to solve not only the problem of Genesis 3 (human fallenness and sin), but also of Genesis 11 (racial dividedness and confusion). This is why it is so important to recognize that the church by its very nature is *part* of the gospel for its existence, for as a community of reconciled sinners from all races it demonstrates the gospel's transforming power.

Two realities from this part of the line inform our theology of mission: first, the presence of the Holy Spirit making available to the people of God the same transforming power that energized the life and ministry of Jesus and raised him from the dead; and second, the existence of the church itself as the missional community of those who have responded to, and entered, the kingdom of God by repentance and faith in Christ, and who now seek to live as a transformed and transforming community of reconciliation and blessing in the world.

4. New Creation

The return of Christ will not only bring to its grand finale that section of the Bible story line that we have called redemption in history, it will also inaugurate the ultimate fulfillment of the whole point of the story—namely, the redemption and renewal of God's whole creation.

The Bible includes in this climactic part of its story line, of course, the reality of judgment. The day of judgment is something that the Bible warns about, from Amos's thunderous reversal of Israel's shallow optimism about "the day of the

Our children are now all grown adults. Recently (perhaps when they thought it was safe to tell us) they told us of a game they used to play as children. They would go in the lounge, when my wife was in the kitchen or garden, or I was out at work, and do everything they knew they weren't allowed to: jumping up and down on the sofa, throwing the cushions at each other, etc., until one of them would call out "Mummy's coming!", at which point they all had to sit down and be quiet and the last one down was "out". For if "Mummy's coming", there will be joy or grief when the moment of judgment arrives. "Let's go play 'Mummy's coming,'" they would say, apparently.

"God is coming", shouts the whole creation again and again, according to the ending of Psalm 96. And then it bursts into odes of joy at the thought of it. For if "Mummy's coming" is a matter of childish fear (or joy, depending on what she sees when she opens the door), what does it mean for the whole creation, for you and me, to know for certain that "God is coming"–to put things right forever?

LORD", through the warnings of Jesus, Paul and Peter about the judgment seat of God, to the terrifying visions of Revelation. The reality of judgment is at one level *part* of the gospel, for it is good news that evil will not have the last word but will ultimately be destroyed by God. And at another level it is the bad news about the wrath of God that makes the gospel such eternally good news for our fallen world.

But the Bible does not end with the day of judgment. Beyond the purging fire of judgment and the destruction of all that is evil and opposed to God's good purpose, there lies the new heavens and new earth, in which righteousness and peace will dwell, because God himself will dwell there with his redeemed people from every nation.

When we take our biblical theology of mission to the end of the line in this way, it generates biblical faith and hope–that irrepressible optimism that should characterize all Christian action in the world. The mission of God's people is not only driven forward by the command of Christ, it is also drawn forward by the promise of God,

> "Look! God's dwelling place is now among the people, and he will dwell with them. They will be his people, and God himself will be with them and be their God. 'He will wipe every tear from their eyes. There will be no more death or mourning or crying or pain, for the old order of things has passed away.'"
>
> He who was seated on the throne said, "I am making everything new!" (Rev. 21:3–5)

This, then, is the grid of the Bible's own story line, which shapes and energizes the mission of God's people. This was the story that the early followers of Jesus knew, and it was their confidence in this story, and the certainty that they had a part to play in it, that led them out into the world in mission. This is the story that we need to know we are part of. For our mission is nothing less (or more) than participating with God in this grand story until he brings it to its guaranteed climax.

As we think through our biblical theology of the church's mission in the light of this story, it has a profoundly illuminating power.

- Creation provides our foundational values and principles.
- The fall brings us down to the realities of the cursed earth and the pervasive tentacles of human and satanic wickedness.
- The Old Testament shows us the scope of God's redeeming purpose, worked out in a specific historical and cultural context, and models for us in amazing detail (from the law, the narratives, prophets, wisdom and worship of Israel) the kind of practical responses that please God (and those that don't).
- The incarnation brings God right alongside us in our struggle and calls us to embody and be agents of the reign of God through Christ.
- The cross and resurrection enable us to experience and share the power of true reconciliation, love, hope and peace, and to seek the atoning, redemptive work of God even in the most apparently irredeemable human situations.
- The Holy Spirit in the church provides the guidance and the power to expect real change in lives and societies, while keeping our eyes on the corporate, not merely individual, dimensions of Christian mission.
- Our great future hope of new creation gives value and worth to all that we do in the present, for our labour is not in vain in the Lord, and shapes our response to the present by the revealed shape of the future.

Through believing the story, we are drawn in to the action and find ourselves caught up in the saving movement of God. We learn to "indwell" the story so looking out from within the biblical world with new eyes onto our postmodern lives and world: we stop trying to make the Bible relevant to our lives and instead begin to find ourselves being made relevant to the Bible. We give up the clumsy attempt to wrench the ancient text into our contemporary world and instead bring our world back into collision with, and cleansing by, the strange new world of the Bible. Through believing the story, we allow our minds to be continuously renewed by the normative narrative of God.... Jesus calls all his disciples away from a faith in which God is available to bless their business into a faith in which disciples are available to God to be part of his business. And God's business is a multi-national company with branches everywhere!

Philip Greenslade[3]

Our mandate for world evangelization is the whole Bible. It is to be found in the *creation of God* (because of which all human beings are responsible to him), in the *character of God* (as outgoing, loving, compassionate, not willing that any should perish, desiring that all should come to repentance), in the *promises of God* (that all nations will be blessed through Abraham's seed and will become the Messiah's inheritance), in the *Christ of God* (now exalted with universal authority, to receive universal acclaim), in the *Spirit of God* (who convicts of sin, witnesses to Christ, and impels the church to evangelize) and in the *church of God* (which is a multinational, missionary community, under orders to evangelize until Christ returns).

John Stott[4]

3. Philip Greenslade, *A Passion for God's Story: Discovering Your Place in God's Strategic Plan* (Carlisle: Paternoster, 2002), 42–43.
4. John Stott, "The Bible in World Evangelization," in *Perspectives on the World Christian Movement* (ed. R. D. Winter and S. C. Hawthorne; Pasadena: William Carey Library, 1981), 4 (italics added).

THE MISSION OF GOD

The story we have just surveyed can be viewed, from another angle, as the mission of God. It is the story of how God in his sovereign love has purposed to bring the sinful world of his fallen creation to the redeemed world of his new creation.

It is the comprehensiveness of Paul's message that is impressive. He proclaimed God in his fullness as Creator, Sustainer, Ruler, Father, and Judge. All this is part of the gospel, or, at least, the necessary prolegomena to the gospel. Many people are rejecting our gospel today, not because they perceive it to be false, but because they perceive it to be trivial. They are looking for an integrated worldview that makes sense of all their experience. We learn from Paul that we cannot preach the gospel of Jesus without the doctrine of God, or the cross without creation, or salvation without judgment, or vice versa. Today's world needs a bigger gospel, the full gospel of Scripture, what Paul later in Ephesus was to call "the entire plan of God" (Acts 20:27 NAB).

John Stott (on Paul's sermon in Athens, Acts 17)[5]

God's mission is what spans the gap between the curse on the earth of Genesis 3 and the end of the curse in the new creation of Revelation 22.

God's mission is what brings humanity from being a cacophony of nations divided and scattered in rebellion against God in Genesis 11 to being a choir of nations united and gathered in the worship of God in Revelation 7.

God's mission, in other words, is what Paul probably meant when he said that he had spent several years in Ephesus teaching the church there about "the whole will [or counsel, or plan, or mission] of God" (Acts 20:27). It was a vast, comprehensive project of cosmic salvation, and even when speaking to a non-Jewish audience, Paul found ways of communicating its universal scope (Acts 17).

In my larger book, *The Mission of God: Unlocking the Bible's Grand Narrative*,[6] I argued that we can read the whole Bible with a missional hermeneutic and then explored some dimensions of what happens when we do. That is where I have examined in more depth the missiological dimensions of such vast biblical themes as monotheism (the uniqueness of YHWH and of Jesus), idolatry, election, redemption, covenant, ethics, ecology, and eschatology.

This present book needs to be read in the light of the substantial exegesis and argument of *The Mission of God*. There is, of course, inevitably some overlap (we are, after all, talking about the same Bible!). But whereas in *The Mission of God* I was making a case for a missional hermeneutic of the whole canon of Scripture, seeing it as the deposit of and witness to the mission of God in all creation and history, in this book we are basically trying to answer the (only slightly!) more limited question, "What are *we* here for? What is the mission of God's *people* as they live in God's world and participate in God's mission?"

5. John Stott, *Through the Bible through the Year: Daily Reflections from Genesis to Revelation* (Oxford: Candle Books, 2006), 334.

6. See footnote 1 in the Preface.

SUMMARY

We began this chapter asking why the first Christians were so indomitably mission-minded—determined at all costs to spread the good news about Jesus Christ to every corner of the world they knew. And the answer, we have seen, is that they understood clearly the dynamic thrust of the Bible's own story line. They saw that story as the story of God's own mission, and they saw their own part in the story, participating in its last great act, as "God's co-workers" (1 Cor. 3:9).

So, in the chapters below, I have sought to follow roughly the outline of the story above, asking as we go along: What challenges and responsibilities face the people of God in their own mission in the light of this or that part of the biblical story? So I have selected texts that seem representative of such missional aspects of our life as God's people. These are by no means all that could have served our purpose, but I hope they show at least two things: first, that we can and should draw our biblical theology of the church's mission from the whole range of the Bible; and second, that when we do so, it becomes clear that the mission of God's people is vast and various.

RELEVANT QUESTIONS

1. Prior to reading this chapter, how relevant were the OT Scriptures for your understanding of the church's mission? How has your view been impacted by the content of this chapter?
2. We tend to explain "the gospel" in the form of a series of propositions or doctrines. In the light of the whole Bible story, as summarized in this chapter, how would you summarize the gospel in more narrative form?
3. What suggestions can you make to help churches (including pastors, leaders, missions committees, etc.) to become more motivated for mission by having a better understanding of "the story we are in"? What impact would better teaching in this area have on our mission awareness and mission commitment?

CHAPTER 3

PEOPLE WHO CARE FOR CREATION

Some people have a hard time connecting their understanding of Christian mission to the Old Testament at all, let alone starting in Genesis. But we really must begin where the Bible begins. For if we don't, we will miss the vital importance of how the Bible ends.

The Bible begins and ends with creation. It opens with the words, "In the beginning God created the heavens and the earth" (Gen. 1:1), and its final great vision opens with the words, "Then I saw 'a new heaven and a new earth'" (Rev. 21:1). The trouble is that some Christians seem to have Bibles that begin at Genesis 3 and end at Revelation 20. They know all about sin from the story of the fall, and they know that God has solved the sin problem through Christ, and that they will be safe on the great day of judgment. The story of creation for them is no more than a backdrop for the story of salvation, and the Bible's grand climax speaks to them only of going to heaven when they die (even though the last chapters of the Bible say nothing about us going anywhere, but eagerly anticipate God's coming here).

But a Bible stripped of its beginning and ending will produce a concept of mission that is distorted in the same way. We will imagine that God's only concern, and therefore ours too, is to save people from sin and judgment. Now of course, there can be no doubting that the Bible gives enormous attention to that issue, and no doubt also that it must be at the heart of our mission in God's name. But it's not the whole story. It's not the whole story of the Bible, and it should not be the whole story of our mission.

The Bible's story is that the God who created the universe, only to see it ravaged by evil and sin, has committed himself to the total redemption and restoration of the whole creation, has accomplished it in advance through the cross and resurrection of Jesus of Nazareth, and will bring it to glorious completion in the new creation when Christ returns. In between the great poles of the original creation and the new creation, the Bible has a great deal more to say about creation.

> Let us rediscover that the gospel, the *good* news, does not begin with Jesus' birth. It begins with the good earth that God made through Jesus. Let us celebrate again that creation in all its richness is the wonderful gift of a good God.
>
> *Dave Bookless*[1]

---

1. Dave Bookless, *Planetwise: Dare to Care for God's World* (Nottingham: IVP, 2008), 25. This book is an excellent short survey of the whole Bible's teaching on creation and its implications for our Christian discipleship, worship, lifestyle and mission.

In fact, creation is one of the major themes in biblical theology. So it would be astonishing if it did *not* have a significant place within a biblical theology of mission. And indeed it *is* astonishing, and very sad, that it has such an insignificant, virtually nonexistent, place in the mission theology and practice of so many Christians who like to claim that they are "biblical" in all things.

We will first of all, then, remind ourselves of the mission of caring for creation, which God gave to humanity in Genesis 1–2 when he first created us on earth. Then we will go on to see what else is said about creation in the Old Testament that reinforces the importance of that task. After that we will move to the New Testament and see how creation is connected to Christ. After all, our mission has to be Christ-centred or it is not even biblical at all. Finally we will suggest some reasons why ecological concern and action can thus be seen as a fully legitimate part of the mission of God's people.[2]

> To be human is to be in proper relationship with God, other people, and the world. Sin has marred and well-nigh destroyed these relationships, but in Christ, the perfect human, they are restored.... Each of these three relationships is restored as we increasingly grow into the image of Christ. Because Christ is the perfect human, the one person who completely fills out the image of God, the more we become like him, the more human we become.... The Christian life, far from transforming us into super-spiritual, quasi-angelic beings, is actually a quest to recover our humanity.
>
> *Michael Wittmer*[3]

SUBDUE AND RULE; SERVE AND KEEP: GENESIS 1 – 2

So let us begin at the beginning by recalling that all of us were created as human beings in God's own image. It may be easy to forget, but we were human beings before we became Christians, and we don't stop being human beings when we do become Christians (though some Christians make you wonder ...). And God will hold us accountable for our humanity as much as for our Christianity. For there are things we have been commanded by God to do as human creatures, from which no other Bible text or teaching exempts us. On the contrary, being God's people and therefore already among the new redeemed humanity surely reinforces and intensifies our obligation to live by his original mandate to the human race. Human beings are people with a mission.

Kings of Creation: Genesis 1:26 – 28

Then God said, "Let us make human beings in our image, in our likeness, so that they may [lit., and let them] rule over the fish in the sea and the birds in the sky,

---

2. Much fuller discussion of the biblical foundation for ecological ethics and mission is available in Christopher J. H. Wright, *Old Testament Ethics for the People of God* (Leicester: IVP, and Downers Grove: IVP, 2004), 103–45; and idem, *The Mission of God*, 397–420.

3. Michael E. Wittmer, *Heaven Is a Place on Earth: Why Everything You Do Matters to God* (Grand Rapids: Zondervan, 2004), 83. Wittmer's book is an excellent survey of key biblical themes, from creation to new creation, that underlie the broad argument of this book.

over the livestock and all the wild animals, and over all the creatures that move along the ground."

> So God created human beings in his own image,
>   in the image of God he created them;
>   male and female he created them.

> God blessed them and said to them, "Be fruitful and increase in number; fill the earth and subdue it. Rule over the fish in the sea and the birds in the sky and over every living creature that moves on the ground."

The first mention of human beings in the Bible states two fundamental things about us, two things that are put so closely together that they are clearly connected: (1) God made us in his image (both male and female), and (2) God intended us to exercise dominion within creation. It is not that having dominion is what *constitutes* the image of God, but rather that exercising dominion is what being made in God's image enables and entitles us to do. We humans have a mission on earth because God had a purpose in putting us on it.

So God instructs the human species not only to fill the earth (an instruction given to the other creatures in their habitats), but also to *subdue the earth* and to *rule over* the rest of the creatures. The words *kabaš* ("subdue") and *radah* ("rule") are strong words, with a sense of imposing of will upon another. However, they are not terms that necessarily imply violence or abuse (though some critics of Christianity lay the blame for ecological disaster at the door of these two words and the freedom they allegedly give to us to rape the environment—a charge that has been well refuted).

The first word, "subduing [the earth]", probably implies no more than the task of agriculture, though it now encompasses many other products of human ingenuity and effort.

The second word, "rule over", is more distinctive. It describes a responsibility for human beings that is entrusted to no other species—the task of ruling or exercising dominion over the rest of creation. With this word, God is passing on to human hands a delegated form of God's own kingly authority over the whole of his creation. Kings and emperors in ancient times (and even dictators in modern times) would set up an image of themselves in far flung corners of their domains. These great statues proclaimed their sovereignty over that territory and its people. The image represented the authority of the king. Similarly God installs the human species as his image within creation and authorizes humans to exercise authority. But that is an authority that finally belongs to God, the creator and owner of the earth.

But if human beings are meant to function as kings within creation, then what kind of king is God? How does God exercise his kingship within creation? We need to know the answer in order to be able to say what it means for humanity as God's image to behave as king within creation.

Psalm 145 is one place to find out, for it is addressed to "my God the King" and calls on all creation to praise him. There we discover that the reign of God in creation is characterized by wisdom, power, goodness, grace, compassion, faithfulness, generosity, provision, protection, justice and love. If that is what it means for *God* to act as king, then the same qualities should be seen in the way we who are made in God's image exercise the dominion that God has entrusted to us. We are given the mission of ruling over creation, but we are to do it in ways that are modeled on the character and values of God's own kingship.

So then, human dominion over the rest of creation is to be an exercise of kingship that reflects God's own kingship. The image of God is not a license for arrogant abuse, but a pattern that commits us to humble reflection of the character of God.

> This understanding [of the image of God] turns our supremacism upside-down, for if we resemble God in that we have dominion, we must be called to be "imitators of God" (Eph. 5:1) in the way we exercise it. Indeed, far from giving us a free hand on the earth, the *imago Dei* constrains us. We must be kings, not tyrants – if we become the latter we deny, and even destroy, the image in us.
>
> *Huw Spanner*[4]

Servants of Creation: Genesis 2:15

> The LORD God took the man and put him in the Garden of Eden to work it and take care of it.

Here we find two more verbs to describe the mission of human beings. God took the human creature he had made and put him in the special environment within the earth that he had made – the garden in Eden – with a simple task: *to serve it and keep it.* That is the simplest meaning of the two verbs.

The verb *ʿabad* means "to serve", with the connotation of doing hard work in the process of serving. So although most translations render it in this verse with meanings like "to work it", "to till it", or "to cultivate it", the essential core of the word still has the sense of serving. Humans are servants of creation, and that is the way they are to exercise their kingship over it.

The verb *šamar* means "to keep something safe", with protection, care, and watchfulness. It means to treat something (or someone) seriously as worthy of devoted attention (thus, for example, in a moral sense it can mean to keep the way of the Lord, or to keep God's law – i.e., by studying, understanding and obeying it).

So humans are put into God's created environment to serve it and to look after it. This makes it clear that the main point of our ruling the earth is for *its* benefit, not our own. Now of course, there is plenty in the Bible about how creation serves our human needs also, as we will see in a moment. But we need to begin here first. God created us to rule over the rest of his creation by serving and keeping it – that is, by working hard in a way that will care for creation and protect its best interests.

4. Huw Spanner, "Tyrants, Stewards – or Just Kings?" in *Animals on the Agenda: Questions about Animals for Theology and Ethics* (eds. Linzey Andrew and Dorothy Yamamoto; London: SCM, 1998), 222.

Ruling and serving creation is humanity's first mission on earth, and God never repealed the mandate.

The great commission given us by Jesus in the New Testament must be held alongside the very first great commission God gave us at the start of the Bible. In Genesis 1, God's very first words to human beings are about ruling over and caring for creation: the fish, the birds and all the other living creatures, for God's sake. This is, if you like, a universal job description of what it means to be human. To the question "Why are we here?" the ultimate answer has to be: "To worship and serve God." The first element of that worship and service that the Bible talks about is creation care.

Dave Bookless[5]

One of the primary responsibilities of kings in the Old Testament was to act particularly on behalf of the weak and powerless. Psalm 72 prays that God will endow the king with justice so that he can defend the afflicted and the needy. Justice in the Old Testament is not blind impartiality, but intervening to set things right, such that those who have been wronged are vindicated, those who are being oppressed are delivered, and those who are weak and vulnerable have their voices heard and their case attended to.

Here is a challenging piece of advice given to a king by his mother:

Speak up for those who cannot speak for themselves,
    for the rights of all who are destitute.
Speak up and judge fairly;
    defend the rights of the poor and needy. (Prov. 31:8 – 9)

So then, for us as humans to rule over the rest of creation as king, to act as the image of God the king, means to do biblical justice in relation to the nonhuman creation. And doing justice must involve particular concern for the weak and defenseless.

"Speak up for those who cannot speak for themselves." Surely that describes not just what a king should do for his subjects, but what humans should do for the nonhuman creation. To be the voice of the voiceless is very much part of the motivation of Christians involved in ecological action, in protection of species and their habitats, in environmental advocacy, and so on. In fact, it is one mark of a righteous person to be concerned for animals (Prov. 12:10).

So then, the first dimension of our mission as God's people is the mission that we share with the rest of humanity, to rule over creation as God intended by serving and caring for it.

FOR GOD, FOR US, FOREVER

For several years the British Royal Society for the Protection of Birds (RSPB) had as its motto, "For Birds, for People, Forever". It was neat and catchy, and it always struck me as very biblical, except for one missing phrase – "For God".

5. Bookless, *Planetwise*, 136.

As the Old Testament develops the theme of creation, we can identify at least three strong emphases, each of which feeds into our concern for ecological mission.

God's Glory Is the Goal of Creation

The creation exists for the praise and glory of its creator God. We humans, being creatures ourselves, share in that reason for existence. As the Shorter Catechism of the Westminster Confession of Faith states, "Man's chief end is to glorify God and enjoy him forever." Our "chief end", the prime goal of all human life, is to bring glory to God, and *in doing so* to enjoy ourselves because we enjoy God.

But that God-focused goal of human life (to glorify and enjoy God) is not something that sets us *apart* from the rest of creation. Rather, it is something we *share* with the rest of creation. That is the "chief end" of all creation. The only difference is that we *human* beings must glorify our creator in uniquely *human* ways. We are the only creatures who are made in the image of God, and so the praise and glory we bring to God reflects that status. So, as humans we praise God with hearts and hands and voices, with rationality as well as emotion, with language, art, music and craft—with all that reflects the God in whose image we were made. Our praise is explicitly *human* praise.

But all the rest of creation—animate and inanimate—already praises God. Indeed in the Bible, the creatures are summoned again and again to praise God! Just read Psalm 148, and the closing line of the whole book of Psalms: "Let everything that has breath praise the Lord" (Ps. 150:6; cf. 145:10, 21; 148). There is a response of gratitude that befits not just human beneficiaries of God's generosity, but comes from the nonhuman creatures as well (e.g., Ps. 104:27–28).

Now we may be puzzled by this. But that's no reason for not believing it. Since we are human beings, we know only the reality of our human personhood "from the inside", and what it means for *us* to praise God. We cannot put ourselves into the "mind" of the animals, still less into the "being" of a tree or a mountain. Nor can we put ourselves into the mind of God the creator and understand how God relates to his nonhuman creation. But the Bible tells us that God does, and that he receives praise and glory from all of it. We may not be

> This response of gratitude is a fundamental feature of creaturely being which is shared by all the creatures of the earth, humans and animals, landscapes, seas and mountains, earth, wind, fire and rain. The Psalmist charges all things with the first moral duty of the creation, to worship and praise the creator.... In the Hebrew perspective humanity and the cosmos have moral significance, and both are required to make a moral response to the creator, a response to God which reflects his glory and offers the return of gratitude, praise and worship [Ps. 150].
>
> *Michael Northcott*[6]

6. Michael S. Northcott, *The Environment and Christian Ethics* (Cambridge: Cambridge University Press, 1996), 180–81.

able to explain *how* it is that creation praises its maker. But just because we cannot articulate the *how* of creation's inarticulate praise, or indeed the *how* of God's receiving of it, we should not therefore deny *the fact that* creation praises God – since it is affirmed throughout the Bible with overwhelming conviction.

So when we care for creation, we share in its great purpose of giving glory to God. Conversely, of course, when we fail to do so, or when we participate in the destruction, pollution and wasting of creation, we are reducing even further creation's capacity to give glory to God.

Human Life and Creation Are Integrally Bound Together

The close link between human beings and the earth is made clear from the start. The Hebrew word for "man" (generically) is *'adam*. The word for the "ground", or the soil (and sometimes the whole earth), is *'adamah*. So we are indeed "earth-creatures", formed from the dust of the earth, and sharing the same basic "stuff" – particles, proteins, DNA, minerals and so on – as all other creatures and the planet itself. Especially water. "We do not depend on water. We are water", was an arresting opening line in an article in a recent RSPB's magazine. It was making the point that whatever we do to the planet's water resources we do to ourselves.

The Old Testament goes on to emphasize this integral relationship between humans and the earth in two ways.

The Earth Provides for Us

First, God has given the resources of the earth to us for our food and survival. Of course, this is true also of all animal species. But explicit permission is given to human beings in Genesis 1:29–30 and 9:3 to eat what is around us in the world.

The earth feeds us. And clothes us. And shelters us. Think of grass for a moment – possibly the most abundant form of vegetation on the planet, in its myriad varieties in all climates. We eat grass, once it has become meat from grazing animals whose only diet is daily grass. We drink grass, in the form of milk and curds. We wear grass, in clothing made from wool or shoes made from leather. Millions of humans still use grass for effective thatched shelter from sun and rain. Grasses are woven into ropes, baskets and floor coverings. Grass alone provides humans with incalculable benefits and supplies so much of our needs, even before we go on to talk about cultivated grasses that produce the vast variety of nourishing grains we shake into our cereal bowls in the morning.

So really, it is somewhat arrogant for us to go on talking about how we have to "care for the environment", as if it were just a passive object in need of our sympathy. *It is the environment that cares for us,* silently ministering the generous grace of God to us every day we live on the planet, as Psalm 65:9–13 cheerfully remembers with gratitude.

The Earth Suffers with Us

Second, however, the Old Testament insists on a strong moral link between how humans behave on earth and the state of the earth itself—for good or ill. Specifically, human wickedness produces ecological stress. The people of Old Testament times may not have understood the underlying scientific connections between human action and biological effects, but they could observe them and draw theological and ethical conclusions.

Hosea provides the most direct example of the link when he concludes his catalogue of social evils with depressing symptoms in the natural order.

> Hear the word of the LORD, you Israelites,
>   because the LORD has a charge to bring
>   against you who live in the land:
> "There is no faithfulness, no love,
>   no acknowledgment of God in the land.
> There is only cursing, lying and murder,
>   stealing and adultery;
> they break all bounds,
>   and bloodshed follows bloodshed.
> Because of this the land dries up [or, mourns],
>   and all who live in it waste away;
> the beasts of the field, the birds in the sky
>   and the fish in the sea are swept away. (Hos. 4:1–3)

Deuteronomy 28 shows how the obedience or disobedience of the people will have effects, in blessing or curse, that operate within the natural order. Jeremiah 4:23–26 portrays God's judgment in a way that terrifyingly reverses the gifts of creation.

So the point is that we cannot extract ourselves from the natural environment of the earth. We were created as part of it and were created to care for it. Whatever we do on earth, for good or ill, will have ecological impact because of the integration of human life and all other life on earth. That is the way God arranged it, and we reap the consequences of our actions. A greedy humanity will lead to a suffering earth—and a suffering earth will lead to a suffering humanity.

God's Redemption Includes Creation

As we know all too well today, the accumulated effect of our carelessness for generations is causing an environmental crisis of unprecedented proportions. I need not go into details since the facts are well-known and increasingly disturbing (though also confusing). Nor do I want to play at being a prophet and make dire predictions. We cannot know the future, and the combination of God's grace and human ingenuity may yet enable means to be found to avert some of the worst scenarios that assail us, whether from sober science or movie fiction.

However, the Old Testament insists that our future does not depend on human ingenuity, however great that may be (and it is in itself, of course, part of the gift of God's creation in us). We live on a cursed earth (according to Gen. 3), but we also live on a covenanted earth (according to Gen. 9). Our survival ultimately depends not on us but on the promise of God to Noah, after the flood, that God himself would sustain the means of life on the planet—a covenant made not just with human beings, but explicitly with all life on earth. So there is a universal assurance of God's intentions even within the present natural order that is so stressed and spoiled by our greed and destruction.

But beyond that, the Old Testament specifically includes creation within its vision of God's redemptive plans. God intends to bless the nations of humanity, and he has promised Abraham that he will so. That is a theme that will echo again and again through our reflections in the chapters to come. But that blessing is never envisaged as whisking the nations off the planet to some other blessed abode. Rather, it will be a blessing of people *with and within* a creation that is finally redeemed and restored to the state of multiple blessedness that characterized it in Genesis 1–2.

Creation is *not* just the disposable backdrop to the lives of human creatures who were really intended to live somewhere else, and some day will do so. We are not redeemed *out of* creation, but as *part of* the redeemed creation itself—a creation that will again be fully and eternally for God's glory, for our joy and benefit, and forever.

Israel's songwriters spend a lot of time looking forward to the day when God will put all things right. When God finally comes to judge the earth, this does not have only a negative ring (though of course it does mean that the unrepentantly wicked will finally be dealt with), but it means that God will vindicate the oppressed, restore wholesome relationships, and bring peace and justice to earth.

But those Israelite songwriters do not think of people only. The whole of creation will benefit from the climactic redemption of God and will rejoice in it. Psalm 96 comes to its climax proclaiming the coming reign of God, and the impact on creation is unmistakable. There is a great "Ode to Joy" from the whole created order:

> Say among the nations, "The LORD reigns."
>> The world is firmly established, it cannot be moved;
>> he will judge the peoples with equity.
> Let the heavens rejoice, let the earth be glad;
>> let the sea resound, and all that is in it.
> Let the fields be jubilant, and everything in them;
>> let all the trees of the forest sing for joy.
> Let all creation rejoice before the LORD, for he comes,
>> he comes to judge the earth.

He will judge the world in righteousness
  and the peoples in his faithfulness. (Ps. 96:10 – 13; cf. 98:7 – 9)

The prophets share the enthusiasm – especially Isaiah. Isaiah 11:1 – 9 portrays the just rule of the future messianic king and concludes with a picture of harmony and shalom within the created order. Isaiah 35 also envisages transformation within creation when God finally redeems his people. However, the climax of the Old Testament future vision regarding creation is found in Isaiah 65 – 66. The words, "Behold, I am creating new heavens and a new earth" (Isa. 65:17 – the opening word is a participle, suggesting it is something God is already active in doing, not merely a future intention), introduce a wonderful section that simply has to be read in full.

"See, I will create
  new heavens and a new earth.
The former things will not be remembered,
  nor will they come to mind.
But be glad and rejoice forever
  in what I will create,
for I will create Jerusalem to be a delight
  and its people a joy.
I will rejoice over Jerusalem
  and take delight in my people;
the sound of weeping and of crying
  will be heard in it no more.

"Never again will there be in it
  infants who live but a few days,
  or older people who do not live out their years;
those who die at a hundred
  will be thought mere youths;
those who fail to reach a hundred
  will be considered accursed.
They will build houses and dwell in them;
  they will plant vineyards and eat their fruit.
No longer will they build houses and others live in them,
  or plant and others eat.
For as the days of a tree,
  so will be the days of my people;
my chosen ones will long enjoy
  the work of their hands.
They will not labor in vain,
  nor will they bear children doomed to misfortune;

for they will be a people blessed by the LORD,
    they and their descendants with them.
Before they call I will answer;
    while they are still speaking I will hear.
The wolf and the lamb will feed together,
    and the lion will eat straw like the ox,
    but dust will be the serpent's food.
They will neither harm nor destroy
    on all my holy mountain,"
    says the LORD. (Isa. 65:17–25)

This inspiring vision portrays God's new creation as a place that will be joyful, free from grief and tears, life-fulfilling, with guaranteed work-satisfaction, freedom from the curses of frustrated labour, and environmentally safe! It is a vision that puts most New Age dreams in the shade.

This naturally leads us on to the way the New Testament sees the fulfillment of these great hopes for creation in the redemption accomplished by Jesus Christ. But before going there, let's briefly summarize where we have gone so far.

When God created the earth, he created human beings in his own image with the express mission of ruling over creation by caring for it—a task modeled on the kingship of God himself. That human mission has never been rescinded, and Christians have not been given some exemption on the grounds that we have other or better things to do.

As we participate in that task of ruling and caring for creation, we are participating in the creation's own giving glory and praise to the creator, which in turn is a proper response to the fact that the creation, by God's intention, provides for our needs in such abundance.

But even as we do so, we are conscious of the appalling suffering and desecration of creation that is the consequence of our sin, greed and violence. So we not only look back to the principles of creation that *push us out* in ecological mission, but we also look forward to the redemption of creation, which *pulls us forward* with hope and the assurance that our labour is not in vain in the Lord.

BY CHRIST, FOR CHRIST, THROUGH CHRIST

Perhaps with a sigh of relief and some impatience, we move to the New Testament. Here, after all, is where we find Christ, the Christ whose Great Commission drives our mission, the Christ in whose name alone our mission is authorized and effective. And once our minds turn to Christ, a number of well-known texts flood in.

"You are to give him the name Jesus, because he will save his people from their sins" (Matt. 1:21). "Christ Jesus came into the world to save sinners" (1 Tim. 1:15). Saving sinners was the mission of Jesus and the meaning of the cross. Surely, then, it constitutes the parameters of our mission too. For if our mission flows from the redeeming work of Christ and his cross, where does creation fit into that? Saving sinners, not saving whales or trees — is that not what we should concentrate on?

But once again we have to point out that although it is gloriously true that sinners are saved through the cross of Christ, it is not actually the whole gospel or the whole achievement of the cross — not according to the New Testament itself.

All Things Reconciled by the Cross

Listen to Paul expounding his grand vision of the work of Christ, in a passage that seems to be definitive of "the hope of the gospel". It is very clearly and carefully constructed.

> The Son is the image of the invisible God, the firstborn over all creation. For in him all things were created: things in heaven and on earth, visible and invisible, whether thrones or powers or rulers or authorities; all things have been created through him and for him. He is before all things, and in him all things hold together. And he is the head of the body, the church; he is the beginning and the firstborn from among the dead, so that in everything he might have the supremacy. For God was pleased to have all his fullness dwell in him, and through him to reconcile to himself all things, whether things on earth or things in heaven, by making peace through his blood, shed on the cross.
>
> Once you were alienated from God and were enemies in your minds because of your evil behavior. But now he has reconciled you by Christ's physical body through death to present you holy in his sight, without blemish and free from accusation — if you continue in your faith, established and firm, and do not move from the hope held out in the gospel. This is the gospel that you heard and that has been proclaimed to every creature under heaven, and of which I, Paul, have become a servant. (Col. 1:15–23)

There are several things we should note in this wonderful text.

Paul is talking about the whole of creation. He first says "all creation" (v. 15), and then uses the phrase "all things in heaven and earth" (v. 16). It could not be clearer that Paul has in mind *the whole of the created universe* — not just human beings.

Paul links *Christ and creation* in the most comprehensive way. Christ was there, of course, as the Son of God, even before creation existed (v. 17). Christ is the source of the creation of the universe (v. 16). Christ is beneficiary or heir of all creation ("the firstborn" [v. 15], "for him" [v. 16]). Christ sustains creation in existence (v. 17).

Paul includes creation in *the saving power of the cross.* Christ has redeemed creation (v. 20). It is vital to see here that the blood of Christ, shed on the cross, is the means of the reconciliation of *creation* to God, not only of *sinners*. "All things" that are reconciled in verse 20 must have the same universal meaning as the "all things" that were created in verse 16.

The order of Paul's argument here is also revealing and runs counter to the way we tend to describe the gospel. We start from the other end.

We tend to start with individuals who need to have their sin problem dealt with. The cross is the answer to that individual problem, so that you can be saved and go to heaven. Meanwhile, you need fellowship and company on the way to heaven, and that's what the church is for, so you'd better join one. As for the world out there, we have to live in it until we get to heaven, but we should not get too obsessed with it, since only what is "heavenly" really counts.

Individual → church → world → heaven. That is our trajectory, with its built-in dualism.

But Paul's gospel works in the exact opposite direction. God has a very big plan indeed. Paul starts with creation – and relates that to Christ as its creator and sustainer. Then he moves to the church (v. 18), which will be the people of the new creation, because they are in Christ, who is the firstborn of the new creation just as he is the firstborn of the original creation. That is to say, the church belongs to Christ because all things belong to Christ, but also because the church is already, in this creation, the anticipation of the redeemed people of God in the new creation. Then, having spoken of all creation and of the whole church, Paul sums up their totality in the reconciling work of the cross (v. 20). Finally, having sketched the grand plan of God for the whole universe and emphasized the centrality of the cross within it, Paul adds – "Oh yes, even you too ["and you" at the beginning of v. 21 is emphatic], you get to be part of this! You who were Gentile outsiders [as described in Eph. 2:11 – 12] can be among the reconciled, through faith in this gospel, which is now for everybody everywhere" ("proclaimed to every creature under heaven", v. 23, could be better translated as "proclaimed in the whole creation / in all creation under heaven" [as in REB and ESV]; Paul sees the whole created earth as the sphere of gospel proclamation).

Good News for All Creation

Paul's vision of the gospel is as wide as creation itself, and that is because his understanding of the cross includes the whole of creation in the reconciling work of Christ. Now our mission is founded on the gospel and needs to reflect the length, breadth and depth of the gospel. If, then, the cross of Christ is good news for the whole creation, our mission must include being and bringing good news to the whole creation.[7]

---

7. In the so-called "longer ending" of Mark's gospel, Jesus told his disciples to "go into all the world and preach the good news to all creation" (Mark 16:15). This may not have been in the original text that left the hands of Mark, but it certainly reflects a truly biblical insight. The gospel of the death and resurrection of Jesus is indeed good news for the whole creation, as the author of Psalm 96 would doubtless have agreed.

So our care for creation is motivated not solely by the fact that it was created by God and we were commanded to look after it, but also by the fact that it has been redeemed by Christ, and we are to erect signposts towards its ultimate destiny of complete restoration in Christ. God's redemptive mission includes creation. Our mission involves participating in that redemptive work as agents of good news to creation, as well as to people.

Other parts of the New Testament add to this great vision for the future. Paul connects the redemption of creation with the redemption and resurrection of our bodies in Romans 8 – a highly significant passage.

> The creation waits in eager expectation for the children of God to be revealed. For the creation was subjected to frustration, not by its own choice, but by the will of the one who subjected it, in hope that the creation itself will be liberated from its bondage to decay and brought into the freedom and glory of the children of God.
>
> We know that the whole creation has been groaning as in the pains of childbirth right up to the present time. Not only so, but we ourselves, who have the firstfruits of the Spirit, groan inwardly as we wait eagerly for our adoption, the redemption of our bodies. (Rom. 8:19 – 23)

Peter too looks forward beyond the purging judgment of God that will destroy all that is evil in the present world order to a new, redeemed creation.

> But in keeping with his promise we are looking forward to a new heaven and a new earth, where righteousness dwells. (2 Peter 3:13)

The language of fire and destruction does not mean that the whole of creation will be *obliterated*. Rather, it is parallel to the same terms used to describe the way the sinful world was "destroyed" by water in the flood (2 Peter 3:6 – 7). What was destroyed in the flood was not the whole planet, but the world of sin and rebellion. Likewise, what will be destroyed in the final judgment is not the universe, but the sin and rebellion of humanity and the devastation they have caused. It will be a conflagration that purges and purifies, so that the new creation will be a place devoid of sin but filled with righteousness, because God himself will dwell there among his redeemed people (Rev. 21:1 – 4).[8]

As a result, our mission as created human beings is to care for the earth God created. And that mission is intensified for us as redeemed human beings because we look forward to the redemption of creation as well. Our ecological activity as Christians thus has both a creational and a redemptive dimension. It is a missional response to what our biblical theology teaches us about God's purpose for creation, from the very beginning and the very ending of the Bible.

---

8. See Wittmer, *Heaven Is a Place on Earth*, 201 – 3.

SUMMARY

I hope that our brief survey of the biblical theology of creation has provided sufficient justification for saying that Christians ought to be in the forefront of caring for creation. We have far more profound reasons for doing so, drawn from our faith and worldview, than merely prudential or self-serving ones (we'd better do something or we'll all fry or drown). So, yes, Christians should seek to live on the planet in ways that are now generally approved as "green"—avoiding wasteful use of energy, reducing our carbon footprint, recycling rather than trashing, preventing pollution, and supporting political and economic initiatives that protect the environment from further needless destruction.

But is there more than that? What about ecological *mission*? Is it legitimate to apply our biblical theology for life at this point by saying that some people are called and sent by God with the specific mission of creation care, scientific research in the ecological arena, habitat conservation, and so on? I believe that the answer is yes, and will suggest some reasons why when we come to reflect on relevance in chapter 15.

RELEVANT QUESTIONS

1. If the Bible's story runs from creation to new creation, what should that mean for your church's mission agenda, if it is to be fully biblical?
2. In what ways has this chapter enriched your understanding of Jesus—especially in relation to the significance and scope of his accomplishment through the cross and resurrection?
3. How does the inclusion of earth care in the church's mission affect your perception of the Christian's/church's responsibility in environmental issues?
4. Are there specific patterns of behaviour and stewardship that you feel should change in your own life as a result of this perspective?

CHAPTER 4

PEOPLE WHO ARE A BLESSING TO THE NATIONS

Who was the greatest missionary in the Bible? Some might say Jesus, but most would probably answer, Paul. He certainly stands as the one who, as "apostle to the nations", envisaged and accomplished the great transition of the gospel across the divide between Jews and Gentiles and thus set in motion the movement that would see the gospel spread to every corner of the world.

How did Paul understand his own missionary life and work? What was he trying to accomplish? What kept him going through all the battering and bruising (literally) of his missionary career?

THE OBEDIENCE OF FAITH AMONG ALL NATIONS

Paul tells us in a phrase that comes at the beginning and end of his greatest letter. His calling as an apostle was, he says, "to bring about the obedience of faith for the sake of his [Christ's] name among all the nations" (Rom. 1:5; repeated at 16:26 ESV).

Now that is an ambition that resonates with strong echoes of Abraham. For Abraham is the Old Testament character par excellence who was the model of faith and of obedience – as Paul, James and the author of Hebrews all testify. And the horizon of "all the nations" goes back to God's promise to Abraham that through him all the nations on earth will be blessed.

So Paul is indicating, by this prominently placed phrase, that his lifetime's service of the gospel was all about producing communities of Abraham look-alikes in *all* the nations, not just in the nation physically descended from Abraham. An ambitious goal, for sure, but profoundly rooted in his reading of God's mission as expressed in his promise to Abraham.

But it goes deeper than that. Paul did not just mean that Abraham was a rather fine *example* that he could use to illustrate the doctrine of justification he was about to expound in the rest of the letter. God's promise to Abraham was not merely a random *illustration* of something else. It was the thing itself – God's own agenda for saving the world. God's promise to Abraham was, in short, the gospel. It is very good news indeed.

That is how Paul describes God's promise to Abraham in Galatians.

> Scripture foresaw that God would justify the Gentiles [the nations] by faith, and announced *the gospel* in advance to Abraham: "All nations will be blessed through you." (Gal. 3:8, italics added)

So the gospel, the good news, from God's own mouth, is that God intends to bless all nations, and to do so through Abraham and his descendants.

Who are we then? We are like the Galatians to whom Paul was writing. If we are among the Gentile nations and have come to believe in Jesus as the Messiah of Israel and saviour of the world, we have entered into the blessing of Abraham. Indeed, we have become part of the people of Abraham. To be in Christ is to be in Abraham, according to Paul – no matter what ethnic, social, or gender identity you have.

> There is neither Jew nor Gentile, neither slave nor free, neither male nor female, for you are all one in Christ Jesus. If you belong to Christ, then you are Abraham's seed, and heirs according to the promise. (Gal. 3:28 – 29)

But what does this mean for our mission? If we are the people of God now in Christ and therefore also "in Abraham", how will that affect our understanding of who we are and what we are here for? We need first of all to see just how important God's choice of Abraham was for the implementing of God's own mission of redemptive blessing. Then we'll need to scan some of the echoes of Abraham through the Old and New Testaments, showing that it is in fact a major theme of biblical theology. Finally we can apply all this to our own practice of mission. In what ways are we to be people who model our mission practice on the faith and obedience of Abraham? What does it mean to say that we are people chosen to bless the nations?[1]

But first, we need to see the connection with the last chapter. There we explored the great biblical arch from creation to new creation. It was human rebellion that spoiled God's good creation and led to God's restoration project that now begins with Abraham. And the story that begins here is the first step on the road that leads to the new creation itself. We are standing at a very key moment in the Bible's story.

ABRAHAM – IN THE BLEAK CONTEXT OF GENESIS 1 – 11

The great promise of God to Abraham, often called the Abrahamic covenant, comes in Genesis 12:1 – 3. But Genesis 12 comes after Genesis 1 – 11. That may seem obvious, but it is crucially important. For the whole point of what God initiates with

---

1. For a much fuller study of this theme of the election of Abraham and its implications for mission, see the two chapters devoted to it in *The Mission of God*, chs. 6 and 7. Some of the sections that follow in this chapter draw extensively on that survey.

his promise to Abraham only becomes clear when we see it against the darkening background of those chapters.

After the grand opening chapters of creation, the biblical story goes awry in Genesis 3, when God's human creatures choose to rebel against their creator, distrusting his benevolence, disobeying his authority and disregarding the boundaries he had set for their freedom in his world. This produces radical brokenness in all the relationships established in creation. Human beings hide from God in guilty fear. Men and women can no longer face one another without shame and blame. The soil comes under the curse of God, and the earth no longer responds to human touch as it should.

The following chapters (chs. 4–11), then, combine an escalating crescendo of human sin alongside repeated marks of God's grace. The serpent's head will be crushed. Adam and Eve are clothed. Cain is protected. Noah and his family are saved. Life goes on, and creation is preserved under covenant. The great creation project is still moving forward, but it is limping under the crippling weight of human sin.

After the flood, God renews his promise to creation, and human beings are again sent forth under God's blessing to multiply and fill the earth (Gen. 9:1). However the story runs into trouble yet again in chapter 11. The human decision to settle and to build a city with a tower in the land of Shinar seems to combine arrogance (in wanting to make a name for themselves) and insecurity (in wanting not to be scattered over the whole earth as God intended). The Babel story presents us with people who seem intent on invading the heavens even while resisting God's will for them on earth.

The result is chaotic dividedness. Genesis 3–11 show how every dimension of life is tragically adrift from the original goodness of God's purpose. The earth lies under the sentence of God's curse because of human sin. Human beings are adding to their catalogue of evil as the generations roll past—jealousy, anger, murder, vengeance, violence, corruption, drunkenness, sexual disorder, arrogance. Animals are being killed for food, with God's permission but hardly with their creator's best pleasure. Women enjoy the gift of childbirth along with suffering and pain. Men find fulfillment in subduing the earth, but with sweat and frustration. Both enjoy sexual complementarity and intimacy, but along with lust and domination. Every inclination of human hearts is shot through with evil. Technology and culture are advancing, but the skill that can craft instruments for music and agriculture can also forge weapons of violent death. Nations experience the richness of their ethnic, linguistic and geographical diversity along with confusion, scattering and strife.

Where can the mission of God go from here? What can God do next? Whatever it may be, it will have to tackle a broad redemptive agenda. Genesis 1–11 poses a cosmic question to which God must provide a cosmic answer. The problems so graphically spread before the reader in Genesis 1–11 will not be solved just by finding a way to get human beings to heaven when they die. Death itself must be destroyed if the curse is to be removed and the way opened to the tree of life. The love and power of God must address not only the sin of individuals, but the strife and strivings of nations; not only the need of human beings but also the suffering of animals and the curse on the ground.

It will take the whole of the rest of the Bible's story, from Genesis 12 to Revelation 21–22, to accomplish all this. Biblical theology encompasses this comprehensive span of problem and solution. So our biblical theology of mission must stretch alongside the same span.

What can God do next? Something that only God could have thought of. God sees an elderly, childless couple in the land of Babel itself and decides to make them the launch pad of his whole mission of cosmic redemption. One can almost hear the sharp intake of breath among the angels when the astonishing plan was revealed. They knew, as the reader of Genesis 1–11 now knows, the sheer scale of devastation that serpentine evil and human recalcitrance have wrought in God's creation. What sort of an answer can be provided through Abram and Sarai? Yet that is precisely the scale of what now follows.

The call of Abram is the beginning of God's answer to the evil of human hearts, the strife of nations, and the groaning brokenness of his whole creation. It is the beginning of the mission of God and the mission of God's people.

ABRAHAM AND GOD'S SURPRISE – BLESSING TO THE NATIONS

The LORD had said to Abram, "Go from your country, your people and your father's household to the land I will show you.

"I will make you into a great nation,
    and I will bless you;
I will make your name great,
    and you will be a blessing.
I will bless those who bless you,
    and whoever curses you I will curse;
and all peoples on earth
    will be blessed through you." (Gen. 12:1–3)

It is not hard to see what the central theme of these verses is. The words *bless* and *blessing* shine through it like a golden thread. The root word (*barak*) actually occurs five times in the three verses. And it is sudden and surprising good news!

Apart from the words of God to Noah immediately after the flood, we have not heard much about blessing since the opening chapters of Genesis, when God's blessings bathed the whole creation. The story has lurched through sin and rebellion to judgment and curse. But now, God speaks again, as he spoke at creation, with words of blessing, first for Abraham, but then through him for all nations on earth.

No wonder Paul read this text as "the gospel in advance" (Gal. 3:8). It is God's glorious surprise. In spite of all that has occurred in the previous chapters, God still intends blessing for the nations. And he will launch that great mission of blessing through Abraham.

But what is meant by "blessing"? All too easily our minds as Christians slip quickly into spiritual mode, and verses like Ephesians 1:3 pop up: "Praise be to the God and Father of our Lord Jesus Christ, who has blessed us in the heavenly realms with every spiritual blessing in Christ." We may be tempted, then, to think that only spiritual blessings are contained in God's promise to Abraham. But of course we must take the words in their wider and fuller biblical context. When we do so, we find that there are several rich and complementary ingredients in the biblical concept of "blessing".

Blessing and the Goodness of Creation

In the majestic account of creation in Genesis 1, God's blessing is pronounced three times: on day five he blessed the fish and the birds; then on day six he blessed human beings; and finally on day seven he blessed the Sabbath. The first two blessings are immediately followed by the instruction to multiply and fill the seas and the earth. The third blessing is followed by the words of sanctification and rest that define the Sabbath.

Blessing, then, at the very beginning of our Bible, is constituted by fruitfulness, abundance and fullness on the one hand, and by enjoying rest within creation in holy and harmonious relationship with our Creator God on the other. Blessing is off to a good start. We find the same themes in God's words of blessing to Noah in Genesis 9 (vv. 1–3, 9–17).

So when we come to 12:1–3, the word of blessing must, from the context so far, include at least the concept of fruitfulness, multiplication, spreading, filling and abundance. It is a richly life-affirming word. This is what God wants for the nations of humanity.

However, there is nothing mechanical about being blessed in this way. Blessing is set within relationships that are both vertical and horizontal. That is, blessing is dependent on relationship with God, and blessing is something to be shared in relationship with other human beings.

On the one hand, *vertically*, those who are blessed know the God who is blessing them, and they seek to live in faithful relationship with their God. The patriarchs knew that the blessings that accompanied them all their lives were all wrapped up with their relationship with God. When blind and aged Jacob blesses the two sons of Joseph, he acknowledges this. Jacob knew from whom his blessing had come:

> May the God before whom my fathers
>   Abraham and Isaac walked faithfully,
> the God who has been my shepherd
>   all my life to this day,
> the Angel who has delivered me from all harm—
>   may he bless these boys. (Gen. 48:15–16)

On the other hand, *horizontally*, the relational element of blessing reaches out to those around. Genesis has several instances of other people being blessed through contact with those whom God has blessed. Those who inherit the Abrahamic family blessing are then found to fulfill God's purpose that they should be a blessing to others.

- Laban is enriched by God's blessing on Jacob (30:27–30).
- Potiphar is blessed through the presence of Joseph (39:5).
- Pharaoh is blessed by Jacob (47:7, 10).

Thus, the blessing of Abraham becomes self-replicating. Those who are blessed are called to be a blessing beyond themselves—and this is one feature that makes it so profoundly missional. For if we see ourselves (as we should, according to Paul in Galatians) as those who have entered into the blessing of Abraham through faith in Christ, then the Abrahamic commission becomes ours also—"be a blessing".

Blessing and Hope within History

When we combine the dark picture of Genesis 3–11 with the promise of blessing in chapter 12, we can anticipate that the story to follow will involve both realities. We know that we will be watching two scenarios unfolding together—just as Jesus said in his parable of the wheat and the weeds growing in the same field. On the one hand, we know that history will be the arena of human sin getting even worse. But on the other hand, we will now be watching for the footprints of God's blessing and looking forward to how he will keep his vast promise to bring about blessing for all nations through the nation to emerge from the loins of Abraham. Blessing will take on a historical dimension, injecting hope and faith into an otherwise dark and depressing narrative.

And that means also, then, that blessing will be missional. For it is precisely this promise that all the nations on earth will find blessing through God's election of Abraham that drives forward the mission of God, and the mission of God's people that flows from it.

At the most fundamental level, who were these people called Israel in the Old Testament, and what were they there for? To be the vehicle of God's mission of extending his blessing to the nations.

So who are we and what are we here for? The same answer has to be given—and is indeed given in the New Testament as we will eventually see. We also are to be a people through whom the nations are blessed. The history of mission is the history of the spread of God's blessing, the history of God keeping his promise to Abraham.

Blessing, Salvation and Obedience

God promised to bless Abraham within a covenant relationship in which Abraham responded in faith and obedience. That remained the pattern for Israel too. Bless-

ing was not automatic or mechanical. Blessing flowed from all that God had already done for Israel in the grace of redemption, provision and protection. And blessing flowed only as Israel responded to God's grace in covenant obedience. *The blessing of salvation called for the response of covenantal obedience in order for the blessing to go on being enjoyed.*

Deuteronomy comes to its climax with a powerful appeal to Israel to "choose life", that is, to sustain their enjoyment of God's blessing (in which they already stood by God's redeeming grace). They could do this only by living in loving, trusting and obedient relationship with their God (Deut. 30). This did not mean, of course, that Israel ever did or ever could *deserve* the blessing of God or any of his great saving acts. It is a fundamental mistake to think that in the Old Testament blessing or salvation came as something *earned* through obedience (this is a mistaken way of reading Deut. 28:1 – 14). On the contrary, blessing is *intrinsic* to the covenant relationship established by God's saving grace. The pattern is clear in Deuteronomy 26:

Blessing is the way God enables his creation to be fertile and fruitful, to grow and to flourish. It is in the most comprehensive sense God's purpose for his creation. Wherever human life enjoys the good things of creation and produces the good fruits of human activity, God is pouring out his blessing. Wherever people bless God for his blessings, to that extent God is known as the good Creator who provides for human flourishing. God's blessing is universal. But it is not the case that blessing is God's goodness in creation as distinct from his goodness in salvation, as has sometimes been proposed. . . .

Salvation too is God's blessing, since salvation is the fulfillment of God's good purposes for creation, purposes already expressed in creation. But salvation is the fulfillment of God's purposes in spite of the damage evil does to God's creation. The Abrahamic blessing is more than the blessing of creation because it is designed to contend with and to overcome its opposite: God's curse. . . .

The ultimate goal of God's promise to Abraham is that blessing will prevail over curse. It does so when the seed of Abraham, the singled-out descendant of Abraham, the Messiah, becomes "a curse for us . . . so that in Christ Jesus the blessing of Abraham might come to the Gentiles" (Galatians 3:13 – 14). It is in this light that Paul can call the promise to Abraham that the nations will be blessed the gospel. . . .

The gospel is that in Christ Jesus the curse has been set aside and God's creative purpose for the blessing of his creation is established beyond any possibility of reversal.

Richard Bauckham[2]

the initial redemptive blessing of God has been experienced as a matter of grateful rejoicing (vv. 1 – 11). This leads on to responsive obedience (vv. 1 – 14). And that in

---

2. Richard Bauckham, *Bible and Mission: Christian Mission in a Postmodern World* (Carlisle: Paternoster; Grand Rapids: Baker Academic, 2003), 34 – 36.

turn is the context in which further blessing can be anticipated (v. 15), within the framework of mutual covenant commitment (vv. 16–19).

We affirm that there is a biblical vision of human prospering, and that the Bible includes material welfare (both health and wealth) within its teaching about the blessing of God. This needs further study and explanation across the whole Bible in both Testaments. We must not dichotomize the material and the spiritual in unbiblical dualism.

However, we reject the unbiblical notion that spiritual welfare can be measured in terms of material welfare, or that wealth is always a sign of God's blessing (since it can be obtained by oppression, deceit or corruption), or that poverty or illness or early death, is always a sign of God's curse, or lack of faith, or human curses (since the Bible explicitly denies that it is always so).

Lausanne Theology Working Group[3]

Obedience, then, is the means of *living within* the sphere of blessing and enjoying it; obedience is never the means of *earning or deserving* the blessing. Israel had already been redeemed by God (in the exodus), so their obedience could never earn that. It was already accomplished. However, their obedience was necessary in order to go on enjoying the benefit of their salvation. Otherwise, through disobedience they would find themselves thrown out of the land, out of the place of God's blessing.

This ethical dimension of blessing within the covenant relationship is another feature that protects biblical blessing from degenerating into the parody that is paraded in Prosperity Theology. Blessing is not just an automatic reflex, routinely doled out in response to certain prescribed inputs—prayers or faith or money. Blessing is not like a great heavenly cashbox of miracles stored up for you and just waiting to be claimed. We will have some more to say on the Prosperity Gospel in chapter 15.

ABRAHAM – GOD'S MISSION AND OURS
God's Universal Mission – All Nations

Genesis 10 and the first part of chapter 11 focus on the nations of humanity. In Genesis 10 they are scattering across the earth in order to fill it, as they were told to. In Genesis 11 they are scattering, but in a state of confusion and division that thwarts their arrogant attempt at self-built unification. So it is natural and fitting that God's great promise and plan announced in chapter 12, though it involves one man initially, has all the nations in view. God's promise to Abraham in Genesis 12 is God's answer to the problem of the nations in Genesis 10 and 11.

The bottom line (literally and metaphorically) of the Abrahamic covenant is that "all peoples on earth will be blessed through you" (Gen. 12:3). There is some dispute

---

3. "A Statement on the Prosperity Gospel", by the Africa Chapter of the Lausanne Theology Working Group, paragraph 2 (italics in original). The whole statement can be read at *www.lausanne.org/ all-documents/a-statement-on-the-prosperity-gospel.html*.

over the precise exegesis of the verb,[4] but there can be no doubt about the extent of God's intention – "all peoples". The word varies between "all kinship-groups" (*mišpeḥot*) and "all nations" (*goyim*), but the intention is clear and emphatic.

In fact, it is so emphatic that this promise is repeated five times in Genesis (12:3; 18:18; 22:18; 26:4; 28:14). There is a universal end in view. If humanity as a whole is subject to God's curse, then humanity as a whole must be reached by God's blessing. And therein lies the great thrust of God's mission and the mission of God's people.

From the perspective of biblical theology we can draw a great trajectory – from the "tribes, languages and nations" of Genesis 10, who stood in need of redemptive blessing, to that "great multitude that no one could count, from every nation, tribe, people and language", who will constitute the redeemed humanity in the new creation (Rev. 7:9).

The Abrahamic covenant is therefore one of the key unifying threads in the whole Bible. As I've said before, no wonder Paul could simply call it "the gospel in advance". What could be more "gospel" – more good news – in the light of Genesis 3 – 11 than that God has committed himself to bless all the people of the earth?

God's Particular Means – One Nation

But this same text that ends with such universality begins in singular particularity. God addresses one man, Abraham, and promises to bring his blessing to humanity through one nation – his descendants. At Genesis 12:1 – 3 we stand at the fountainhead of Old Testament Israel's self-consciousness of being God's elect people. That is, they believed they were a people uniquely chosen by God for a relationship with himself that would later be consolidated in the form of the Sinai covenant. But it is utterly crucial to see that this divine election of one man and one people takes place in the context of, and on the global stage of, God's dealings with all the nations, who have been the main focus of the narrative in chapters 10 and 11.

One nation is chosen, but all nations are to be the beneficiaries of that choice. In our biblical theology, we know, of course, that in the end that one nation would be represented by one man, the Messiah Jesus, through whom God's redemptive blessing would become available to all nations. That was the way Paul understood God's mission through Christ and the spread of the gospel as the fulfillment of God's promise to Abraham in Galatians 3.

---

4. The form of the Hebrew verb is known as "Niphal," which can be reflexive or passive. Translations vary, therefore, between "by you the nations will bless themselves" (reflexive) or "through you the nations will be blessed" (passive). The meaning of the former is that the nations would see in Abraham and his people such a signal demonstration of God's blessing that they would use Abraham or Israel as a model for blessing one another: "May you be blessed like Abraham." In this case, "you will be a blessing" (at the end of verse 2) means that Abraham would become the name on people's lips when they uttered blessings. This is certainly possible and fits with other cases of such practice (e.g., Gen. 48:20; Ruth 4:11 – 12; Ps. 72:17; Zech. 8:13). However, the ancient translations, including the Greek Septuagint (LXX), and the apostle Paul (Gal. 3:8) all render it with the passive sense. In any case, if the sense is reflexive ("all the nations will bless themselves *by you*"), then it implies that the nations have come to know about Abraham and Abraham's God and seek blessing from that source. God promises to bless such people in the first line of Gen. 12:3, so ultimately a reflexive sense comes to include and imply the passive, "will be blessed."

Election for Mission

This affects the way we understand the whole biblical doctrine of election. There is a tendency to speak of it solely as a doctrine of *salvation*—that is to say, the elect are those who get saved. That then leads to all kinds of controversy through the centuries as to whether God is fair in choosing some to be saved and not others. I don't want to get bogged down in that ancient but still potent debate. All I want to point out here is that the first time we really see God choosing and calling someone—i.e., putting election into action—it is precisely not so that Abraham and his family alone get saved, but rather that by being blessed he should become *the agent of blessing to others.*

Election of one is not the rejection of the rest, but ultimately for their benefit. It is as if a group of trapped cave explorers choose one of their number to squeeze through a narrow flooded passage to get out to the surface and call for help. The point of the choice is not so that she alone gets saved, but that she is able to bring help and equipment to ensure the rest get rescued. "Election" in such a case is an instrumental choice of one for the sake of many.

In the same way, God's election of Israel is instrumental in God's mission for all nations. Election needs to be seen as a doctrine of *mission*, not a calculus for the arithmetic of salvation. If we are to speak of being chosen, of being among God's elect, it is to say that, like Abraham, we are chosen for the sake of God's plan that the nations of the world come to enjoy the blessing of Abraham (which is exactly how Paul describes the effect of God's redemption of Israel through Christ in Gal. 3:14).

Missional Church

It all started with one man, Abraham. But the promise was to him and his seed, or his descendants. *Who are the descendants of Abraham now?* Paul is totally explicit on this point: people of any and every nation who believe in Jesus as Messiah and saviour are included in the seed of Abraham and are inheritors of the promise made to Abraham. Abraham, as God promised, has become the father of many nations—in and through Jesus Christ. Abraham is, in short, "the father of us all"—all of us who share his faith (Rom. 4:16–17). The church, then—that multinational community that includes believing Jews and Gentiles—is the people chosen and called in Abraham to be God's people.

But if that is so, and I cannot read the New Testament in any other way than to affirm that it is so, an important conclusion follows. If we are in Christ, we not only share in the blessing of Abraham, *we are commissioned to spread the blessing of Abraham.* The last phrase of Gen. 12:2 is actually an imperative in Hebrew—"Be a blessing!", though it is most often translated simply as a consequential statement from the preceding phrases, "so that you will be a blessing". My own exegetical understanding of the structure of Gen. 12:1–3 sees it as two fundamental commands, each followed by three subordinate or explanatory clauses, climaxing in the last line of verse 3.

The skeleton message of Genesis 12:1 – 3 is this:

"Go...
and be a blessing...
and all nations will be blessed through you."

Is that not a "great commission"? Is it not, in fact, the foundation on which the whole thrust of God's mission, including what is usually referred to as "The Great Commission" in Matthew 28, is based? And if so, this has serious consequences for our understanding of the church as well as of mission.

When God set about his great project of world redemption in the wake of Genesis 12, he chose to do so not by whisking individuals off up to heaven, but by calling into existence a community of blessing. Starting with one man and his barren wife, then miraculously transforming them into a large family within several generations, then into a nation called Israel, and then, through Christ, into a multinational community of believers from every nation – all through the story God has been moulding a people for himself. *But also a people for others. "Through you ... all nations."*

In other words, the missional thrust of Genesis 12:1 – 3 is also ecclesiological. The origins of *the church* go back, not just to Pentecost, but to Abraham. And the missionary impulse that we find in Acts was no sudden change, but the outworking of the logic of biblical faith and history. The command of Jesus and the leading of the Holy Spirit combined to send the church out in mission to the ends of the earth, as those who, having received the blessing of Abraham, must now be the means of passing it on. That was how the story worked, and that was the story they knew they were in.

So the idea of "missional church" is far from a new idea. It may have taken on a particular cultural form in recent years in reaction to an institutionalized church that has lost touch with its own raison d'être. But really, if we understand the church from our biblical theology as that community of people chosen and called since Abraham to be the vehicle of God's blessing to the nations, what else can the church be but missional? This is who we are and what we are here for.

Indeed, as a friend of mine said recently, "All this talk of 'missional church' sounds to me like talking about a 'female woman'. If it's not missional, it's not church."

ECHOES OF ABRAHAM
IN BIBLICAL THEOLOGY

We are attempting to do biblical theology in this book and series, so we need to show that a theme we are putting so much weight on actually does find support through a variety of biblical texts in both the Old and New Testaments. Once again, a fuller exposition of all the following texts and many more can be found in *The Mission of God* (read especially chs. 6, 7 and 14), but a selection of some of the most revealing ones should make our point clear. Do take time to read these texts. Their cumulative effect will greatly strengthen our biblical theology of mission at this point.

The Nations Drawn to Israel's Worship and Israel's Salvation

The Psalms are the songs of Israel's faith imagination in worship. They not only soar into the presence of God in adoration, confession, thanksgiving, praise and protest, they also take wings and fly to the ends of the earth and bring the nations of the world into the scope of their vision. Whatever God is doing in and through Israel itself must ultimately impact the nations, for that is the reason for Israel's existence in the first place.

It would be worthwhile to read the following passages carefully and note the echoes of the Abrahamic promise in their reference to all nations of the world ultimately coming to worship YHWH the God of Israel, or being the venues where the praises of God are sung. These are some of the places in the book of Psalms where we see the universality of Israel's faith in relation to the nations. Some of them seem clearly to be echoes of the Abrahamic covenant, but even where they are not directly alluding to it, they draw from its deep source a powerful message of God's overarching mission of blessing that extends way beyond the borders of Israel itself.

- Psalm 22:27–28
- Psalm 47:9
- Psalm 67
- Psalm 72:17
- Psalm 86:9
- Psalm 87
- Psalm 96
- Psalm 102:15, 21–22
- Psalm 117

The prophets, like the historians and psalmists, focus most of the time on Israel in relationship with God, but when their vision widens to the nations and the earth, the results are sometimes stunning, and the echoes of Abraham are unmistakable. Again, take some time and read these passages, savouring the universality of their vision. These are the kind of texts that feed the New Testament theology of mission to the nations.

- Isaiah 19:19–25 (esp. vv. 24–25)
- Isaiah 45:22–23
- Isaiah 56:3–8

- Isaiah 60
- Jeremiah 4:1 – 2
- Amos 9:11 – 12
- Zechariah 2:10 – 11

Abraham in the Gospels

Matthew is often portrayed as the gospel for the Jews. But Matthew sees clearly that the very existence of the Jews, as the people of Abraham, is for the sake of all nations. Matthew shows this in the way he begins with Abraham and ends with all nations.

Luke also puts an Abrahamic envelope around his gospel by seeing the coming of Jesus as the fulfillment of that promise, with its relevance to Israel and to all nations. He begins and ends on that note of Scripture fulfillment (Luke 1:55, 73; 2:29 – 32; 24:46 – 47).

But Luke also mentions Abraham by name in four short but significant incidents in his narrative – three in the gospel and one in Acts.

- Luke 13:10 – 16 – the crippled woman
- Luke 16:19 – 31 – the poor beggar Lazarus
- Luke 19:1 – 10 – the tax collector Zacchaeus
- Acts 3:1 – 26 – the lame man at the temple

What these stories have in common is that in each of them somebody who was excluded – by demonic bondage, or poverty and injustice, or deserved social contempt, or crippling illness – is brought into saving blessing. None of the characters is a Gentile (though Luke has plenty to say about them too). But they illustrate the healing, transforming, restoring power of God that is entailed by receiving the blessing of Abraham.

> Matthew frames the whole story of Jesus between the identification of him as a descendant of Abraham in the opening verse of the Gospel and, in the closing words of Jesus at the end of the Gospel, the commission to the disciples of Jesus to make disciples of all nations. Matthew's genealogy of Jesus begins with Abraham (1:1 – 2), not with Adam, as Luke's does (3:38), nor with David, which would have been sufficient to portray Jesus the Messiah the son of David, which certainly is an important theme in Matthew's Gospel. However, for Matthew, Jesus is the Messiah not only for Jews but also for Gentiles. He is the descendant of Abraham through whom God's blessing will at last reach the nations.
>
> *Richard Bauckham*[5]

Abraham in Paul's Gospel

It would not be exaggerating to say that Abraham is the most important figure in Paul's understanding of the gospel – second only to Jesus Christ. For what God had accomplished in Christ was nothing less than what God had promised to Abraham, to bring about the blessing of all nations on earth. That universal hope had been a mystery (as Paul puts it) for centuries – not a mystery in terms of *what* was expected, for that was clear in the text itself, but a mystery in terms of *how* it could ever be

---

5. Bauckham, *Bible and Mission*, 33.

accomplished. That, says Paul, has now been revealed through the gospel of Christ, by what he accomplished in his cross and resurrection (Eph. 3:4–6).

So, as we saw at the start of this chapter, Paul's personal mission was to replicate Abrahamic faith and obedience among all nations, to bring about what God had originally promised Abraham. Paul's theology of the gospel and his theology of mission are both Abrahamic. In Christ, the promise to Abraham is accomplished in principle, for salvation is now open to people of all nations. In mission, the promise to Abraham is worked out in the ongoing history of the church in its proclamation of the good news.

Thus, though we cannot now study the passages in detail, Paul's argument from Romans 3:29 to the end of Romans 4, and even more so in Galatians 3, is not (as sometimes suggested) merely using Abraham as an illustration of his doctrine of justification by faith, but constitutes precisely his exposition of what that doctrine means. God has demonstrated his righteousness and his trustworthiness by keeping his promise to Abraham through providing, in Christ, the means by which people of all nations, not just Jews, can enter into the blessing of a right relationship with God by God's grace through faith.[6]

Paul's doctrine of justification is essentially missional for it extends the blessing of the gospel, with no ethnic privileges or barriers, to all nations in principle, and therefore demands that it be extended to them in practice – that is, in the practice of evangelism, church-planting and discipling communities who walk in "the obedience of faith" among all nations.

Mission Accomplished in Revelation

How else could we finish a biblical survey of such an important theme other than in the Bible's climactic final book, Revelation? And there indeed the echoes of Abraham resound loud and clear.

Revelation 5:9–10

Why is Jesus worthy to unlock the seals on the scroll in the right hand of God? Because he is "the Lamb who was slain". It is the crucified Christ who holds the key to the unfolding purpose of history and its final destination. So when the elders sing out their answer to the question as to who is worthy to open the seven-sealed scroll, they celebrate the cross as redemptive, universal and victorious. And that universal phrase, "with your blood you purchased for God members of every tribe and language and people and nation", is an instantly recognizable allusion to the context of Genesis 10, the world of nations, for whose blessing and salvation God had called Abraham.

---

6. The doctrine of justification is the subject of considerable recent controversy, between proponents and opponents of the so-called "New Perspective" on Paul. I do not wish to enter that discussion here, but it is clear to me that for Paul, what God has accomplished through the death and resurrection of the Messiah, Jesus, constitutes God's fulfillment of his promise to Abraham, such that the inclusion of people from *all* nations in the blessings previously enjoyed only by Old Testament Israel is at the heart of Paul's understanding of the gospel.

Revelation 7:9 – 10

The same language surfaces again here, as the great song of God's salvation is sung by "a great multitude that no one could count, from every nation, tribe, people and language."

Revelation 22:2

Who benefits from the healing power of the tree of life by the river of life in the new creation? *The nations.* They have already been pictured as bringing their splendour, glory and honour into the city of God—redeemed and purified of all sin and evil (Rev. 21:24–27). But the final picture of the nations that we have in the Bible is *healing*: "The leaves of the tree are for the healing of the nations." Nations that have been fundamentally sick since Genesis 3–11 will at last experience that international healing that the world longs for. The blessing of Abraham will bring all nations into the *shalom* of Christ, the redeemer, saviour and healer of all.

And as redeemed humanity, together with all angels and all creatures in creation, joins to celebrate that great achievement, I picture God turning to Abraham and saying, "There you are. I kept my promise. 'All nations,' I said, and all nations it is. Mission accomplished."

ABRAHAM AS A MODEL FOR OUR MISSION

I hope it has been inspiring to see the wonderful biblical panorama of God's promise to Abraham and how it generates the biblical theology of God's mission to all nations. But we are thinking in this book not only of the mission of God but the mission of God's people. And so we need to ask also what relevance Abraham has to our own concept and practice of mission.

If we are those who inherit not only the privilege of Abrahamic blessing, but also the responsibility of being a blessing to the nations, then what is required of us? Surely, that we respond as Abraham did to the promise and command of God. For Abraham, that meant leaving and going, believing and obeying.

Leaving and Going

God's opening word to Abraham was, in essence: "Get up and go, away from your land...." It is a clear command to leave a particular place and go elsewhere. He had to leave *his* land and people, in order that God would bless *all* lands and peoples. Only Abraham's leaving released the nations' blessing.

The story of Babel had brought an end to the hope and attempts of humankind to find their own means of blessing. Blessing will not come from within that world itself. Abraham must relinquish all that ties him to the land of Babylon before he can be the vehicle of blessing to the whole earth. Babel, the climax of the problem portrayed in Genesis 3 – 11, cannot be the source of the solution to the problem.

In this way, even the great Mesopotamian empires are relativized and negated. The greatest human civilizations cannot solve the deepest human problems. God's mission of blessing the nations has to be a radical new start. It requires a break, a radical departure from the story so far, not merely an evolutionary development from it. So Abraham is commanded to get up and leave.

God's mission required leaving and going. And of course, it still does.

Now at one level, we can see this as an obvious parallel to the opening of the so-called Great Commission, "Go and make disciples of all nations" (Matt. 28:19) – though it needs to be pointed out that the first word is not a command in itself, but a participle – "As you go. . . ." Nevertheless, it is clear that if the nations were to be discipled, the disciples had to go to them. So we can certainly detect in God's first command to Abraham an anticipation of the dynamic that would eventually explode in centrifugal missional "going" to the ends of the earth. And that would be an appropriate connection to make.

But at another level, such "leaving and going" need not necessarily mean actual travel from one geographical place to another. Christians who commit themselves to the mission of God *in* the world have to start with a certain going out *from* the world. For we still live in the land of Babel and Sodom. We need to recognize the idolatrous nature of the world and all its claims and ideologies. This is not so that we become "other-worldly", for as we will see in chapter 13, our mission must also take place in the public arena of the place where God has put us. Nevertheless, there is a form of leaving and going that is spiritual, mental and attitudinal – even when it is not physical. For it involves the abandonment of the worldview through which the world tells its own usurped story, and adopting, in faith and hope, the worldview of the story we are in – the biblical story of God's mission. That brings us to our next point.

Believing and Obeying

We began this chapter with Paul's ambition to bring about "the obedience of faith ... among all the nations", and that indeed is what the Bible emphasizes most of all about Abraham, in both the Old and New Testaments – his "faith-obedience".

There is an old dispute among biblical theologians as to whether the covenant with Abraham was unconditional or conditional. But really, that is far too simplistic because, in different respects, it was both. On the one hand, it was *unconditional*, in the sense that it did not depend upon any *prior* condition that Abraham had fulfilled. God simply announces his choice of Abraham and his amazing intention to bless the nations through him. Abraham had done nothing to deserve or trigger that action on God's part.

Yet on the other hand, God's first words imply *a condition*. Everything hinges on the opening command (lit.), "Get yourself up and go from here to the land I will show you." All that God goes on to promise depends on that. No leaving, no blessing. Bluntly put, if Abraham had not got up and left for Canaan, if he had not trusted God enough to obey him, the story would have ended right there. The Bible would be a thin book indeed.

But Abraham's faith and obedience were repeatedly tested in the chapters that follow. The severest test came in Genesis 22, which is really the climax of the whole story of Abraham. God commanded Abraham to take his son Isaac and sacrifice him. Abraham's willingness to obey even up to that point and to trust God for the aftermath, was then built into God's most solemn confirmation of his promise, reinforced by an oath on his own existence.

> It is not that the divine promise has become contingent upon Abraham's obedience, but that Abraham's obedience has been incorporated into the divine promise. Henceforth Israel owes its existence not just to YHWH but also to Abraham. Theologically this constitutes a profound understanding of the value of human obedience – it can be taken up by God and become a motivating factor in his purposes towards humanity.
>
> *Walter Moberly*[7]

> By myself I have sworn, oracle of YHWH,
>> *it is because of the fact that you have done this thing*
>>> and have not kept back your son, your only one,
>>>> that I will most surely bless you,
>>> and I will most surely multiply your offspring [seed],
>>>> like the stars in the heavens and like the sand on the seashore,
>>> and your offspring will possess the gate of your enemies.
>> And in your offspring all the nations of the world will find blessing,
> *on account of the fact that you obeyed me.*
>>>> (Gen. 22:16 – 18; my translation and italics)

This remarkable text explicitly binds together God's promised intentions for the nations, on the one hand, and Abraham's faith and obedience on the other. The two are integrally bound together. God's speech emphatically begins and ends by making Abraham's obedience the reason why God now binds himself irrevocably on oath to keep his promise to bless the nations.

Now of course this does not in any way mean that Abraham has *merited* God's covenant promises. We are not slipping into "works righteousness" here. As we just said, Abraham had done nothing to *deserve* God's promise, which came "out of the blue", as it were. But Abraham's sustained response of faith and obedience not only moves God to count him as righteous (Gen. 15:6), but also enables God's promise to move forward towards its universal horizon.

When we come to the New Testament, we find that Paul, James and the writer to the Hebrews between them capture both poles of Abraham's response to God.

---

7. R. W. L. Moberly, "Christ as the Key to Scripture: Genesis 22 Reconsidered," *He Swore an Oath: Biblical Themes from Genesis* *12–50* (eds. R. S. Hess et al.; Carlisle: Paternoster and Grand Rapids: Baker, 1994), 161.

- Paul focuses on the faith that led Abraham to *believe in the promises of God*, however impossible they seemed, and that was thereby counted as righteousness (Rom. 4; Gal. 3:6–29).
- James focuses on the faith that led Abraham to *obey the command of God*, thus demonstrating in practice the genuineness of his faith (James 2:20–24).
- Hebrews actually captures *both* dimensions (as, of course, Paul and James would have both agreed), by repeatedly emphasizing Abraham's faith while going on to show that he proved his faith through his obedience, from his initial departure from his homeland to the classic account of his obedience in Genesis 22 (Heb. 11:8–19).

For ourselves, with our concern for a missiological reading of these texts, the important point to notice is the way God's intention to bless the nations is combined with human commitment to obedience, which enables us to be the agent of that blessing.

The *glorious gospel* of the Abrahamic covenant is that God's mission is ultimately to bless all the nations. The *enduring challenge* of the Abrahamic covenant is that God planned to do that "through you and your descendants". The faith and obedience of Abraham, therefore, are not merely models for *personal* piety and ethics. They are also the essential credentials for effective participation in all that is meant by the command, "Be a blessing".

There is no blessing, for ourselves or for others, without faith and obedience. Those whom God calls to participate in his redemptive mission for the nations are those who exercise saving faith like Abraham *and* demonstrate costly obedience like Abraham.

So then, *what God promised Abraham* becomes the ultimate agenda for God's own mission (blessing the nations), and *what Abraham did in response to God's promise* becomes the historical model for our mission (faith and obedience).

SUMMARY

In "Queuing the Questions" (the title to part 1 of this book), we asked the fundamental question about the church: "Who are we and what are we here for?" Getting a correct answer to that question is essential if we are to build a sound biblical theology of the church's mission. Rather than begin with the book of Acts, we have gone back to Abraham, because that is where we find God launching his great redemptive, restorative project – God's answer to the bleak situation presented in Genesis 3 – 11.

In a world where God's curse is operating in response to human sin and rebellion, God launches a program to bring blessing, and we have explored what a rich and comprehensive content there is in the biblical word "blessing". But God's blessing was not for Abraham and his family only. He would be the father of a particular nation through whom blessing would come universally to all nations. "We", then, if we are in Christ, are part of that family of Abraham, no matter what nation we come from.

But if, in Christ, we inherit Abraham's blessing, we also inherit Abraham's mission – that is, to go and be a blessing, to be the means by which God's blessing comes to others. At a fundamental level, starting right here in Genesis, that is "who we are" – the children of Abraham; and that is "what we are here for" – to participate in God's promised mission of bringing people from all nations on earth into the sphere of God's redemptive blessing through Christ.

However, in "Queuing the Questions" we also asked, "What kind of people are we to be?" Abraham was called not only to trust God but also to obey him. There is an ethical dimension to being a people of blessing that also derives from the great Abrahamic tradition. That is a dimension of the mission of God's people that we must explore further in the coming chapters. In the next chapter we will see that it was in God's mind even when he chose and called Abraham.

RELEVANT QUESTIONS

1. What does the word "blessing" usually bring to mind for you? In what ways has your concept changed in the light of this chapter?
2. "Being a blessing" might not seem an adequate description of "the mission of God's people" (and indeed, by itself it isn't!), but what aspects of our mission would be challenged or improved by thinking in such Abrahamic terms?
3. Abraham was called to "leave and go". Whether or not you are called to physically leave your country and go overseas as a missionary, what elements of your present cultural and social context do you need to "leave" if you are to follow Abraham in "faith-obedience"?
4. Does the notion of the demand of obedience to the mission of the church sound like legalism to you? How might this unbiblical notion be biblically rebutted?

CHAPTER 5

PEOPLE WHO WALK IN GOD'S WAY

GOD'S SELF-REMINDER

> For I have known [chosen] him [Abraham] for the purpose that he should instruct his children and his household after him that they should keep the way of the LORD, by doing righteousness and justice, for the purpose that the LORD may bring about for Abraham what he has spoken [promised] to him.
>
> Gen. 18:19 (my translation)

"All peoples [nations] on earth will be blessed [or will bless themselves] through you" (Gen. 12:3). This is the grand, sweeping scope of God's promise to Abraham. As we explored in chapter 4, if we ask what is the mission of God's people, the first thing the Bible tells us, when God's people had not yet even been conceived in the womb of Sarah, is that they will be a people of blessing for the nations. Indeed, says Paul, that is the good news, the gospel (Gal. 3:8). Blessing the nations is the declared mission of God, and that is the reason why he calls this people into his existence – to be the vehicle of that mission of God in the historical world of nations.

The history of God's saving work began with the call of Abraham and the promise that through his descendants, *blessing would come to all nations on earth*.

But how?

That, of course, is the question that we will be answering in different ways as we explore the many dimensions of the task God lays on his people in the Bible. But here in this single verse, in delightfully human language, God reminds himself of what he had in mind when he chose Abraham in the first place.

Genesis 18:19 is a remarkable text, for it puts together in a single sentence God's *choice of* Abraham, God's *moral demand on* Abraham's community, and God's *promise to* Abraham (which the immediately preceding verse 18 has spelled out yet again, that "all nations on earth will be blessed through him"). *Election*, *ethics* and *mission* all in one verse – that's biblical theology for life! In this chapter we will be looking at how these three great biblical themes are inseparable – integrally intertwined with each other.

How was Abraham going to be a blessing to the nations? First of all, as we saw in the closing section of chapter 4, only by trusting and obeying God himself. So the first thing we have to say, if we hold up Abraham as the father of God's people and the embodiment of the mission of God's people, is that he reminds us that our mission has to start with justifying faith in God and practical obedience to God. That's an important lesson, but it's only the starting point of the missional significance of Abraham.

After all, Abraham had only the one lifetime, so how could *his* faith and obedience constitute a means of *blessing to the nations* (i.e., have a missional impact), other than by the story of his example? Genesis 18:19 gives us the answer. The power of Abraham's personal example was to be reinforced and multiplied by direct instruction and moral formation. Abraham's family, and then his whole household after him – that is, the whole community of Abraham's descendants who would be the people of God – were to be taught to walk in the way of the Lord, by doing righteousness and justice.

Now in terms of biblical theology, we have already pointed out that "the community of Abraham" includes Old Testament Israel along with all those who are in Christ – Jew and Gentile believers (Rom. 4; Gal. 3). So the ethical stretch of Genesis 18:19 is long indeed and extends right to where you and I sit right now. For if we are in Christ, we are in Abraham, heirs of the promise God made to him and the responsibility God laid on him. And if we inherit Abraham's blessing, we inherit his mission also.

What then is the mission of God's people? According to this text, it is to be the community who live by the ethical standards of the ways of God, so that God can fulfill his promise to Abraham and bring about the blessing of the nations. Our ethics and God's mission are integrally bound together. That is why God chose us in the first place.

However, before we look more carefully at what that means in practice, we need to pay attention to the context of our text. God's conversation with himself here comes in the middle of the story of God's judgment on Sodom and Gomorrah, a story that comprises Genesis 18 and 19.

So God's universal promise of *blessing* here is actually nested within the story of one particularly notorious instance of God's historical *judgment*. That's an important context. It reminds us that the mission of God operates within this fallen world, that the most glorious promise of blessing stands alongside the most terrible

> The scope of God's purpose [in telling Abraham his plans] must be carefully noted. His will, as made known to Abraham, bound all Abraham's descendants. Certainly God does not make his will known to us so that knowledge of him should die with us. He requires us to be his witnesses to the next generation, so that they may in turn hand on what they have received from us to their descendants. . . . In this way we must propagate God's truth. It was not given for our private enjoyment; we must mutually strengthen one another according to our calling and our faith.
>
> *John Calvin*[1]

---

1. John Calvin, *Genesis* (The Crossway Classic Commentaries; Wheaton, IL: Crossway, 2001), 177.

words and actions of judgment, and that the people of God are called to live like Abraham in a world like Sodom.[2]

SODOM: A MODEL OF OUR WORLD

Disobedience of the Nations

Sodom represents the way of the fallen world. It stands in Scripture as a proverbial prototype of human wickedness and of the judgment of God that ultimately falls on evildoers. With Sodom, we seem to come again to a story like the Tower of Babel—stories that illustrate the horrendous capacity of human societies for evil, in the wake of Genesis 3. It is the disobedience of Adam, Eve, Cain and their descendants multiplied to a national level.

In order to make this clear, let's do a condensed "biblical theology of Sodom" and trace the theme through several texts.

Starting in *Genesis 18:20*, we hear the "outcry" (*ze'aqah*) that comes up to God from Sodom—a word that immediately tells us there was cruelty and oppression going on there.

> Then the LORD said, "The outcry against Sodom and Gomorrah is so great and their sin is so grievous that I will go down and see if what they have done is as bad as the outcry that has reached me." (Gen. 18:20–21)

The term *ze'aqah*, or *se'aqah*, is a technical word for the cry of pain, or the cry for help, from those who are being oppressed or violated.[3] It is the word used for Israelites crying out under their slavery in Egypt (Ex. 2:23). Psalmists use it when appealing to God to hear their cry against unjust treatment (e.g., Ps. 34:17). Most graphically of all, it is the scream for help by a woman being raped (Deut. 22:24, 27). As early as Genesis 13:13 we were told that "the men of Sodom were wicked and were sinning greatly against the LORD." Here that sin is identified as oppression, for that is what the word "outcry" immediately indicates. Some people in or near Sodom were suffering to such an extent that they were crying out against its oppression and cruelty.

In *Genesis 19* we read further of the hostile, perverted and violent sexual immorality that characterized "all the men from every part of the city of Sodom—both young and old" (19:4).

In *Deuteronomy 29:23* the future fate of Israel under God's anger and judgment for their idolatry is compared to that of Sodom and Gomorrah, which suggests that

---

2. The exposition of Gen. 18:19 that follows is abbreviated from a much fuller discussion of it in *Mission of God*, 358–69. Used and quoted with permission.

3. See Richard Nelson Boyce, *The Cry to God in the Old Testament* (Atlanta: Scholars Press, 1988).

part of the sin of the twin cities was unbridled idolatry, along with their social evils (cf. Lam. 4:6).

Isaiah portrays the Jerusalem of his own day in the colours of Sodom and Gomorrah when condemning it for its bloodshed, corruption and injustice (Isa. 1:9–23). He further portrays the future judgment of God against Babylon (another prototypical city) for its pride as a replay of God's destruction of Sodom and Gomorrah (Isa. 13:19–20).

Ezekiel even more caustically compares Judah unfavourably with Sodom, describing Sodom's sin as arrogance, affluence, and callousness to the needy. They were overproud, overfed, and underconcerned–a very modern sounding list of accusations (Ezek. 16:48).

So, from this wider Old Testament witness, it is clear that Sodom was used as a paradigm–a model of human society at its worst. At the same time, the name Sodom spoke of the inevitable and comprehensive judgment of God upon such wickedness. Sodom was a place filled with oppression, cruelty, violence, perverted sexuality, idolatry, pride and greedy consumption, and it was a place empty of compassion or care for the needy. A model, indeed, of the fallen world in which we still live.

When we draw the theme through into the New Testament, we find a similar "Sodomic catalogue" in Paul's portrayal of human wickedness in Romans 1:18–32. Though Paul does not name Sodom, his devastating list of human sin reflects all of the above items in the sin of Sodom, and that is probably what is in the back of his mind from his own Jewish traditions.[4] Significantly, Paul begins his list with the statement, "the wrath of God is being revealed from heaven against" all such behaviour, and he ends it with the statement that "those who do such things deserve death". It was indeed from heaven that fire and brimstone rained death upon Sodom and Gomorrah (Gen. 19:24).

Now, if that was the world as Paul saw it in his day–a world of nations typified by Sodom–that was also the world into which Paul was called to engage in mission. What a world of evil! How, then, did Paul see his mission in such a world? He tells us twice, at the beginning and end of Romans. Paul's mission was nothing less than to bring about "the obedience of faith ... among all the nations" (Rom. 1:5; 16:26 ESV).

Obedience among the Nations

Haven't we heard that language already? As we emphasized in chapter 4, Paul saw his mission in Abrahamic terms. His mission was to carry on what God commanded Abraham in our text–to create communities of faith and obedience, communities

---

4. Philip Esler ("The Sodom Tradition in Romans 1:18–32", *Biblical Theology Bulletin* 34 [2004]: 4–16) suggests that this catalogue of vice and evil that characterized Sodom had shaped the Jewish mind in relation to sin and judgment and was well-known to Paul.

committed to walking in the ways of the Lord in a world of nations that were walking in the ways of Sodom–transformed communities that would present a stark contrast to the Sodom all around them.

Paul's mission, therefore, had a strongly ethical content. There was mission beyond evangelism. It was the mission of teaching the new communities, of moral transformation into the ways of God. This was fundamentally Abrahamic, and in line with our text in this chapter.

Our mission, in line with Paul's and Abraham's, is the same. And it requires no less of the miraculous transforming grace of God in the gospel to even contemplate what it means.

The world has not changed much from the world of Sodom. The mission of God's people has therefore not changed either. We are still called to be those who are taught by Abraham's example and who are committed to "walking in the way of the LORD" by "doing righteousness and justice". What those phrases mean, we will come to in a moment. But for now, it is unavoidably clear from this text that the ethical distinctiveness of God's people is an integral part of the role they are called to play in God's mission of bringing blessing to a world that otherwise stands under his judgment, like Sodom. Indeed, according to Genesis 18:19, that ethical quality of life is part of the very purpose of our election in Abraham.

If the nations are to be blessed, God's people must walk in God's ways.

ABRAHAM: A MODEL OF GOD'S MISSION

God's conversations with himself and with Abraham in Genesis 18, then, are set within the context of the wickedness of Sodom. It was that wickedness that had led to the investigation being conducted by God with his two angels, an investigation that seemed certain to end in judgment. God's conversation with *himself* begins in Genesis 18:18 with a recapitulation of the original covenant promise: "Abraham will surely become a great and powerful nation, and all nations on earth will be blessed through him."

Immediate Judgment: Ultimate Blessing

By repeating this overarching missional goal for the world, God explains why he had just renewed his promise to Abraham and Sarah that they would have a son (which he had done a little earlier in the story, over dinner; Gen. 18:10, 14). Whatever God is about to do–judgment for Sodom and Gomorrah, or a son for Abraham and Sarah–must be seen in the light of this purpose. God, while he is on his way to act in immediate judgment on a *particular* evil society, stops to remind himself of his ultimate purpose of *universal* blessing to all nations. It is almost as if God cannot do the one (judgment) without setting it in the context of the other (redemption).

The immediate particular necessity was judgment. The ultimate universal goal is (as it always was) blessing. This is an important part of our biblical theology of mission. Never forget Paul's definition of the gospel in Galatians 3:8 – God's will that the nations of the earth should be blessed. That's the good news to bear in mind even in the contexts of awesome judgment such as this one.

A Promise for the World

So then, God stops for a meal with Abraham and Sarah. God need not have done so, of course, any more than he needed to "go down" to discover what was going on in Sodom. The reason that God and his two angels choose to stop off and have a meal with Abraham just as if they were three travelers (as Abraham at first thought they were, 18:2) is not because they know Sarah is a good cook. It is because God saw in this elderly and still childless couple, camped there on the hills above the cities of the plain, the key to his whole missional purpose for history and humanity.

The story reminds the reader (just as God reminds himself in vv. 17 – 19) of the centrality of Abraham in the biblical theology of the mission of God. Abraham and Sarah will have a son, promises God. Why? Not just as a special treat when they both thought it was too late for all that kind of thing (Gen. 18:10 – 13 seem deliberately humorous). No. They must and they will have a son because God's whole plan for the evangelization of the world to bring blessing to all nations depends on it. After all, the whole idea that God's people should have the mission of being a blessing to the nations does rather depend on such a people of God actually existing. And that can't even begin until Abraham and Sarah are blessed with the promised son.

So we need to give full attention to the global scope of verses 17 – 19. God's promise to Abraham is the foundation stone, or mainspring, of all the mission of God's people throughout history.

- When individuals came to saving faith in the God of Israel within the Old Testament itself (such as Ruth, Naaman, the widow of Zarephath), God was keeping his promise to Abraham.
- When Solomon prayed that people from the ends of the earth could come and have their prayers answered by God in the temple, he was praying for God to keep his promise to Abraham.
- When psalmists, prophets, apostles and gospel writers all saw the extension of the good news of God's saving love to the Gentiles, they knew that God was keeping his promise to Abraham.
- When the gospel moved north to Asia Minor, west to Europe, south into Africa, and East to Arabia (within the New Testament era itself), God was keeping his promise to Abraham.

- When the gospel stretched further over all the centuries, reaching the very ends of the earth (like my home country, Ireland, from Israel's perspective), God was keeping his promise to Abraham.
- And when the gospel reaches you and me and embraces us within this great multinational community of Abraham's faith and obedience, God is still keeping his promise.

That is what constitutes the mission of God's people – to be those who, having received the blessing of Abraham, continue the task of reaching those who have not yet been touched by it.

Abraham and Sarah may have not seen much beyond their tent door and their longing for a son, but God had a long-term vision in mind that lunchtime.

"THE WAY OF THE LORD": A MODEL FOR GOD'S PEOPLE

Returning to the key central verse (Gen. 18:19), we find *ethics* in the middle of it, with *election* (God's choice of Abraham) on one side and *mission* (God's promise to Abraham) on the other. So we need to examine what the key phrases: "the way of the LORD" and "doing righteousness and justice" actually mean. Then we will take note of the strong missional logic that runs through the verse. And we will finish up with some challenging practical reflections.

An Ethical Education

God says that he had chosen Abraham to be a teacher, specifically a teacher of the way of the Lord, and a teacher of righteousness and justice. This ethical education will start with his children and then pass on to "his household after him". That means that there will have to be transmission of the teaching down through the generations – which is exactly what we find in later Old Testament Israel (e.g., Deut. 6:7 – 9). Two phrases summarize the content of the Abrahamic family curriculum:

"The Way of the LORD"

The expression "keeping the way of the LORD" or "walking in the way of the LORD" was a favourite metaphor used in the Old Testament to describe a particular aspect of Israel's ethics. A contrast is implied: that is, walking in *YHWH's* way, as distinct from the ways of other gods, or the ways of other nations, or one's own way, or the way of sinners. Here, the contrast is clearly between the way of *YHWH* and the way of *Sodom* that immediately follows.

As a metaphor, "walking in the way of the LORD" seems to have two possible pictures in mind.

One picture is that of following someone else on a path, watching his footsteps and following along carefully in the way he is going. In that sense, the metaphor suggests the imitation of God: you observe how God acts and you try to follow suit. "O let me see thy footsteps and in them plant my own," as the hymn says about following Jesus. It is a way of talking about the imitation of God, or better, of reflecting his character.

The other picture is of setting off on a path following the instructions that someone has given you—perhaps a sketch map (if that is not too anachronistic for ancient Israel), or a set of directions to make sure you stay on the right path and do not wander off on wrong paths that may turn out to be dead ends or dangerous. This use of the metaphor is most commonly linked to obeying God's commands, which is one dimension of reflecting God himself.

The commands of God are not just arbitrary rules; they are frequently related to the character or values or desires of God. So to obey God's commands is to reflect God's character in human life.

One of the clearest examples of this dynamic at work is Deuteronomy 10:12–19. It begins with a rhetorical flourish, rather like Micah 6:8, summarizing the whole law in a single chord of five notes: fear, walk, love, serve and obey:

> And now, O Israel, what does the LORD your God ask of you but to fear the LORD your God, *to walk in all his ways*, to love him, to serve the LORD your God with all your heart and with all your soul, and to observe the LORD's commands and decrees that I am giving you this day for your own good? (Deut. 10:12–13, italics added)

And what are the ways of YHWH in which Israel is to walk? The answer is given first in broad terms. His was the way of condescending love in choosing Abraham and his descendants (vv. 14–15), so that Israel should respond in repentance and humility (v. 16).

But when the passage goes on *specifically* to define the ways of YHWH, it focuses on his character and actions.

> [He] shows no partiality and accepts no bribes. He defends the cause of the fatherless and the widow, and loves the alien, giving him food and clothing. *And you are to love those who are aliens,* for you yourselves were aliens in Egypt. (vv. 17–19, italics added)

To walk in the way of the Lord, then, means doing for others what God wishes to have done for them, or more particularly, doing for others what (in Israel's case) God has already done for you (deliverance from alien status in Egypt and provision of food and clothing in the wilderness). You know what God is like because you have experienced him in action on your behalf. Now go and do likewise!

The contrast with Sodom stands out now even more clearly. For these things were exactly what the people of Sodom were *failing* to do, in their callous oppression and lack of care for the needy. So Abraham is to teach his people to be fundamentally *different*. "To keep the way of the LORD" would mean renouncing the way of Sodom. It still does. And it is a fundamental part of the mission of God's people that we do so.

The phrase "keep the way of the LORD", then, would have been enough for any experienced reader of the Old Testament to understand the full, rich significance of God's point here. But to make absolutely sure we get the message, our text explains it further with two more words.

Doing Righteousness and Justice

Here is a pair of words that stands right at the top of the Old Testament's ethical vocabulary. Each of them individually, in various verbal, adjectival and noun forms, occurs hundreds of times, and they are often found together as here. Let's look at the two root words.[5]

(1) The first is the root *sdq*, which is found in two common noun forms, *sedeq* and *sedaqah*. These words are usually translated "righteousness" in English Bibles, but that word, with its somewhat religious flavour, does not convey the full range of meaning that the words had in Hebrew. The root meaning is probably "straight": something that is fixed and fully what it should be. So it can mean a norm or standard – something by which other things are measured.

It is used literally of actual objects when they are, or do, what they are supposed to: for example, accurate weights and measures are "measures of *sedeq*" (Lev. 19:36; Deut. 25:15). Safe paths for sheep are "paths of *sedeq*" (Ps. 23:3). So it comes to mean *rightness*, that which is as it ought to be, that which matches up to the standard.

When applied to human actions and relationships, it speaks of conformity to what is right or expected. But this is not in some abstract or absolute way, but rather according to the demands of the particular relationship or situation one is in. It means doing what is right in *this* relationship, or according to the priorities and expectations of *this* situation. It is not an abstract norm, but a particular sense of what it means to do the right thing, as a parent, as a child, as a judge, as a king, as a brother, as a farmer, as a spouse, as a friend, as a worshiper, and so on. Righteousness is doing all that one ought to do in the given circumstances and relationships.

(2) The second is the root *špt*, which has to do with judicial activity at every level. A common verb and noun are derived from it. The verb *šapat* refers to legal action over a wide range. It can mean: to act as a lawgiver; to act as a judge by arbitrating between parties in a dispute; to pronounce judgment by declaring who is guilty and who is innocent respectively; and to execute judgment in carrying out the legal consequences of such a verdict. In the widest sense, it means "to put things right", to intervene in a situation that is wrong, oppressive, or out of control, and to fix it. So

---

5. A much fuller analysis and discussion of these terms, with relevant bibliography, can be found in my *Old Testament Ethics for the People of God*, 253–80.

when the psalmists looked forward to God's coming "to judge the earth", they were not thinking just of his condemning the wicked, but of God's putting all things right that have gone so badly wrong in society and creation.

The derived noun *mišpat* can describe the whole process of litigation (a case), or its end result (the verdict and its execution). It can mean a legal ordinance, usually a case law based on past precedents. Exodus 21–23, known as the Covenant Code, or Book of the Covenant, is called in Hebrew, simply, the *mišpat.im*.

But *mišpat* can also be used in a more personal sense as one's legal right, the cause or case one is bringing as a plaintiff before the elders. The frequent expression, "the *mišpat* of the orphan and widow", means their rightful case against those who would exploit them, their just cause in an unfair world. It is from this last sense in particular that *mišpat* comes to have the wider sense of "justice" in a more active sense, whereas *sedeq/sedaqah* has a slightly more static flavour.

There is a great deal of overlap and interchangeability between the two words, but if there is any distinction, one might put it like this: *mišpat* is what needs to be *done* in a given situation if people and circumstances are to be restored to conformity with *sedeq/sedaqah*. *Mišpat* is a *set of actions* – something you do. *Sedeq/sedaqah* is a *state of affairs* – something you aim to achieve. But actually both words can be used for practical actions.

Here in Genesis 18:19 the two words are paired, as they frequently are, to form a comprehensive phrase. This pairing is what is technically called a *hendiadys* – that is, a single complex idea expressed through the use of two words paired together (like "law and order"). Possibly the nearest English expression to the Hebrew double word phrase would be "social justice". Even that phrase, however, is somewhat too abstract for the dynamic nature of this pair of Hebrew words. For *sedaqah* and *mišpat* are concrete nouns, unlike the English abstract nouns used to translate them. That is, in Old Testament thinking, righteousness and justice are actual actions that you *do*, not concepts you reflect on or an ideal you dream about.

Abraham, then, was to teach his household the way of the Lord and about doing righteousness and justice. And this ethical education was to pass down through the generations. That, says God, is what I chose him for.

But how would Abraham himself come to learn what he was supposed to teach? He gets his first lesson from God in Genesis 18. Who better than God himself to teach the way of the Lord and what it means?

The first point that YHWH draws to Abraham's attention is God's own concern about the suffering of the oppressed in the region at the hands of Sodom and Gomorrah. In the careful account of the conversation, Genesis 18:17–19 are soliloquy – that is, God speaking *to himself*. But at verse 20 God speaks again *to Abraham*, and the very first word that God speaks in that sentence is: *ze'aqah* ("cry for help"). The trigger for God's investigation and action is not only the appalling sin of Sodom, but especially the protests and cries of its victims.

Now this is an exact anticipation of what motivated God in the early chapters of Exodus (see Ex. 2:23–25; 3:7). God hears the cry for help from the Israelites under slavery. In fact this incident in Genesis is highly programmatic in the way it defines God's character, actions and requirements. When God acts in the story of the exodus, it will be in the same way as God tells Abraham he is about to act on Sodom and Gomorrah, and for the same reasons—his compassion for the suffering and his anger at injustice.

So the way of the Lord, which Abraham is about to witness and then to teach, is to do righteousness and justice for the oppressed and against the oppressor. The psalmist says that God taught this to Moses. He could easily have added, "and to Abraham".

> The LORD works *righteousness*
> and *justice* for all the oppressed.
> He made known *his ways* to Moses,
> his deeds to the people of Israel. (Ps. 103:6–7, italics added)

The Missional Logic

Returning again to our key text, we must also give attention to its grammatical structure and logic. Genesis 18:19 is a compact statement, and the order of clauses and the connections between them are important. Let's work through it in order:

Gen. 18:19 falls into three clauses, joined by two expressions of purpose—"so that...."

"I have known him"—which is frequently used for God's choosing to bring a person or people into intimate relationship with himself (e.g., also Am. 3:2). That is why it is usually translated, "I have chosen him".

God then states the purpose of his choice of Abraham: *"for the purpose that[6] he will command/teach his children and household after him to keep the way of YHWH by doing righteousness and justice."* This is what we have been exploring in the last section.

This in turn is then followed by another purpose clause, *"for the purpose that YHWH may bring about for Abraham what he has spoken/promised to him."* This is the final clause, expressing the long-term goal of both the previous clauses. God intends to keep his promise of blessing the nations through Israel's descendants (just referred to in v. 18). That's why he chose Abraham, and that's why Abraham must teach his descendants to live in the way of the Lord.

In terms of our biblical theology, as we said above, this one verse thus binds together *election*, *ethics* and *mission* into a single sequence located in the will, action and desire of God. It is fundamentally a *missional* declaration, which *explains the reason for election* and *explains the purpose of ethical living*. It is enormously rich and significant.

---

6. The expression of purpose is emphatic, since the clauses are not merely joined (as they might easily be in Hebrew) by the ubiq- uitous conjunction *w*, but by the purposive conjunction, *lema'an*, which means, "in order that ..." or "for this purpose that...."

We should particularly notice the way *ethics stands as the mid-term between election and mission.* Ethics is the purpose of election and the basis of mission. That is to say, God's election of Abraham (line 1) is intended to produce a community who are taught and committed to ethical reflection of God's character (line 2). And the result of such a community actually existing will be the fulfillment of God's mission of blessing the nations (line 3).

This builds on the link that we saw in chapter 4 between Abraham's election for the blessing of others and Abraham's own *personal* obedience to God. Both Genesis 22:18 and 26:4–5 make that link, connecting God's intention to bless the nations with Abraham's tested obedience. The personal obedience of Abraham was to be the model for his descendants, as God's promise goes on being fulfilled. But here in this text, that personal obedience of Abraham is to be passed on by teaching to his whole community. They will become a model community, taught by the model of Abraham himself.

Another way to make this clear is to approach the missional logic of Genesis 18:19 from either end of the verse. Either way you read the verse, ethics stands in the middle.

Reading from the end:

- *What is God's ultimate mission?* To bring about the blessing of the nations, as he promised Abraham (**mission**).
- *How will that be achieved?* By the existence in the world of a community that will be taught to live according to the way of the Lord in righteousness and justice (**ethics**).
- *But how will such a community come into existence?* Because God chose Abraham to be its founding father (**election**).

Or reading from the beginning:

- *Who is Abraham?* The one whom God has chosen and come to know in personal friendship (**election**).
- *Why did God choose Abraham?* To initiate a people who would be committed to the way of the Lord and his righteousness and justice, in a world going the way of Sodom (**ethics**).
- *For what purpose should the people of Abraham live according to that high ethical standard?* So that God can fulfill his mission of bringing blessing to the nations (**mission**).

Here, then, is another passage that shows us the important link, in our biblical theology, between our ecclesiology and our missiology. We have already pointed out how important it is to see the missional reason for the very existence of the church as the people of God. In this age, the church is missional or it is not church.

But now we see more clearly that this link between church and mission is also *ethical.* The community God seeks for the sake of his mission is to be a community shaped by his own ethical character, with specific attention to righteousness and justice in a world filled with oppression and injustice. Only such a community can be a blessing to the nations.

With such a strong biblical link, it is not surprising that Jesus spent so much time training his community of disciples in what it meant to follow him in all the demanding ethical choices of life – turning away from the ways of their surrounding culture (repentance), exercising faith in him and obeying his teaching. Thus, when he sent them out to the nations, it was with the same emphasis on the *obedience* of discipleship: "teaching them to observe all that I have commanded you." Mission to the nations is ethical at its core, for it demands lives committed to obedience to the Lord, which become self-replicating through the work of evangelism (baptism) and discipling (teaching).

The combined missional and ethical thrust of the Great Commission is entirely consistent with what we have seen in this single verse in Genesis. According to Genesis 18:19, *the ethical quality of life of the people of God is the vital link between their calling and their mission.* God's intention to bless the nations is inseparable from God's ethical demand on the people he has created to be the agent of that blessing.

There is no biblical mission without biblical ethics.

SUMMARY

There would be nothing new in complaining about the state of the church around the world. Everybody does. We are all painfully aware that Christians everywhere, and institutional forms of Christianity worldwide, fall far short even of our own ideals, let alone the requirements of God. But what the exegesis and standards of this text make even more painfully plain for us to see is that it is the moral state of those who claim to be God's people that is a major hindrance to the mission we claim to have on his behalf.

While I lived in India, I was frequently told by Indian Christians themselves that the greatest obstacle to the evangelization of India was not the state of the nation or the resistance of Hinduism, but the state of the church itself.

Our text tells us that God judged Sodom. Yes, and we can see the marks of Sodom all around us still. But God called Abraham and his people to be *different*, to live by different standards, to reflect the God who is radically different from all the flawed gods of the nations. Our problem is that so often the church is *no different* from the world, and in some respects even worse.

A divided, split and fighting church has nothing to say or to give to a divided, broken and violent world. An immoral church has nothing to say to an immoral world. A church riddled with corruption, caste discrimination and other forms of social, ethnic, or gender oppression has nothing to say to the world where such things are rampant. A church with leaders seemingly obsessed with wealth and power has nothing to say to a world of greedy tyrants. A church that is bad news in such ways has no good news to share. Or at least, it has, but its words are drowned out by its life.

This is what makes it so important to take seriously what God said to Abraham in the first Great Commission and what Jesus said to his disciples in his later version. God's people must be taught and must pass on that teaching, about what it means to walk in God's ways and demonstrate righteousness and justice. There is an unavoidable ethical dimension to the mission of God's people.

This is what is at stake in all those ethical choices we have to make in life—whether at an individual level or as communities of God's people. It is always linked to the effectiveness of our mission. It is never merely a matter of me and my conscience and God. The moment we fail to walk in the way of the Lord, or fail to live lives of integrity, honesty and justice, we not only spoil our personal relationship with God, we are actually hindering God in keeping his promise to Abraham. We are no longer the people of blessing to the nations.

We cannot fit into the last line of Genesis 18:19 unless we fit into the middle line. We cannot fulfill line 1 of the Great Commission unless we also obey line 3.

This does not mean, of course (and I am not suggesting), that the church has to be morally perfect before anybody can engage in mission. If that were so, no mission would ever have happened, for even the church in the New Testament was all too human and flawed. The point is: What is our goal? Where is our heart? Are we obsessed with making converts only, or are we committed to teaching God's people to walk in his ways, so that the nations are blessed?

RELEVANT QUESTIONS

1. What impact does Sodom's paralleling of modern society have on your sense of the need of the world?
2. How does the link between the church's mission and godly ethics challenge your own life and the life of the church?
3. Abraham was called to "teach" his household and community to keep the way of the Lord by doing righteousness and justice. How much does *ethical* teaching in your church connect with the church's sense of mission and calling?
4. If ethics is the middle term between our calling and our mission (in Gen. 18:19), what difference should that make as we go about our daily lives in the world—in our choices, actions, attitudes and relationships?
5. How different might the history of Christian mission have been if the church had been as concerned about the middle section of this verse (doing righteousness and justice—i.e., its own ethics) as it has been about the final section (fulfilling God's promise of blessing all the nations—i.e., its evangelism)?

CHAPTER 6

PEOPLE WHO ARE REDEEMED FOR REDEMPTIVE LIVING

"Are you redeemed?" was a question that earnest "personal workers" would ask complete strangers on the streets of Belfast or in buses. In the Northern Ireland of my youth the amazing thing is that most people would know you were talking about the gospel, about the need for personal salvation, about getting saved and going to heaven. That was in the days when "redeeming" was still a Christian word, and not something you do with reward points on your supermarket loyalty card or frequent flyer miles.

But even if at that time we thought of the church as God's redeemed people, it was seen largely as a collection of redeemed individuals, not as a whole community redeemed for a purpose, redeemed for mission. Mission meant helping others to get redeemed; it was not intrinsically connected to the whole purpose of redemption in itself for the people of God.

Biblically, however, when we first encounter the language of redemption,[1] it is in the mouth of God addressed as a promise to the whole Israelite community in bondage in Egypt (Ex. 6:6). Next we find it on the lips of Moses celebrating God's redemption of the whole people for himself (Ex. 15:13). It is unambiguously corporate—God redeemed the whole Israelite nation out of Egypt. And God did so with clear purpose—that they should be his people, committed to him by covenant, knowing him as YHWH, and serving him as a holy priesthood in the midst of the nations. Israel was redeemed to fulfill the promise God had made to Abraham, that all the nations on earth should find blessing through his descendants. Israel was redeemed for a reason. They had a mission in the world as the people God had redeemed for himself, for his glory and for his mission.

So in this chapter we will think about what it means to be that redeemed people of God. We will see that God's idea of redemption is exodus-shaped. So we need to ask what the experience of redemption meant for Israel, and how that great Old Testament story is built into the foundations of the biblical theology of the cross, and must therefore affect what it means for us as Christians to say that we are redeemed.

---

1. With the single exception of Gen. 48:16, where Jacob recalls God's protection throughout his life.

Second, we need to observe how deep and wide was the influence of the exodus on Israel's life and faith. Redemption was not merely a past event, but a reality that required practical response in the present. Remembering the exodus was not confined to the annual Passover rituals, but performed some powerful functions in Israel's faith—sometimes in reproach but also for encouragement and hope.

Finally, we must ask what it means, then, to live redemptively in mission. *For what* have *we* been redeemed?

EXPERIENCING GOD'S REDEMPTION

If our earnest Northern Irish evangelist had asked an Old Testament Israelite, "Are you redeemed?" the answer would have been an immediate, "Yes". And if our good Ulster man or woman had persisted, "How do you know?" the answer would probably not have been a *personal testimony* (though if the Israelite happened to be writing a psalm at the time, it might have been), but a *national epic*—the story of the exodus. For, as noted above, the first and strongest use of the language of redemption in the Bible is applied to the exodus.

In the exodus God acted as redeemer and the event itself is called an act of redemption. In both respects (what it said about God and what redemption actually was for Israel), the exodus provides one of the key ways in which the New Testament interprets the achievement of the cross of Christ—most significantly through the actions of Jesus himself in the final meal with his disciples before his crucifixion, which all the Gospels connect in some way to the Passover—the celebration of God's great act of redemption.

The meal itself [The Last Supper] said two very specific things.

First, like all Jewish Passover meals, the event spoke of leaving Egypt. To a first-century Jew, it pointed to the return from exile, the new exodus, the great covenant renewal spoken of by the prophets. . . .

Second, however, the meal brought Jesus' own kingdom-movement to its climax. It indicated that the new exodus, and all that it meant, was happening *in and through Jesus himself*. . . .

Jesus intended this meal to symbolize the new exodus, the arrival of the kingdom through his own fate. The meal, focused on Jesus' actions with the bread and the cup, told the Passover story, and Jesus' own story, and wove these two into one.

N. T. Wright[2]

So the exodus redemption is clearly a major theme for our biblical theology for life, and it certainly impacts the mission of God's people. For those who have been redeemed are called to live redemptively in response. This is another way in which the biblical story line that we are following impacts our understanding of the mission of God's people. Who are we and what are we here for? We are the people whom God has redeemed, and redeemed for a purpose.

2. N. T. Wright, *Jesus and the Victory of God* (London: SPCK, 1996), 557–59.

The Redeemer – A Champion Who Does Whatever It Takes

We need to ask first what the words mean. In applying the words "redeem" to God's action in the exodus, Israel drew on a concept and practice that was an integral part of their culture and used it as a metaphor for what God had done for Israel. The English word "to redeem", from its Latin roots, means to "buy back" something or someone. In Israel the practice might involve that, but had wider cultural meaning.

The Hebrew verb is *ga'al*, and the noun for a person who performs that action is a *go'el*. In Israel, somebody acted as a *go'el* whenever they took it upon themselves to act in defence of another member of their own family who had been wronged or was facing some danger or threat. So the word is sometimes translated "kinsman-redeemer" or "family guardian". Here are three examples of how somebody might act as a *go'el* in Old Testament Israel:

Bringing a Murderer to Justice

If someone was murdered, it was the duty of some member of the victim's wider family to seek out the guilty person and bring him or her to justice before the elders. This did not give free rein to revenge and blood feuds; it was built into a careful system of legal process that took account of accidental killing and the need for courts to decide in cases of doubt (cf. Num. 35:6–34, where the *go'el* is described as "the avenger of blood").

Helping a Family Member out of Debt or Slavery

If someone was struggling against adverse economic circumstances and had no option but to sell some land, or even to sell dependents into bonded labour, in order to obtain or pay off debts, it became the duty of a member of the family to buy that land in order to keep it in the wider family, or to pay off the debt so that family members enslaved for it could be freed. The descending degrees of such impoverishment and the rules to cope with it are laid out in Leviticus 25, where we find the language of redemption in its most literal sense. It required somebody to pay the cost of the restoration of a brother's land or of a family's freedom.[3]

Keeping a Brother's Family Name Alive

If a man died without having a son who would inherit his name and property, there was a strong moral obligation (though it does not seem to have been a legally enforced duty) on a brother or some other male relative to take his widow into his

---

3. For detailed discussion of Leviticus 25, its various provisions, and wider context in Old Testament economics and Christian ethics, see Christopher J. H. Wright, *God's People in God's Land:* *Family, Land and Property in the Old Testament* (Grand Rapids: Eerdmans and Carlisle: Paternoster, 1990); and *Old Testament Ethics for the People of God*, 146–81.

own family, and to seek to have a son by her. Then that son would inherit the name and property of the deceased brother.

Deuteronomy 25:5 – 10 refers to this practice (though the word *ga'al* is not used), and indicates that it was probably an unpopular duty. The story of Ruth, by contrast, shows Boaz exercising "faithfulness" in acting as *go'el* for Ruth and Naomi, whereas a nearer kinsman exercised what we might call his "right of first refusal". The other man's action indicates that taking on the role of *go'el* did indeed involve considerable personal cost and risk (Ruth 3:9 – 13; 4:1 – 8).

So then, when God promised he would *ga'al* his people (Ex. 6:6), and when Moses celebrates that he had done so (Ex. 15:13), it speaks powerfully of YHWH's adopting a significant role in relation to Israel. It means God is as committed to his people as any family member to another. He accepts a kinship relationship with all its obligations. God is prepared to do whatever it takes, to pay whatever it costs, in order to protect, defend and liberate his people.

Are they being murdered (as they were under Egyptian genocide)? He will avenge them and see that justice is done. Are they languishing in economic bondage, without land or freedom? He will restore them to both. Are they in danger of dying out without posterity (as the Egyptian killing of all male sons threatened)? He will take them to himself in a covenant bond that will ensure that all future generations of firstborn sons belong to him by right of redemption (Ex. 13:1 – 16).

Those are the rich dimensions of meaning that filled Israel's minds when they spoke of YHWH as "redeemer". God was their champion, protector, liberator, avenger and defender. It was the foundation for prayer and praise in the Psalms (e.g., Pss. 19:14; 69:18; 72:14; 74:2; 77:15; 78:35; 103:4; 106:10; 107:2; 119:154). And it reaches its crescendo in the poetry of Isaiah (e.g., Isa. 41:14; 43:1, 14; 44:6, 22 – 24; 48:20; 52:9; 62:12; 63:9).

But what exactly did this God do when he chose to act as redeemer? He did the exodus.

So we need to look carefully at that event to see the scale and scope of God's idea of redemption in action. Remember, the reason we need to do this is that if our mission is connected to God's redemption, we need to understand the Bible's teaching on what redemption actually means. That will affect how we understand what it means to live redemptively in response to God's redemption.

The Exodus – Deliverance from Whatever Enslaves

It is hard to imagine a sequence of events more comprehensive in effect than the story of the exodus presented to us in the book of that name. The texts portray at least four dimensions of the bondage that Israel suffered in Egypt – political, economic, social and spiritual – and goes on to show how God redeemed them in every one of these dimensions.

Political

The Israelites were an immigrant, ethnic minority in a large imperial state. They had come originally as famine refugees and found a welcome (as they remembered; Deut. 23:7–8). But government policy did a U-turn in a later generation, and economic asylum turned into a prison house of political hatred, unfounded fears, exploitation and discrimination. Exodus 1 echoes through the stories of many such ethnic minorities in the modern era, suffering the suspicion and systematic oppression of host states.

God's redeeming work included bringing this political enslavement to an end, enabling Israel eventually to become established as a free people. Provisional asylum for temporary survival had kept the promise of Abraham going. But permanent slavery under political oppression was intolerable since it prevented the promise to Abraham going any further. So to liberate them, God confronted the state power of an empire.

Redemption operated on the political stage.

Economic

The sharpest pain of the oppression was economic. Israelites were being exploited as slave-labour, on land not their own, for the economic benefit of the host nation, in its agricultural and construction projects (Ex. 1:11–14). It was their outcry (*se'aqah*) against this that precipitated the compassionate intervention of God as their *go'el*.

But it was not enough just to get Israel out of Egypt into some kind of tenuous freedom in the wilderness. The objective of their redemption (also stated in Ex. 6:6–8) was to give them land of their own–along with an economic system that was intended to outlaw such oppression within Israel itself. As we will see in a moment, it was particularly in the economic realm that the Israelites themselves were to live redemptively, in response to what God had done for them.

Redemption was strongly economic in content.

Social

The horror story of Exodus 1 moves on from economic exploitation (which failed as a tool of population control), to attempted subversion from within (via the Hebrew midwives), and finally to state-sponsored genocide (extermination of all male Hebrew babies by orders of the government; Ex. 1:22). Thus, lack of political freedom and endurance of economic oppression are now compounded by vicious invasion of normal family life and the denial of fundamental human rights. Once again, we don't have to look far to see Exodus 1 thriving in our modern world.

So when God redeemed his people from this intolerable hell of suffering, it led to the inauguration of a society in which limitation on government power, respect for human life and basic rights, and passion for social justice were built into the founding documents—though sadly their history would show rapid decline from the post-exodus ideals of the Sinai covenant.

Redemption was a social transformation.

Spiritual

Hebrew uses the same word, *ʿabodah,* for service as a slave and for worship. The word occurs frequently in Exodus 1–2 for the Hebrew slaves serving Pharaoh. But when God says to Pharaoh, "Israel is my firstborn son, and I told you, 'Let my son go, so he may worship me'" (Ex. 4:22–23), the ambiguity is evident as different English versions show: some render the last word "serve me", others "worship me". For indeed the Israelites' slavery to Pharaoh was a massive hindrance to their worship of the God of their fathers. Israel's bondage had a spiritual dimension; it was not merely political, economic and social.

In fact, Moses' specific request to Pharaoh was that the Israelites be allowed to go and worship their own God, and God had already told Moses that they would do so on the same mountain as he had received his commission at the burning bush.

As the story develops, it becomes a massive power encounter between YHWH and Pharaoh—who was acclaimed among the gods of Egypt. So the victory over Egypt was not merely at the socioeconomic and political level, but was God's judgment on "all the gods of Egypt" (Ex. 12:12). So the supreme moment comes when Moses proclaims at the climax of his song after the crossing of the Sea of Reeds, "The Lord [YHWH] reigns for ever and ever" (Ex. 15:18)—with the clear implication, "and not Pharaoh".

So when God redeemed Israel at the exodus, it was not just *out of* the several dimensions of their bondage, but also *into* a covenant relationship with God himself. It was not the case that Israel was physically enslaved and needed to be freed (in which case God could have led them out and then waved farewell as they made off to whatever destiny they might choose in their freedom). The problem was not just that the Hebrews were slaves, but that they were slaves to the wrong master and needed to be transferred into the service of the living God.

The exodus was not a movement from slavery to freedom, but from slavery to covenant. Redemption was for relationship with the redeemer, to serve his interests and his purposes in the world.

Redemption had clear spiritual intent and results.

The Exodus—A Holistic Model

Political, economic, social, spiritual—all of these dimensions are integral to the Bible's first great act of redemption. God did whatever it would take to rescue Israel out of whatever form their bondage took.

So the exodus narrative tells us comprehensively *what* God did when he redeemed Israel. But it also tells us the reasons *why* he did so.

The clear motivation for the exodus explained in Exodus 1–2 was twofold. First, it was because of God's compassionate concern for people suffering under cruel oppression – that is God's passion for justice. Second, it was because of God's faithfulness to his covenant promises to Abraham. In other words, this is simply the biblical God acting on mission and acting in character.

In the exodus God responded to *all* the dimensions of Israel's need. God's momentous act of redemption did not merely rescue Israel from political, economic and social oppression and then leave them to their own devices to worship whom they pleased. Nor did God merely offer them spiritual comfort of hope for some brighter future in a home beyond the sky while leaving their historical condition unchanged. No, the exodus effected real change in the people's real historical situation and at the same time called them into a real new relationship with the living God. This was God's total response to Israel's total need. . . .

So here we have the prime, opening, definitive case study of the Redeemer God acting in history out of his own motivation, achieving comprehensive objectives, and pinning his own identity and character to the narrative as a permanent definition of the meaning of his name, YHWH.

Chris Wright[4]

Now, if the mission of God's people flows from the mission of God, what do we learn from the Bible's first story of redemption about the shape of our own mission in God's world?

If then, redemption is biblically defined in the first instance by the exodus, and if God's redeeming purpose is at the heart of God's mission, what does this tell us about mission as we are called to participate in it? The inevitable outcome surely is that *exodus-shaped redemption demands exodus-shaped mission*. And that means that our commitment to mission must demonstrate the same broad totality of concern for human need that God demonstrated in what he did for Israel. And it should also mean that our overall motivation and objective in mission be consistent with the motivation and purpose of God as declared in the exodus narrative.[5]

The exodus, then, as a model of redemption is part of the biblical foundation for the holistic understanding of mission that seems to me to be demanded from a holistic reading of the Bible.

We should not fall into unbalanced interpretation of the exodus. We may be tempted, for example, to spiritualize its meaning into merely an Old Testament "picture" of personal deliverance from the power of sin. Or we may be inclined instead to politicize it into merely a picture of political or economic action for justice without reference to the spiritual demands of knowing and serving the living God through faith and obedience directed to Jesus as Lord.[6]

The best way to avoid such unbalanced interpretation is to move forward in our biblical theology to the way the New Testament sees the exodus as finding its ultimate counterpart in the cross of Christ.

---

4. Wright, *The Mission of God*, 271–72.
5. Ibid., 275–76.
6. There is no space here to discuss these flawed alternatives, but I have explored them and their impact on Christian mission thinking and practice in *The Mission of God*, 253–80.

The Cross – God's Victory over
Whatever Opposes and Oppresses

The New Testament presents the redeeming death of Jesus through the lens of the exodus. Both the person and the event match the Old Testament picture of redemption. Jesus as redeemer is the champion who will do whatever it takes to achieve rescue for his people. It took the surrender of his own life. And the cross, as the supreme moment of redemption, was God's victory over all that opposes him and enslaves his creation.

The clearest reference to the exodus in the Gospels comes when Jesus met with Moses and Elijah on the Mount of Transfiguration. According to Luke "they were talking about his exodus that he intended to fulfill in Jerusalem" (Luke 9:31, my translation). Unfortunately the significance is lost in English versions that translate the Greek word *exodos* as "his departure" (how do you "fulfill" a departure?). The two great representatives of the Law and the Prophets were hardly chatting about Jesus' death merely as an "exit", but about the fulfillment of the Scriptures they had played such a part in. Specifically, they were referring to the fulfillment of "exodus", achieved for national Israel under Moses, now to be achieved for the world by Jesus. His imminent and fully intended death would constitute God's great act of redemption. God in Christ would pay the cost of delivering the whole creation from the bondage of sin and evil, leading his people out of the darkness of captivity into the light and liberty of God.

Other gospel writers see exodus motifs elsewhere. Matthew sees events in the infancy of Jesus as exodus replayed (Matt. 2:13 – 15). Mark uses the new exodus imagery of Isaiah 40 – 55 in his understanding of the life and accomplishment of Jesus (Mark 1:3; 4:35 – 5:13). Luke does the same in recording the song of Zechariah, with its rejoicing in the anticipated redemption of God's people from the tyranny of their enemies (Luke 1:67 – 79). Jesus died at Passover time, with its memory of the historical exodus deliverance and its hopes that God would deliver his people again.

Paul uses the language of redemption, sometimes in its more literal sense of ransom, the purchase of freedom for those in bondage (probably with the Greek and Roman practice of slaves gaining freedom or prisoners of war being ransomed, e.g., 1 Tim. 2:6), but sometimes also with the Old Testament exodus in the background. In Romans, for example, he looks forward to the whole creation being liberated from its bondage to decay, as we anticipate the redemption of our bodies (Rom. 8:18 – 25). Redemption is both the accomplishment of Christ through his death for our forgiveness (Eph. 1:7; Col. 1:14), and also the future complete liberation to which we look forward (Eph. 1:14; 4:30). As the Israelites did at Passover, so Christians can look back to the cross as God's historic rescue mission and look forward to final redemption of ourselves and all creation.

Just as the exodus was God's great defeat of the usurped claims and power of Pharaoh, so the cross was God's victory over the principalities and powers (Col. 2:15). The exodus imagery is perhaps strongest in Colossians.

The exodus event is one of the archetypal narratives of the Bible for it informs the beginning, middle and end of the biblical account of redemptive history. God inaugurates the nation of Israel in the exodus from Egypt. He establishes his covenant with the nation at Mount Sinai, provides for his people's needs in the wilderness for forty years, and finally leads them into the Promised Land. . . .

In the middle of God's plan of redemptive history we find Jesus Christ's incarnation, life, death and resurrection. . . . The four New Testament evangelists frame at least parts of their gospel narratives in exodus terms and patterns. Christ's teaching of his disciples is often informed by the exodus experience and his actions among the multitudes have exodus overtones . . . exodus themes and patterns help explain the events of Christ's life and death.

At the end of redemptive history is the Apocalypse. John makes use of exodus allusions and patterns in the Apocalypse to bring the biblical narrative to its conclusion. The ancient Israelites entered Canaan, their Promised Land. New Testament Christians enter the promised rest of their salvation and freedom from their sins. At the end of it all, the redeemed of all ages will enter the New Jerusalem and their exile will finally be over. They will be home. The exodus is never far from the readers of the Old and New Testaments.

Richard Patterson and Michael Travers[7]

> For [God the Father] has rescued us from the dominion of darkness and brought us into the kingdom of the Son he loves, in whom we have redemption, the forgiveness of sins. (Col. 1:13 – 14)

In other words, in the Old and New Testaments, redemption is the act of God in which he stands up as the great champion of his people, exerts his mighty strength, and pays the full cost of rescuing them from all that opposes and oppresses them. It involves the defeat of all oppressive power and the reversal of all dimensions of bondage that afflict people. It brings his people "out from under" and brings them into a new relationship with God. And that new relationship calls for the practical response of redemptive living in mission for God in the world.

RESPONDING TO GOD'S REDEMPTION
Called to Rejoice

The first instinctive response to the great exodus deliverance was to break out in songs of rejoicing, as Moses and Miriam did (Ex. 15:1 – 21). The song of Moses celebrates God as redeemer, emphasizing that he has won a great victory over his enemies, that he is beyond comparison with any of the gods of the nations, that he has redeemed his people, and that other peoples will be affected by the news of

---

7. Richard Patterson and Michael Travers, "Contours of the Exodus Motif in Jesus' Earthly Ministry," *Westminster Theological Journal* 66 (2004): 25 – 27 (also 46 – 47). This article has a fine and comprehensive summary of the exodus theme in both Old and New Testaments.

this great event. The song is a celebration of the reign of God demonstrated in his mighty act of redemption.

But rejoicing in redemption was not to die away like the cheering and applause at the end of a great sporting victory. It was to become a habit of personal life and embedded in Israelite culture. The redemptive reign of God, in a sense, continued to be actualized in the worshiping life of Israel.

> You are the Holy One,
> Enthroned upon (or dwelling in) the praises of Israel.
> > (Ps. 22:3, my translation, in preference to the NIV/TNIV)

The life of Israel was permeated by the times of rejoicing in God that punctuated the annual calendar. The Passover in the spring, of course, was the most specific celebration of the exodus deliverance. But the autumn harvest provided another opportunity for telling the old, old story of YHWH and his love and singing the songs of redemption (Deut. 26:5 – 11).

Rejoicing in redemption was thus not only personal, but also communal (all sections of society were to be allowed to join in), and also commanded. It was not so much an optional emotional bonus as an inculcated community responsibility and benefit (Deut. 16:11; cf. Neh. 8:10 – 12). Old Testament Israelites would have agreed with the lines in the Anglican Eucharistic prayer, "It is not only right, it is our duty and our joy at all times and in all places to give you thanks and praise...."[8]

Peter, then, is being authentically scriptural and Israelite when he quotes the book of Exodus to tell his readers, most likely predominantly Gentile believers, that they have also had their exodus experience, and he immediately adds that their first practical response to it should be to live lives of declarative praise, as the God-centred context in which they should also be living lives of practical goodness among the nations. Praise and practice together are missional functions, and both are what we are called to in response to God's redeeming love.

> But you are a chosen people, a royal priesthood, a holy nation, God's special possession, that you may declare the praises of him who called you out of darkness into his wonderful light. (1 Peter 2:9)

We shall consider the missional importance of such praise and prayer in chapter 14.

Called to Imitate

The exodus permeated Israel's laws and customs. It is mentioned many times as motivation for obedience to a range of social requirements. This is where the experience of redemption blends into the practice of redemptive living.

---

8. The phrases properly capture the biblical emphasis that thanksgiving is both a command we are to obey ("our duty") and a pleasure we are to enjoy ("our joy").

The exodus is not merely an event in history. It becomes a model for behaviour. As a redeemed people, Israel must live out the same qualities that motivated YHWH to act as their divine *go'el*. Part of the mission of God's redeemed people is to reflect the character of their redeemer in the way they behave to others. And that means especially the chief requirements of any *go'el*: costly compassion, commitment to justice, caring generosity, redemptively effective action. Those are the things that are involved in redemptive living.

Slave Release

So it is not surprising to find that the first laws given to Israel—a bunch of escaped slaves—immediately after the Ten Commandments, have to do with the way they were to treat those who, in their own society, would find themselves in some form of bonded labour (Ex. 21:1–11). "Hebrew servants" were probably not ethnic Israelites, but a vulnerable class of landless people in the ancient Near Eastern culture who lived by selling their services as labourers, soldiers, or whatever was available. Israel's law required that after six years of service they were to be granted the option of freedom—an "exodus" provision.

The same body of law makes Israel's experience in Egypt an explicit motivation for *not* treating foreigners in their midst in the way they had suffered in Egypt (Ex. 23:9).

Deuteronomy 15:1–18 is possibly the warmest chapter in the Old Testament about the economics of generosity. It preaches compassion for the needy in a highly relational manner.

> If anyone is poor among your people in any of the towns of the land that the Lord your God is giving you, do not be hardhearted or tightfisted toward them. Rather, be openhanded and freely lend them whatever they need.... There will always be poor people in the land. Therefore I command you to be openhanded toward those of your people who are poor and needy in your land. (Deut. 15:7–11)

Generosity

When the passage from Deuteronomy moves on immediately to its command to show generosity to released slaves, it explicitly cites the exodus as the model and motivation for such behaviour:

> And when you release them, do not send them away empty-handed. Supply them liberally from your flock, your threshing floor and your winepress. Give to them as the Lord your God has blessed you. *Remember that you were slaves in Egypt and the Lord your God redeemed you. That is why I give you this command today.* (Deut. 15:13–15; italics added)

Those who know what it is to be redeemed must live redemptively towards others—especially those who are now in the same kind of need as Israel was when God redeemed them.

Redemption and Jubilee

The most literal use of the language of redemption is in Leviticus 25, where it applies to the buying back of land that had been (or was about to be) sold as collateral for a loan, and to the buying back of family members who had been sold to work off debts. Interwoven with these redemption procedures was the Year of Jubilee, which aimed at restoration of families to their ancestral land and to productive participation in the community.[9]

All of these mechanisms were fundamentally redemptive and restorative in a broader economic and social sense – intended to intervene and reverse the otherwise relentless downward spiral of debt, poverty and dispossession. Once again, we find that God's great redeeming act, the exodus, stands as the repeated model and motivation for all such behaviour. Theology and economics do not inhabit separate universes but combine in the biblical experience and practice of redemption.

Micah put the two together with devastating logic. Read Micah 6:4–5, 8 and notice how it moves through the history of redemption, to God's revelation of explicit and universal moral demands.

Forgiveness and Debts

The same dynamic principle of reflecting our redeemer through redemptive living permeates the New Testament also. How many times can we say the Lord's Prayer and not notice this principle? "And forgive us our sins, for we ourselves forgive everyone indebted to us" (Luke 11:4; NRSV).[10]

In Matthew's version, the word is "debts" in both parts of the petition, though Jesus explains it in terms of "transgressions" – affirming that God's forgiveness of our transgressions is linked to our willingness to forgive the transgressions of others. But in a society where poverty and debt were endemic and a major cause of social unrest, the prayer that God would "release for us our debts" had a strongly economic ring, as well as pointing to the reality of our sins against God. There is no need to opt for either an exclusively spiritual or exclusively financial interpretation of the prayer at this point. The link between sins and debts crops up elsewhere in Jesus' teaching as we shall see.

The more crucial point we are making here is that the forgiving action of God and the compassionate action of those who pray to him are integrally linked. As those who know God's forgiveness, we are to behave in like manner to those who have offended us – especially those who have debts.

The joy of being released from debt (one of the meanings of redemption, as we have seen) should produce a willingness to release others from debt, an act that

---

9. For fuller analysis of these economic measures in Old Testament Israel, see my *Old Testament Ethics for the People of God*, 146–211, and *God's People in God's Land*, and the bibliography cited in both books.

10. Inexplicably, the NIV and TNIV, which so often use different English words for the same Hebrew or Greek, thus obscuring important verbal *connections* in the original, here choose to use the same English word, "sins," where the text deliberately uses different words, thus obscuring an important verbal *distinction* in the original.

It is not that we can earn forgiveness by being forgiving. It is rather that our experience of God's great mercy should make us merciful people. . . .

The experience of grace transforms us into gracious people. It is not just about inter-personal conflict. It is about how we treat other people. It is about economic generosity. While God forgives our *sins*, we forgive our *debtors*. Luke could have used the word "sin" in both cases, but he chose to highlight the economic implications of Jesus' words. . . .

In the Old Testament Year of Jubilee debts were forgiven and slaves were set free as the people celebrated God's grace to them in providing atonement (see Lev. 25 and Deut. 15). Now the Lamb of God who takes away the sins of the world has come. In the light of God's forgiveness, a new era of economic and social relations has begun among those forgiven and set free by Christ's death. The followers of Jesus are to live as both recipients of, and participants in, a permanent jubilee.

Tim Chester[11]

reflects the generosity of the original redeemer. This is precisely the point of Jesus' parable in Matthew 18:21–33, which Jesus told to explain the radical meaning and scope of forgiveness within God's kingdom.

Experience of redemption must generate redemptive living. This is the missional outflow of what God has done for us. The mission of God's people has such intensely practical dimensions.

The principle of reflecting our experience of God's redeeming grace in how we live and especially in our treatment of others is found throughout the New Testament. A few examples make the point clear:

- Be merciful, just as your Father is merciful (Luke 6:36).
- Love each other as I have loved you (John 15:12).
- Be kind and compassionate to one another, forgiving each other, just as in Christ God forgave you (Eph. 4:32).
- Accept one another, then, just as Christ accepted you (Rom. 15:7).
- See that you also excel in this grace of giving. . . . For you know the grace of our Lord Jesus Christ, that though he was rich, yet for your sake he became poor, so that you through his poverty might become rich (2 Cor. 8:7–9).
- This is how we know what love is: Jesus Christ laid down his life for us. And we ought to lay down our lives for one another. If any one of you has material possessions and sees a brother or sister in need but has no pity on them, how can the love of God be in you? (1 John 3:16–17).

LIVING REDEMPTIVELY IN MISSION

How then can we relate this survey of some dimensions of the biblical theology of redemption, with its exodus roots and its fulfillment at the cross, to life in mission for the people of God?

We have seen that in both Old and New Testaments, redemption was not just a historical fact of the past, nor just a personal experience to be enjoyed in the present,

---

11. Tim Chester, *Good News to the Poor: Sharing the Gospel through Social Involvement* (Leicester: IVP, 2004), 96–97.

but a status that was to be lived out in ethical response. God's redeemed people are called to redemptive living in the world. And in view of our exodus understanding of the full breadth of what it means when God acts to redeem, there must be equally broad implications for our understanding of a quality of mission that responds to, reflects, and in some ways embodies the redeeming purposes of God.

The exodus has been seen as the biblical foundation par excellence for theologies of mission that emphasize the importance of social, political and economic concern and action alongside the spiritual dimensions of personal forgiveness. Or rather, and with greater biblical faithfulness, it is the biblical basis for the integration of all these dimensions within the comprehensive good news of the biblical gospel. Such holistic, or integral, understandings of mission point to the totality of what God accomplished for Israel in the paradigmatic redemptive event – the exodus. And I believe they are right to do so.[12]

Once upon a time there were certain banks who, though their own great folly, found themselves in danger of collapse under mountains of toxic debt that they could not repay or even understand. So they went to their governments, who had mercy on them and took their debts away with thousands of billions of dollars and pounds taken from their taxpayers. Then those same banks came across many individuals whose taxes had rescued them, who owed them small debts of a few thousand dollars or pounds, but they showed them no mercy at all and took away their homes because they couldn't pay up. Which goes to show that redemption in our fallen world seems to work very nicely for the rich and powerful but is hard to come by if you're poor. Jesus' idea of redemption in the kingdom of God operates differently.

Keeping the Cross Central

However, I have stressed in this chapter that we must see the exodus in the light of the cross, and vice versa. God's redemption is in reality one great redeeming achievement – even though spread across centuries of human history. The redeemed in the new creation sing the song of Moses and the Song of the Lamb (Rev. 15:3), because essentially it is one song celebrating one great redeemer and his one great redemptive work in history.

For this reason, when we think of the mission of God's people in holistic or integral terms as described above, *it is vital that we keep the cross central to every dimension of mission* that we engage in. The following section is an extract from *The Mission of God* in which I expressed a passionate concern for this, and since I don't think I can say it any better, I quote it here.

All Christian mission flows from the cross – as its source, its power, and as that which defines its scope.

It is vital that we see the cross as central and integral to every aspect of holistic, biblical mission – that is, of all we do in the name of the crucified and risen Jesus. It is a

12. I have discussed such a holistic understanding of mission, with particular reference to the exodus and also the jubilee, in *The Mission of God*, 265–323.

mistake, in my view, to think that, while our evangelism must be centred on the cross (as of course it has to be), our social engagement and other forms of practical mission work have some other theological foundation or justification.

A church without social ethics rooted in the moral vision of the Scripture with its emphasis on justice, mercy, and humility before God is in no condition to avoid irrelevance in relation to the great problems that affect humankind. At best it will concentrate on empty ritualism and private morality, but will remain indifferent to the plight of the poor and the rape of God's creation. At worst it will fail to recognize its own captivity to the culture-ideology of consumerism and will be used by the powerful to provide religious legitimization to their unjust socioeconomic and political system and even to war.

Rene Padilla[13]

Why is the cross just as important across the whole field of mission? Because in all forms of Christian mission in the name of Christ we are confronting the powers of evil and the kingdom of Satan – with all their dismal effects on human life and the wider creation. If we are to proclaim and demonstrate the reality of the reign of God in Christ – that is, if we are to proclaim that Jesus is king, in a world which likes still to chant "we have no king but Caesar" and his many successors, including mammon – then we will be in direct conflict with the usurped reign of the evil one, in all its legion manifestations. The deadly reality of this battle against the powers of evil is the unanimous testimony of those who struggle for justice, for the needs of the poor and oppressed, the sick and the ignorant, and even those who seek to care for and protect God's creation against exploiters and polluters, just as much as it is the experience of those (frequently the same people) who struggle evangelistically to bring people to faith in Christ as Saviour and Lord and plant churches. In *all* such work we confront the reality of sin and Satan. In all such work we are challenging the darkness of the world with the light and good news of Jesus Christ and the reign of God through him.

By what authority can we do so? With what power are we competent to engage the powers of evil? On what basis dare we challenge the chains of Satan, in word and deed, in people's spiritual, moral, physical and social lives? Only through the cross.

- Only in the cross is there forgiveness, justification and cleansing for guilty sinners.
- Only in the cross stands the defeat of evil powers.
- Only in the cross is there release from the fear of death and its ultimate destruction altogether.
- Only in the cross are even the most intractable of enemies reconciled.
- Only in the cross will we finally witness the healing of all creation.

The fact is that sin and evil constitute bad news in every area of life on this planet. The redemptive work of God through the cross of Christ is good news for every area of life on earth that has been touched by sin – which means every area of life. Bluntly, we need a holistic gospel because the world is in a holistic mess. And by God's incredible grace we have a gospel big enough to redeem all that sin and

---

13. Rene Padilla, "The Biblical Basis for Social Ethics," *Transforming the World? The Gospel and Social Responsibility* (eds. Jamie A. Grant and Dewi A. Hughes; Nottingham: IVP, 2009), 187–204 (esp. 191).

evil have touched. And every dimension of that good news is good news utterly and only because of the blood of Christ on the cross.

Ultimately all that **will** be there in the new, redeemed creation will be there because of the cross. And conversely, all that will **not** be there (suffering, tears, sin, Satan, sickness, oppression, corruption, decay and death), will not be there because they will have been defeated and destroyed by the cross. That is the length, breadth, height and depth of God's idea of redemption. It is exceedingly good news. It is the font of all our mission.

So it is my passionate conviction that holistic mission must have a holistic theology of the cross. That includes the conviction that the cross must be as central to our social engagement as it is to our evangelism. There is no other power, no other resource, no other name, through which we can offer the whole Gospel to the whole person and the whole world, than Jesus Christ crucified and risen.[14]

The Church as an Exodus and Jubilee Community

But while we keep the cross central to all that we mean by the mission of God's people, we need to view it from the Mount of Transfiguration, in conversation with Moses and Elijah, as "the exodus that Jesus intended to fulfill". That is to say, we do not see the cross as that which *replaced* the exodus (as if all the socioeconomic and political aspects of the exodus simply drop away, leaving only a spiritual significance). Rather, we see the cross as the *fulfillment* of the exodus, including within its total redemptive accomplishment final liberation from *all* that enslaves and oppresses humanity and creation. Of course, we do not yet see the completion of that redemptive work in present history, but we look forward to it in its ultimate totality, as Paul does in Romans 8. The "day of redemption" still lies ahead, even though the achievement of redemption has been won at the cross.

Our biblical theology for life has to build the span of its great arch of redemption from the Torah to Revelation.

SUMMARY

We have seen, then, that our biblical theology of redemption portrays God as the divine Redeemer. He is the one who undertakes to do whatever it takes and to pay whatever it costs to deliver his people from all that oppresses them. He is the great champion who wins the victory that sets his people free. The exodus provides the Old Testament model of redemption and shows how broad and comprehensive a thing it is when God steps in as redeemer. The New Testament presents the cross and resurrection of Jesus as the grand exodus *par excellence* – the crowning accomplishment of God's redeeming will and power, his victory over all powers, human and satanic, that oppose him and oppress his people.

---

14. Wright, *Mission of God*, 314–16.

So what then is the mission of God's people? Surely it is to live as those who have experienced that redeeming power of God already, and whose lives—individual and corporate—are signposts to the ultimate liberation of all creation and humanity from every form of oppression and slavery.

For that reason, we engage in redemptive living that seeks to bring the different dimensions of *God's* idea of redemption—as expressed in the exodus and Year of Jubilee—to bear on all such manifestations of oppression as surround us. And that is why we too must converse with Moses and Elijah, for it is the Law and the Prophets that provide us with so many resources to put flesh and blood on what it means to live redemptively, to be moved by compassion, justice and generosity in a world of cruelty, exploitation and greed.

That, after all, is what the Scriptures are for, according to Paul (referring to the Old Testament):

> All Scripture is God-breathed and is useful for teaching, rebuking, correcting and training in righteousness, so that all God's people may be thoroughly equipped for every good work. (2 Tim. 3:16–17)

I am not suggesting that the church should seek to reenact literal exoduses or promote legislation for enforcing a literal jubilee. Rather, we need to see these as models of the kind of comprehensive redemptive response to human need that God himself enacted and then demanded of his people.

Where there is political injustice, economic exploitation, social oppression and spiritual bondage, what actions are appropriate for those who share God's compassion and justice, demonstrated at the exodus?

Where people are torn apart by an upward spiral of debt and a downward spiral of poverty, with all the human indignity and social exclusion that go with them, what actions reflect the theological principles of the jubilee, with its insistence that debt should not have eternal life and that the failures of one generation should not condemn all future generations to poverty?

Will we, in other words, choose to define our own mission with some degree of similarity to the way Jesus defined his own, drawing on the prophet's reframing of the language and the hopes of exodus and jubilee?

> "The Spirit of the Lord is on me,
>   because he has anointed me
>   to proclaim good news to the poor.

The Christian community is both a sign and a promise of God's coming liberation. We are the presence of God's liberating kingdom in a broken world. We are the place where liberation can be found, offering a home for exiled people. We are to welcome the broken people to a community of broken people. We are the community among whom liberation is a present reality—the jubilee people who live with new economic and social relationships. We are the light of the world, a city on a hill. The challenge for us is to articulate Jesus' message of liberation in a way that connects with people's experience and offers a place of liberation in the Christian community.

Tim Chester[15]

15. Chester, *Good News to the Poor*, 97.

He has sent me to proclaim freedom for the prisoners
>   and recovery of sight for the blind,
to set the oppressed free,
>   to proclaim the year of the Lord's favor." (Luke 4:18–19)

As we do so, we become communities that are like exodus and jubilee signposts, pointing to the redeeming work of God in the past and to the only hope of liberation that our world can have for the future.

RELEVANT QUESTIONS

1. How does understanding the cross and resurrection of Jesus as the fulfillment of the exodus pattern impact how you understand redemption and the church's mission?

2. When we think of "being redeemed", we tend to equate it simply with having our sins forgiven, which is right and good. But what other dimensions of God's redeeming (delivering, liberating) work, as we have considered it in this chapter, can you point to in your own life experience?

3. We also tend to think of redemption in individual terms (being redeemed persons). But how should it change your perception of the church to think of it as a redeemed *community*? And in what ways could your church function as such, in reflecting the redemptive compassion and justice of God in the world around?

4. What difference will it make to your understanding of the mission of God's people if you now believe that it is not just about sending missionaries to other countries so that other people can be redeemed, but includes God's people everywhere living redemptively in the world, as reflectors and messengers of God in Christ, our redeemer?

PEOPLE WHO REPRESENT GOD TO THE WORLD

REMEMBERING THE STORY
The Story That Provides a Reason for Living

Who are we and what are we here for? These could be said to be the questions we are seeking to answer in the whole of this book: What is the mission of God's people? But even at the personal level such questions are challenging. What is your sense of identity and what is the purpose of your existence in this world?

The answer depends on what story you think you are part of. We all live the little stories of our own lives on the assumption of some larger story that makes sense to us, or that makes enough sense to allow us to think it is probably, on balance, worth going on living. That is true even if you have to make such a story up for yourself rather than seeing yourself within a grand story that transcends your own life, and transcends even the material universe. That is certainly what atheists have to do, though one wonders if they manage to make a satisfying job of it. They don't have much of a story to tell.

If we step back again to the Old Testament, we could ask the same questions about the Israelites. Who were *they*, and what were *they* there for? And the way we answer has to come out of the big story they were part of. So at this point we take another step forward in seeing the significance of the grand biblical narrative that we surveyed in chapter 2. This is why it matters so much to have a grasp of it.

Here, then, is God's own answer to those questions for the Old Testament Israelites: "Who are we and what are we here for?" It comes in one of the most influential verses in the Bible.

> Then Moses went up to God, and the LORD called to him from the mountain and said, "This is what you are to say to the house of Jacob and what you are to tell the people of Israel: 'You yourselves have seen what I did to Egypt, and how I carried you on eagles' wings and brought you to myself. Now if you obey me fully and keep my covenant, then out of all nations you will be my treasured possession. [5b] *For*

indeed the whole earth is mine, and you will be for me a kingdom of priests and a holy nation.' These are the words you are to speak to the Israelites."

Ex. 19:3–6 (my italics and translation in v. 5b)

Now the story that formed the immediate context for these words was, of course, the story of the exodus, as we saw in chapter 6. But even that is not a big enough story. That was just one part of God's great drama that shapes the whole Bible, that spans the whole universe, and that includes the past, present and future. It was the early episodes of the big story that told the Israelites who they were.

It is also the story that tells us who *we* are and why, for it is part of the story that gave us Jesus of Nazareth and *his* story. Indeed it was the story that confirmed to Jesus who *he* was and what he was there to be and to do. And as we saw in chapter 2, it is the story that drove the New Testament church out in its mission to the world.

So then, in thinking about what it is about our identity as the people of God that necessitates our involvement in mission, we need once again to pay attention to the story – as God surveys it in this text.

In early 2009 an advertisement appeared on the sides of London's red buses, sponsored and paid for by various humanist and atheist societies and individuals, such as Richard Dawkins – televangelist of atheist fundamentalism: *"There probably is no God. Now stop worrying and enjoy life."* A curious misunderstanding, I thought when I saw it, for it suggests that belief in God only makes people worried or spoils their enjoyment. All the research and statistics, however, have shown that people with Christian faith are *less* stressed than average and have a markedly greater sense of life-fulfillment. But my main response to the slogan was, "Well, that's not much of a story. In fact, no story at all. It gives nobody a positive reason to live (or die)." Contrast the gospel. "God so loved the world that he gave his only Son, that whoever believes in him shall not perish but have everlasting life" (John 3:16). Now there's a story! It has a subject, a problem, an action, a solution and a happy ending.

The Story So Far

So as we turn in this chapter to study Exodus 19:3–6, remember that all the way through this book we are building biblical theology for life – which means that the theology we dig out of this story and God's comment on it can be applied to our own lives precisely because this is part of *our* story, part of the big story that gives meaning and purpose to *our* lives as God's people.

We know the story so far. The Israelites had been oppressed as an ethnic minority in Egypt. God, out of compassion and faithfulness, sent Moses to deliver them. After a series of plagues on Pharaoh and Egypt, they had escaped, and God sealed their deliverance by a miraculous crossing of the sea, celebrated by Moses and Miriam in Exodus 15. Then God had provided them with food, with water, with protection from their enemies, and with a bit of organizational common sense from Moses' father-in-law (Exodus 16–18).

But now at last, God had got the Israelites to himself, as it were, gathered at the foot of Mount Sinai, as he had promised Moses (Ex. 3:12). It was time to explain. Time to make sense of the story so far. Time to help them understand the point of it all. Time to tell them who they were, and what they were to be and do for God in this new world situation in which they found themselves.

That is the thrust of Exodus 19:1–6. The speech of God at this point is a crucial hinge between the great story of redemption in the first half of the book and the making of the covenant, the giving of the law, and the construction of the tabernacle in the second half of the book. It is explanatory, encouraging and challenging all at once.

Most of all, this text gave to Israel (and gives to us, as we will see once we build it into our biblical theology) an identity, a role, and a mission in the world, along with the privileges and the responsibilities that go along with them.

So then, in verses 4–6 God points in three directions. He points *back* to Israel's recent past. He points *forward* to his future vision for all nations. And he points to the *present* responsibilities of Israel. And in every direction we find God's grace at work.

PAST GRACE: GOD'S SALVATION – EXODUS 19:4

The first words God tells Moses to speak to the Israelites are a reminder. "You your-selves have seen what I did...." And of course, so they had. It was a recent memory. Only three months previously (v. 1) they had been slaves in Egypt, enduring systematic state-sponsored genocide as an ethnic minority. But now, as we explored in the last chapter, they are comprehensively liberated. A bit footsore and weary, perhaps. A bit bored of manna already, perhaps. But free, with the Egyptian oppression already fading into the past. And all of that was because God had taken the initiative. He had acted out of his compassion, love and faithfulness to his promise to their ancestors.

So God points emphatically to this as his opening words. He points to his grace in action, caring for them enough to liberate them, to exercise his mighty hand and outstretched arm in defeating their oppressors and rescuing them from the place of slavery and death. God's grace has been proved in history. God's justice has been done, the mighty put down and the poor lifted up. God was their great redeemer, as we saw in chapter 6.

Whatever is going to come next in the story (which the reader knows, of course, but the Israelites in the story do not yet) will thus be founded on that historical grace of God. Soon we will be in the world of the Ten Commandments (ch. 20), the wider law in the Book of the Covenant (chs. 21–23), and the making of the

Sinai covenant (ch. 24). But all of that will be a matter of responding to the grace of redemption already experienced.

I emphasize this point because of a misunderstanding that is still sadly common about the difference between the Old and New Testaments. Many Christians think that it can be summed up by saying that in the Old Testament people tried to get saved by obeying the law, whereas in the New Testament (thank God), we know that we can only get saved by grace through faith. But the first is a distorted idea. Some form of that view (though not nearly so blunt as that) was what Paul was combating in his arguments with some of the Jews who disagreed with his missionary theology and practice. But as Paul himself pointed out, salvation had always been, even in the Old Testament, a matter of God's promise and grace, received by faith (like Abraham).

Grace came first, faith next, and obedience to the law a necessary third, as a believing response in action to what God had already done.

So here in our text, God reminds the Israelites that he had *already* delivered them, and only then did he say, "Now let's talk about your obedience in response to what I have done." The very shape of the book of Exodus as a whole implicitly supports the theology that is explicit in this text. We have 18 chapters of salvation before we get a single chapter of law. Law is the response to grace, not the means of earning it.

The same basic principle flows through biblical theology, ethics and mission. Commands follow grace. *Generosity* is commanded in Deuteronomy, but obedience to that command is motivated by blessing already received. "Give to them as the LORD your God has blessed you" (Deut. 15:14). *Love* is commanded by Jesus, but our obedience starts with his love for us: "We love because he first loved us" (1 John 4:19). *Mutual forgiveness* is commanded by Paul, but our obedience is based on being forgiven ourselves: "forgiving each other, just as in Christ God forgave you" (Eph. 4:32). We are *sent out in mission* by the command of Christ. But the prior reality was God's grace in sending Jesus into the world (John 17:18).

Already in Ex. 4:31 these people believe the gospel word of God spoken by Moses and bow down and worship YHWH. The Passover materials continue this worshiping theme (12:27), and it comes to a climax in the worship activity of 15:1–21. The people who are delivered from Egypt are the elect people of God, a community of faith already worshiping YHWH. It is as such a people of God that they "fear the LORD" and "believe in the LORD" (14:31). God's saving actions, undertaken at the divine initiative, have drawn the community into a new orbit of life and blessing, to which the people have responded in faith/worship. Before there is any talk of obeying the law, what God has done fills their lives.... The covenant at Sinai is a specific covenant with an already existing covenant [i.e., Abraham] with an elect, redeemed, believing, worshiping community.

Terence E. Fretheim[1]

---

1. Terence E. Fretheim, *Exodus* (Interpretation: A Bible Commentary for Teaching and Preaching; Louisville: John Knox, 1991), 209.

If we were to transpose God's words to Israel into a New Testament theological context, it would be as if God were to point to the cross of Christ and say to us, "You have seen what I have done...." After that, whatever action we take, in ethical or missional obedience, is a matter of grateful response.

Like the Israelites, we need to remind ourselves of God's past grace demonstrated in historical redemption and then go on to understand our identity and our mission in the light of it.

FUTURE GRACE: GOD'S MISSION – EXODUS 19:5B

I wonder what the view was like from the top of Mount Sinai. In the pictorial, metaphorical language of the story, that is where God "was". That is where he spoke from. That is where Moses, and later the elders, had to go to meet with him (Ex. 24:9 – 11).

Down at the foot of the mountain, the only people around were the Israelites. The Amalekites had been scattered in defeat. It may have been easy for Israel to imagine they were the only people God was interested in. They were the ones who had been rescued, fed, watered, protected and brought to this place for an awesome encounter with the living God. And of course, at one level they were right.

A Special People, but Not the Only People

There was indeed a unique and special relationship between God and this people, established through Abraham. Israel was, as God had instructed Moses to tell Pharaoh, "my firstborn son" (Ex. 4:22). And God would reinforce that special relationship in 19:5 ("my treasured possession"), and then consolidate it in the Sinai covenant a few chapters later. But it was far from being *exclusive* in the sense that YHWH could be considered as merely the local god of one particular people.

YHWH never had been and never would be the God of Israel alone (cf. Rom. 3:29). On the contrary, from his elevated mountain-top altitude, as it were, God surveys "the whole earth", and "all the nations", and they all belong to him. In other words, that unique and special relationship with Israel must be placed within the wider universal framework of God's global ownership.

Yes, God had just rescued *one* particular nation out of bondage. But his ultimate goal was to offer salvation to *all* nations. Yes, God had just demonstrated his sovereign power in *one* particular land, the land of Egypt. But even while doing so, he had made it repeatedly plain to Pharaoh himself that his intention was to prove that the *whole earth* belongs to him and his sovereignty knows no boundaries (Ex. 9:14, 16, 29). This is the universal scope of God's mission, as we have been seeing repeatedly so far in our survey.

Now of course, we can grant that the references to all the nations and the whole earth in Exodus 19:5 serve primarily to emphasize the special status, identity and role that *Israel* will have in that wider context. Nevertheless, in such an important context, at such a crucial juncture in Israel's pilgrimage, at such a pivotal point in God's historical address to them, the *double reference* to this universal dimension ("all nations", "the whole earth"), is very telling.

The view from the top of Sinai is 360-degree, wide-angle panoramic. God's vision and intentions span the whole earth and all nations. The people and the place are particular (Israel at Sinai). The God who addresses them is awesomely universal. God's agenda is global.

Unfinished Business

"But of course it is!" we might exclaim. For who is this God who is speaking, after all? This is the God who introduced himself to Moses at this very place, at the burning bush on Mount Sinai, with the words, "I am the God of your father, the God of Abraham, the God of Isaac and the God of Jacob" (Ex. 3:6). And we know enough now about the God of Abraham to understand that his intentions include all nations. As we explored in chapter 4, this is the God who spoke repeatedly in Genesis of his promise to bless Abraham and through him all nations on earth.

So God's business with Israel is really his unfinished business with the rest of the world, as it has been ever since Genesis 10 and 11. This part of the story is no exception, but rather the continuation of that great drama. Exodus 19:5b, even while it focuses primarily on Israel's distinctive role, won't let the story of Israel proceed without a reminder of God's wider agenda and the ultimately universal scope of his saving sovereignty.

That, then, is the big picture. That is the reminder of the big story, which is the long-term biblical story of God's bringing all nations into the sphere of his blessing. That's what told the Israelites who they were. That's what made sense of the part of the story they had just lived through, and that was the foundation for what God now expected from them.

Putting our first and second main sections together now, we see here the *future grace* of God's ultimate mission to the nations alongside the *past grace* of God's historical act of redemption. And the whole story of Old Testament Israel is slung between these two poles.

And so is the story of our own lives as disciples of Christ in every generation. This is what frames the mission of God's people. All our missional response to God lies between the past and the future, between grace and glory, between historical salvation and ongoing mission, between what God has done and what God will yet do, between where we have come from and where we are going.

Who, then, are we and what are we here for? We are the people (1) whom God has redeemed out of bondage and sin (past), and (2) through whom God is working to bring blessing to all nations on earth (future).

Speaking personally, that is the story within which I make sense of that little slice of space, time and matter that I call my own life. It makes a great deal more sense, and brings a great deal more significance, than the philosophy expressed on the London buses by Richard Dawkins and his atheist friends. It gives a meaning and purpose to this tiny bundle of intelligent DNA because it locates my personal existence within a story that has God at its beginning and its end. That is a story worth living in. That is a story with a purpose worth living for.

But so what? What, then, did such a location within the past and future grace of God mean for Israel, and by extension, for us? Between the past and the future lies the present, and so we move on to our third observation in this text.

PRESENT GRACE: GOD'S PEOPLE IN GOD'S WORLD – EXODUS 19:6

"You will be for me a kingdom of priests and a holy nation."[2]

These phrases are not immediately obvious to us. First, "kingdom" and "nation" are more or less neutral. God is saying, "Of course you will be a nation and probably also a kingdom. But the point is, *what kind of* nation and kingdom?" The emphasis, then, is on the descriptive words. Israel was to be *priestly* and *holy*. These are the words we need to work at understanding properly.

Priestly

To understand what it meant for Israel as a whole to be called God's priesthood in relation to the nations, we have to understand what Israel's priests were in relation to the rest of the people. Priests stood in the middle, between God on the one hand and all the rest of the people on the other. In that intermediate position, priests had a twofold task, a job that meant working in both directions:

Teaching the law of God to the people. The job of the priests was to teach God's law to the people (see Lev. 10:11; Deut. 33:10; Jer. 18:18). They were appointed to make known the ways, word and commands of God. Through the priests God would be known to his people. That's why, when the people went so badly astray, the prophets said it was because there was no knowledge of God in the land. And whom did they blame? The priests, for failing to teach (Hos. 4:1–9; Mal. 2:6–7).

---

2. This was a highly influential text, not only within the Old Testament, but for Jewish people in their diaspora among the nations after the exile. It inculcated a conviction that they had an ethical mandate that would be attractive to non-Jewish peoples, and that this was part of their "mission". For a full discussion of this concept in post-OT Judaism, see John P. Dickson, *Mission-Commitment in Ancient Judaism and in the Pauline Communities: The Shape, Extent and Background of Early Christian Mission* (WUNT 2.159; Tübingen: Mohr Siebeck, 2003), 51–60.

Bringing the sacrifices of the people to God (Lev. 1 – 7, etc.). Israelites who had sinned in some way would bring their animal to the sanctuary, lay their hands on its head, and slaughter it. The priest would take the blood and throw it against the altar, representing God. Then the priest would declare to the worshipers that their sins were atoned for and that they could come back into covenant fellowship with God. So then, through the priests and their work of atonement, the people could come to God.

The job of priests, then, was to bring God to the people and bring the people to God. So now, with rich significance, God says to Israel as a whole people:

"You will be for me to all the rest of the nations what your priests are for you. Through you I will become known to the world, and through you ultimately I will draw the world to myself."

That is what it meant for Israel to be God's priesthood in the midst of the nations. As the people of YHWH they would have the historical task of bringing the knowledge of God to the nations, and of bringing the nations to the means of atonement with God.

In addition to those twin tasks, it was also a prime privilege and responsibility of the priests to *bless the people* in the name of YHWH (Num. 6:22 – 27). So the Abrahamic task of being a means of blessing to the nations also constituted being a priesthood in the midst of the nations. Just as it was the role of the priests to bless the Israelites, so it would be the role of Israel as a whole ultimately to be a blessing to the nations.

This dual movement in the priestly role (from God to people, and from people to God) is reflected in prophetic visions concerning the nations, which included both centrifugal and centripetal dynamics. There would be a going out from God and a coming in to God. On the one hand, the law, or the justice, or the light of YHWH would go out to the nations from Israel or from Zion (e.g., Isa. 42:1 – 4). On the other hand, the nations could be pictured as coming to YHWH, or to Israel or to Jerusalem/Zion (e.g., Isa. 2:2 – 5; 60:1 – 3; Zech. 2:11).

> Israel as a "kingdom of priests" is Israel committed to the extension throughout the world of the ministry of Yahweh's presence . . . a kingdom not run by politicians depending upon strength and connivance but by priests depending on faith in Yahweh, a servant nation instead of a ruling nation.
>
> *John I. Durham*[3]

The priesthood of the people of God, then, is a *missional function*, which stands in continuity with their Abrahamic election and impacts the nations. Just as Israel's priests were called and chosen to be the servants of God and his people, so Israel as a whole is called and chosen to be the servant of God and all peoples. Exodus 19:4 – 6 carries forward the intention of Genesis 12:1 – 3, in the saving purposes of God for the world.

---

3. John I. Durham, *Exodus* (Word Bible Commentary; Waco, TX: Word, 1987), 263.

The mission of God's people, then, includes being God's priesthood in the world. We are a representative people. Our task is to represent the living God to the world, and to bring the world to acknowledge the living God. This fits exactly with the way the New Testament also presents our responsibility as Christians.

Certainly this was exactly how Paul saw his own life's work as a missionary to the Gentiles — the nations. He reminds the Romans of

> the grace God gave me to be a minister of Christ Jesus to the Gentiles. He gave me *the priestly duty* of proclaiming the gospel of God, so that the Gentiles might become an offering acceptable to God, sanctified by the Holy Spirit. (Rom. 15:15 – 16; italics added)

In other words, Paul saw his role as bringing God to the nations and bringing the nations to God, and he pictures himself as a priest in doing so. Paul could never, of course, have functioned as a priest in Jerusalem. He was of the tribe of Benjamin, not Levi. But he says he had a priestly job — not in some professional ordained function *within* the church, but in his evangelistic missionary work among the Gentiles. *Evangelism is a priestly task.*

But we must not confine this task only to cross-cultural missionaries. Peter applies our very same text (Ex. 19:6) to all believers, writing probably to a mixture of Jewish and Gentile believers scattered over several provinces in Asia Minor. Notice in this rich text how Peter combines several Old Testament references, including Exodus 19:6, and goes on to insist that it affects how we are to live among the nations.

> You are a chosen people, a royal priesthood, a holy nation, God's special possession, that you may declare the praises of him who called you out of darkness into his wonderful light. Once you were not a people, but now you are the people of God; once you had not received mercy, but now you have received mercy.
>
> Dear friends, I urge you, as foreigners and exiles, to abstain from sinful desires, which war against your soul. [12] Live such good lives among *the nations* that, though they accuse you of doing wrong, they may see your good deeds and glorify God on the day he visits us. (1 Peter 2:9 – 12, my italics and translation in v. 12)

"You [plural] are that priesthood," says Peter. We are God's representatives in the world.

The fact that Exodus 19:3 – 8 is a form of reworking of Genesis 12:1 – 3 reminds us that this designation links with Yhwh's lordship over the whole world and works toward the world's inclusion rather than its exclusion. The stretching of the royal priesthood to include other peoples (Rev. 1:6) is in keeping with the Abrahamic vision.

John Goldingay[4]

If somebody reads on the side of a London bus, "There probably is no God . . . ," they should think, "That can't be right. I know Sally, and she's a Christian, and God is very clearly alive and well in her life." We are called to be the living proof of the living God, to bring God to people and to bring people to God. That is our priesthood. That is part of the mission of God's people.

---

4. John Goldingay, *Old Testament Theology: Volume One: Israel's Gospel* (Downers Grove, IL: IVP, 2003), 374.

But how can we function in that way? What sort of life can produce that kind of effect? That is where the second of our two phrases becomes crucial.

To be God's priesthood, we have to be holy.

Holy

In Old Testament terms, being holy did not mean that the Israelites were to be a specially *religious* nation. At heart, the word "holy" (in Hebrew, *qadoš*) means *different or distinctive*. Something or someone is holy when they get set apart for a distinct purpose in relation to God and then are kept separate for that purpose. For Israel, it meant being different by reflecting the very different God that YHWH revealed himself to be, compared with other gods. Israel was to be as different from other nations as YHWH was different from other gods.

There were several aspects to Israel's holiness in the Old Testament that we must understand before we consider how they apply to us as Christians and to our mission.[5]

Holiness – a Given Fact

First of all, *holiness was a given* – a fact of Israel's existence. That is to say, God had set apart Israel for himself. It was God's initiative and choice: "I am the LORD your God, who has sanctified you" (Lev. 20:24, my trans.) – that is, the God who has made you holy, separate, distinct from the nations. Just like the choice of Abraham and the exodus experience of redemption, holiness is a prior gift of God's grace. Israel's own priests were set apart by God as holy within Israel (Lev. 21:8, 15, 23). The same thing is also said of Israel as a whole in relation to the nations:

> You are to be holy to me because I, the LORD, am holy, and *I have set you apart from the nations to be my own.* (Lev. 20:26; italics added; cf. Lev. 22:31 – 33)

The same thing is said about Christians in the New Testament. We are those whom God, in his grace, has chosen to "sanctify" (which is the same basic word), that is, to set apart for himself. This is the New Testament meaning of the word "saints". It does not refer to especially religious people, or those who have achieved higher status than anybody else through great spiritual exertion or supremely moral living. It simply means those whom God has identified as his own.

Holiness – A Given Task

But then second, holiness was an imperative. Israel was required to live out in daily life the practical implications of their status as God's holy people. "Be what you are," was the message. "Be different!" It could not be put more clearly than in this text:

---

5. Fuller exegesis and discussion of the points in the following section may be found in *The Mission of God*, ch. 11, "The Life of God's Missional People", 369 – 75.

You must not do as they do in Egypt, where you used to live, and you must not do as they do in the land of Canaan, where I am bringing you. Do not follow their practices. You must obey my laws and be careful to follow my decrees. I am the Lord your God. (Lev. 18:3–4)

Israel as a "holy people" then represents a third dimension of what it means to be committed in faith to Yahweh [i.e., in addition to being a treasured possession and a kingdom of priests]: they are to be a people set apart, different from all other people by what they are and are becoming—a display-people, a showcase to the world of how being in covenant with Yahweh changes a people.

John I. Durham[6]

The two country references are more than geographical. Egypt was characterized by the idolatry of military power and empire. "Don't mimic the world I rescued you from," said God to Israel. "Be different from the Egypts of the world." Canaan was characterized by the idolatry of fertility and all that Baal was supposed to bring by way of sex, success, prosperity, and the like. "Don't go down that road either. Be different from the Canaans of the world." These idolatries are still with us in potent and seductive forms, and part of the mission of God's people is to be different.

So too in the New Testament, holiness is a calling. Many times the apostles tell their readers to live out what is true of them, to demonstrate in practice the holiness of life that is consistent with the holiness of their status as God's people. Peter's first letter is virtually a whole tract on exactly that point.

Holiness—In All of Life

The strong ethical demand of holiness in Old Testament Israel meant living lives of integrity, justice and compassion in every area—including personal, family, social, economic and national life. The most comprehensive single text that articulates this ethical dimension of holiness in Israel is Leviticus 19.

Leviticus 19 is the finest commentary we have on Exodus 19:6. *"You shall be holy, for I am holy"* (Lev. 19:2). The opening verse expresses God's fundamental demand. It could be translated more colloquially, "You must be a different people, because YHWH is a different God." YHWH is utterly unique and distinct as God. YHWH is not simply one of the gods of the nations, and not even like them.

For Israel to be holy, then, meant that they were to be a distinctive community among the nations. Or to be more precise, Israel was to be "YHWH-like", rather than like the nations. They were to do as YHWH does, not as the nations do (Lev. 18:3–4). Holiness for Israel meant reflection on earth of the transcendent holiness of YHWH himself.

So what did this reflective holiness mean for Israel? What would it mean for them, in their historical and cultural circumstances, to be holy in a way that would reflect the holiness of YHWH? What content might we expect to be suspended under the stark headline of Leviticus 19:2, "You shall be holy …"?

6. Durham, *Exodus*, 263.

Perhaps we would expect a list of religious rituals. But we find few "religious" laws in this chapter. The bulk of the Leviticus 19 shows us that the kind of holiness that reflects God's own holiness is *thoroughly practical, social and very down-to-earth.* Simply listing its contents highlights this dominant note.

Holiness in Leviticus 19 involves:

- respect within the family and community (vv. 3a, 32)
- exclusive loyalty to YHWH as God; proper treatment of sacrifices (vv. 4, 5–8)
- economic generosity in agriculture (vv. 9–10)
- observing the commandments regarding social relationships (vv. 11–12)
- economic justice in employment rights (v. 13)
- social compassion to the disabled (v. 14)
- judicial integrity in the legal system (vv. 12, 15)
- neighbourly attitudes and behaviour; loving one's neighbour as oneself (vv. 16–18)
- preserving the symbolic tokens of religious distinctiveness (v. 19)
- sexual integrity (vv. 20–22, 29)
- rejection of practices connected with idolatrous or occult religion (vv. 26–31)
- no ill-treatment of ethnic minorities, but rather racial equality before the law and practical love for the alien as for oneself (vv. 33–34)
- commercial honesty in all trading transactions (vv. 35–36)

And all through the chapter runs the refrain: "I am the LORD", as if to say, "*Your* quality of life must reflect *my* character. This is what I require of *you* because this is what reflects *me*. This is what I myself would do."

That, then, was what it would look like for Israel to be different from the nations. Not just that they worshiped a different God from their gods, but that they actually lived and behaved differently in every dimension of personal and social life.

The call to distinctiveness is heard strongly also in the New Testament. Perhaps the simplest and clearest example is Jesus' telling his disciples that they were to be salt and light.

> You are the salt of the earth. But if the salt loses its saltiness, how can it be made salty again? It is no longer good for anything, except to be thrown out and trampled underfoot.
>
> You are the light of the world. A city on a hill cannot be hidden. Neither do people light a lamp and put it under a bowl. Instead they put it on its stand, and it gives light to everyone in the house. In the same way, let your light shine before others, that they may see your good deeds and glorify your Father in heaven. (Matt. 5:13–16)

Salt and light are distinctive, penetrating, transforming–utterly contrasting to corruption and darkness. That is what Christians are called to be, as Israel was called to be holy. Once again, then, we find that an essential part of the mission of

God's people is nothing other than to be what they are—by living out the holiness of God in practical everyday living. Mission is not something that happens when you go somewhere else. It starts in your own home and neighbourhood. That is where we are called to be holy.

But once again we ask the question, How? How are we to be such a holy people?

And that brings us back to our text, this time to verse 5a. "Now if you obey me fully and keep my covenant ..." (Ex. 19:5a). *Obedience* is the key to being priestly and holy.

Covenant Obedience

In the Old Testament context, of course, Exodus 19:5a means obedience to the law of God that follows immediately (in the Decalogue and Book of the Covenant). That law comes in the context of the covenant-making ceremony of Exodus 24 (in which the Israelites did indeed undertake to do all that the Lord commanded them, with some irony in view of the history that followed).

But at this point it is vital that we remember again *the double context of grace* that we established in our first two major sections—the grace of God's past act of salvation and the grace of God's concern for all the nations. That is the vitally important context in which obedience is called for. We are called to obedience because of what God has already done and because of what God wants to do in and through us.

Most of all, we should read verses 5 and 6 carefully and notice that obedience is *not* made a condition of salvation. That is, God did not say, "If you obey me and keep my covenant, I will save you and you will be my people." He already had saved them and they already were his people. No, obedience to the covenant was not a condition of *salvation*, but a condition of their *mission*.

Only through covenant obedience and community holiness could Israel claim or fulfill the identity and role here offered to them. The mission of priesthood among the nations was covenantal, and like the covenant itself, its fulfillment and enjoyment were inseparable from ethical obedience. God was saying, "If you live in this way, you can fulfill this role." In other words, for Israel (as also for us), obedience was a matter of grace and response.

What we have in these verses is the grace of obedience, responding to the grace of salvation and living in the grace of mission. Obedience, here as throughout the Bible, is ultimately for the sake of God's purpose of bringing salvation and blessing to the world of nations.

There is no biblical mission without biblical holiness.

SUMMARY

Who are we and what are we here for? Those are the questions we started with. The answer from the texts we have studied in this chapter should now be clear.

Like Old Testament Israel, we are people who have experienced past grace—God's historical acts of redemption, at the exodus and supremely, of course, at the cross.

Like Old Testament Israel, we are people whom God wants to use for the mission that is driven forward by his future grace—bringing people of all nations in the whole earth into that multinational family of those who know him, love him and worship him alone.

Like Old Testament Israel, we are people who are called to live in response to that grace, with lives that represent God to the world and that show the difference between the holiness of the living God, seen especially in the face of Jesus Christ, and the degraded ugliness and impotence of all the false gods that surround us.

In other words, we are exactly as Peter describes us, with the same identity, the same mission, and the same ethical responsibility.

> You are a chosen people, a royal priesthood, a holy nation, God's special possession, that you may declare the praises of him who called you out of darkness into his wonderful light. Once you were not a people, but now you are the people of God; once you had not received mercy, but now you have received mercy.
>
> Dear friends, I urge you, as foreigners and exiles, to abstain from sinful desires, which war against your soul. Live such good lives among the pagans that, though they accuse you of doing wrong, they may see your good deeds and glorify God on the day he visits us. (1 Peter 2:9–12)

Peter applies Exodus 19:4–6 directly to Christians: "You've had your exodus experience [out of darkness]," he says. "You've tasted God's grace and mercy. You are his precious, treasured possession, his very own people. Now then, live by *that* story. Live out *that* identity. And live with such attractive obedience of 'good lives' that people will be attracted to the God you worship, and whatever they say about you, they will come to glorify him."

RELEVANT QUESTIONS

1. "Live such good lives among the nations," said Peter, echoing Exodus 19:4–6. What does that mean in your context? And how can we avoid sliding into Pharisaism or legalism?

2. This chapter has stressed ethical obedience, and yet the key word throughout has been "grace". Did this surprise you? How would you now express and live by the twin truths that, on the one hand, grace comes before the response of obedience, and yet, on the other hand, obedience as a necessary response is inseparable from grace received by faith?

3. How does the summary of holiness in Leviticus 19 inform how the mission is to be accomplished? Which items in the list of instructions in that chapter do you find most challenging and relevant to your own context?

CHAPTER 8

PEOPLE WHO ATTRACT OTHERS TO GOD

If I were to propose that the mission of God's people is *cosmetic*, I would be open to serious misunderstanding. As the word is used today, it has come to mean something merely external and superficial, something just to make you look good, polishing your image.

But the original meaning of the word, and the Greek from which it comes (*kosmeo*), is to adorn something or someone so that they are seen to be beautiful and attractive. That is the sense that Paul means when he tells Christian slaves to behave well so that they can thereby make the teaching about God's salvation attractive. This assumes that slaves want their masters to be saved, and so Paul says, "Here's a way to make it more likely to happen."

> Teach slaves to be subject to their masters in everything, to try to please them, not to talk back to them, and not to steal from them, but to show that they can be fully trusted, so that in every way *they will make the teaching about God our Savior attractive.* (Titus 2:9 – 10, italics added; lit. "so that they may adorn [*kosmosin*] the teaching").

We have thought a lot in the preceding chapters about the ethical dimension of the mission of God's people. We are to be a people committed to blessing others (ch. 4), walking in the way of the Lord, doing righteousness and justice (ch. 5), working for holistic redemptive blessing for the oppressed (ch. 6), and representing God by living lives of practical holiness in the midst of the world (ch. 7).

This does not, of course, exclude the importance of verbal witness, the message we have to proclaim. We will come to that soon enough (in ch. 10). But so far we have been following the Bible's own emphasis on the kind of people God's people are meant to be rather than the kind of things they are meant to say. All of this practical demand, we have seen, is part of the mission that God has for us as his people in the world.

But why?

Well, one big reason is that such quality of life is attractive. Actually, in another sense, it also repels people and leads to persecution and suffering, but that's a theme for another chapter (ch. 13). Our main point in this chapter is to explore through a variety of texts the theme that God's people are to live in such a way that they become *attractors* — not attractors to themselves, but to the God they worship.

God longs to draw people to himself. God seeks the lost, invites the stranger to come on home. But a primary means that he does so is by living in the midst of his own people in such a way that they attract others.

Now this can happen in various ways, and our selection of texts will illustrate that variety. But what all these texts will show is that part of the mission of God's people is to have God so much at the centre of who they are and what they do, that there is a centripetal force, God's own gravitational pull, that draws people into the sphere of his blessing.

Missional magnetism is our theme in this chapter.

God be gracious to us and bless us [Psalm 67:1]. If only Aaron's blessing would come true! If only God were specially to bless them, and the light of His smile were to be upon them and with them always! Surely then the nations would see for themselves? Then the nations would have visual proof of the existence, activity and grace of God? Then the nations would come to know His way and His salvation. . . .

The same principle operates today. Non-Christian people are watching us. We claim to know, to love and to follow Jesus Christ. We say that he is our Saviour, our Lord and our Friend. "What difference does he make to those Christians?" the world asks searchingly. "Where is their God?" It may be said without fear of contradiction that the greatest hindrance to evangelism in the world today is the failure of the church to supply evidence in her own life and work of the saving power of God. Rightly may we pray for ourselves that we may have God's blessing and mercy and the light of his countenance — not that we may then monopolize His grace and bask in the sunshine of His favour, but that others may see in us His blessing and His beauty, and be drawn to Him through us.

John Stott[1]

ATTRACTING CURIOSITY – DEUTERONOMY 4:5 – 8[2]

Deuteronomy presents Moses as a preacher, keen to motivate the Israelites, who were on the verge of crossing into Canaan, to be loyal to God when they get there by keeping his covenant law. The book has a great variety of what are called "motive clauses" for obedience. Most of these motivations appeal either to Israel's own benefit ("for our good"), or to some feature of God's activity (in blessing or in punishment) that Israel needs to take into account.

Here in Deuteronomy 4 we encounter a motivation that is remarkable in its wider perspective. It puts Israel's obedience on a wide open stage and invites them to envisage *what the nations will think* as they observe the national life of the people whose God is YHWH.

---

1. John Stott, *Favourite Psalms* (London: Candle Books, 1988), 68; commenting on Psalm 67.

2. A much fuller discussion of the whole of Deuteronomy 4, from which the section below is adapted, will be found in *The Mission of God*, 378 – 80.

See, I have taught you decrees and laws as the LORD my God commanded me,
so that you may follow them in the land you are entering to take possession of it.
Observe them carefully, for this will show your wisdom and understanding to the
nations, who will hear about all these decrees and say, "Surely this great nation is a
wise and understanding people." What other nation is so great as to have their gods
near them the way the LORD our God is near us whenever we pray to him? And
what other nation is so great as to have such righteous decrees and laws as this body
of laws I am setting before you today? (Deut. 4:5–8)

Open to Be Seen

Old Testament Israel lived on a very public stage. All that happened in their history
was open to the observation and reaction of the surrounding nations—as in any vibrant
international community such as the ancient Near East certainly was. At one level,
this was just a fact of geography, living as they did on the land bridge between three
continents (Africa, Asia and Europe), at the crossroads of great powers to the west and
east, and surrounded by other smaller nations like themselves. But at a theological
level it was even more significant. As God's priesthood among the nations, they were
even more "on display" in relation to all that happened between them and God.

This visibility to the nations could be positive or negative. In this passage it is
hoped that it should be positive. But more realistically Deuteronomy foresaw that
the nations would be shocked by the severity of God's judgment on Israel when
they abandoned his ways and fell into idolatry (Deut. 28:37; 29:22–28). Either way,
faithful or unfaithful, the people of God were an open book to the world.

The nations are portrayed as taking an interest in the phenomenon of Israel as
a society, with all the social, economic, legal, political and religious dimensions of
the Torah. And that social system will lead the nations to the conclusion that Israel
as a people qualifies as a "great nation",[3] to be deemed "wise and understanding".

But what would such a reputation be based on? First (v. 7), it is based on the
nearness of God to his people. Second (v. 8), it is based on the *righteousness of the
Torah*. Israel would have an intimacy with God and a quality of social justice that
no other nation could match. These would be the inner facts that would produce
the external reputation. As far as the nations could see, the thing that was different
about Israel was simply the wisdom of their social system. The inner reality was the
presence of God and the justice of God's Torah.

The key point was *something had to be seen* by those beyond the limits of God's
people. That in itself is a missional perspective. Invisibility is not much help in mission. Of course mission means bearing a message (as we will see in due course). But

---

3. The TNIV somewhat distorts the meaning with its translation "what other nation is so great as to have...." The text actually says, "what other great nation has...?" The point is not that no other nation is *greater* than Israel. Rather, the text assumes that Israel is a great nation like the others, but then *defines* that greatness in surprising terms—not military might, nor geographical or numerical size, but rather their greatness lies in the nearness of the living God in prayer and the social justice of their constitution and laws.

those who bear the message must themselves be transformed by it. It is not enough to be heard only; we must be seen as well.

Open to Comparison

The force of the two rhetorical questions in verses 7 and 8 is to *invite comparison*. But Moses has no fear that anything will invalidate the claim he is making for God and Israel's law. No nation has such a God or such a social system, he claims.

Now this bold claim for Israel's social uniqueness was being made on a crowded stage. There were plenty of other claimants for admirable systems of law in the world of that day. Israel itself knew of the ancient and acclaimed legal traditions of Mesopotamia, like the Code of Hammurabi. In fact they had borrowed and adapted some of them. Yet this claim for Old Testament law is advanced: "You won't find anything better than this."

Old Testament law explicitly invites—even welcomes—public inspection and comparison. But the expected result of such comparison is that Israel's law will be found superior in wisdom and justice. This is a monumental claim. It grants to the nations and to the readers of this text, including ourselves, the liberty to analyze Old Testament law in comparison with other social systems, ancient and modern, and to evaluate its claims.

Indeed, the humaneness and justice of Israel's overall social and legal system have been favorably commented on by many scholars who have looked at it in great detail in comparison with other ancient codes of law in the contemporary world of Old Testament times. And even as Christians we still go on finding the social relevance of Old Testament law today.

> There was a gathering of the Lausanne Committee on World Evangelization at Pattaya, Thailand, in 1980, under the title, "How Shall They Hear?" A comment went around among those committed to the church's role in issues of justice and compassion alongside evangelistic proclamation, suggesting that the conference also needed to ask, "What Do They See?" The need to be seen to be different was expressed in the final statement, however, in a call for *Integrity*—a concern for "the character and conduct of the message bearer. Our witness loses credibility when we contradict it by our life or lifestyle. Our light will shine only when others can see our good works (Matt. 5:16). In a word, if we are to speak of Jesus with integrity, we have to resemble him."[4]

Open to Challenge

The point is, then, that if *Israel* would live as God intended, *the nations* would notice. The missional challenge, therefore, as we have seen in earlier chapters, is that the ethical quality of life of the people of God (their obedience to the law, in this context) is a vital factor in the attraction of the nations to the living God—even if only at first out of curiosity.

---

4. "The Thailand Statement," *Making Christ Known: Historic Mission Documents from the Lausanne Movement 1974–1989* (ed. John Stott; Grand Rapids: Eerdmans, 1996), 160–61.

But the challenge then becomes, of course, *would* God's people live in that way? Sadly we know from the rest of the story that Israel failed lamentably in this role. Not only did they *not* show the nations what righteous laws God had given them, but they failed even to live by the standards of the nations themselves—according to Ezekiel (see Ezek. 5:5–7).

The same challenge still faces God's people today. Our mission is, to say the least, to make those around us curious about the God we worship and the lives we live. But notice that it is the second (our lives) that leads to the first (curiosity about God).

After all, what would the nations actually *see*? The nearness of God is by definition invisible. What, then, would be *visible*? Only the practical evidence of the kind of society that was built on God's righteous laws. The world will be interested in our claims about God (and how near he is when we pray to him) only when it sees the visible evidence of a very different way of living.

Or, to put it the other way round, the world will see no reason to pay any attention to our claims about our invisible God if it sees no visible difference between the lives of those who make such claims and those who don't.

ATTRACTING SEEKERS – 1 KINGS 8:41 – 43, 60 – 61

The great day had come. It had taken seven years to build, but now it was complete. Solomon's temple was at last a splendid reality, and now it must be dedicated to the Lord so that he could be invited to allow at least his name to dwell there. First Kings 8 records the celebrations attending the arrival of the ark of the covenant, followed by Solomon's great prayers of dedication and his exhortation to the people.

In many ways this is the climax of the reigns of David and Solomon. This would be the place that replaced the tabernacle in the wilderness and the sanctuary at Shiloh. This would be the place that symbolized the presence of the living God in the midst of his people, the place where they could come before him in worship and prayer, and for the cleansing and rectifying work of the sacrifices and ministry of the priests. This building would generate a theology and an outpouring of the worshiping poetry of affection and hope in the following centuries. It would be the heartbeat of Israel's unique faith in YHWH their God.

So what would Solomon's prayer express on this momentous occasion—the dedication of the temple?

The God Who Keeps His Promises (vv. 14 – 21)

Solomon begins where so many of the prayers of the Bible begin, by acknowledging something of the character of God for which he is to be praised. In this case, Solomon focuses on how God had kept the promise he made to David that one of his sons would succeed him as king and would build the temple for YHWH. At first he records that as a kind of testimony, or public affirmation (vv. 14–21).

But then Solomon goes on, as he starts addressing God directly in prayer, to turn this truth about God into a feature of the uniqueness of YHWH the God of Israel. In the language of Deuteronomy (cf. Deut. 4:35, 39), he affirms,

> LORD, the God of Israel, there is no God like you in heaven above or on earth below—you who keep your covenant of love with your servants who continue whole-heartedly in your way. (1 Kings 8:23)

Of course, in this context, Solomon has in mind particularly God's faithfulness to his covenant with David, but his words have wider resonance. If we could have got alongside Solomon in the banquet afterward and asked him for further examples of God's "keeping his covenant of love", he would undoubtedly have pointed back to the covenant at Sinai, and above all to the covenant with Abraham.

Three elements of God's promise to Abraham had been spectacularly fulfilled by the time of Solomon's reign, and the account of the reign of his father David had highlighted them. Israel had become a *great nation*, as God promised. God had abundantly *blessed* them, as their friends and even enemies recognized. And God had given them security in the *land* he had promised them.

But then, as we've been remembering repeatedly, the promise to Abraham included God's promise that the blessing of Abraham would be a blessing ultimately shared with *all nations*—in some as yet unforeseeable way. Would that wider perspective of God's covenant promise find a place in Solomon's prayer? Remarkably, yes.

The Outsider Who Seeks God's Blessing (vv. 41–43)

Solomon's prayer lists a number of situations in which Israelites might need to come to the temple and pray for God's help: in disputes, after defeat in battle, in drought, famine, disease, or siege. And in each case he asks that God would hear their prayer and respond.

But then come the words, "As for the foreigner [the word is generic singular], who does not belong to your people...." We might expect something like this to follow: "Drive him out and keep him far from your clean and holy sanctuary." But no. Solomon's request on behalf of the foreigner is most surprising. Well, it is surprising because of the false assumptions we often bring to the Old Testament, but perhaps not so surprising after we have worked through the last few chapters of this book.

> As for the foreigners who do not belong to your people Israel but have come from a distant land because of your name—for they will hear of your great name and your

mighty hand and your outstretched arm – when they come and pray toward this temple, then hear from heaven, your dwelling place. Do whatever the foreigners ask of you, so that all the peoples of the earth may know your name and fear you, as do your own people Israel, and may know that this house I have built bears your Name. (1 Kings 8:41 – 43)

There is an amazing openness, compassion and vision in this prayer. One commentator goes so far as to say (though I think Isaiah would disagree) that this is "possibly the most marvelously universalistic passage in the Old Testament."[5] Here, at the most focused point of Israel's sense of unique particularity in relation to God, the very steps of the temple itself, Solomon's prayer anticipates *the nations* being blessed by the God of Israel and the fame of their God spreading far and wide.

Our short text is noteworthy for its assumptions, its content and its motivation.

The Assumptions

In asking what he does, Solomon makes some assumptions that are significant in themselves from a missiological point of view. He *assumes* that people of other lands will hear of the reputation of YHWH the God of Israel ("your great name"). He *assumes* that people from afar will be attracted to come and worship Israel's God for themselves and seek answers to prayer from that God. He *assumes* that Israel's God can and will hear the prayers of such foreigners and will actually want to answer them.

These assumptions proved true in biblical history. Apart from the fact that Jerusalem was a cosmopolitan city from the days of Solomon, with many foreigners there for commercial or political reasons who were doubtless curious to witness what went on in Solomon's new temple (the Queen of Sheba being only the most celebrated of Solomon's tourists), we have Old Testament stories of individuals attracted to Israel's God (such as Ruth or Naaman). And then later there was the widespread phenomenon of groups of so-called "God-fearers" scattered around the first-century world, attached to Jewish synagogues. These were Gentiles who were attracted to the God of the Jews and came to worship him – people like the Roman centurion in Luke 7:1 – 5, Cornelius in Acts 10, or those who heard Paul gladly in Acts 13:16, 46 – 48.

When we think about the mission of God's people, such assumptions need to encourage us too. The living God whom we worship can draw people from the ends of the earth to himself. God *attracts* worship and prayer – even from those who do not yet fully know him in all his biblical revelation. And God hears and answers the prayers of those who do not yet belong to his covenant people. If that were not so, Solomon could not have prayed in this way – without fear of rebuke or contradiction.

5. Simon J. DeVries, *I Kings* (Word Biblical Commentary; Waco, TX: Word, 1985), 126.

The question is, do we see it as part of *our* mission to be the living face of that attractiveness of God, drawing people to come and find him for themselves? That is a challenge we will return to below.

The Content

What Solomon actually asked God to do is no less surprising. Israelites knew that God heard and answered prayer. Indeed it was a mark of their distinctiveness, as we saw above (Deut. 4:7). But at no time in the Old Testament era did God ever promise in quite so many words to do for Israel *whatever they might ask of him*. When Jesus spoke in this way to his disciples, there was something new and fresh about his promise precisely for that reason (John 15:7; 16:24).

Yet here Solomon asks this very thing, long before Jesus, but for people who did not even belong to Israel. Solomon asks God to do for foreigners what God had not even guaranteed to do for Israel. And who knows what foreigners might ask! Who would control the question box? It is an utterly open-ended prayer to an utterly open-handed God.

The Motivation

And why should God answer Solomon's prayer? It is one of the features of Old Testament prayers (often found in the Psalms) that people like to suggest to God a few reasons why it would be in God's own best interests to step up and deliver what was being asked for – just in case the prayer might appear a bit selfish, you understand. In this case, Solomon proposes that if God answers *his* prayer by answering *the foreigners'* prayers, then *God's own reputation* will spread even further – which is the reason why people would come to the temple in the first place.

Solomon the entrepreneur spots a multiplication opportunity. God should not be content with just a few foreigners even from distant lands, when there was limitless scope for expansion until *"all the peoples of the earth may know your name"*. Isn't that what God had promised Abraham, after all?

Is this a missionary prayer, or what? Not that I'm suggesting Solomon was a "missionary" in our sense of the word. His marital arrangements would have disqualified him with any mission selection board. But the scope of the vision that motivated his prayer here is outstandingly missional in its implications. He wants the whole world to know the name of the one true living God.

And is the mission of God's people any less than that? Or for any lesser reason than that?

Surely the greatest motivation for our mission has to be that the name of the Lord, which for us means the name of the Lord Jesus Christ, should be known to the ends of the earth; that he should be the one to whom people come in prayer and from whom they receive the blessings of answered prayer, especially prayer for forgiveness and salvation.

But if that is our motivation, then our attitudes and practice need to match it. Sadly, Israel did not always match in practice the open spirit of Solomon's prayer here, but became negative, hostile and exclusive towards foreigners. Some think that books like Ruth and Jonah were written, at least in part, to combat such attitudes and reveal the heart of God more clearly. Likewise, it is not always easy for us to accept God's acceptance of outsiders. Even Jesus got into trouble in his hometown for suggesting such a thing, with biblical precedents (Luke 4:23–30).

Perhaps we need reminding that all of us start out as "outsiders", who have been brought near and welcomed by God, as Paul told the sophisticated Gentile believers in Ephesus (Eph. 2:11–13). Then we need to look for ways in which we can do for others what God has done for us, in drawing others into his magnetic field rather than repelling them still further.

The People Who Keep God's Commands (vv. 60–61)

And that is where we come back, as we so often do, to the ethical response that is needed if the world is to see God's attractiveness.

Solomon finished his prayer and then addressed the Israelites once more. He repeats what he has said about God, and then he urges the people to walk in his ways, for the same remarkably missional reason,

> so that all the peoples of the earth may know that the LORD is God and that there is no other. And may your hearts be fully committed to the LORD our God, to live by his decrees and obey his commands, as at this time. (1 Kings 8:60–61)

If only what Solomon urged on his people had remained true of Solomon himself. Sadly, as we know, it did not, and the accumulated social and economic oppression of his later reign in the end cost his son Rehoboam more than half his kingdom in the great rebellion under Jeroboam. But the record stands against him in advance, out of his own mouth as it were.

The combination of mission (v. 60) and ethics (v. 61) is clear—as clear as in Genesis 18:19. If the world is to know who God is, then the character of the living God must be seen in the behaviour of his living people. Only as we reflect the character and ways of God can we attract others to want to know him, to come to pray to him.

God *will* keep his promises, and he has been doing so since long before Solomon. Outsiders *will* seek God's blessing, and all around us they are doing so even now. The question is whether we might miss out on the excitement and joy of sharing in God's attraction by failing to have hearts that are fully committed to the Lord God in practical daily living according to his ways and standards. For our mission begins as we seek to live in that way—a way that enables God to attract outsiders to himself.

ATTRACTING ADMIRATION – JEREMIAH 13:1 – 11

It was shopping day again for Jeremiah. Not to the potter's shop this time (ch. 18), but to the tailor's. He needed a new sash, and God told him what kind to buy.

> Thus the LORD said to me, "Go and buy yourself a linen waistband, and put it around your waist, but do not put it in water." So I bought the waistband in accordance with the word of the LORD and put it around my waist. (Jer. 13:1 – 2, NASB)

The word "belt" in TNIV does not really describe the piece of clothing in question. It would have been a sizeable piece of cloth, worn around the waist and loins, over the lower garment.[6] In sparkling fresh white linen, it would have been a very attractive piece of sartorial elegance, and probably rather out of character for Jeremiah. Walking round Jerusalem with that on would have attracted attention, and perhaps some grudging admiration.

But then God told him to go and bury it in the soil by a river – which he dutifully did, doubtless with reluctance! Months later he is told to go and dig it up again, and to nobody's surprise, the piece of cloth, once so decorative, has become a soiled, rotten rag, "ruined and completely useless". He wasn't going to be seen around the city wearing that – though probably the message he now had to give meant that he carried it around and showed the disgusting thing to the people who had once admired him when it was pristine (vv. 3 – 8).

And the point was?

> "These wicked people, who refuse to listen to my words, who follow the stubbornness of their hearts and go after other gods to serve and worship them, will be like this belt – completely useless! For as a belt is bound around the waist, so I bound the whole house of Israel and the whole house of Judah to me," declares the LORD, "to be my people for my renown and praise and honor. But they have not listened." (Jer. 13:10 – 11)

The imagery is striking. God compares his covenant with Israel to a man binding a piece of clothing around himself.

God wants to wear his people!

But the imagery goes further. This is not just underclothing or factory overalls. This is clothing worn for show. God uses three words here – *renown, praise and honor* – that come together as a triplet in another verse, about Israel itself. This is God's covenantal purpose for Israel:

---

6. It is a rather rare word (*ʾezor*) and in some places it may refer to an undergarment wrapped around the loins. But the implication of verse 11, where Israel is compared to such a piece of clothing as something for "renown and praise and honour", suggests that in this context it is an outer sash that is meant. A similar metaphorical use is Isa. 11:5, where God puts on righteousness as a belt and "faithfulness the sash (*ʾezor*) round his waist".

> He [God] has declared that he will set you [Israel] in *praise, fame and honor* high above all the nations he has made and that you will be a people holy to the Lᴏʀᴅ your God, as he promised. (Deut. 26:19)

In that text, the fame is for Israel, but it is clear that the ultimate beneficiary is God himself. Whatever levels of renown, praise and honour may come Israel's way among the nations is actually for YHWH, the God who chose them as his covenant people and wants to look good wearing them in public, as it were. The imagery of Jeremiah's acted parable in Jeremiah 13 expresses this well. The bright new waistband was beautiful in itself, but the point of wearing it was to bring pleasure and praise to the wearer.

When my wife puts on a beautiful new dress, I may well say how nice the dress looks, but my praise is really for *her*, whose beauty the dress has enhanced even more. If I praise the dress, it is really her that I am praising. So, if the nations come to praise Israel, it is YHWH who is really the one being praised. Israel is simply the decorative clothing that God is wearing to display his own glory and beauty.

This puts another interesting perspective on election. God had chosen Israel, yes. But he had done so as a person might choose a particular piece of clothing for a special occasion. It is not so much a privilege for the piece of clothing in being chosen as the purpose behind it—to make the wearer look good. When I choose one particular shirt rather than another, the point is not to privilege that shirt above all others, but because that is the one in which I will look best for the purpose for which I will wear it. Likewise, in choosing to wear Israel, God had a wider agenda, namely, the exaltation of his own name among the nations through what he would ultimately accomplish, "dressed with" Israel.

And it was that wider purpose of God that the Israelites were frustrating by their disobedience. They had become as corrupt as a new waistband that has lain in wet soil for many months—to return to Jeremiah's graphic acted-out parable. God simply couldn't wear them anymore. Far from bringing him praise and honour, they brought him shame and disgrace.[7] How could God attract admirers dressed in the filthy rags of such people? Their rottenness would bring him into contempt.

For that reason, if God's purpose for the nations were to proceed, God would have to deal with Israel first. And so it is significant that the next time we come across that little triplet of words, it is in a promise—the promise that God will once again make his people fit to bring him admiration and praise.

> I will cleanse them from all the sin they have committed against me and will forgive all their sins of rebellion against me. Then this city [the city of Jerusalem, standing for the people of God] will bring me *renown, joy, praise and honor* before all the nations on earth that hear of all the good things I do for it, and they will be in awe and will

---

7. This is what Ezekiel means in Ezekiel 36 when he speaks of Israel "profaning the name of YHWH"—i.e., "bringing YHWH into disrepute".

tremble at the abundant prosperity and peace I provide for it. (Jer. 33:8–9; italics added; "joy" is added to the original three, "renown/name, praise and glory/honor")

Thus we have to ask, how does our mission as God's people fit this metaphor? Are we living in such a way that the God we claim to worship attracts admiration from those around? Or does God look at us and think, "I can't be seen wearing people like that!"

"Attracting admiration". I hope it is clear that the admiration is *for God, not for us*. But it still has to be said that if there is fundamentally nothing in the least admirable about the lives of Christians individually, or the collective witness of the church, then there is small hope of the world finding anything to admire in the God we represent, the God who wants to put us on like a dress suit or a party gown.

ATTRACTING WORSHIP – ISAIAH 60

Isaiah 60 is a chapter that begins (vv. 1–3) and ends (vv. 19–20) in light. And it is a powerfully attractive light, for it welcomes home not just a weary traveler, but the nations of the world. It is a rich chapter that speaks of God's intentions for his own people and the universal implications for the world as a whole. The overall thrust of this passage is that when God comes to redeem his people, the nations will come to worship God, and the world will come to know peace and justice.

So Isaiah 60 has a strongly missional message in connecting the light of God himself, the light of God's people in the world, and the light that the world will come to live and walk in.

This is missional light. It is the light of God attracting the worship of the world.

God Is Coming to His People (vv. 1 – 2)

In order to appreciate the scale and scope of this great chapter of Isaiah, we need to step back a bit and recall the flow of the book of Isaiah to this point.

In chapters 1–39 the book highlights God's demand for righteousness, Israel's utter failure to show it, and the resultant judgment of God that ended in exile.

In chapters 40–55 we are awestruck at the great act of God's redemption and restoration of his people, portrayed as a new exodus, promising to bring them back from exile in Babylon.

I used to live at All Nations Christian College in a house on campus that was set in quite thick woodland. Every time I would return home at night from some journey, my heart would quicken as I drove round the bend from which I could see the lights of my home twinkling through the trees, telling me that my wife and family were at home and a welcome awaited me there. Light is attractive. It draws you in out of the darkness. Ask any moth. Thankfully, the missional light of God attracts people out of darkness to a destiny very different from moths.

From chapter 56 on we find that even after the return from exile, the people of Israel are still living in a state of sin and failure. The climax of that situation is reached in the tragic description of the people by the prophet in 59:12–15.

> For our offenses are many in your sight,
>   and our sins testify against us.
> Our offenses are ever with us,
>   and we acknowledge our iniquities:
> rebellion and treachery against the LORD,
>   turning our backs on our God,
> inciting revolt and oppression,
>   uttering lies our hearts have conceived.
> So justice is driven back,
>   and righteousness stands at a distance;
> truth has stumbled in the streets,
>   honesty cannot enter.
> Truth is nowhere to be found,
>   and whoever shuns evil becomes a prey. (Isa. 59:12–15a)

So what possible hope can there be? Only in God. Only if God himself acts decisively in righteousness, to judge and to save. And that is exactly what God says he will do in 59:15b–20.

> "The Redeemer will come to Zion,
>   to those in Jacob who repent of their sins,"
> declares the LORD. (Isa. 59:20)

God will come and bring redemption to a people who certainly don't deserve it, but who are willing to repent and receive it.

That, then, is what Isa. 60:1 announces – the arrival at last of God himself. In the prophet's vision, God has come, the light has dawned, the sun has risen, and the glory of God himself is being shared with his people Israel.

> Arise, shine, for your light has come,
>   and the glory of the LORD rises upon you.

But the opposite of light is darkness, so if God has come as the light of revelation and redemption to *Israel*, then *the rest of the world* must still be in the darkness of ignorance of sin. But in their present state, Israel needs to remember that they were at that time in darkness too, as they were all too aware when they faced up to reality.

> So justice is far from us,
>   and righteousness does not reach us.
> We look for light, but all is darkness;
>   for brightness, but we walk in deep shadows.

Like the blind we grope along the wall,
    feeling our way like people without eyes.
At midday we stumble as if it were twilight;
    among the strong, we are like the dead. (Isa. 59:9 – 10)

Israel was no better than the Gentile nations around them. There is no difference; all have sinned, as Paul would later put it (Rom. 3:22 – 23).

So, then, the only hope *for Israel and for the world* is that God would come as redeemer and saviour, bringing light out of darkness for both alike. And that is exactly what the prophet envisages:

See, darkness covers the earth
    and thick darkness is over the peoples,
but the LORD rises upon you
    and his glory appears over you. (Isa. 60:2)

Now as Christians, of course, we read this text in the light of the coming of the Lord Jesus Christ. Indeed this is one of the Old Testament texts commonly read at Christmas, and even more at Epiphany (the revelation of Christ to the Gentiles, with the coming of the Magi).

In Jesus of Nazareth, God himself came to be the saviour of his people. "The arm of the LORD" has been revealed (Isa. 51:5, 9; 52:10; 53:1; 59:16) in the person of God's servant and Son. "Today," said Jesus, quoting a passage only a short distance from our text, "this scripture has been fulfilled in your hearing" (Luke 4:21, quoting Isa. 61:1 – 3).

This, to remind ourselves of chapter 2, is the story. This was Israel's story. This is our story. The story of the mission of God and of God's people to the end of the world. It is the story of God's promised coming, bringing the light of salvation.

The World Is Coming to God (vv. 3 – 16)

But then the prophet goes on to the next logical thing. If God has come to save his people, *the nations will come to this saving God.* For when the light goes on in Israel, those still in darkness will be attracted to come to the light, that is, to the saving work of God accomplished in Israel.

Nations will come to your light,
    and kings to the brightness of your dawn. (Isa. 60:3)

This echoes two earlier prophecies in Isaiah: the nations flowing up to the mountain of the Lord (Isa. 2:1 – 5), and the light dawning on those who sit in darkness (Isa. 9:2). But here it is filled out in three ways. When the nations come to God's light, they will come bringing Israel's children, bringing gifts, and bringing worship.

Coming with Israel's Children from the Nations (vv. 4, 9a)

Remember, Israel had experienced exile and scattering among the nations, so the prophet pictures the nations bringing their children (the next generation) back home—indeed, so many there will be hardly room for them (Isa. 49:19–22).

But in wider Old Testament perspective, *who will these children of Israel be*, returning to Zion? Not just ethnic Israelites, but people of all nations, as God had promised Abraham. So Psalm 87, for example, sees people of many nations registered as native-born citizens of Zion. And this ingathering of the nations happens, of course, in the New Testament as the gospel goes out to the nations and gathers them through faith in Jesus into the family of Abraham (Gal. 3:26–28).

Coming with the Gifts of the Nations (vv. 5, 9a, 11)

The prophet pictures nations from all points of the compass bringing their most precious wealth in gratitude to God for the salvation that has come to them—from north and west (the sea trade of Phoenicia, v. 5); from south and east (Midia and Arabia, vv. 6–7); and from the ends of the earth (the [Atlantic?] islands beyond Tarshish—probably Spain, v. 9). It was this vision that the Magi symbolized when they brought their gifts to Jesus, prototypical of the gifts of all nations. Paul may have seen his collection among the Gentiles as also symbolizing the fulfilling of this prophecy (Rom. 15:25–29).

The wealth of the whole world ultimately belongs to God and will one day beautify the place of God's dwelling with his redeemed people. So beyond the judgment and purging of the nations lies the prospect of the redemption (not the obliteration) of all that human civilization, culture, work and trade will have produced. It will be brought as cleansed gifts into the city of God. Revelation builds Isaiah's imagery into its own vision of the same thing (Rev. 21:23–27).

Coming with the Worship of the Nations (vv. 6, 7, 9b, 13)

We need to read those verses seeing the emphasis on worshiping *God*, the God of Israel. The nations are coming not to flatter *Israel*, or to enrich Israel, or to be enslaved by Israel. The language could sound a bit that way, but we should remember the context—long years of exile, oppression and suffering. That will all be turned upside down, the prophet says. But the main point is this: since it is the God of Israel who has brought salvation and light to the nations, it will be this same God of Israel to whom the world will come in praise and worship.

And above all, the result will be that the whole world will know who the living God is—which is the goal of all God's mission.

> Then you will know that I, the LORD, am your Savior,
>   your Redeemer, the Mighty One of Jacob. (Isa. 60:16b)

So, when the light of salvation dawns as it did when Jesus came, the prophet's vision is that the nations will be attracted to that light as a great multinational community bringing their praise and worship to the living God. And that is exactly what has been happening for two thousand years since Pentecost, through the mission of God's people to the ends of the earth.

Peace Is Coming to the World (vv. 17 – 22)

But the vision is not quite over, and indeed, there is an element of it that lies ahead of us yet. If God has come to redeem his people, and if the nations are coming to God, then transformation is coming to the world. As in the visions of Isaiah 9, 11 and 32, we hear what it will be like when God comes to reign. It is a glorious picture of peace with justice (60:17b), of the end of violence and war (v. 18), of the beautifying presence of God (vv. 19 – 20), and of the moral goodness of God's people (v. 21).

This is a picture of new creation reality, which, as we know, is not yet. As God says in Isaiah 60:22, "in its time I will do this swiftly." That is the assurance with which we wait in faith and hope.

There is an intriguing sense in which Isaiah 60 covers all the horizons of the New Testament:

- *Verses 1 – 2* lead us to the Gospels, Christmas and Easter: God has come, the light has dawned, salvation has been accomplished in Christ.
- *Verses 3 – 16* lead us to Acts and the epistles, the mission of the church, the gospel reaching out to bring light to all nations, attracting them to come in out of the darkness, and bringing their worship to the living, saving God.
- *Verses 17 – 22* lead us to Revelation 21 – 22, the end of the present world order of wickedness, violence and injustice, and the new creation of perfect peace and righteousness.

But where does this leave us here and now? What does this tell us about our mission as the people of God? We are to shine as God's light to the nations.

We go back to the very start and listen to the first verse again (Isa. 60:1). It is not just a prediction, but a *summons– "Arise! Shine!"* God's people are to shine with the light of God, to live out the attractiveness of God's saving light, in lives that are being transformed in the present. God has brought the light; we are to do the shining. We often sing, "Shine, Jesus, Shine." I sometimes hear a voice from heaven muttering, "Shine yourselves, why don't you?"

The light with which we are to shine is not just the light of a verbal proclamation of the gospel (though it includes that as we will see), but the light of demonstrated justice and compassion–as Isaiah 58:8 – 10 had made very clear.

If you do away with the yoke of oppression,
> with the pointing finger and malicious talk,
and if you spend yourselves in behalf of the hungry
> and satisfy the needs of the oppressed,
then your light will rise in the darkness,
> and your night will become like the noonday. (Isa. 58:9 – 10; italics added)

That's what it means to be people who attract others to the worship of God. That's part of the mission of God's people.

ATTRACTING APPROVAL

From Isaiah 60 it is but a short step to the New Testament. There too we see that part of the mission of God's people is to live in such a way that they are attractive to the outside world and draw others to find him.

"You," said Jesus one day to a bunch of scruffy and probably rather astonished disciples, "you are the light of the world." Imagine the surprise of such a statement to people who knew scriptures like Isaiah 58 and 60 very well – not to mention what God had said to his Servant who would embody the mission of Israel itself –

I will also make you a light for the nations,
> that my salvation may reach to the ends of the earth. (Isa. 49:6)

Then Jesus went on to explain exactly what he meant by being such light. Here is as missional a statement as any:

> You are the light of the world. A city on a hill cannot be hidden. Neither do people light a lamp and put it under a bowl. Instead they put it on its stand, and it gives light to everyone in the house. In the same way, let your light shine before others, that they may see your good deeds and glorify your Father in heaven. (Matt. 5:14 – 16)

Disciples of Christ are to shine with a light that is visible and attractive, and the light consists of "good deeds". And the quality of that ethical light is to be such that it attracts people ultimately to God himself, so that he is glorified. It is all the same dynamic that we have observed in the Old Testament passages above. And it is the same dynamic that Peter, who heard that teaching from Jesus, passed on in his own letter (1 Peter 2:12).

Now in the same chapter, of course, Jesus has warned his disciples that if they live the life of God's kingdom, they will also suffer persecution. But alongside that reality of persecution we must also set this teaching about the missional attractiveness of shining in the world with ethical Christlikeness.

The church in Acts was persecuted, certainly. But Luke records that it also attracted approval and favour in some quarters. And he makes that point specifically after commenting on the quality of its social and economic life. In caring for one another and ensuring that there were no needy people among them, the early believers demonstrated a new quality of living that was appealing. And it was that quality of life that reinforced the evangelistic preaching of the apostles, so that people joined the church in great numbers.

> We are sent into the world, like Jesus, to serve. For this is the natural expression of our love for our neighbours. We love. We go. We serve. And in this we have (or should have) no ulterior motive. True, the gospel lacks visibility if we merely preach it, and lacks credibility if we who preach it are interested only in souls and have no concern about the welfare of people's bodies, situations and communities. Yet the reason for our acceptance of social responsibility is not primarily in order to give the gospel either a visibility or a credibility it would otherwise lack, but rather simple uncomplicated compassion. Love has no need to justify itself. It merely expresses itself in service whenever it sees need.
>
> *John Stott*[8]

> All the believers were together and had everything in common. They sold property and possessions to give to anyone who had need. Every day they continued to meet together in the temple courts. They broke bread in their homes and ate together with glad and sincere hearts, praising God and *enjoying the favor of all the people.* And the Lord added to their number daily those who were being saved. (Acts 2:44–47; italics added)

Paul also saw Christian behaviour as a shining light in a dark world, possibly having in mind what Daniel had said about wise believers leading many to righteousness (Dan. 12:3):

> Do everything without grumbling or arguing, so that you may become blameless and pure, "children of God without fault in a warped and crooked generation." *Then you will shine among them* like stars in the sky as you hold firmly to the word of life (Phil. 2:14–16; italics added).

Peter was not suggesting that Christian wives of unbelieving husbands should be *unattractive* when he told them not to let their beauty be a matter of hairstyle and jewelry. Rather, he wanted their beauty (and he assures them they *are* beautiful) to shine through their character and behaviour, so that they may "win" their husbands to faith in Christ (1 Peter 3:1–4). That would be their most important attractiveness.

SUMMARY

But let's finish the chapter where we began, with slaves and the remarkable power they had, according to Paul, to apply some cosmetic appeal to the doctrine of salvation (Titus 2:9–10). What a remarkable privilege! The evangelistic work of the

8. John Stott, *Christian Mission in the Modern World* (London: Falcon, 1975), 30.

church was teaching the world about a saviour God – not the Roman emperor (who claimed exactly those titles), but Jesus, the crucified Messiah of Israel. What a joke! The whole thing was ridiculous to sophisticated Greek citizens, until they noticed the change that had come over their slaves (many of whom were converted in early Christianity). If *slaves* were transformed in their behaviour, there could be something appealing in this teaching after all.

Thus, Paul goes on to a general exhortation to all Christians to live in ways that respond to the saving grace of God, as we live between two "epiphanies" – between Christ's first "appearing" for salvation, and his second "appearing" in glory.

> For the grace of God has appeared that offers salvation to all people. It teaches us to say "No" to ungodliness and worldly passions, and to live self-controlled, upright and godly lives in this present age, while we wait for the blessed hope – the appearing of the glory of our great God and Savior, Jesus Christ, who gave himself for us to redeem us from all wickedness and to purify for himself a people that are his very own, *eager to do what is good*. (Titus 2:11 – 14; italics added)

But could it work? Do good works have sufficiently transforming and attracting power, as Jesus, Luke, Paul and Peter tell us? Do they really contribute to, let alone constitute, mission? Here is the opinion of John Dickson.

> Humanly speaking, no one would have thought it possible to bring the nations to the worship of God through simple good deeds. How on earth could "good deeds" change a realm as mighty as the Roman Empire, let alone the whole world? As unlikely as it may have sounded at the time, Jesus' call to be the light of the world was taken seriously by his disciples. They devoted themselves to quite heroic acts of godliness. They loved their enemies, prayed for their persecutors and cared for the poor wherever they found them.
>
> We know that the Jerusalem church set up a large daily food roster for the destitute among them – no fewer than seven Christian leaders were assigned to the management of the program (Acts 6:1 – 7). The apostle Paul, perhaps the greatest missionary/evangelist ever, was utterly devoted to these kinds of good deeds. In response to a famine that ravaged Palestine between AD 46 – 48 Paul conducted his own decade-long international aid program earmarked for poverty-stricken Palestinians. Wherever he went, he asked the Gentile churches to contribute whatever they could to the poor in Jerusalem.
>
> Christian "good deeds" continued long after the New Testament era. We know, for instance, that by AD 250 the Christian community in Rome was supporting 1,500 destitute people every day. All around the Mediterranean churches were setting up food programs, hospitals and orphanages. These were available to believers and unbelievers alike. This was an innovation. Historians often point to ancient Israel as the first society to introduce a comprehensive welfare system that cared for the poor and marginalised within the community. Christians inherited this tradition but opened it up to Jew and Gentile, believer and unbeliever, alike.

And the result of all this? Well, within two and a half centuries Christians had gone from being a small band of several hundred Palestinian Jews to the greatest social force in world history. In fact, the influence of Christian good works was so great in the fourth century that Emperor Julian (AD 331–363) became fearful that Christianity might take over the world forever by the stealth of good works.[9]

Sadly, Emperor Julian's fears have proved unfounded. But what if he'd been right?

RELEVANT QUESTIONS

1. Someone has said that whereas God wanted the life of his people to arouse questions, the church today only arouses suspicion. What kind of questions do you think people are asking as they watch your life, or the life of your church?
2. Who are the "outsiders" in relation to your community? In what ways do you think they are "seeking God", consciously or otherwise? What does Solomon's prayer teach us about how we should pray for them and live in relation to them?
3. In what way does the image of God "wearing" Israel as a garment affect your understanding of the importance of covenant faithfulness as a Christian?
4. Jesus probably had Isaiah 58–60 in mind when he described his disciples as "the light of the world" and told them to "let their light shine". Read Isaiah 58 (as a whole, but notice vv. 8 and 10) and reflect on the radical nature of what that means today.

9. John Dickson, *The Best Kept Secret of Christian Mission: Promoting the Gospel with More Than Our Lips* (Grand Rapids: Zondervan, 2010), 92–93.

INTERLUDE – PAUSE FOR THOUGHT

We have reached the half way point in our journey through this book, so this seems a suitable spot to take a break and survey the road we have traveled, remember the scenery we have viewed, and get ready for the road ahead.

We have taken the title *The Mission of God's People* as asking two fundamental questions about ourselves, "Who are we and what are we here for?" So far, the main emphasis we have found in a wide range of texts that talk about God's people is that they are created and called to *live* in certain ways in their relationship to God, to the world and to others.

What have we learned so far?

We started in chapter 2 by recognizing how important it is to read the whole Bible as the story of the mission of God, from creation to new creation, and to see that we exist as God's people within that great story, to serve God's purpose in creation itself and in the midst of the nations. It is not so much that God has a mission for his church as that God has a church for his mission. We exist to serve God's mission. That's why it is so important to know what that mission is, from the whole of the Bible he has given to us.

Then in chapter 3 we paid attention to the way the Bible begins and ends – with creation itself. Even as God's people we remain human beings, mandated to serve and care for the earth in which he has put us. That is a part of our mission that derives from our humanity itself. But it points onward also towards the redemption of all things. We have not been saved *out of* creation, but rather creation itself will be redeemed *along with us*.

From our exploration of God's covenant with Abraham in chapter 4, we know that the chief agent of God's mission is the people of God. In order to bring blessing to all nations, God created the people of Abraham, and in Christ we belong to that people. The reason for our existence and the mission entrusted to us is the same in principle for us as Christians as it was for Old Testament Israel.

From Genesis 18:19 we learned in chapter 5 that God's requirement of the people of Abraham (which includes all who are in Christ) is that they should keep the way of the Lord by doing righteousness and justice, in order for God to keep his promise of blessing the nations. How we live (ethics) is the connector between our election and our participation in God's mission.

From the story of the exodus itself in chapter 6, we understand more comprehensively God's idea of redemption, and we should not lose those broad dimensions when we see God the redeemer accomplishing our total liberation through the cross and resurrection of Christ. Those whom God redeemed are then called to reflect his action and the motivation behind it, in living redemptively in the world in the way we behave to others.

From Exodus 19 and Leviticus 19, we saw in chapter 7 that Israel's *identity* (to be a priestly kingdom) constituted a *mission* (to bless the nations by bringing God to them and bringing them to God). That remains the mission of God's people in Christ, to be the living proof of the living God. And Israel's *mission* demanded an *ethic* (to be a holy nation, i.e., to be fundamentally different from the surrounding nations). The same demand underlies our mission. We are called to be different. *There is no biblical mission without biblical ethics.*

Living in ways that reflect God's own character should make God's people as attractive as God himself is. So we explored in chapter 8 a number of places in the Bible where God's people have the task of attracting others to God, to find his blessing and salvation. The most powerful metaphor for this is light, which is used both to signify the joyful good news of the salvation that God brings when he comes, and to picture the world-transforming quality of the lives and deeds of those who come to that light and live by it.

So it should be abundantly clear by now that the mission of God's people in the Bible is to *be* the people whom God created us to be and to *do* the things that God calls us to do. We have a life to live, and if we are not living as God's people, there is not much point saying anything.

However, we are, of course, also called to speak up and to speak out. There is a message to be communicated. There is a word to be heard. There is truth to be known and passed on. There is good news to be shared!

And so we come to the second half of the book, where that becomes one of our key themes. We will explore the great missional themes of "bearing witness" (chapter 10) and of "proclaiming the gospel" (chapter 11), and discover (perhaps to our surprise) that both of them originated in the Old Testament (that's the value of doing Biblical Theology for Life). People in the Bible were "sent" to do both of those tasks, along with a wide range of other "missions" – whether they were sent directly by God or sent by the church.

Since the word *mission* comes from the Latin word for "sending", we will trace this theme too (chapter 12). But in case we still imagine that mission is only for missionaries (people literally sent out across cultural boundaries), we will think also of the mission of all (i.e., most of us) who live and work in the arena of ordinary public life and work (chapter 13). Finally, in this part of the book, we will remind ourselves that the goal of all mission is the glory of God; thus, in chapter 14 we will see how praise and prayer are also missional actions of God's people.

Foundational to all of these dimensions of our mission, however, is that we must know the God of whom we speak, and we must be totally committed to non-negotiable loyalty to him. This, we will see in our next chapter, was required of Old Testament Israel, and triumphantly demonstrated in the apostles' courageous testimony to the uniqueness of the Lord Jesus Christ.

CHAPTER 9

PEOPLE WHO KNOW THE ONE LIVING GOD AND SAVIOUR

Knowing God is one of the most pervasive themes in biblical theology. People have even been known to write whole books on it.[1] But one might be tempted to ask what it has to do with the mission of God's people. Knowing God seems to have more to do with personal devotion and spiritual experience than with mission. But when we think like that, it just shows how far we have individualized and privatized our Christian faith, and how much we need the corrective of biblical theology – especially biblical theology that is applied to the mission of God's people.

In the Bible, it is true that knowing God was a deeply personal experience, but it was never merely private and it was never merely spiritual. Coming to know God could be exhilarating or devastating, depending on the state of your life when the encounter takes place. When a whole community was called to know God, as Old Testament Israel was, it was a comprehensive social agenda, not just a badge of nominal national religion.

And most of all, knowing God was a responsibility. It generated an agenda, a mission.

The thing about all biblical experience of God is that it never stays merely "intransitive" (something that happens to you and stays there). It always has a "transitive" dynamic (it has to affect somebody or something else). We have seen this in some of our earlier chapters. If God blesses you, it is so you can bless others. If God redeems you, it is so you can demonstrate redemptive grace to others. If God loves you, feeds and clothes you, then you should go and do likewise for others. If God brings you into the light of salvation, it is so you can shine with a light that attracts others to the same place. If you enjoy God's forgiveness, then make sure you forgive others. And so on.

In this sense, *all* our biblical theology is, or should be, missional. Biblical theology is, by definition, "theology for life".

---

1. The classic, of course, is J. I. Packer, *Knowing God* (Downers Grove, IL: IVP, 1979). See also Christopher J. H. Wright, *Knowing Jesus through the Old Testament* (Oxford: Monarch, and Downers Grove, IL: IVP, 1992); idem, *Knowing the Holy Spirit through the Old Testament* (Oxford: Monarch, and Downers Grove, IL: IVP, 2006); and idem, *Knowing God the Father through the Old Testament* (Oxford: Monarch, and Downers Grove, IL: IVP, 2007).

Likewise, then, to know God is to be challenged to make God known. It is to be entrusted with knowledge that God wants to be shared. That is what makes it missional. For behind all our mission stands the unshakeable determination of God to be known throughout his whole creation as the living God. God's will to be known is what makes our mission not only imperative but also possible.[2]

All our missional efforts to make God known must be set within the prior framework of God's own will to be known. We are seeking to accomplish what God himself wills to happen. This is both humbling and reassuring. It is humbling inasmuch as it reminds us that all our efforts would be in vain but for God's determination to be known. We are neither the initiators of the mission of making God known to the nations nor does it lie in our power to decide how the task will be fully accomplished or when it may be deemed to be complete. But it is also reassuring. For we know that behind all our fumbling efforts and inadequate communication stands the supreme will of the living God, reaching out in loving self-revelation, incredibly willing to open blind eyes and reveal his glory through the treasures of the gospel delivered in the clay pots of his witnesses.

Christopher Wright[3]

So in this chapter we will look at two texts in which those who had come to know God, or to know something unique and exciting about God, were confronted with the challenge of that knowledge and the missional implications of being stewards of it. We will also diverge from our practice so far of looking at an Old Testament text first and then moving to the New Testament. This time we will move back and forward between our two texts, seeing the connections and resonances between them and building our biblical theology from both together.

Our two texts are Acts 4:1–22 and Deuteronomy 4:32–39. It would be helpful to read both texts through one after the other and then keep them open. Now would be good.

CHALLENGING CONTEXTS

We might ask what the two texts have in common, with each other or with the mission of God's people—then or now. Answer: the context in both cases was one of conflict and challenge. There was a clash of ideas, of worldviews, of religious zeal.

In Acts, the conflict was between those, on the one hand, who claimed that Jesus of Nazareth was Messiah and that even though he had been crucified only weeks earlier, he was now risen and exalted Lord, and those, on the other hand, who rejected any such idea as dangerous nonsense.

In Deuteronomy the conflict was between the faith of Israel in YHWH as their unique covenant God and Lord and the polytheistic religion and culture of Canaan that lay ahead of them.

---

2. This determination of the one living God that he should be known throughout his whole creation is a key driver for biblical mission. I have discussed it in greater depth in *The Mission of God,* 75–135.

3. Ibid., 129–30.

In both cases, the speakers in the texts refer to unique events that have been witnessed and that lead to certain conclusions about God – things that are to be known and made known. And in both cases claims are made, whether about Jesus or about the God of Israel, that are presented as nonnegotiable in content and universal in significance.

In today's world, the context of our mission is just as challenging. The Christian faith is required to express its identity and its distinctiveness in the face of all kinds of rival claims and loyalties – whether those of other religious faiths, or of resurgent atheism.

As in the days of the apostles, there are many today who do not accept that Jesus is the only saviour and Lord. There are even more who have never even heard of Jesus, let alone been able to make such a decision about his claims. And as in the days of Deuteronomy, the people of God live surrounded by multiple cultures that manifest all the idolatries that human beings are capable of. The sheer seductive power of the world around us makes loyalty to the one living God an enormous challenge. Like the Israelites of old, we do not even recognize the syncretism we easily fall into, or how easy it is simply to "worship the gods of the people around".

In such contexts, we are commanded to acknowledge what we know and whom we know, and to bear witness to both. That is what makes knowing God, and for us, knowing the Lord Jesus Christ, the profoundly missional reality that it is.

Acts – We've Seen a Man Raised

In Acts 3, Luke tells us the story of how a man, who had been crippled for life and survived on the alms of worshipers at the temple, was healed by Peter and John in the name of Jesus. Taking immediate evangelistic advantage of the crowd's amazement, Peter

I wish now that I had taken it to the checkout, paid for it, and then stamped on it before leaving the bookstore of the Christian church where I saw it. It horrified me as a piece of blasphemous syncretism. It was a small statue of a cross wrapped in the American flag. What were its manufacturers thinking? What message was any purchaser supposed to read into it? It seemed to say, "You can have the cross of Jesus, and all your sins forgiven, and have it wrapped in patriotism too. You don't even need to think that the cross might cut across the very thing your patriotism idolizes, or that the cross was where the patriots of Jesus' day put traitors and terrorists."

Or was it saying, "Jesus died for Americans". That's true, but did he not also die for people of all nations, of all flags and none? In other words, even the most charitable interpretation of such symbolism was confusing. That's syncretism: mixing the supposed worship of the living God of the Bible with all kinds of other loves and loyalties. It is not something that happens only in foreign countries with "other religions".

deflects all credit from John and himself and explains that Jesus of Nazareth (none other than the one they had crucified some weeks earlier) was in fact the Messiah God had promised to their ancestors. But God had now vindicated him by raising him from the dead, thus keeping his promise to Abraham. The healing of the cripple was a signpost to what God could now do for them spiritually. Even as Israelites, the blessing of Abraham could come to them only through repentance and faith in Jesus.[4]

Acts 4 describes the shockwave this sent through the Jewish religious and political authorities, who were certain they had dealt with that troublemaker from Nazareth with brutal but effective finality. So they call Peter and John to account for their actions, which gives Peter a second opportunity to preach the gospel of salvation in Jesus Christ (to which we'll return).

But the one thing the authorities could not do was to deny the evidence of their own eyes and of the whole citizenry of Jerusalem. The guy they'd all passed at the gate for years was running and leaping around in the streets, and here he was now *standing* (a posture he hadn't achieved all his life) in the court!

Since they could see the man who had been healed standing there with Peter and John, there was nothing they could say. So they ordered them to withdraw from the Sanhedrin and then conferred together. " 'What are we going to do with these men?' they asked. 'Everyone living in Jerusalem knows they have performed a notable sign, and *we cannot deny it*' " (Acts 4:16; italics added).

Now, what is significant in the narrative is that Peter proclaims the resurrection of Jesus on exactly the same basis as the healing of the cripple – namely, a factual witness to it as an undeniable event. For Peter, the fact that Jesus was risen was as much a matter of eyewitness testimony as the fact that the man was healed: "You killed the author of life, but God raised him from the dead. *We are witnesses of this*" (Acts 3:15; cf. 4:2, 9 – 10; italics added).

"You've seen a man *healed of disease*, and you can't deny it," say Peter and John. "We've seen a man *raised from the dead*, and we can't deny that either." "As for us, we cannot help speaking about what we have seen and heard" (Acts 4:20). [5]

It is important to remember that the whole of our Christian faith is based on publicly testified witness of historical experience, not on religious speculation or theorizing, however spiritual. The gospel is *good news* about something that has happened; it is not a *good idea* or good advice. We will come back to the "whole Bible" content and dynamic of the gospel as good news in chapter 11.

Deuteronomy – You've Seen God in Action

Deuteronomy presents Moses addressing the people of Israel on the verge of entering the land of promise, and reminding them of the witnessed events of their history:

---

4. Acts 3:25 – 26 is an important text in the vexed question of who the descendants of Abraham are today. Peter makes the key point that the promised blessing of Abraham comes even to the ethnic Israelites (his own fellow Jews) only through repentance and faith in Jesus. Physical descent from Abraham in itself does not release the promise; rather, submission to Jesus does.

5. Perhaps this was John speaking, rather than Peter at this moment, since "what we have seen and heard" is typical of Johannine testimony (1 John 1:1, 3).

Ask now about the former days, long before your time, from the day God created human beings on the earth; ask from one end of the heavens to the other. Has anything so great as this ever happened, or has anything like it ever been heard of? Has any other people heard the voice of God speaking out of fire, as you have, and lived? Has any god ever tried to take for himself one nation out of another nation, by testings, by signs and wonders, by war, by a mighty hand and an outstretched arm, or by great and awesome deeds, like all the things the LORD your God did for you in Egypt *before your very eyes?*[6] (Deut. 4:32–34; italics added)

A research project of truly cosmic scale is imagined in verse 32, encompassing the whole of human history hitherto and the whole of universal space. Such is Moses' confidence that the questions he is about to pose in verses 33 and 34 will find no answer. Moses refers to both the Sinai theophany and the exodus deliverance, and his claim is that nothing like them has ever happened. What God did in the events of the exodus and Sinai was unprecedented (God had never done such a thing at any other time) and unparalleled (God had never done such a thing anywhere else for any other nation).

Moses is insisting, then, that Israel's experience is utterly unique. YHWH has spoken to Israel in a way no other people have experienced (cf. Ps. 147:19–20), and YHWH has redeemed Israel in a way that no other people have ever known as yet (cf. Amos 3:1–2).

The two events Moses refers to are, of course, the foundations of Israel's status as God's redeemed and covenant people. They are events of salvation and revelation combined.

Salvation

The exodus was the greatest undeniable experience of all. Whereas they had once been slaves in Egypt, they were now a free people on the edge of the Promised Land. Whatever they now knew about YHWH as a God mighty to save they knew on the basis of this fact.

Revelation

Sinai had been the overwhelming experience of God's self-revelation. At Sinai YHWH had revealed his name, his personal character, his moral demands, and his covenant commitment. All this was a matter of record, and there was a rather important gold-covered box being carried around by the Levites with stone tablets inside it – the ark of the covenant – physical evidence and proof of what had transpired on that awesome occasion.

---

6. Strictly speaking, of course, it had not happened before the eyes of those whom Moses was addressing (except if they had been young children at the time), since this was the generation after the one that had come out of Egypt. But the Old Testament sees the generations united together in historical memory, and what had been witnessed by their parents was now held up as publicly testified events for them to reflect upon.

So then, *both* our texts appeal to facts, to publicly witnessed experiences, to undeniable events, as the basis for the claims and challenge that follow. What the disciples now know about Jesus, what the Israelites now know about YHWH, had all arisen out of historical experience.

When we talk, then, about part of the mission of God's people being to share what they know about God, it is not some kind of esoteric or speculative opinion about God, or the results of some prolonged spiritual pilgrimage, or the fruit of eons of religious reflection. Whatever we know, we know on the basis of things that have happened and the understanding of them that is given to us in Scripture.

The gospel we share is good news about real events. There is a "having-happened-ness" at the core of the gospel. There is a story to tell, about real people, and above all about the real person, Jesus of Nazareth.

This is one reason why confidence in the Bible is also so important. For that is where we have the recorded testimony of those who experienced these events first-hand. Peter and John could speak about "what we have seen and heard", because they were there. We can't speak in exactly the same way. So we depend on their testimony, and that testimony is in the Bible—and indeed that was the very reason why John says he wrote his gospel (John 20:30–31; 21:24).

UNCOMPROMISING CLAIMS

Both our texts move on from the undeniable historical event that underlies each of them to an uncompromising claim that is then made in unambiguous language. The expression "*there is no other . . .*" is another feature that both texts have in common. And as it turns out, although the texts are separated by centuries, in terms of biblical theology it is ultimately said about the same person.

Deuteronomy – No Other God

The great rhetorical questions of Moses that had affirmed the uniqueness of Israel's experience in Deuteronomy 4:33–34 were not for nostalgia or feel-good comfort. They had a clear message. There was something Israel must emphatically now know, in the sense that they must actively acknowledge it and build it into their hearts and lives:

> You were shown these things *so that you might know* that the LORD is God; besides him *there is no other.* (Deut. 4:35; italics added)
> *Acknowledge* [lit., "know!"] and take to heart this day that the LORD is God in heaven above and on the earth below. *There is no other.* (Deut. 4:39; italics added)

All that Israel had so uniquely experienced was so that they would learn something utterly vital—the *identity* of the living God. YHWH, and YHWH alone, is

God, and there is no other anywhere else in the universe. This is the theological freight that the rhetorical rolling stock is carrying.

Because Israel alone had experienced the unique acts of God's redemption (exodus) and God's revelation (Sinai), Israel had a knowledge of God that was correspondingly unique: "*You* [the pronoun is emphatic] were shown these things so that *you* might know." In a world of nations that did *not* know YHWH as God, Israel was now the one nation that had been entrusted with that essential knowledge.

Old Testament Israel knew God as no other nation did, because they had experienced God in ways that no other nation had at that time.

Now, although the language of "no other god" immediately tells us that we are here in the realm of what is often called "Old Testament monotheism", it is important to see clearly that the text is not merely affirming monotheism in itself. Moses does not say, "You were shown these things so that you would know that there is only one God." The question was not merely one of *arithmetic* (how many gods are there?), but of *identity* (who truly is the living God?). Merely believing that there is only one God is fine, but it gets you no further than the demons, as James would say (Jas. 2:19).

The true and living God is the God who is revealed as YHWH, through the narrative just experienced. "These things" (the events of exodus and Sinai) show God, as YHWH, to be the God of compassion and justice, the God of salvation and revelation, the God who had redeemed Israel by his grace and now calls them to love and serve him exclusively. The story shows, then, not just who really is God, but what God is really like. It reveals not only his existence and identity, but also his character. This God is *like this*, in a way that no other god is. How do you know? Because of what this God (and no other) has done in your publicly witnessed history.

The thrust of these verses in Deuteronomy 4 is filled out in many other Old Testament passages, where we find a combination of the assertion that YHWH is *incomparable* (there is no other god *like* him), and the assertion that YHWH is *unique* (there is actually no other god beside him at all, in the sense of his transcendent deity). For the sake of our biblical theology, and also in order to feel the full impact of what Peter and John calmly claimed for Jesus in Acts 4, it is worth pausing to read the following texts and let their staggering claims sink in.

Moses states the uniqueness of YHWH by simply asking the question "Who is like you?"

> Who among the gods
>   is like you, O Lord?
> Who is like you —
>   majestic in holiness,
> awesome in glory,
>   working wonders? (Ex. 15:11)

Elsewhere in the Old Testament the same rhetorical question is asked to express wonder and admiration for YHWH as the God like no other. YHWH is beyond all comparison ("none like him/you"):

- in keeping promises and fulfilling his word (2 Sam. 7:22)
- in power and wisdom, especially as seen in creation (Jer. 10:6–7, 11–12)
- in the heavenly assembly (Ps. 89:6–8)
- in ruling over the nations (Jer. 49:19; 50:44)
- in pardoning sin and forgiving transgression (Mic. 7:18)
- in saving power on behalf of his people (Isa. 64:4)

And because there is none like YHWH, all nations will eventually come and *worship him* as the only true God (Ps. 86:8–9). There is already, therefore, a missional dimension of this great truth. What we will see Peter and John affirming about Jesus was already being said about YHWH centuries earlier and with the same missional relevance.

Here (in YHWH, in Jesus) is the only source of salvation and the only focus of worship – for all the nations of the world.

But the Old Testament goes beyond saying merely that YHWH is not like any other god. In the end, the simple reason why YHWH is incomparable is that there is nothing in reality to compare him with. YHWH stands in a class of his own. He is not just one of a generic category – "gods". He alone occupies the place of transcendent deity – as *the God*.[7]

In addition to Deuteronomy 4:35 and 39, this truth is affirmed in various other places, and of course it underlies all the worship and prophecy of Israel.

> There is no one holy like the Lord; there is no one besides you; there is no Rock like our God. (1 Sam. 2:2)

· · ·

> So that all the peoples of the earth may know that the Lord is God and that there is no other. (1 Kings 8:60)

· · ·

> I am the Lord, and there is no other; apart from me there is no God. (Isa. 45:5, 6, 18)

· · ·

> Then you will know that I am in Israel, that I am the Lord your God, and that there is no other. (Joel 2:27)

---

7. For further discussion of the question of whether "the gods" in the Old Testament were regarded as something, or nothing, and in what senses, see the much fuller analysis in *Mission of God*, 75–104, 136–90.

Acts – No Other Saviour

If Moses exhorts Israel about what they must "*know*" on the foundation of what they have experienced of God's miraculous power, then Peter does exactly the same, in the same words. Regarding the miracle of the healing, Luke writes:

> Then Peter, filled with the Holy Spirit, said to them: "Rulers and elders of the people! If we are being called to account today for an act of kindness shown to a man who was lame and are being asked how he was healed, *then know this,* you and all the people of Israel: It is by the name of Jesus Christ of Nazareth, whom you crucified but whom God raised from the dead, that this man stands before you healed." (Acts 4:8 – 10; italics added)

From that he goes on to draw his great evangelistic conclusion:

> "Salvation is found in no one else, for there is *no other name* given under heaven by which we must be saved." (Acts 4:12; italics added)

Here [Psalm 96] we arrive at the fundamental equation of mission, the driving force behind all our efforts to bring the news of the one true Lord to our friends and neighbours: If there is one Lord to whom all people belong and owe their allegiance, the people of that Lord must promote this reality everywhere. Monotheism and mission are intimately related. The existence of just one God makes our mission to the many essential.

John Dickson[8]

This is a famous verse and rightly so. But what makes it so astonishing is that *Peter was talking about Jesus.* For of course, if "the name" he meant had been the name of *YHWH*, Acts 4:12 could easily have been a verse from the Old Testament. Just read the verse again without thinking of the story in which it is set. Don't you think you could as easily be reading Isaiah? In fact, it is almost precisely what Isaiah *did* say about YHWH (or rather, what YHWH says about himself through Isaiah):

> There is no God apart from me,
> a righteous God and a Savior;
>   there is none but me.
> Turn to me and be saved,
>   all you ends of the earth;
>   for I am God, and there is no other. (Isa. 45:21 – 22)

Every one of Peter's judges in the Sanhedrin would have agreed with Peter's statement if that had been what he meant: "There is no other name under heaven by which we can be saved than the name of YHWH the God of Israel."

"Absolutely. No question about that. We all know the Scriptures. Preach it, fisherman."

But of course, the shock and offence of Peter's affirmation is that he was not talking about YHWH. Or was he? He was talking about Jesus of Nazareth. But Peter knew his Scriptures too, and he could not have used such language as Acts

---

8. Dickson, *Best Kept Secret*, 31.

4:12 without fully knowing what he was doing. He was taking truths that he and everybody in the room believed about *YHWH*, and calmly applying them to *Jesus*. *Jesus* now occupies the place of being the unique saviour of all. "Jesus" is now the name that carries the same unique, divine, saving power as the name of "the LORD God of hosts".

Peter had made similar claims already. In his message on the day of Pentecost he had affirmed, "God has made this Jesus, whom you crucified, both Lord and Messiah" (Acts 2:36). And Paul later took Old Testament texts about YHWH and applied them to Jesus. In 1 Corinthians 8:4–6, he builds Jesus Christ into the most monotheistic of all Old Testament texts–the *Shema* of Deuteronomy 6:4. And in Philippians 2:9–11, he probably quotes an early Christian hymn in which words originally spoken by YHWH about himself (in Isa. 45:23) were calmly sung about Jesus, as the one to whom "every knee should bow ... and every tongue acknowledge that Jesus is Lord, to the glory of God the Father."

UNDIVIDED LOYALTY

So then, putting our two main texts together, we find that the Old Testament affirms the uniqueness of Israel's historical experience as the foundation for Israel coming to know who the living God is, and to know YHWH as the unique and universal God that he is. And in the same way, using the same kind of language, the New Testament affirms that Jesus of Nazareth is the one who embodied both the uniqueness of Israel (whom he embodied as Messiah) and the uniqueness of Yahweh (whom he incarnated as Lord). This is what we are called on to know and to make known.

> Monotheism remains the essential basis for mission. The supreme reason why God "desires *all men* to be saved and come to the knowledge of the [same] truth" is that "there is *one God* and there is one mediator between God and men, the man Jesus Christ, who gave himself as a ransom for all ..." (1 Tim. 2:4–6). The logic of this passage rests on the relation between "all men" and "one God". Our warrant for seeking the allegiance of "all men" is that there is only "one God", and only "one mediator" between him and them. Without the unity of God and the uniqueness of Christ there could be no Christian mission.
>
> *John Stott*[9]

This is the knowledge to which we are called to be loyal–holding fast to it for ourselves and making it known to others without compromise. Our mission is an inevitable reflex from the truth of biblical monotheism–the uniqueness of YHWH in the Old Testament and the uniqueness of Jesus in the New Testament (speaking, of course, of one and the same divine reality).

There is, then, an uncompromising claim at the heart of biblical proclamation

---

9. John Stott, *Our Guilty Silence* (London: Hodder and Stoughton, 1967), 23.

and witness. But it is not a claim about Christians or about Christianity as a religion. When we go out into the world affirming that Jesus is Lord and Christ and Saviour, it is not some arrogant claim about *ourselves* or what wonderful religion we have. It is simply our acceptance of the testimony of both the Old and New Testaments about the one true living God, and about how, and where, and through whom this one God has acted to bring salvation to us and the whole world. And that testimony, in both Testaments, is founded on historical events and a historical person.

For those who have come to share the undeniable experience of God's salvation and revelation, with its uncompromising explicit claim about God and Jesus, there follows naturally an undivided loyalty to the Lord himself. This is found in both texts we have been examining. And it is a loyalty that fuels the mission of God's people. For the knowledge that there is no other God and no other name leaves no other choice than to make him known.

Acts – We Cannot Help Speaking

It is not surprising that the religious authorities told Peter and John to be quiet about Jesus. For if what they were saying was true, it changed everything in their world. It meant the end of the whole system on which their power and status rested.

But Peter and John would not betray or deny the truth of what they had experienced. And so they make their majestic reply: "Which is right in God's eyes: to listen to you, or to him? You be the judges! As for us, we cannot help speaking about what we have seen and heard" (Acts 4:19 – 20).

If Christ has been crucified for us, if Christ has been raised from the dead, if God was in Christ reconciling the world to himself, then such world-changing realities cannot be silenced.

Either Jesus is the only saviour and Lord, or he is not. And if he is, then, with Peter and John we are called to stand up for him with total loyalty and unwavering witness.

Deuteronomy – "You Shall Love the LORD Your God"

The great truths of Deuteronomy 4, which Israel was to "know and take to heart", are combined in the clinching affirmation and command of Deuteronomy 6:4 – 5: the Shema:

> Hear, O Israel: The LORD our God, the LORD is one. Love the LORD your God with all your heart and with all your soul and with all your strength.

> Such love is a total commitment of intellect, will, emotions, and energy. One Lord, one love, one loyalty – that is the challenge of Deuteronomy. One Lord, one name, one saviour – that is the challenge of Acts.

Notice the reason Jesus gives for getting involved in this mission. It is made clear by the all-important "therefore": "All authority in heaven and on earth has been given to me. *Therefore* go and make disciples ..." (Matt. 28:18–19). The reference to "heaven and earth" obviously recalls Genesis 1:1 and refers to every part of creation. The one true God has given universal authority to the one true Lord, and for this reason we are to make disciples throughout the world. At the risk of sounding like a scratched CD, let me repeat the mission equation: if there is one Lord to whom all people belong and owe their allegiance, the people of that Lord must promote this reality everywhere.

We promote God's glory to the ends of the earth not principally because of any human *need* but fundamentally because of God's/Christ's unique worthiness as the Lord of heaven and earth. Promoting the gospel to the world is more than a rescue mission (though it is certainly that as well); it is a reality mission. It is our plea to all to acknowledge that they belong to one Lord.

John Dickson[10]

SUMMARY

The biblical gospel, then, announces to us the story of undeniable experiences of unique events, culminating in the life, death, and resurrection of Jesus of Nazareth. It goes on to make the uncompromising claim that in these events the living God has acted to save humanity and redeem his whole creation, and that there is no other God or source of such salvation. It therefore claims the undivided loyalty of the hearts, minds, and lives of those who know these things.

What else is the mission of God than bearing witness to such cosmic realities? That is where we must go next in the following chapter.

RELEVANT QUESTIONS

1. "Undivided loyalty". What are the things in your cultural context that threaten your loyalty to the one true living God and the uniqueness of Jesus Christ? What do you now recognize as subtle forms of syncretism?

2. This chapter calls for a robust refusal to renounce the claims of Christ, even under threats. What are the pressures – cultural, secular, or religious – that could tempt you to do that? How do the texts studied in this chapter help you resist?

3. How do you hold together the challenge of this chapter to be loyal to the uniqueness of Christ in the face of other religions, with the call in earlier chapters to be people of blessing, love and compassion to all people, including those of other faiths? In contexts of religious plurality, how can we simultaneously sustain love for people along with loyalty to the truth?

10. Dickson, *Best Kept Secret*, 34–35.

CHAPTER 10

PEOPLE WHO BEAR WITNESS TO THE LIVING GOD

"At last!" you might be thinking. "Why have we had to wait so long before getting to a chapter that tackles the fundamental task of mission – preaching the gospel? Surely the real mission of God's people is to get out there and spread the Word, witness, evangelize, tell people about Jesus and how to get saved."

Our mission most certainly includes that, and this chapter will show the important place such spoken testimony has in the Bible. But not even the Great Commission itself focuses solely or primarily on the *proclamation* task. "Go and make disciples of all nations," said Jesus, immediately explaining what such discipling included, "baptizing them ... *and teaching them* to obey everything I have commanded you" (Matt. 28:19 – 20; italics added).

It takes disciples to make disciples, and Jesus had spent three years teaching his disciples what it meant to be one. It involved practical and down-to-earth lessons on life, attitudes, behaviour, trust, forgiveness, love, generosity, obedience to Jesus, and countercultural actions toward others. This was what it meant to live in the kingdom of God – now.

In short, you had to *live* under the reign of God if you wanted to go *preach* about the reign of God.

The same thing is noticeable in Paul's church planting and nurturing strategy. Paul's own passion was preaching the gospel (and we will look at that in detail in chapter 11), but there is comparatively little in his letters to the churches he founded about *their* task of preaching the gospel to outsiders in evangelistic mission. This is not at all to suggest that Paul did not want them to do that; it is clear that Paul expected his churches to be hubs of evangelistic witness. Rather, Paul also knew that the gospel message needed to be embodied in people whose own lives were radically changed by it. So all Paul's teaching about how believers ought to live was not just "the ethical bit at the end," but a fundamental part of the transformative work of the gospel itself. Gospel witness had to flow from gospel transformation.

Coming back to the order of this book, however: I have been trying to follow the Bible's own order in answering the questions, *What are we here for as believers?*

What is the mission of God's people? And as we have traced the question along the Bible's own story line so far, we have found a rich list of answers:

- We are here as human beings to care for God's creation.
- We are chosen in Abraham to be a people though whom God's blessing reaches all nations.
- We are called to walk in the ways of God, in justice and righteousness, in a corrupt world.
- We are to live out the dynamic of our own redemption in our compassionate treatment of others.
- We are to represent God to the world and draw the world to God.
- We are to be people whose lives demonstrate the character of God and attract others to come to faith in him.
- And above all, we are to know the living God and be uncompromisingly loyal to the Lord Jesus Christ in our worship and witness.

Ah, at last, *witness*! Yes indeed. For, as we pointed out in the last chapter, those who know God are required to make God known. And that requires the medium of words as well as deeds. There are things to be said; there are stories to be told; there are affirmations and truth claims, warnings and challenges, announcements and appeals.

And so we come in this chapter and the next one to consider this verbal dimension of the mission of God's people. We will do so by considering two major terms that the Bible uses for such word-focused mission: *bearing witness* (ch. 10) and *announcing good news* (ch. 11). And as before, we will launch our study from careful examination of Old Testament texts that have major echoes in the New.

"We're not all called to be evangelists, but we are all called to be witnesses." That's something I heard often as a young Christian. The point of it was that although some Christians are specially gifted for evangelistic ministry, not all are (as Paul says in Eph. 4:11, and by implication, 1 Cor. 12:29–30). However, even those of us who are not called to be evangelists are all called to be faithful witnesses to the Lord Jesus Christ and to be willing to speak up for him when opportunities arise.

The instructions of Jesus to his disciples on the Mount of Ascension provided initial support for this understanding: "You will be my witnesses in Jerusalem, and in all Judea and Samaria, and to the ends of the earth" (Acts 1:8). Like its companion verse in Luke 24:48, this probably refers primarily to the special place of the original disciples/apostles as *eyewitnesses* of the life, death and resurrection of Jesus himself.[1]

However, I was taught (rightly I think) that even though the apostolic witness had a unique function in authenticating New Testament Christianity, witnessing

---

1. That is how it is used in the first half of Acts. See Acts 1:22; 2:32; 3:15; 4:33; 5:32; 10:39–41; 13:31.

to Christ was something that went beyond the apostles. All following generations of believers were enlisted in the ongoing task of bearing witness to the same Lord Jesus Christ, in whom they had come to believe through the apostolic witness. We would have quoted 2 Timothy 1:8 to support that, and of course (being well-taught youngsters) we knew that the word for "martyrs" in Revelation is the same as "witnesses" (so it might get a bit rough).

What I didn't learn in those young days was the connection (which I believe was intentional) between the words of *Jesus* to his disciples on both occasions in Luke 24 and Acts 1 and the words of *YHWH* to Israel in the book of Isaiah (Isa. 43:10, 12; 44:8). But doing biblical theology for life enables us to spot that connection immediately and draw out its implications for our witnessing mission. For after all, what else was Jesus doing according to Luke (Luke 24:27, 45–47) but biblical theology for life—the ongoing life of his disciples for all generations to come?

Let's take our minds back, then, from the resurrection of the Messiah to the world of the book of Isaiah and study a key text in which the concept of God's people as his witnesses is found, namely, Isaiah 43:8–13:

Lead out those who have eyes but are blind,
    who have ears but are deaf.
All the nations gather together
    and the peoples assemble.
Which of their gods foretold this
    and proclaimed to us the former things?
Let them bring in their witnesses to prove they were right,
    so that others may hear and say, "It is true."
"You are my witnesses," declares the LORD,
    "and my servant whom I have chosen,
so that you may know and believe me
    and understand that I am he.
Before me no god was formed,
    nor will there be one after me.
I, even I, am the LORD,
    and apart from me there is no savior.
I have revealed and saved and proclaimed—
    I, and not some foreign god among you.
You are my witnesses," declares the LORD, "that I am God.
    Yes, and from ancient days I am he.
No one can deliver out of my hand.
    When I act, who can reverse it?" (Isa. 43:8–13, my italics)

We must put these words into their historical context.

A DOUBLE PROBLEM FOR GOD

The story of Old Testament Israel had reached its lowest ever point – the exile in Babylon. After centuries of recurring generations of rebellion against YHWH, disloyalty to the covenant between God and Israel, disobedience to God's laws, and disregard for the warnings of prophet after prophet, God's patience had come to an end. In the trauma of 587 BC, the Babylonians had captured and destroyed Jerusalem, burnt YHWH's temple, and carried off the bulk of the Israelite population into exile in Babylon.

Two generations had passed. It seemed that all hope had gone. But these words in the central portion of Isaiah (chs. 40 – 55 especially) address the exiles with a message of amazing grace. YHWH is on the move again. Babylon's time is almost over. There will be a new exodus as God once again delivers his people from slavery, and God's mission to bring blessing to the whole world through these descendants of Abraham will move forward to its great climax.

However, there are two great problems that stand in the way of God's great plan.

The Ignorance of the Nations

All through these chapters, YHWH engages in a running argument with the nations and their gods. According to the cultural assumptions of the day, the gods of big and powerful nations were bigger and more powerful than the gods of the little nations they defeated. The natural assumption, therefore, was that if Babylon had defeated and captured *Israel*, then *YHWH* the God of Israel was likewise defeated and defunct.

Not at all, says the prophet. YHWH is the *only* sovereign living God, and he has been as much in control of the events that led to the exile as he would be in bringing it to an end. The gods of the nations are nonentities, with illusions of power and grandeur created by their worshipers, but ultimately powerless to do anything good or ill, let alone to act in sovereign salvation, as YHWH was about to (Isa. 41:21 – 24).

Now, we know that the God of Abraham wills to bring blessing to all nations. And these chapters rise to great heights in their anticipation of all humanity (lit., "all flesh") coming to see the glory of God (Isa. 40:5), knowing God (45:6), and being saved by God (45:22). But the nations' blind devotion to their non-gods stands in the way of that (44:9 – 20). There is an ignorance (44:18) that has to be penetrated. The gods need to be radically unmasked and dethroned and those whose oppressive power rests on them need to be brought low (Isa. 46 and 47). The nations need to see and hear the truth. But how can they?

That is where Israel comes in, for it had from the start been God's intention that through Israel he would make himself known to the nations, for their blessing and salvation. That, indeed, was why he had chosen and called Israel to be his servant (Isa. 41:8 – 10), a servant whose mission would include being "a light to the Gentiles" – i.e., the nations (Isa. 42:6; 49:6b).

But that solution, which was nothing less than the long-term mission of God ever since his promise to Abraham, seemed to have run into the sand. And that was God's second big problem: Israel itself seemed no better than the nations.

The Blindness of Israel

Isaiah 42, the immediate prelude to the words of our text in this section, presents a terrible paradox. Look carefully at the sharp contrast between the opening section (vv. 1 – 9), and the closing section (vv. 18 – 25). The Servant of YHWH, who is to embody the identity and mission of Israel (Isa. 41:8), is described in 42:1 – 9 with a wonderful mission of justice, compassion, enlightenment and liberation. But the *actual* servant of YHWH at that time, namely historical Israel in exile, is blind and deaf!

Isaiah 42:18 – 25 portrays the terrible reality: Israel was in exile, "plundered and looted", because of God's judgment on them for their disobedience. God had given them plenty to see (all the great acts of past salvation), but they were willfully blind. God had given them plenty to hear (all his great revealed teaching and covenant law), but they were willfully deaf. There is a strong echo here of Isaiah's call vision in Isaiah 6:9 – 13. All the preaching of the preexilic prophets had gone unheeded, and even in exile their condition seemed unchanged.

Any hope for the *nations*, then, would have to depend not on *Israel's* natural capacity to respond and obey, but on a miracle of God's grace and transforming, healing power. But such a miracle was indeed what was anticipated when God himself would return and do his great new thing in saving power:

" … your God will come,
    he will come with vengeance;
with divine retribution
    he will come to save you."
Then will the eyes of the blind be opened
    and the ears of the deaf unstopped. (Isa. 35:4 – 5)

And that seems to be exactly what happens next. God summons the blind and deaf into court (Isa. 43:8) – *as witnesses*!

A DOUBLE ROLE FOR ISRAEL

For, indeed, it is a court scene that is envisaged in Isaiah 43:8 – 13 (as several times already in these chapters). It is the metaphor by which the prophet portrays the reality that there is a conflict between YHWH and the gods of the nations.

A great assembly of nations is pictured in verse 9. These nations had their many gods. But how can the court decide which god is "real" or "in the right"? YHWH chooses his pitch, and it is the same as in the earlier court case in Isaiah 41:21–24, namely, the ability to predict the future, interpret the past and explain the present in sovereign detail and across the centuries.

So the other gods are invited to bring in *their* witnesses, if they have any, to give evidence of their power to do the same and so "prove they were right" (43:9; lit., "justify themselves"). The witnesses for the gods of the nations are the nations themselves, but they have nothing to say, because of course, the gods they will defend are "less than nothing" (Isa. 41:24).

So who will speak for YHWH, then, in this great international court of nations and alleged gods? Who will testify to his reality and power? The shock of the next word is stunning. YHWH turns to the people whom he has just described as blind and deaf, and says,

"You!" [the word is emphatically placed first], "you are *my* witnesses" (43:10).

My Witnesses

Now being a witness was a serious matter in Old Testament Israel. A great deal is said about the responsibility of it. It was actually regarded as a sin to fail to speak up and testify about any matter that you had seen or heard if it was a matter before a court (Lev. 5:1). The duties of witnesses were solemnly laid out (Ex. 23:1–3). Witnesses must take primary responsibility for the execution of the court's verdict (Deut. 17:7), and perjury could cost you your life (Deut. 19:16–21)–two laws that would stamp out frivolous false accusations. To bear false witness was among the most serious covenant offences–prohibited in the ninth commandment (Ex. 20:16). And false witness was among the things that God hates most (Prov. 6:19).

But even apart from law court cases, witnesses were most important to establish the truth of statements or claims, so that such claims could never be called into dispute (e.g., Ruth 4:9–11; Jer. 32:10–12). Earlier in Isaiah, the prophet himself had used witnesses who could later verify the truth of when the prophetically significant naming of his son had taken place, and who would testify to his message in the time of its later fulfillment (Isa. 8:1–2, 16–18).

So God is here summoning Israel as a nation to exercise, in the international court of nations and gods, a responsibility that was deeply and reverently rooted in their own social culture–the task of bearing witness.

There is not only shock here, but profound irony. For one of the main reasons that Israel had been exiled under God's judgment was precisely their collective social failure to uphold the standards of justice in court that their own covenant law called for. Instead, their judicial system had become a playground for lying witnesses–so much so that Amos raged that "there are those who hate the one who reproves in court and detest the one who tells the truth" (Amos 5:10).

And now YHWH calls the descendants of such liars to be *his* witnesses? The miracle of mercy is matched only by the risk that God takes in relying on such people. But there is no Plan B, because of the other thing that is said here about Israel in Isaiah 43:10.

My Servant

"... and my servant whom I have chosen". The middle phrase of Isaiah 43:10 deliberately echoes what God had said about Israel in 41:8–10. All the content of those verses is here reaffirmed. Israel as God's servant had been chosen in Abraham, and God was not going back on all the promises and commitments of that past. So this repetition of the key word "servant" emphasizes that, in spite of all the negative reality described in 42:18–25, God's original commission remains.

Israel is God's servant for God's purpose for God's future for God's glory. God's mission goes on. So Israel's mission has to go on too.

The mission of God's people is not a matter of how great we are at doing things for God, but a matter of how patient and persistent God is in doing things through us.

The striking parallelism in Isaiah 43:10, however, means that being God's servant and being God's witness are now integrated. Or to put it another way, the reason that God had chosen and called Israel to be his *servants* was in order that they should be his *witnesses*.

Witnessing to the truth about YHWH as the one true living God is at the heart of the role and mission of the servant—always was and still is.

And that servant is God's people—Israel/Jacob, descendants of Abraham. The mission of God's people, then, according to this passage, is to be witnesses for the living God in a world of competing claims by multiple gods. That witnessing function is at the heart of their election. We have been chosen *in order* to be witnessing servants of the living God.

Servanthood exercised through witnessing, the thrust of Isaiah 43:10, however, not only gives *content* to the role of servant, it also describes the *quality* of the witnessing. Witness to YHWH is to be given, not by those who wield imperial power and claim his backing (not, in other words, like Babylon or Cyrus), but by the gentle, noncoercive nature of the servant, so counter-culturally described in Isaiah 42:2–3. To accept the role of God's servant, then, necessarily involves bearing witness to him. And the task of bearing witness must be done in the spirit of servanthood—as servants of God, of God's people, and of the world that waits for God.

This was a combination that the apostle Paul saw clearly and demonstrated in his own mission and ministry. In fact, he records that these were the very two words that Jesus used to summarize the mission that lay ahead of him. "Now get up and stand on your feet. I have appeared to you to appoint you *as a servant and as a witness* of what you have seen and will see of me" (Acts 26:16, italics added). The relevance of both words to our own practice of mission needs to be radical and penetrating, and it points towards something we need to discuss further in part 3.

THE DOUBLE PURPOSE OF BEARING WITNESS

So Israel is summoned as the servant of God to give their witness on God's behalf. But the paradoxes continue. One might have thought that the purpose of bearing witness would be to convince *the nations* of the truth about YHWH as God. True, but there is a prior purpose.

Restoring Trust in God

The *witnesses themselves* need to be convinced, and the act of bearing witness will generate such conviction in the witnesses:

> so that *you* may acknowledge and trust in me
>   and understand that I am he. (Isa. 43:10; my translation)

The three verbs in the sentence are important and have many echoes in the book of Isaiah. God's complaint against Israel was precisely that they had failed to *acknowledge* him, whether in the gifts of his grace (Isa. 42:20–21) or in the experience of his punishment (42:23–25). From the start the prophet has been reminding Israel, with some surprise, of things they ought to have *known* but needed to be told afresh (40:21, 28). And throughout the book, Israel's failure to *trust* in God was a major source of grief to God and his prophet (7:9; 30:1–5, 15–18; 31:1–3). Their lack of *understanding* of God made even the dumbest beasts look wise (1:3).

Such failure, however, was exactly what the ministry of Isaiah had anticipated. In the enigmatic sequel to Isaiah's call vision in Isaiah 6, God had pointed out that the people were in such an advanced state of rebellion that the presence of a prophet in their midst would only serve to underline their refusal to acknowledge or understand (the same verbs of Isa. 43:10 are used in 6:9–10). That state would continue through the terrible destructive judgment of exile (6:11–12).

But now, says God in Isaiah 43:10, a new thing is happening. There is a new dawn and a renewed summons to Israel. They are recalled to their original mission of being witnesses to YHWH, and in that task they will themselves be restored to recognize their God, to put their trust in him, and to understand him. God calls them back to their task as a way of calling them back to himself.

The thrust of this verse is that the power of testimony lies not only in what it does in the hearts of those who hear it, but also in what it does for the faith of the one who gives it. The task of convincing others reinforces the convictions of the witness.

Establishing the Truth about God

What, then, is the substance of the testimony that God's people must bear before the nations? Three key truths are embedded in the great claims that YHWH makes in Isaiah 43:10b, 11 and 12. Make sure these verses are open in front of you as you read on.

That YHWH Alone Is the Transcendent, Eternal God

"I am he" (v. 10) – "I am God" (v. 12). This is the great affirmation of Old Testament monotheism: not just the abstract conception that there is only one deity, but that YHWH alone is "the God". He is eternal, for there was no god before him, nor one to come after him. The expression "Before me no god was formed" is ironic, for it acknowledges the fact that in the surrounding culture of Babylon gods were indeed "formed" – that is, constructed.

Not only was this obviously the case with the idols and statues of the gods, but of their very origin as gods. Ancient mythologies are rich in stories of the origins of the gods in one way or another. YHWH's point is double-edged, then. He alone is *un*formed. "Form" is a verb that can only have YHWH as its subject (as in the creation narrative and creation psalms repeatedly), never as its object. But also, before all other gods were formed (human constructs that they are), YHWH was there – God before all gods.

[Isaiah portrays] Yhwh intending Jacob-Israel to function as witnesses to the world. That is for the world's sake, so that it may see the truth, for Yhwh's sake, so that Yhwh's unique deity may be acknowledged, but also for Jacob-Israel's sake, so that they may be convinced through their own being chosen to witness. Paradoxically, they are not convinced so that they may witness. They are chosen to witness, so that they may be convinced.

John Goldingay [2]

That YHWH Alone Is In Sovereign Control of History

The assertion of Isaiah 43:9 – that it was YHWH alone who had interpreted the past and proclaimed the future – is repeated in verse 12, but with the added emphasis that no strange god in their midst had given such historic revelation to Israel. The sequence, "revealed and saved and proclaimed", reflects the great paradigmatic narrative of Israel's salvation – the exodus. Back then, God first revealed what he intended to do; then he did it; then he interpreted, explained and taught his people on the foundation of both his faithfulness to his promise and his actual saving fulfillment of it. Only the God who is actually in control of events from beginning to end could claim such comprehensive mastery of history and its meaning. The story is God's story because it is the story he is writing. The author controls the story.

---

2. John Goldingay, *The Message of Isaiah 40–55: A Literary-Theological Commentary* (London, New York: T&T Clark, 2005), 201.

That YHWH Alone Is Saviour

The saving power of YHWH was already proven, of course, in the past history of Israel, but could it be trusted for the future, in the wake of the apparent defeat of 587 BC and the exile? The future lies as much in the sole saving power of YHWH as the past. That is why the affirmation "apart from me there is no savior" follows immediately on the claim, "nor will there be any [god] after me".

God has insisted that Israel has witnessed the evidence that he alone is God. What had that evidence been? The promise to make Abraham a great nation; the promise to deliver his descendants from Egypt; the promise to give them the land of Canaan; the promise to make the dynasty of David secure on the throne of Jerusalem, and so on. What had the fulfillment of those promises required again and again? Deliverance, often over impossible odds. In the process of demonstrating his character as Yahweh to his people, he had demonstrated to them over and over his inclination and his capacity to save. What Israel had witnessed and could not escape was the realization that "Yahweh" meant "Savior", and that as Yahweh was the only God, he was the only Savior. In the first part of his book, Isaiah had demonstrated that God alone can be trusted, that all other resources, especially the nations, would fail. Now he is showing that when we have refused to trust and have reaped the logical results of our false dependencies, God alone can save.

John N. Oswalt [3]

In other words, it is not a question of hoping that some other god will come along after YHWH to rescue Israel (or anybody) out of the mess that their sin has landed them in. No, the God whose righteousness put them in exile is the same (and only) God who will deliver them from it. There is no other saving God, for there is no other God, period. This truth that Israel needed to learn applied equally to all nations, whom the prophet will shortly invite to turn around, abandon the false gods that cannot save, and turn to the only God who can—and will (Isa. 45:20–22).

These, then, are the great truths about YHWH to which Israel is to testify. Actually, they are the greatest truths in the universe. What is more important than the identity, sovereignty and saving power of the living God?

And yet—in the greatest paradox of all—this God entrusts such vast cosmic truth into the mouths of human witnesses—witnesses whose untrustworthiness he had endured for a thousand years. There is incredible vulnerability and risk here—not in relation to God's own self or survival, but in the great project of making these truths known to the world.

How will the nations come to know the living, revealing, saving God, the one who is their creator, sovereign, judge and saviour? *"You are my witnesses,"* says God, to a community of the spiritually blind and deaf, languishing in exile. Only the miraculous, life-giving and transforming power of God's Spirit could ever give such

---

3. John N. Oswalt, *The Book of Isaiah: Chapters 40–66* (New International Commentary on the Old Testament; Grand Rapids: Eerdmans, 1998), 148.

people any hope of a future at all, let alone a renewed calling to be God's chosen servant and witness. But that is exactly what God promised (Isa. 42:1; 44:3). And when the Spirit came, it would be nothing short of a resurrection, a resurrection into the assured knowledge of God (Ezek. 37:1–14).

THE DOUBLE ROLE OF WITNESSES IN THE NEW TESTAMENT

"You will be my witnesses," said the resurrected Jesus to an equally unpromising group of people, whose flaws and failings he had lived with for three years and suffered most painfully at his death. One of the people Jesus had chosen as a witness had denied any knowledge of him at all! The rest had just run for cover. And yet they had been chosen and called by Christ for this very purpose, to fulfill the servant role of Israel, to be a light to the nations that God's salvation should go to the ends of the earth. And that was an election for mission that Jesus would not rescind, just as God had not rescinded his election of Israel because of their failure. Rather, as in the Old Testament, Jesus reinforced it with the matching promise of the gift and power of God's Spirit to empower them for it (Luke 24:49; Acts 1:8).

For what greater truths are there in the universe than the identity, sovereignty and saving power of the Lord Jesus Christ?

There on the Mount of Ascension, Jesus calmly assumed the YHWH position in words drawn straight from Deuteronomy 4:39: "All authority in heaven and on earth has been given to me. Therefore go. . . ." It is as if Jesus says to them,

You know who I am now; *you* know my identity as the one who has come (as YHWH said he would come) and has accomplished all that only YHWH could accomplish. *You* know that I am He. And you are witnesses to the events that demonstrate these things–my life, death and resurrection.

So how will all *the nations* whom God has promised to bless ever since Abraham come to the saving knowledge of these truths about me? You are *my* witnesses. You stand in the place of Israel bearing witness to YHWH, bearing witness to the one who embodies YHWH, as sovereign and saviour.

So as the New Testament develops the rich Old Testament theme of God's people as YHWH's witnesses, it does so in two ways, both of which remain crucially important for our own mission as God's people today.

Original Eyewitnesses of the Historical Jesus

"You are witnesses of these things," said Jesus (Luke 24:48).

What things?[4]

4. As Jesus innocently asked the two disciples on the road to Emmaus, in what must be one of the most richly ironic–even comic–lines in the Bible: Jesus, who had been the very focal point of all that had happened in Jerusalem that weekend, pretends that he doesn't even know what they are talking about. "What things?" indeed! (Luke 24:19).

The events that had just been described – the coming of the Messiah, his suffering, death and resurrection. One of the prime privileges and responsibilities of apostleship was exactly this – to have known Jesus of Nazareth in his earthly life and ministry and to have been a witness of his death and resurrection. So when the disciples needed to replace Judas Iscariot after the resurrection, they were quite explicit that candidates for selection needed to have this minimum qualification:

> … it is necessary to choose one of the men who have been with us the whole time the Lord Jesus went in and out among us, beginning from John's baptism to the time when Jesus was taken up from us. For one of these must become a witness with us of his resurrection. (Acts 1:21 – 22)

And in chapter 9 we saw how vital this personal eyewitness testimony was in the early preaching of the apostles. They refer to it again and again:

> You killed the author of life, but God raised him from the dead. We are witnesses of this. (Acts 3:15)

•   •   •

> As for us, we cannot help speaking about what we have seen and heard. (Acts 4:20)[5]

The same Peter and John, who presented their credentials as eyewitnesses at the start of their life of apostolic ministry, never lost the wonder of that privilege. Peter describes himself not merely as "a fellow elder" (which speaks of what he shared with his readers) but also as "a witness of Christ's sufferings" (which distinguished him from them as an apostle, without stating it as a matter of rank; 1 Peter 5:1; cf. also 2 Peter 1:16 – 18). John emphasizes the visual, audible and tangible nature of his testimony to Christ:

> That which was from the beginning, which we have heard, which we have seen with our eyes, which we have looked at and our hands have touched – this we proclaim concerning the Word of life. The life appeared; we have seen it and testify to it, and we proclaim to you the eternal life, which was with the Father and has appeared to us. We proclaim to you what we have seen and heard. (1 John 1:1 – 3)

Well, we might think, this was clearly important to those first gospel missionaries of Jesus Christ. *They* could stand up and say, "We were there. We knew him. We saw him die. We saw him raised to life by God. We are witnesses of these things." But *we* can't say that. So what relevance has this point got to the mission of God's people today?

It is vitally important, for where did all that eyewitness testimony about Jesus end up? In the Bible, of course! In the New Testament documents that trace their origin and their authenticity back to those first eyewitnesses. And since all our

---

5. See also: Acts 1:22; 2:32; 4:33; 5:32; 10:39 – 41; 13:31.

witnessing to the gospel is founded on the Bible, it is vital that we should be able to have confidence in the trustworthiness of those documents.

Indeed we can have such confidence. Luke tells us that he did his research carefully and checked those eyewitness sources, precisely so that we can have confidence in the certainty of what we believe:

> Many have undertaken to draw up an account of the things that have been fulfilled among us, just as they were handed down to us by *those who from the first were eyewitnesses* and servants of the word. With this in mind, since I myself have carefully investigated everything from the beginning, I too decided to write an orderly account for you, most excellent Theophilus, so that you may know *the certainty of the things you have been taught.* (Luke 1:1–4; italics added)

What was true for Luke was doubtless true of the others who compiled what we now hold in our hands in the New Testament. Indeed, Richard Bauckham has argued with enormous scholarly research and conviction that the impact of contemporary eyewitness testimony on the documents of the New Testament is far greater than many imagine. Certainly he explodes the popular caricature that all the stories about the life and sayings of Jesus were embroidered by years of free-flowing oral imaginings before they were ever written down.[6]

All our witness to the Lord Jesus Christ and the saving power of the gospel is dependent on the trustworthiness of the Bible. The Scriptures point to him. Indeed Jesus himself used the language of witness to speak of the Scriptures that we now call the Old Testament: "You study the Scriptures diligently because you think that in them you possess eternal life. These are the very Scriptures that testify about me" (John 5:39). The Old Testament bore its witness to the one who came to fulfill God's promise. The New Testament bears witness to him through those who were, as Peter put it, "witnesses whom God had already chosen–by us who ate and drank with him after he rose from the dead" (Acts 10:41).

The mission of God's people, then, is a witnessing mission–bearing witness to the Lord Jesus Christ. But all our witnessing is authenticated by the witness of those who were God's own chosen eyewitnesses. And their testimony is in our hands–God's Word through their words–our Bible.

Ongoing Testimony to the Gospel of Christ

So the first witnesses were those who had seen and heard the earthly Jesus. However, as Jesus pointed out to Thomas, "blessed are those who have not seen and yet have believed" (John 20:29). Jesus prayed not for his first disciples alone, but for "those who will believe in me through their message" (17:20). So Jesus clearly envisaged that the witnessing work of his community would continue beyond the first

---

6. Richard Bauckham, *Jesus and the Eyewitnesses: The Gospels as Eyewitness Testimony* (Grand Rapids: Eerdmans, 2008).

generation of eyewitnesses, to the ongoing testimony of those who would come to faith. Faith comes through hearing the testimony of those who have seen and heard; but faith also demands to be passed on through continuous testimony.

Jesus had also warned his disciples that they would face persecution and arrest by religious and political authorities, but this would provide them with all the more opportunities to testify about Jesus in the public arena. Or rather, it would be one of the ways through which the Holy Spirit would bear witness to Jesus through the words of his followers on trial. Indeed it would be one means by which the gospel would spread to all nations (Mark 13:9–11; cf. also Matt. 10:17–20; Luke 21:12–15). So, Jesus clearly envisaged this as an ongoing witness by the community of believers beyond the immediate lifetime of his first eyewitness disciples.

The ministry of the apostle Paul falls somewhat into both categories. He knew well that he had not been among the original disciples of Jesus during his earthly ministry, nor had he been there at the cross or on the day of resurrection. So his inclusion among the original band of apostles had to be endorsed by his personal, direct and overwhelming encounter with the risen Christ on the road to Damascus. He saw that event as authenticating his apostleship alongside those who had been there when it happened.

But Paul was also conscious of his duty to testify to Jesus. That is how he describes the commission he received at conversion (Acts 22:14–15; 26:16) and how he summed up his life's ambition: "I consider my life worth nothing to me; my only aim is to finish the race and complete the task the Lord Jesus has given me – the task of testifying[7] to the good news of God's grace" (Acts 20:24).

John is fond of the concept of bearing witness. His whole gospel is written as the testimony of one who was there at the cross and the empty tomb and who bears witness so that others may come to believe (John 19:35; 20:8; 21:24). He emphasizes the role of John the Baptist in bearing witness to the identity of Jesus as the Messiah (John 1:7–8, 15, 19, 32, 34). And he portrays Jesus engaged in prolonged debate with Jewish leaders over the range of testimony to his identity (John, his Father, his works, the Scriptures, himself).

John also provides two "witness" passages that provide a model and an encouragement – the Samaritan woman and the Holy Spirit.

It is often said that the Samaritan woman at the well in John 4 was the first evangelist. And this is all the more amazing in that she seemed to suffer triple disqualification for such a role – being a foreigner, a woman (whose testimony was not counted valid in Jewish courts at that time), and someone with serious moral and social questions hanging over her domestic circumstances.[8] But she did what any

7. "Testifying" is an alternative English translation for "bearing witness." Similar words are used with little difference in Greek (*martyreo* and *diamartyromai*).

8. She is often blamed for the fact that she had had five husbands and was living with someone who was not her own husband. It was no way for a woman to live, of course, and she would have suffered considerable social stigma. But in the culture of the day and its divorce practices, it is likely that this was just as much a case of serial abuse by unfaithful men as a case of serial promiscuity by a loose woman.

witness should do – nothing more nor less. She went and told her town about Jesus. And the power of her testimony became a self-replicating evangelistic force. It seems clear that John intends this as a model for all who come to faith:

> Many of the Samaritans from that town believed in him *because of the woman's testimony*, "He told me everything I ever did." So when the Samaritans came to him, they urged him to stay with them, and he stayed two days. And because of his words many more became believers.
>
> They said to the woman, "We no longer believe just because of what you said; now we have heard for ourselves, and we know that this man really is the Savior of the world." (John 4:39 – 42; italics added)

John's second "witness" passage, with equally strong evangelistic intention, is his record of the words of Jesus about the role of the Holy Spirit:

> When the Advocate comes, whom I will send to you from the Father – the Spirit of truth who goes out from the Father – he will testify about me. And you also must testify, for you have been with me from the beginning. (John 15:26 – 27)

The immediate surrounding context of this is the warning that Jesus gives about the world's hatred and persecution of his followers. So the atmosphere is dark with conflict and accusation. As in Isaiah, the metaphorical background is a court, only this time it is Jesus himself in the dock. Jesus is maligned, attacked, hated. Who will stand up for him? Who will speak in his defence? The Holy Spirit will, claims Jesus, for that is his primary task – to testify to Jesus.

In the next chapter, Jesus will portray the Holy Spirit in the role of prosecuting counsel, with the world in the dock, being convicted of its guilt and sin before

Jesus stands on trial, not now before Pontius Pilate, but at the bar of world opinion. The "world", which in biblical language means secular, godless, non-Christian society, is in the role of judge. The world is judging Jesus continuously, passing its various verdicts upon Him. The devil accuses Him with many ugly lies and musters his false witnesses by the hundred. The Holy Spirit is the *Parakletos*, the counsel for the defence, and He calls us to be witnesses to substantiate His case. Christian preachers are privileged to testify to and for Jesus Christ, defending Him, commending Him, bringing before the court evidence with they must hear and consider before they return their verdict.

How is the Christian to react when faced with the opposition of the world? He is certainly not to retaliate. Nor is he to lick his wounds in self-pity. Nor is he to withdraw into safe and sheltered seclusion away from the disagreeable enmity of the world. No, he is bravely to bear witness to Jesus Christ before the world in the power of the Holy Spirit. Here is the world – sometimes indifferent and apathetic on the surface but underneath actively aggressive and rebellious. How are they to hear, to understand, to repent and to believe? How are they to be brought to give sentence in favour of the Jesus who stands on trial before them? The answer is: through our testimony. It is because of the unbelieving world's opposition to Christ that the Church's witness to Christ is needed.

John Stott[9]

9. John Stott, *The Preacher's Portrait* (Grand Rapids: Eerdmans, 1961), 61 – 63. This book is describing the work and character of preachers, of course, using five biblical images. But what it says about "A Witness" in chapter 3 applies to all Christians. It is well worth reading for its comprehensive survey of the New Testament term and its sharp relevance to this aspect of our Christian mission.

the righteous judgment of God (John 16:8–11). But here in John 15, his brief is to bear witness to Jesus *through the witness of his disciples.* Once again we see that the primary reference is to those who were eyewitnesses of Jesus' earthly life ("with me from the beginning"), but there is no doubt that such testifying to the truth about Jesus, in the power of the Holy Spirit, is the ongoing privilege and responsibility of all his faithful followers through the generations.

SUMMARY

In chapter 9 we saw how part of the mission of God's people is to give undivided loyalty to the God we know in Christ as Lord and Saviour. Part of that loyalty includes being willing, like the apostles, to stand up for him in open court, as it were. In this chapter we have explored what that means through the biblical category of bearing witness. Jesus lays this responsibility on his disciples, but he drew the idea and its content from his Scriptures – our Old Testament.

In a world where the nations of humanity have constructed gods for themselves and do not know the living God, God's people are summoned to bear witness to his uniqueness, sovereignty and saving work. That is a fundamental reason for our election and part of the meaning of being God's servants. But the task of bearing witness is not only for the benefit of those who do not yet know God, it also strengthens the faith and understanding of the witnesses themselves.

The mission of God's people, then, includes verbal testimony, standing up to speak the truth about who is truly God and about what God has done through the Lord Jesus Christ to bring salvation to the nations. The task of being a "servant and a witness" continues to define our mission as much as it did for Israel, for Paul, and for all those whose testimony has even included martyrdom "because of the word of God and the testimony of Jesus" (Rev. 1:9).

The content of our testimony is above all good news. And that leads us in the next chapter to ask what that good news is and what it means to be a messenger of it.

RELEVANT QUESTIONS

1. What does the expression "giving your testimony" bring to mind? How does the popular practice relate to what the Bible means about "bearing witness"? How can we resist the tendency to make "our testimony" be mostly about us, rather than about the great truths of God in Christ?
2. Can you point to ways in which the task of witnessing has resulted in strengthening your own Christian faith and understanding?
3. Courts sometimes speak of someone as "a credible witness" (or not, as the case may be). What constitutes a "credible witness" for Christ?

CHAPTER 11

PEOPLE WHO PROCLAIM THE GOSPEL OF CHRIST

Evangelism, evangelists, evangelical, evangelistic, evangelization – words that are at home in many Christians' vocabulary, but very much misunderstood and abused in the world at large.

We are "gospel people", we like to say, and sharing the gospel in all possible ways is of the essence of the mission of God's people. And most of us are aware that the old English word "gospel" means "good news", which is also the core of all the "evangel-" words in Greek in the New Testament.

The mission of God's people is to bring *good* news to a world where *bad* news is depressingly endemic.

Now we could immediately launch into a survey of the use of the *"evangel-"* root in the New Testament, where it occurs about one hundred times as a verb and a noun, and build a convincing enough portrait of our evangelistic mandate and method there. However, we are doing biblical theology for life, and so we will follow our established practice hitherto and step back first to the Old Testament. And there are two good reasons for doing that.

The first reason is that Paul tells us that the gospel is "in accordance with the Scriptures" (1 Cor. 15:1–4); that is to say, the gospel message of the death and resurrection of Jesus is to be understood in the light of the Old Testament. Paul can even say that the gospel was *preached* in the Old Testament. The Scripture, he says, "pre-evangelized Abraham" – when God promised him that all nations would be blessed through him (Gal. 3:8).

The biblical gospel begins in Genesis, not in Matthew. That certainly puts "the gospel" into our framework of biblical theology.

"Gospel" is one of those words that is so basic, so fundamental to Christian life that it can be taken for granted. It can become the term for just about anything at all in the Christian faith. "Gospel" can become so full of the meaning I want to put into it that it can be emptied of meaning altogether. Like the word "love" in popular music, "gospel" can mean everything and nothing at the same time. I've heard people describe congregations as "gospel churches", and ministers as "gospel men", when all they really mean is "Bible-based", or "we like them".

John Dickson[1]

---

1. Dickson, *The Best Kept Secret*, 111–12.

The second reason is that it seems probable that the New Testament *vocabulary* of gospel and evangelism actually has its roots in the Old Testament, specifically in the book of Isaiah (and some psalms, as we will see). The "gospel" words go back, in fact, to the good news that came to the exiles in Babylon.

GOOD NEWS FOR THE EXILES

As we saw in chapter 10, we need to go back to that time in Israel's history when the unthinkable had happened—the exile, with the loss of land, city, temple and hope. Then, if ever, Israel needed to hear some good news. And that is what they did hear in the soaring words recorded in Isaiah 40–55.

Four times in those chapters we hear about "good news" on its way. Check them out, since they are the origin of our gospel language: Isaiah 40:9; 41:27; 52:7; and 61:1. In each case, the Hebrew word is *baśar,* and in three cases the Greek translators in Septuagint texts chose to use the verb *euangelizomai.* And this, of course, is the word that entered into the New Testament usage, especially when those texts were quoted by Jesus or the apostles. The good news that the prophet looked forward to has actually arrived with the coming of Jesus. So the language of "good news" or "gospel" uses the Septuagint verb from the Old Testament Scriptures and gives us the whole range of "evangel-" words in the New Testament.

Baśar means to bring or announce good news. It was common enough in everyday life in Old Testament Israel. Probably the most exciting and revealing use of it is in 2 Samuel 18:19–32—the story of how the news of Joab's victory over Absalom was brought to David—good news that was ruined for David by the death of Absalom himself.[2] The participle, *m^ebaśer,* then meant somebody who announces such good news, a messenger of *good* news (as distinct from the ordinary word for messengers in general—*mal'ak*).

And it is exactly such a messenger of *good* news whom we meet in the opening verse of the passage that will lay the foundation for our study in this chapter, Isaiah 52:7, a verse that was much quoted in the hopes of the Jewish people around the time of Jesus and also in the New Testament—except that in the New Testament it is no longer a hope for the future but a glad celebration of an event that had arrived at last.[3]

---

2. Other examples of ordinary use of *baśar,* bringing good news, include: 1 Sam. 31:9; 2 Kings 7:9—a verse which has given rise to the saying that evangelism is a matter of one beggar telling other beggars where to find bread. An interesting case comes in Ps. 68:11, which seems to speak of a great victory, achieved by God's decisive word, being broadcast by those who proclaim the good news of it. In fact the "company of those who proclaimed it" is the *feminine* plural of *m^ebaśer,* suggesting the picture of happy women telling the good news of the victory after the battle had been fought and won by their men folk (cf. ESV). This is a finer point of grammar that seems to have

eluded the earnest leader of a Brethren assembly I used to attend as an undergraduate. He liked to use the verse in the translation of the Book of Common Prayer, "The Lord gave the word; great was the company of the preachers," as warrant for the plurality of speakers in their meetings. He might have been shocked to learn that the "preachers" in the text were women. But neither he nor I at that time knew Hebrew.

3. For a full discussion of the influence of this text in post-OT Judaism and on Paul's understanding of the gospel, see John P. Dickson, *Mission-Commitment in Ancient Judaism and in the Pauline Communities,* 153–77.

How beautiful on the mountains
    are the feet of the one who brings good news,
who proclaims peace,
    who brings good tidings,
    who proclaims salvation,
who says to Zion,
    "Your God reigns!"
Listen! Your watchmen lift up their voices;
    together they shout for joy.
When the LORD returns to Zion,
    they will see it with their own eyes.
Burst into songs of joy together,
    you ruins of Jerusalem,
for the LORD has comforted his people,
    he has redeemed Jerusalem.
The LORD will lay bare his holy arm
    in the sight of all the nations,
and all the ends of the earth will see
    the salvation of our God.
(Isa. 52:7 – 10; my translation in v. 7; the messenger is singular in Hebrew)[4]

So we return to the exiles in Babylon. This chapter, Isaiah 52, has begun by summoning Zion to wake up and believe that the bad days of its desolation and captivity are coming to an end. And in verse 7, the prophet calls on the exiles (and us, his later readers) to exercise our imagination. We see ourselves back in the ruins of Jerusalem, anxiously gazing out toward the East, where the exiles were languishing in captivity, waiting every day for news that God has won the victory he had promised, that the exiles are coming home.

At last, in verse 7, we see the running feet of a messenger speeding across the mountain ranges to the east, toward Jerusalem. A *single* running messenger will mean good news of a victory rather than the straggling remains of a defeated army limping home. And so it proves.

The messenger's good news consists of three words in verse 7 that could be presented in quotation marks as the words he gasps out as he runs nearer: "It's peace!" "It's good!" "We're saved!" until at last he reaches the city itself and calls out to those within, "Your God reigns!"

> Feet can be not a pretty sight. Jeremiah had once imagined Rachel watching her children trudging past her tomb as captives. The contrasting vision here is of feet bringing good news, a point implicit in the fact that they are lovely. The people had sinned with their feet (Prov. 1:16), had been punished with feet (Jer. 13:16), but now are comforted with feet.
>
> *John Goldingay* [5]

---

4. Cf. the earlier use of the same imagery in Nahum 1:15, where the message is one of the victory of God over the Assyrians (Nineveh).

5. Goldingay, *The Message of Isaiah*, 452.

God Reigns (Isa. 52:7)

This is the key message, and it is the truth that explains all the other three items in the messenger's good news. For what does it mean to say that YHWH, the Lord God of Israel, reigns? What does the good news of the kingdom of God bring with it? Everything the messenger has said, but with all their additional Old Testament resonance.

What does God's rule entail? It entails a condition where all things are in their proper relation to each other, with nothing left hanging, incomplete or unfulfilled (*peace, šalom*); it entails a condition where creation purposes are realized (*good, ṭob*); it entails a condition of freedom from every bondage, but particularly the bondage resultant from sin (*salvation, yešuʿah*). Where God reigns, these follow. Of course, this is exactly congruent with what the Christian faith considers its good news (*euangelion*) to be. This is the content that Christ instructed his disciples to preach from village to village (Matt. 10:1–7): that which Isa. 52:7–10 had spoken of was now present and at hand. Christianity understood itself to be about what Isaiah was about, declaring the good news of the universal rule of God in the world, with concomitant peace, good, and salvation.

John Oswalt[7]

The Reign of God Means "Shalom"

It will be a reign of peace. It will mean the end of the violence and conflict, and all the brokenness and shattering that war brings. God's reign will bring wholeness and fullness of life, when all things are as God intended them to be, when we are at peace with God, with ourselves and with the world.

This was an Old Testament longing and vision[6] that of course expressed a literal desire for the end of actual physical warfare. But it went deeper to the levels of restored peace and harmony in all relationships, and in that sense the image of the messenger who "proclaims peace" took deep root in Jewish hopes and informed New Testament understanding of the work of Christ, as we will see (Acts 10:36; Eph. 2:17).

The Reign of God Means "Good"

When God acts in the way the prophet has been saying, it will be good news for the whole creation, for it will be restored to what God said when he first created it: "It is very good." When God reigns over all creation and over all humanity, it will be good, for God is good.

The Reign of God Means "Salvation"

The victory of God means the ending of all that holds people in slavery. It will be the great rescue, deliverance—from the literal captivity of the Israelite exiles to all forms of oppression, addiction and bondage. The reign of God breaks the chains of evil, sin and Satan and removes the ultimate dangers of judgment and death. Salvation is an incredibly rich and complex word throughout the Bible. It was the

6. Cf. Ps. 46:9–10; Isa. 9:5–7.   7. Oswalt, *The Book of Isaiah Chapters 40–66*, 368.

distinctive, defining character of YHWH in the Old Testament and the personal name of Jesus in the New.[8]

So when God reigns, there will be peace, life will be good and we will be saved. This is the summary content of the "evangel" borne by the beautiful feet of the Lord's messenger. This is gospel truth.

God Returns (Isa. 52:8)

In verse 8 the single voice of the running messenger is joined by an ensemble of watchmen. These are the imaginary sentries on the broken down walls of Jerusalem. They now join together in a great chorus of joy. Why? Because they can now see beyond and behind the messenger and what they see is YHWH himself.

The Lord is on his way home! And so the God who reigns is the God who returns. God is coming back to his city–coming back to, and coming back with, his own people.

When Nebuchadnezzar destroyed Jerusalem and took its people into captivity, the exiles were not the only ones to leave the city. In a sense, God himself had departed as well. Ezekiel, in the terrible vision that was probably the lowest point of his whole ministry (second only to the death of his wife), had witnessed the glory of YHWH leaving the temple and moving away, deserting the city (Ezek. 8–11). God had left the building. Would he ever come back?

Already Isaiah has given the answer in Isaiah 40:3. God is on the move–so get the roads ready. In fact, this has already been heralded as "good news to Zion" (Isa. 40:9). Now the watchmen in Jerusalem are singing because they see him on his way! God is returning to Zion!

As indeed he did, when the exiles returned in 538 BC, with the permission and sponsorship of the new king on the block, Cyrus of Persia. The city was inhabited again. The temple was rebuilt. Worship was restored.

He would return to Zion again, in a more significant way, when the Lord entered his temple on the first Palm Sunday.

And he will do yet again, when the Lord returns to claim the whole creation as his temple and to dwell with his redeemed humanity forever. But our biblical theology is running ahead of us. That's what happens when you see these resonances and connections within the Bible.

God Redeems (Isa. 52:9–10)

This song is infectious. From the gasped gospel of the single running messenger (v. 7), it has spread to the small choir of sentries (v. 8). But now the ruins of Jerusalem

---

8. For a survey of the breadth of the biblical understanding of salvation, see Christopher J. H. Wright, *Salvation Belongs to Our God* (Nottingham: IVP, and Downers Grove, IL: IVP, 2007).

are given personified voice to sing of their own redemption (v. 9), and in verse 10 it will have rippled out to the ends of the earth. And the theme of the song remains the same – the Lord God himself, who not only reigns and returns, but also redeems.

What does it mean? *Comfort* and *redemption*.

It means being comforted and liberated. The two words that describe what God has done for his people (note that the parallelism makes it clear that "Jerusalem" is not just the city itself, but stands for "the people" – the redeemed people of God) are repetitions of phrases that the prophet has used most emphatically already and filled with rich meaning. The opening words of Isaiah 40 double up "comfort, comfort my people", and expand it with "speak tenderly", which is literally, "speak to the heart". Comfort brings relief to pain and grief, bereavement and sorrow. The exiles have suffered their great loss and trauma long enough. God is pouring in his comfort (Isa. 49:13; 51:3).

But comfort by itself can be impotent – mere words, as we say. So the second word is crucial. God has *redeemed* his people. Again, this is a word (*ga'al*) already used several times (Isa. 41:14; 43:1, 14; 44:22, 24; 48:17, 20). It comes from the world of Israel's economic life, as we saw in some detail in chapter 6. We saw there that the word "redeem" in Israel spoke of the commitment of a family member to stand up and champion other members of the family who were in some situation of loss, danger or threat. It implied decisive, powerful action, payment of whatever cost was needed (literally or in the sense of effort), and the achievement of liberty, release or restoration.

This is the term and the role that YHWH applies to himself repeatedly on behalf of Israel – especially in these chapters of Isaiah. It is an exodus-flavoured word, since its earliest use in a theological sense with YHWH as the subject comes in God's declaration of intent to "redeem" Israel out of Egypt (Ex. 6:6–8), and in Moses' celebration of that event in song (Ex. 15:13). The return from exile will be exodus reloaded – God's redeeming his people out of captivity.

How will it be accomplished? By the "holy arm" of the Lord. Verse 10 hints at how God will accomplish this great redemptive work. "The LORD will lay bare his holy arm." We recognize this immediately as an anthropomorphic metaphor. You roll up your sleeves for vigorous work. Or the imagery may come from the battlefield, as a soldier throws off his cloak, baring his right arm for combat with the enemy.

Yes, but actually we have met "the arm of the LORD" before in this prophecy, and there are other flavours to the metaphor.

- In Isaiah 40:10–11, the arm of the Lord is a combination of sovereign power combined with tender compassion – the compassion of a shepherd who takes up struggling lambs in his arm and carries them close to his heart.
- In Isaiah 51:9, the arm of the Lord is identified with YHWH himself in his great demonstration of saving power in bringing the Israelites out of Egypt and through the sea.

- In Isaiah 51:5, however, the arm of the Lord is described in exactly the same terms as had been used for the servant of the Lord in 42:1–4, which suggests that God will accomplish his redeeming work through that servant; the servant will be the personified arm of the Lord.
- In Isaiah 53:1, the so-called fourth Servant Song that follows immediately on our text, this impression is strengthened as the arm of the Lord is identified with that servant who would live a life of rejection and die a death of horrendous injustice – but ultimately be vindicated and glorified by God. The Servant is the arm of the Lord.

So it is a rich picture, then. The good news is that God will act and will accomplish redemption for his people. In one sense, he will do so unaided, acting solely by the power of his own arm, as at the exodus. And yet, we are led to expect that the arm of the Lord will be embodied in the servant whose calling, ministry, suffering and victory so fill these chapters.

Who will benefit? All the nations.

From a single runner to the ends of the earth, the good news spreads. Verse 10 does what this prophet does so characteristically – that is, he opens up the promise of God from being a word directly for his own historical people (Old Testament Israel in exile) into a word that has universal scope and power. Verse 10 takes a word intended to bring hope to the exiles, centuries before Christ, and turns it into a promise of salvation to the world, quoting verbatim as he does from Psalm 98:3.

No wonder it is described as "gospel". This is *good news for the world*, not just for Israel. Israel's gospel is gospel for all nations – as it was always intended to be (a point that Paul will build into the very essence of the gospel he preached to the Gentiles).

Now since we are thinking of Isaiah 52:7–10 particularly as a "*gospel*" declaration (because of its use of the verb *baśar* and its influence on the gospel vocabulary of the New Testament, through the LXX *euangelizomai*), it is worth pointing to Psalm 96, where the same language is used. Strikingly, it is employed with the same universal intent – proclaiming the good news about YHWH and all his works to the nations.[9]

Sing to the LORD a new song;
    sing to the LORD, all the earth.
Sing to the LORD, praise his name;
    proclaim his salvation day after day.

---

9. Many psalms use other verbs, but have the same theme of universal proclamation to the nations of the works of YHWH, or celebration of YHWH in the midst of the nations, or invitation to all nations to praise YHWH; , e.g., Pss. 9:11 (where it is linked to God's judgment on all nations); 22:27–28; 47:8–9; 49:1; 57:9–10; 66:8; 67; 68:32; 87; 98:2; 99:2–3;102:21–22; 105:1–2; 108:3; 117; 126:2; 138:4–5; 148:11. The remarkable quantity of this material that brings the nations into the orbit of the praises of Israel is worth far more attention than it usually gets (sadly, even here all it gets is a footnote. But you can compensate by reading carefully through that list of references and absorbing their staggeringly universal scope). For a more in-depth analysis of it in relation to the wider Old Testament theology of the nations and God's mission to them, see Wright, *Mission of God*, 454–500.

Declare his glory among the nations,
    his marvelous deeds among all peoples. (Ps. 96:1–3; italics added)

"Proclaim" is *baśar*, and the LXX translates it as *euangelizesthe*—"*proclaim this as good news*". The message of YHWH's name, salvation, glory and marvelous deeds constitutes good news, a *gospel message* that the nations need to hear. Psalm 96 goes on to expose the futility of the idolatry of the nations and to invite them to abandon their non-gods and join in the worship of the only living God, in the beauty of his holiness.

And what is the content of this "new song" that is to be sung among the nations? Nothing less than the same truth we find in our Isaiah text—"YHWH reigns" (Ps. 96:10). And if YHWH reigns, then the old order of the world is turned upside down, transforming the whole creation into a place of reliability, righteousness and rejoicing (Ps. 96:10–13).

Gospel truth, then, is generated in the prophets and psalms of Israel. That is what we have found so far.

The good news of the kingdom of God that is to go out to the ends of the earth, to bring comfort and joy to all nations, is the good news of the living God who reigns, who returns to his rightful inheritance, and who redeems the whole world. And all of these things God will accomplish through his mighty arm—his Arm (his Servant), outstretched in gentle compassion, outstretched in suffering love, and outstretched in cosmic victory.

The gospel is on its way.

GOOD NEWS IN JESUS

"Go tell it on the mountain that Jesus Christ is born," sings a popular Christmas song, drawing its imagery from the messenger on the mountain in our text and in Isaiah 40:9. And its instinct is right. For beyond the horizon of the exiles was the horizon of that greater arrival of God among his people in the person of Jesus of Nazareth. And all three parts of the gospel according to Isaiah's messenger in 52:7–10 are even more gloriously good news in Christ.

Jesus Was and Is God Reigning

The first gospel written opens with "the beginning of the good news [*euangelion*] about Jesus the Messiah" (Mark 1:1) and goes on to quote from Isaiah 40. Mark sees John the Baptist as the initial herald bringing good news, but both Mark and John quickly make it clear that John was not the one who fulfilled the prophecies—they both point to Jesus in that role.

Thus Jesus, when he begins his public ministry, functions as the messenger of good news, announcing that it has arrived. The reign of God is beginning—with his arrival (Mark 1:14–15).

Luke records that among the earliest acts of Jesus was to take upon himself precisely the role of the anointed preacher of good news whom we find in Isaiah just a few chapters after our text, using the same verb (Isa. 61:1–3).

> [Jesus] stood up to read, and the scroll of the prophet Isaiah was handed to him. Unrolling it, he found the place where it is written:
>
> > "The Spirit of the Lord is on me,
> >> because he has anointed me
> >> to *proclaim good news*[10] to the poor.
> > He has sent me to proclaim freedom for the prisoners
> >> and recovery of sight for the blind,
> > to set the oppressed free,
> >> to proclaim the year of the Lord's favor." (Luke 4:16–19; italics added)

How many years had that Scripture been read in that synagogue? How many times would the local rabbi have encouraged the people to go on praying and trusting for the day when the one of whom it spoke would come and do those things? May he come soon, O Lord! Bring us this good news in our lifetime. Perhaps tomorrow …

Then one Sabbath morning, the local carpenter's son shocked the whole town with the electric word, "*Today!*" No more waiting. What you have hoped and longed for all these years is here, in the one standing before you. The prophetic voice of the ancient text has become the living voice of the one now reading it to you. "Today this scripture is fulfilled *in your hearing*" (Luke 4:21; italics added).

And the things the text spoke of were exactly the things that Jesus pointed to as evidence that the kingdom of God had indeed come. God was reigning in and through Jesus, through his words and his works: "If I drive out demons by the finger of God, then the kingdom of God has come upon you" (Luke 11:20). When John the Baptist wondered if perhaps he had backed the wrong messiah, Jesus pointed to the same things, this time supported by yet another text of Isaiah (Isa. 35:5–6), but adding the significant words, "and the good news is proclaimed to the poor" (lit., "and the poor are being '*evangelized*' "; Matt. 11:4–5).

And that reign of God, inaugurated by Jesus and indeed embodied in him, continues to work within human history in the ways that Jesus said it would—like seed growing, like yeast rising, like fish being caught. The kingdom of God is at work in and through the lives of those who have "entered" it, that is, in whose lives God is reigning through repentance and faith in Christ, in those who are committed to the ways of Jesus Christ by submitting to him as Lord, in those who seek first the kingdom of God and his justice, in those who hunger and thirst for justice.

---

10. The word is *basar* in the Hebrew original; *euangelisasthai* in Luke's Greek, following the LXX.

In short, the reign of God is found among those who understand their mission, to make *peace*, to do *good*, and to proclaim God's *salvation*. For those are the things, as Isaiah's gospel messenger called out, that constitute the good news that "our God reigns". The gospel is *good news about God,* as a foundation for all that makes it *good news for us.*

At the heart of the gospel message (in the Old and New Testaments) is the idea of God's rule as king, in other words, his kingdom. When the first Christians proclaimed this gospel of the kingdom, they were not copying the "gospel" of the Roman kingdom; they were exposing it as a fraud. It was God, not any human king, who ruled over all. This is the central theme of the Christian gospel. . . .

What is the single most important idea driving our mission to the world? . . . The answer has to do with monotheism (one God) or, more correctly, Christological monotheism—the lordship of the one true God through his Messiah. . . . To put it in simple and practical terms, the goal of gospel preaching—and of gospel promoting—is to help our neighbours realise and submit to God's kingship or lordship over their lives.

[However] the Christian gospel does not just announce the concept "God reigns"; it outlines exactly how that reign has been revealed to the world ... the core content of the gospel is the work of God's anointed king, Jesus. Through his birth, miracles, teaching, death and resurrection God's kingdom has been manifested (and will be consummated upon his return). Telling the "gospel", then, involves recounting the deeds of the Messiah Jesus.

John Dickson[11]

The gospel, then, is fundamentally good news of the reign of God. It was the good news for which Israel had waited for centuries. They knew *what* the kingdom of God would mean; the question was, *when* would it arrive? Jesus announced the good news: "It has come!"

It is also the good news for which the world is waiting still. "And this gospel of the kingdom will be preached in the whole world as a testimony to all nations, and then the end will come" (Matt. 24:14).

Jesus Was and Is God Returning

Our text from Isaiah was not the only place in the Old Testament where God promised to come, or to come back. It is a theme found in several places, particularly in the postexilic period when there was the feeling that, although the temple had been rebuilt, God himself had never really brought the exile to a true end by returning to his temple and keeping all the great prophetic promises. But he would do so, and would send a messenger to prepare the way for his return (Zech. 9:9; Mal. 3:1; 4:5).

Jesus himself identified John the Baptist as the one who fulfilled that role of the Elijah to come (Matt. 11:14). But since Elijah was to come before YHWH himself arrived, and if John was Elijah, who then was Jesus (who everybody knew had come after John)? The day of the Lord had arrived, for the Lord himself was here in the person of Jesus.

As a result, in a dramatic and totally deliberate piece of prophetic theatre, Jesus came into Zion riding on a donkey. Having walked from Galilee he had no need to ride the last few hundred yards. It was as clear as he could make it for all who had

11. Dickson, *Best Kept Secret,* 114–15.

eyes to see and knew their Scriptures. The king was coming home, bringing God's righteousness and salvation.

So the horizon of our text stretches first to the return of the Lord to Jerusalem with the exiles, but then to the return of the Lord in the person of Jesus Christ in his first coming. And of course the rest of the New Testament points to a further horizon when "this same Jesus, who has been taken from you into heaven, will come back in the same way you have seen him go into heaven" (Acts 1:11).

The gospel is good news of the God who came, who came back as he first promised, and who will come again, bringing both judgment for those who reject him and salvation for those who heed his call to repent and believe the good news.

Jesus Was and Is God Redeeming

The name Jesus means "salvation", or "YHWH is salvation". And the gospels festoon the story of Jesus' birth and ministry with scriptural quotations to show the full significance of that. He was indeed "the one who was going to redeem Israel" (Luke 24:21), though the two on the road to Emmaus thought such hopes had been dashed at Calvary when in fact they had been fulfilled there.

For at Bethlehem "the arm of the Lord" was rolling up his sleeves for

But what does it mean for *them* I thought, as I prepared my sermon on Isaiah 52:7–10 and took the text for a walk (as I often do). I was walking on Tottenham Court Road, near my home, and I thought, "What about these people on the streets of London in their thousands? What does it mean for them that Jesus is the reigning Lord of history, the returning king of creation, and the redeemer and saviour of the world?"

And the answer seemed to bounce back off the walls of the buildings: *Absolutely nothing.* Nothing at all. How can it mean anything if they don't know about it, if they have never heard about Jesus, if nobody has ever told them?

And then my text itself seemed to bounce off the walls also, only this time through the words of Paul, who quoted Isaiah 52:7 in the midst of a similar list of questions.

> For there is no difference between Jew and Gentile—the same Lord is Lord of all and richly blesses all who call on him, for, "Everyone who calls on the name of the Lord will be saved."
>
> How, then, can they call on the one they have not believed in? And how can they believe in the one of whom they have not heard? And how can they hear without someone preaching to them? And how can anyone preach unless they are sent? As it is written: "How beautiful are the feet of those who bring good news!" (Rom. 10:12–15)

Actually, there is nothing very beautiful about feet. The only thing that makes feet beautiful is when they are wearing the running shoes of the gospel (Eph. 6:15). Then they are feet that belong to people who are willing to

- "Go, tell it on the mountain"—the mountain of human arrogance, that Jesus Christ is born and is reigning;
- "Go, tell it on the mountain"—the mountain of human despair, that Jesus Christ is born and is returning;
- "Go tell it on the mountain"—the mountain of human bondage, that Jesus Christ is born, and is redeemer, saviour and Lord.

Christopher Wright[12]

12. Christopher J. H. Wright, *The God I Don't Understand: Reflections on Tough Questions of Faith* (Grand Rapids: Zondervan, 2008), 180–81.

Calvary. Finally he went to Calvary, and the arm of the Lord was indeed stretched out there, stretched out on the cross for the redemption of the world.

But God raised him from the dead, delivering his decisive "No" to death and his decisive "Yes" to Jesus, "Yes" to creation, and "Yes" to all those for whom the risen Christ is the firstfruits from the dead. In Christ, "we have redemption, the forgiveness of sins" (Col. 1:14).

In other words, the gospel of Isaiah's messenger becomes the gospel of Christ, which is also of course, as Paul said just as easily, the gospel of God.[13] In Christ the good news of Isaiah is realized.

Jesus Christ is the reigning, returning, redeeming God. God has kept his promise.

GOOD NEWS FOR PAUL

How then did Paul think and speak of the gospel?

How did he not! It is almost impossible to summarize concisely the rich, vibrant, dynamic ways in which Paul uses the term "gospel" in a variety of contexts. But at least in attempting to do so we may rid ourselves of oversimplistic, sound-bite definitions that fail to do him justice. And we will certainly have a better foundation for what we understand to be the mission of God's people for the sake of the gospel.

In search of an answer to this question, I read through all of Paul's letters, noting every use of the word "gospel". My broad analysis of this suggests that Paul uses "the gospel" as shorthand for at least the following six things.

The Gospel Is the Story of Jesus in the Light of the Scriptures

First, the gospel for Paul is above all else the historical facts about Jesus of Nazareth through whom God has accomplished salvation. The gospel is an account of the events of Jesus' death and resurrection, understood in the light of the Scriptures of the Old Testament. The good news is what God promised in Scripture and then completed in Jesus.

Paul tells us that he "received" this — that is to say, it was not an idea original to him, but rather, he entered into an understanding of the significance of the life, death and resurrection of Jesus of Nazareth that had already been articulated within the earliest community of Jesus' followers, though he claimed that he "received it", not secondhand, as it were, from them, but by direct revelation from God, and later confirmed by his meetings with the believers in Jerusalem:

---

13. Paul speaks of "the gospel of God" seven times, and "the gospel of Christ" ten times.

Now, brothers and sisters, I want to remind you of the gospel I preached to you, which you received and on which you have taken your stand. By this gospel you are saved, if you hold firmly to the word I preached to you. Otherwise, you have believed in vain.

For what I received I passed on to you as of first importance: that Christ died for our sins according to the Scriptures, that he was buried, that he was raised on the third day according to the Scriptures... (1 Cor. 15:1–4; cf. also Gal. 1:11–2:10)

What Paul means by "according the Scriptures" is summarized in the opening verses of his letter to the Romans, making it clear that for Paul "the gospel" was essentially the scriptural (i.e., Old Testament) identity, narrative and accomplishment of Jesus (Rom. 1:2–4; cf. 2 Tim. 2:8).

Basically, in line with all that we have seen from our Old Testament survey, Paul in effect declares his gospel as saying:

The God of Israel, who is the only true and living God, has been faithful to his covenant promise, originally made to Abraham and then amplified and testified all through the Law and the Prophets (Rom. 3:21). In and through the Messiah Jesus of Nazareth, God has decisively acted to deal with the problems of human sin and division (Gen. 3 and 11). Through the death and resurrection of Jesus, according to the Scriptures, God has borne our sin and defeated its consequences–enmity and death. And in Christ's exaltation to God's right hand (the place of government), the reign of God is now active in the world, so that we now live under the kingship of Christ, not of Caesar. Jesus, the Messiah of Israel, is Lord, God and Saviour of the world. So turn from your futile idols to the living God who alone can save you, repent of your sins and believe in Jesus.

The gospel for Paul, then, is rooted in Scripture and shaped by the kingdom of God. It is constituted by the accomplishment of Jesus as Messiah in fulfilling the first and embodying the second. The good news is that the reign of God, promised and defined in the Scriptures, has now come through the person and work of Jesus the Messiah. This is seen not only in Paul's letters, but also in the way Luke ends the book of Acts, describing Paul's ongoing gospel ministry as one of proclaiming the kingdom of God by teaching about the Lord Jesus Christ (Acts 28:23, 30–31).

The Gospel Is a New Redeemed Humanity, a Single Family of God

And where was he doing that, Luke? In Rome! The very heart of the empire, the place from which almost all the nations of the known world were ruled. And there in the seat of the most powerful kingdom of this world, Paul was cheerfully teaching about "another king, one called Jesus" (Acts 17:7). For indeed, the good news about Jesus was a universal message for all the nations. That too, as we have seen so clearly, had deep Old Testament roots. God's plan, announced to Abraham, had always been to bring blessing through Israel to all the nations of the world. But the great problem had been – how? How could all the nations of *the world* enter the sphere of God's blessing through *Israel*?

The nations, it would seem, were utterly outside and alienated from the heartlands of God's family. God had entered into covenant with *Israel*, had redeemed them, had given them his law, had given them promise and hope, had stooped to make his dwelling place among them. The nations, by contrast, could be accurately described by Paul as follows:

> Therefore, remember that formerly you who are Gentiles by birth and called "uncircumcised" by those who call themselves "the circumcision" (which is done in the body by human hands) – remember that at that time you were separate from Christ, excluded from citizenship in Israel and foreigners to the covenants of the promise, without hope and without God in the world. (Eph. 2:11–12)

But this dismal status of hopeless alienation was precisely what the gospel had brought to an end for those of any nation who put their faith in Jesus Christ and his blood:

> But now in Christ Jesus you [Gentiles] who once were far away have been brought near by the blood of Christ.
>
> For he himself is our peace, who has made the two [Jew and Gentile] one and has destroyed the barrier, the dividing wall of hostility, by setting aside in his flesh the law with its commands and regulations. His purpose was to create in himself *one new humanity* out of the two, thus making peace, and in one body to reconcile both of them to God through the cross, by which he put to death their hostility. He came and preached peace [lit. "evangelized peace" – quoting Isa. 52:7] to you who were far away and peace to those who were near. For through him we both have access to the Father by one Spirit. (Eph. 2:13–18; my italics and additions).

It is important to see how this "peacemaking" work of the cross – reconciling Jews and Gentiles and creating one new humanity – is *not just a by-product* of the gospel, but is *at the heart* of the gospel itself (Eph. 3:6). Paul includes it in the work of the cross. In other words, Paul is not merely saying that now that lots of individual sinners of different nations have got saved and are on their way to heaven, they really ought to try to get on with each other in the meantime. He is saying that the creation of a new humanity is the good news that Christ came to accomplish. "Peace" is part of the good news – exactly as Isa. 52:7 announced. And Paul says that Jesus *is* our peace, *made* peace, and *preached* peace (which must in context refer to the apostolic preaching of Christ).

God has only one family (Rom. 3:29; 4; Gal. 3:26–29; and possibly Eph. 3:14). In the Old Testament period, it had been ethnic Israel alone, "the house/family of Israel". But from now on, because of the work of Christ, that one single family includes people from all nations – just as God had promised. And that is gospel – good news for the nations.

So the gospel, then, is "the power of God that brings salvation to *everyone* who believes: first to the Jew, then to the Gentile" (Rom. 1:16; italics added, reflecting, I think, Paul's emphasis). And Paul can then fill out that saving power of the gospel in multiple ways that are familiar to us. By God's grace, through the death and resurrection of Jesus, believers are assured of "every spiritual blessing in Christ" (Eph. 1:3).

- *We are justified;* that is, we receive here and now advance declaration by God of the verdict of his court on the day of judgment, that we are included among those whom he will declare righteous on account of our faith in Jesus and his obedience unto death.
- *We are saved;* that is, we are delivered from the wrath to come, rescued from the anger of God against all wickedness and rebellion.
- *We are reconciled:* that is, the enmity between us and God has been removed, because God himself bore our sins in the person of his own Son on the cross.
- *We are forgiven;* that is, God chooses to "carry" (the Hebrew word usually translated "forgive") our sins, rather than repay them to us, because they have been "carried" by Jesus on the cross. They will never be held against us.
- *We are redeemed;* that is, God has achieved our liberation from all the bondage of sin, as he rescued the Israelites out of Egypt, through the sacrificial blood of Christ.
- *We are adopted;* that is, God includes us among his children, or more specifically, treats us as firstborn sons (whether male or female), and thus as his heirs, sharing in the inheritance that belongs to Christ.
- *We are made alive*; that is, from the death of sin we are given new life, the resurrection life of Christ himself.
- *We have the Spirit*; that is, the promise that God made to Israel, that would bring about their renewal and "resurrection" and obedience (as, e.g., in Ezek. 37), is now poured out in us, bearing the fruit of transformed lives.

The Gospel Is a Message to Be Communicated to the Whole World

Such comprehensively transforming good news cannot be concealed! Indeed the very nature of "gospel" is that it is good news that simply has to be announced, as we saw from its biblical roots in Isaiah 52:7. The gospel, therefore, must be heard as "word of truth" (Eph. 1:13; Col. 1:5, 23), and on being heard, it needs to be received and believed for what it is (1 Thess. 2:13). This message is to be preached to all nations, for, as we have seen, all nations are in view in the scope of what God has done in Christ in fulfillment of his promise to Abraham.

"The work of the gospel" (Phil. 2:22), then, seems to refer primarily to this task of making the good news known by all means of communication possible and at whatever cost. There is an intrinsically verbal dimension to the gospel. It is a story that needs to be told in order that its truth and significance may be understood.

In Paul's self-understanding, his encounter with Jesus on the road to Damascus was not merely a conversion but even more a commissioning to preach the gospel to the nations. He refers to this in his own reports of the event (Acts 22:14–15; 26:16–18; cf. Gal. 1:15–16; 2:7). His early letters give abundant evidence of the passion and commitment that drove Paul in this preaching mission, backed up by manual work and costly suffering. It was a whole-life thing (Gal. 4:13–14; 1 Thess. 2:8–9).

Paul clearly also had a geographical perspective on what it meant to preach the gospel to the nations. His fascinating description of his missionary work up to the point of writing his letter to the Romans indicates that he felt he had completed the task of preaching the gospel in the northeastern quadrant of the Mediterranean basin, and he was planning to head farther west (and possibly to complete the "circle of nations" by returning via North Africa?). Whatever his exact intentions, Paul saw the work of the gospel as a constant "going beyond", to places and peoples as yet unreached by the knowledge of Christ (Rom. 15:19–21; quoting again from a favourite text, Isaiah 52).

The Gospel Is Ethical Transformation

"*Repent* and believe the gospel," said Jesus (Mark 1:15). Radical change of life goes along with faith in the good news. They cannot be separated. When the people asked John the Baptist what he meant by repentance, he was ruthlessly practical (Luke 3:7–14).

Paul agrees. The gospel involves putting off the filthy clothes of the old humanity and putting on the clothes that bear the aroma of Christlikeness. In fact, Paul uses exactly the same words, "new humanity" (*kainos anthropos*), both for the union of Jew and Gentile in God's single new multinational family, accomplished through the cross (Eph. 2:15), and for the new way of life that this community is to demonstrate (Eph. 4:24).[14]

It is not the case that one is "gospel" and the other is "ethics". This common way of summarizing the two "halves" of Ephesians is vulnerable to misunderstanding – as if one can separate the doctrinal believing part of the gospel from the ethical living part of the gospel. Both are intrinsic to the gospel itself, for the second "new humanity" is described as "created to be like God in true righteousness and holiness", which is the work of the gospel of grace (cf. Eph. 2:10). The gospel speaks of a salvation that is *by grace* and *unto good works*. Grace comes first and is received by faith. And faith demonstrates its existence through obedience.

---

14. A fact that even the ESV obscures by translating the former as "new man," and the latter as "new self."

So Paul's missionary goal was not evangelism only, in the sense of communicating a message for mental assent. Rather, his aim was nothing short of ethical transformation among those who received that message and responded to it by faith. His shorthand for this comes in the striking phrase with which he begins and ends his letter to the Romans – "the obedience of faith for the sake of his [Christ's] name among all the nations" (Rom. 1:5; 16:26; ESV).

"The obedience of faith". It is a remarkable single genitive expression – "faith's obedience" – which unfortunately many translations split apart into two distinct verbs ("to believe and obey"), which allows the possibility that one might adequately do the first while failing to do the second. Paul's point is more radical and actually essentially the same as we find in James 2. It is the obedience that proves the reality of the faith.

> Although we cannot be saved by good works, we also cannot be saved without them. Good works are not the way of salvation, but its proper and necessary evidence. A faith which does not express itself in works is dead.
>
> *John Stott[15]*

Compare it with an expression like "the breath of life". How do you know there is any life in somebody? Check if they're breathing! No breath, no life. No obedience, no faith. Faith without works, as James would say, is as dead as a body without breath. Feel the breath and rejoice that they're alive. See the obedience and rejoice that they're believers.

That is exactly how Paul viewed the practical response of the Corinthian believers in giving money for the needs of Jerusalem believers. It was a proof of genuine faith. The gospel had been truly confessed because the gospel was being sacrificially obeyed (2 Cor. 9:12 – 13).

It is actually striking how many times Paul speaks of *"obeying the gospel"*, not just believing it. In fact such obedience to God was the work of Christ himself, in and through Paul's holistic ministry of words, works and wonders. And the Christians in Rome were themselves among those whose obedience brought him joy (Rom. 15:18 – 19; 16:19).

Conversely, the wrath of God rests not merely on un-*believers* in an intellectual sense, but on dis-*obeyers* – those who "do not obey the gospel of our Lord Jesus" (2 Thess. 1:8). Their double condemnation is the negative mirroring of the gospel's double demand of faith and obedience: "all will be condemned who have *not believed* the truth but have delighted in *wickedness*" (2 Thess. 2:12; italics added).

This understanding of the gospel as intrinsically ethical, a matter of obedience not just belief, is shared by Peter (Acts 5:32; 1 Peter 4:17), James (Jas. 2:14 – 26), John (1 John 2:3; 3:21 – 24; 5:1 – 3), and the writer to the Hebrews (Heb. 5:9), and of course it goes back to Jesus himself (e.g., Matt. 7:21 – 27; 28:20; Luke 11:28; John

---

15. John Stott, *Christ the Controversialist* (London: Tyndale, 1970), 127. Stott would accept, of course, as doubtless Paul would have too, that there are circumstances where a person may turn to Christ in repentance and faith and be saved when no possibility exists for that faith to issue in good works – the penitent thief on the cross being the clearest example. But such an exceptional case does not invalidate the integration of faith and obedience that we see in Ephesians.

14:23 – 24). It would be worth pausing to read all these passages. And when you have finished reading through them, is it still possible to say that the gospel is only a matter of saying a prayer of faith?

Given the clear teaching of Jesus, Paul, and other New Testament authors, how can one account for the Gospel-Ethics dichotomy characterizing much Christianity?

How can it be that in churches around the world the Nicene Creed or its equivalent is recited regularly and repeatedly, while no recurring allusion is made to the Sermon on the Mount, the core of our Lord's teaching? How could men and women be sent into exile, thrown into prison, tortured on the rack, burned at the stake or otherwise subjected to agonizing deaths simply for holding doctrinal opinions at variance with those preferred in the centers of power? How, similarly, could "Christians" be characterized chiefly by insatiable greed for the gold and silver of others, by murder, genocide, and the theft of entire continents in the name of Christ in pursuit of that idolatrous obsession? And how could it be that all this was carried out at the behest and with the hearty blessing of "Christian" leaders? How did it come about that those who identified themselves as Christians could devote such prodigious thought to who Jesus *was* in the Godhead, reverencing him in the Eucharist, and yet give such scarce heed to what he actually *said* they should do? How has it become customary for evangelicals to say "Lord, Lord" and ignore the Lord's will for the everyday lives of his followers (Matt. 7:21)?

Jonathan Bonk[16]

So then, while Paul's whole understanding of the gospel is that salvation is entirely the work of God's grace received only through faith in Christ, not the achievement of our works, he is equally adamant that the whole point of grace being at work in us is to produce the fruit of lives that have been transformed – transformed negatively in renouncing evil and positively in tirelessly doing good (Eph. 2:8 – 10). Paul sees the ethical transformation that the gospel accomplishes as the work of God's grace – grace that is at work since Christ's first coming and grace that shapes us to live ethically in the eschatological light of his second coming (Titus 2:11 – 14).

Paul's emphasis in these matters accords precisely, of course, with what we saw in our earlier chapters on the Old Testament. The saving grace of God's work for Israel (in election and redemption) was to be received within the covenantal framework of grateful obedience and reflected in the response of ethical living.

The gospel that is intrinsically verbal is just as intrinsically ethical. These things are as integral as life and breath.

There is no gospel where there is no change.

The Gospel Is Truth to Be Defended

Good news can also be bad news for those whose vested interests are threatened by it. There is, therefore, a battle to be fought to make sure that the truth of the gospel is preserved, clarified and defended against denials, distortions and betrayals.

---

16. Jonathan Bonk, "The Gospel and Ethics" (a paper given at a meeting of the Lausanne Theology Working Group on "The Whole Gospel"), *Evangelical Review of Theology* 33:1 (2009): 55.

- The fact that the gospel of Christ is for all people, and not just the privilege of one ethnic community, threatens those who stake their claim on belonging to the "right people".
- The fact that the gospel is utterly the gift of God's grace offends those who take pride in their own achievements.
- The fact that the gospel locates the glorious salvation of the living God in the person of one who lived in obscurity and died in excruciating shame is a laughingstock to those who want their salvation to come from a more reputable religious emporium.
- The fact that the gospel summons people to repentance and a radically changed personal and social ethic riles those who want the benefits of the gospel but resist its demands.

So there is a polemical dimension to the gospel. The gospel *confronts* things that contradict it or people who deny or reject it. It exists in explicit contrast and conflict with other worldviews and ultimate commitments that people have. So to be a servant of the gospel necessarily involves costly struggle and spiritual battle (2 Cor. 10:4–5).

Paul experienced this from his earliest missionary days and reflects on it in Galatians, where the phrase "the truth of the gospel" comes twice (Gal. 2:5, 14; cf. 1:6–9). Perceiving that the truth of the gospel was at stake could transform what might seem to us a relatively minor thing (whom you would or would not eat with, as when Peter under pressure went back to eating only with Jews) into the trigger for a major defence and explanation of the meaning of justification by faith, rather than by works of the law. If the truth of the gospel was that in Christ there was neither Jew nor Gentile, but one single family of faith in the Messiah, then to act in a way that erected again the barrier of the law between them, by refusing to eat with Gentiles, was to deny the gospel, not just to offend other believers. Peter needed (not for the first time in his life) to be rebuked.

What Paul took as a mandate for himself (Phil. 1:7), he urged on believers as a challenge for their behaviour as well as their witness (Phil. 1:27). He commended two of the women in Philippi, among his fellow workers there, for having contended at his side for the cause of the gospel (Phil. 4:3) – even if they needed now to be helped to agree with each other. Timothy needed similar encouragement (2 Tim. 1:8). The gospel calls for courageous defence.

The Gospel Is the Power of God Transforming the Universe

Finally, the gospel is the power of God at work in history and creation. For Paul this was something to marvel at and celebrate. The gospel seemed to have a life of its own, such that Paul could personify it as being at work, active, spreading and bearing fruit all over the world (Col. 1:6). The great paradox of the cross—something shameful and absurd to Jew and Greek—was nothing to be ashamed of, for it was the saving power of God (Rom. 1:16) that was transforming history and redeeming creation.

In fact, we could have started our survey of Paul's understanding of the gospel here rather than ending with it. Such is Paul's cosmic grasp of the mind and plan of God that he can hold all things from creation to new creation within the scope of the gospel. And the reason he can do that is, of course, because fundamentally the gospel *is* Christ himself.

Christ is not only the messenger of good news (as per Isa. 52:7); Christ *is* the good news, in the sense that the gospel proclaims that Jesus of Nazareth is the Messiah—king and saviour—in fulfillment of the promises of God in all Scripture since Genesis.

Thus, in what is arguably Paul's most eloquent summary of the identity of Christ *and* the scope of the gospel, he proclaims that all things in the universe have been created by Christ, are being sustained by Christ, and will be reconciled to God by Christ through the blood of his cross. That is the breathtakingly universal scope of the reign of God through Christ. And that, says Paul, is the gospel (Col. 1:15–23—read and relish this great passage again!).

And only after the survey of the cosmic significance of Christ, his church, and his cross does Paul move to the personal reconciliation of believers. The Christians in Colossae could stay firm in their faith and hope (v. 23), because their salvation was bound up within a gospel agenda that was cosmic in scope, spanning all of space and time. No wonder Paul says that it is being proclaimed "in all creation under heaven" (v. 23).[17]

The scope of the gospel's power should be the extent of the gospel's proclamation—it is good news for *all* creation.

SUMMARY

We must leave some practical reflections until our final chapter, but I hope this survey of Paul's understanding of the gospel helps to deepen and enrich your understanding of what it means to say that the mission of God's people is to proclaim the gospel. What is the gospel, then, for Paul?

- It is historical *and* also ecclesial; that is, includes facts of history *about* Christ and the reality of a new humanity *in* Christ.
- It is faith *and* obedience.
- It is a message that must be heard *and* a life that must be seen.

---

17. I think "in all creation" is preferable to "to every creature" as a translation of *en pasei ktisei*.

- It is personal *and* cosmic.
- It is above all "the gospel of God" – the grace of God, the promise of God, the faithfulness of God, the salvation of God, the Son of God, the people of God, and the glory of God.

And in urging us to understand all these dimensions, Paul would direct us continually back to what he knew simply as "the Scriptures" – our Old Testament, for it was "in accordance with the Scriptures" that Jesus died and rose again for our salvation. And it was from there that the New Testament draws the very word "gospel", as we saw earlier in this chapter.

Our whole gospel, then, must be drawn from the deep well of the whole Bible, and our mission must be integrated accordingly around its great resonant narrative of saving grace, its transforming demand for, and promise of, covenantal obedience, and its vibrant hope and vision of a new creation in which righteousness dwells, for God will dwell there with his redeemed humanity from every nation.

One final effect of drawing our understanding of the gospel from the whole Bible is that it generates a more humble and sober assessment of our own missional role as proclaimers of the gospel. We are neither the first nor the only agency of gospel proclamation. So let us neither (at one extreme) neglect our evangelistic responsibility by forgetting the vital importance that God places on the witnessing role of the church as God's people, nor (at the other extreme) inflate

Now who is to be the messenger?

The first and fundamental answer to this question is "God himself". The gospel is God's gospel. He conceived it. He gave it its content. He publishes it. The fact that he has committed to us both "the ministry of reconciliation" and "the message of reconciliation" (1 Cor. 5:18 – 19) does not alter this. He acted "through Christ" to achieve the reconciliation and now acts "through us" to announce it. But he still remains himself both reconciler and preacher.

He has used other and more exalted agencies through whom to publish salvation before partially delegating the work to the church. Apart from Old Testament prophets, the first herald of the gospel was an angel, and the first announcement of it was accompanied by a display of the glory of the Lord and greeted by the worship of the heavenly host.

Next, God sent his Son, who was himself both the messenger and the message. For God sent a "word ... to Israel, preaching good news of peace by Jesus Christ" (Acts 10:36). So Jesus not only "made peace" between God and man, Jew and Gentile, but also "preached peace" (Eph. 2:14 – 17). He went about Palestine announcing the good news of the kingdom.

Next, God sent his Spirit to bear witness to Christ (John 15:26). So the Father himself witnesses to the Son through the Spirit. And only now does he give the church a privileged share in the testimony: "and you also will bear witness" (John 15:27, lit.). It is essential to remember these humbling truths. The chief evangelist is God the Father, and he proclaimed the evangel through his angel, his Son and his Spirit before he entrusted any part of the task to men. This was the order. The church comes at the bottom of the list. And the church's witness will always be subordinate to the Spirit's.

John Stott[18]

our evangelistic egocentricity by imagining that God has no other means of communicating his good news.

RELEVANT QUESTIONS

1. In what ways has this chapter expanded your understanding of the biblical gospel? What difference will that make to the way you express it and share it?
2. Which elements of the gospel, as the word is used by Paul, do you feel are most neglected in today's church? What can you do to bring them back into focus?
3. If the essence of the gospel is "good news", how can it be heard in your community as truly good news?

CHAPTER 12

PEOPLE WHO SEND AND ARE SENT

"Everyone who calls on the name of the Lord will be saved."

How, then, can they call on the one they have not believed in? And how can they believe in the one of whom they have not heard? And how can they hear without someone preaching to them? *And how can anyone preach unless they are sent?* As it is written: "How beautiful are the feet of those who bring good news!" (Rom. 10:13–15; italics added).

This wonderful piece of airtight rhetorical logic is the perfect connector between the previous chapter and this one. In chapter 11 we saw how Isaiah's great vision of a messenger bringing good news of the reign of God–proclaiming peace, goodness and salvation (Isa. 52:7, quoted here by Paul)–flows forward into the New Testament preaching of the gospel of Christ–both in vocabulary and in content. And we argued that an essential part of the mission of God's people is to fulfil the role of that messenger, to be the bearers and the embodiment of the good news. Our mission is to be gospel people.

But in everyday life we don't believe every message or messenger that crosses our path. We want to know where it comes from. We ask for an ID. We try to verify the source of the information. In our media-saturated and media-manipulated age, we are used to hearing "unconfirmed reports", passed on from "unnamed sources close to the government", and we are rightly sceptical. But if someone comes to the microphone as an official spokesperson, authorized to make a statement on behalf of the President or Prime Minister, we trust that whatever he or she says has been approved by, and carries the authority of, the person represented. They have been *sent* to deliver a message on behalf of the one we want to hear and (in an ideal world) would like to trust.

That is the dynamic of Paul's argument here.

People need to be saved (both Jews and Gentiles, as Paul has been arguing hitherto). That is possible only through Jesus Christ. People must therefore call on him for salvation, as God had already promised Israel (significantly "the Lord" of Paul's quotation from Joel 2:32 was YHWH, but now clearly means Jesus). But to call on him, they must believe in him. And to believe in him, they must hear him. (That's actually what Paul says, not just "hear of or about him", but "hear *him*"). And how can they hear Christ? Through someone who "heralds" on his behalf. But a herald has to be authorized and sent by the one whose message he bears – that is, Christ himself. Thus, as Paul concludes, saving faith comes through hearing, and what is heard is actually "the word of Christ" (v. 17).

So Christ is there at both ends of the process. He is *the object* of saving faith – the one on whom we must call for salvation. But he is also *the subject*, who sends the authorized messengers with the good news by which we can be saved. Christ's sending is the first link in the chain of Christ's saving.

Paul's meaning is that when any nation is favoured with the preaching of the Gospel, it is a pledge and proof of divine love. There is no preacher of the Gospel who has not been raised up by God in His special providence. It is certain, therefore, that God [i.e., God himself, not just the preacher] visits that nation in which the Gospel is proclaimed. . . . The Gospel does not fall from the clouds like rain, by accident, but is brought by the hands of men to where God has sent it.

John Calvin[1]

The whole work of salvation is from God from beginning to end, and it includes God's purposeful sending of messengers with the good news that salvation is available through Christ. The emphasis of the final verb, "unless they are sent", is on the intentionality of God in this. People do not get saved by accident or at random, but by a process that begins with the authorizing, commissioning, sending action of the saving God.

Paul's quotation of Isaiah 52:7 here should not be seen as merely a conveniently vivid image thrown in to illustrate a point already made. It is a deliberate climax to his argument. Paul's point is this: the fact that people are now being "sent" to "preach" so that others may "hear", "believe", "call" and "be saved" is in itself a fulfillment of precisely this prophetic Scripture that was already regarded as messianic in his day.

Something that fulfills Scripture is de facto authorized by the God of the Scriptures. Sending and preaching, therefore, are activities that have God's approval and biblical warrant. They are, to coin a phrase, part of the story, written into it by the author of the story. The mission of God requires the realities of sending and being sent as part of the mission of God's people.

What, then, is the nature of sending and being sent? Once again, in order to do our biblical theology for life thoroughly, we must start with some significant use of "sending" language in the Old Testament before returning to the New. There is actually a rather rich seam of biblical theology around the concept of "sending" in the whole Bible for us to mine in relation to the mission of God's people.

OLD TESTAMENT SENDINGS

The Hebrew verb *šalah* means to send, and it is used with as broad a range of ordinary meanings as the English word. All kinds of people and things are sent for

---

1. John Calvin, *The Epistles of Paul the Apostle to the Romans and to the Thessalonians* (trans. Ross Mackenzie; Grand Rapids: Eerdmans, and Carlisle: Paternoster, 1960), 231.

all kinds of reasons. But what we are looking for in particular are cases where *God* sends, and where there is a clear theological dimension to the action, its purpose and its results. We are seeking to discern where God sends human beings as agents of his mission in the world, and what range of things he sends people to do.

Broadly speaking, having surveyed the range of Old Testament texts that refer to God sending, it seems to me that two main objectives stand out. When God sends people, it is most often either to act as agents of his deliverance and salvation, or to declare a message that somebody needs to hear (whether they want to or not). Sometimes God sends somebody like Moses to do both.

In other words, God's sending is closely connected to two of the great actions of God in and for Old Testament Israel – salvation and revelation. And, to put it bluntly, it is only because God *sent* deliverers of his people and because God *sent* speakers of his Word that we have the Scriptures at all, including their story of God's salvation and their communication of God's revelation. If God were not a sending God, the Bible would be a very different book indeed.

Let's look at a few famous examples.

Sent to Save
Joseph
The first significant description of a person being sent by God is found in the mouth of Joseph in Genesis 45. It comes at the jaw-dropping moment when he discloses his identity to his brothers, who had sold him into slavery in Egypt years before and probably assumed he was long dead.

> Then Joseph said to his brothers, "Come close to me." When they had done so, he said, "I am your brother Joseph, the one you sold into Egypt! And now, do not be distressed and do not be angry with yourselves for selling me here, because it was to save lives that **God** *sent me* ahead of you. For two years now there has been famine in the land, and for the next five years there will be no plowing and reaping. But **God** *sent me* ahead of you to preserve for you a remnant on earth and to save your lives by a great deliverance.
>
> So then, it was *not you who sent me here, but* **God**." (Gen. 45:4 – 8; italics and bold added; cf. Ps. 105:17)

The triple repetition of "*God* sent" emphatically expresses the same theology that brings the book of Genesis to a close, once more in the mouth of Joseph, namely, the sovereignty of God overruling and working through the actions (including evil actions) of men and women (Gen. 50:20). But equally emphatic is the express purpose of this sending – "to save lives" ("saving of many lives"; 50:20).

God sends because God saves.

What makes this interesting also is that a set of circumstances in which a person is entirely the passive victim of *other people's* wicked actions can be described as "God sending". Joseph was hardly a volunteer missionary. Yet he interpreted his remarkable life's journey as divine sending, in retrospect. The same perspective occurs at the other end of Israel's story when the Israelites were carried off into exile by Nebuchadnezzar's army, wreaking its vicious hatred on Jerusalem and its rebel citizens.

But how does God interpret that? The exiles, says God, are those whom *God* carried into exile (Jer. 29:4, 7, 14), indeed, those whom God had *sent* there (Jer. 29:20). Granted the exile was a sending under judgment, but it was also a sending that could lead to a surprising mission for the welfare of the city of Babylon (Jer. 29:7; see ch. 13 below). A similar reflection applies to the early believers in Jerusalem. It was by being scattered under persecution that God effectively "sent" them beyond the boundaries of Judea and Judaism.

Moses

With considerable irony, the biblical narrative that has shown us Joseph sent by God to save his brothers by getting them *down into* Egypt goes on to show us Moses, sent by God to save his people by getting them *up out of* Egypt. Joseph saved his people from death by famine. Moses saved them from death by genocide.

The event that in 587 B.C. took place in Jerusalem—the defeat and captivity of its people, the destruction of the city and ultimately of the temple too—from the standpoint of world history was little more than the so ordinary fate of many other small centers of government as they were subsumed under the authority of greater powers. But in actual fact it was something quite different, for through Israel the King of kings was preparing the way by which his people would be more than conquerors and the world come to share in this victory.

Richard R. De Ridder [2]

On this occasion there is nothing passive or only retrospective about the sending of Moses. It is entirely upfront from the start, uncomfortably so for Moses, who in classic missionary funk begged God to send somebody else instead (Ex. 4:13). The language of sending permeates the narrative of Exodus 3 and is linked at one end to God's compassion and at the other end to God's identity as the covenant-keeping God. Read Exodus 3:10–15 and take note of the number of times the verb "send" occurs and the reasons given for it.

God sends because God saves because God promised.

This was a commission that Moses relied upon (Ex. 7:16), though early on he questioned its effectiveness (5:22). Part of Moses' legendary humility and self-defence lay in acknowledging that all he had said and done was the result of God's sending, not his own claims (Num. 16:28). In fact, Moses could eliminate himself from the narrative altogether and attribute the great exodus deliverance to God's having sent an angel (Num. 20:16)—which was probably not how Miriam would have described her kid brother. Old and New Testament texts agree that Moses was

2. Richard R. De Ridder, *Discipling the Nations* (Grand Rapids: Baker, 1971), 77.

no self-appointed leader, or elected champion, or fortuitously available super-hero. Moses was sent by God. And he was sent to accomplish God's salvation.[3] What Moses did, therefore, God did. That is of the essence of the sending relationship.

Judges

The judges were also men and women who acted to bring God's deliverance to Israel. The more common language in that book is that "the LORD *raised up* judges" (Judg. 2:16), but the purpose is the same – "to save". Thus, in the formulaic description of Othniel, the first judge, he is "raised up", he "saved" the Israelites from oppression, and he was empowered by the Spirit of YHWH – another feature of divine sending that we will notice later.

However, the language of sending is used of Gideon, with a purpose (deliverance) and a promise ("I will be with you") that strongly echo the sending of Moses (Judg. 6:14).

A Saviour to Come

Getting the Israelites out of Egypt was the work of a saviour – Moses. But what if the Egyptians themselves were to turn to God and cry out under the afflictions of his judgment? In one of the most breathtaking eschatological visions in the Bible, Isaiah envisages exactly that – a day when Egypt (doubtless standing as representative of all nations) will turn to God. At that time, in the midst of a text that is loaded with reminders of the exodus – only with the Egyptians as the ones in need of deliverance – God promises:

> When they [the Egyptians] cry out to the LORD because of their oppressors, *he will send them a savior and defender,* and he will rescue them. So the LORD will make himself known to the Egyptians, and in that day they will acknowledge the LORD. (Isa. 19:20–21; italics added)

The savior foreseen here, of course, is none other than the Lord Jesus Christ, the one whom God sent to seek and to save the lost.

Sent to Speak

Messengers, by their very nature, are sent. And messengers speak on behalf of the one who sends them. In the ancient world, without the mass media we take for granted, the normal means of disseminating a message was by oral proclamation. The role of heralds and ambassadors was of great social and political importance. It is within this cultural context that the prophets of Israel functioned, and they claimed to *speak for* YHWH because they had been *sent by* YHWH, with his authority.

---

3. See Josh. 24:5; 1 Sam. 12:8; Ps. 105:26; Isa. 63:12; Acts 7:35.

Moses

Though, as we have seen, God's major purpose in sending Moses was for the deliverance of his people, he was also sent with the task of communicating God's revelation — a task for which he felt ill-equipped and needed God's reassurance as well as Aaron's assistance (Ex. 4:10 – 17). So Moses was also a prophet. Indeed he was the model prophet. God promised that in the generations after Moses' death, God would raise up "a prophet like Moses", who would carry God's authority and speak God's words (Deut. 18:17 – 20). At one level, this is a generic singular (like "the king", or "the widow"), referring to the whole line of prophets who would bring God's word to Israel. But it was also understood as a prophecy that was fulfilled fully in Jesus, the one who, like Moses, was the agent of both God's salvation and revelation (Acts 7:37 – which reads "send" for "raise up").

Isaiah

Many a missionary sermon has been preached on Isaiah's famous words, "Here am I. Send me." Many a missionary traces their calling to the moment they echoed those words before the Lord. However, I think we get the scene of Isaiah's call and sending rather out of perspective if we put Isaiah himself centre stage, as if he were the main focus of attention, the heroic missionary volunteer.

No, the whole portrayal in Isaiah 6:1 – 7 up to this moment has been of the overwhelming, towering altitude of the throne of God. Isaiah has gone to worship in the temple when he is awesomely confronted with the reality of the God of Israel and his transcendent holiness. That strikes him down in terrified consciousness of his own sin. Isaiah 6:5 is a remarkable confession, since it follows the chapters in which Isaiah has roasted the people around him for their sins. Now in a burst of intense self-consciousness he recognizes that he is no better than those he has condemned. The humility of that moment and the cleansing of his mouth that follows it (vv. 6 – 7) are vital constituents in his sending.

It is from that posture that Isaiah then overhears what is going on around the throne of God. For this is the command and control centre of the universe. This is the seat of government of human history, and the government is at work. There is a world to run, strategies to be planned, decisions being made, and messages to be sent. This is God in control, God at the centre, God on mission, God getting on with God's business. And in the midst of it Isaiah hears a question, "Right. Who will deliver this one? Whom shall we send on this mission?" And Isaiah raises a hand off the floor from the outer edges of the scene, "Excuse me … Yes over here … I'm available, you could send me if you like.…"

Isaiah is not the centre of the picture; God's throne still is.

What is happening here is a recentering of Isaiah's life and ministry to God, God's agenda and God's Word — which the rest of his book will show to be mysterious and paradoxical, but ultimately embracing not only his own generation but all future ones, and not only Israel but the whole world. But for Isaiah himself, the experience has been one of being awesomely confronted with God's reality, then terrifyingly conscious of his own sin, and then radically recentered on God's mission.

Only then, as a humbled, cleansed, recentered sinner, is he ready to be sent. Only then does God say, "Go. . . ."

Jeremiah

Jeremiah also felt the touch of God on his mouth, but in his case not to cleanse it but to fill it with the words of God himself (Jer. 1:9). If Isaiah needed God's touch because he felt his own sinfulness, Jeremiah needs it because he feels his own youthful inadequacy. God's explanation of the gesture quotes exactly from what he promised to Moses, "I have put my words in your mouth" (cf. Deut. 18:18), indicating that Jeremiah stands in that authentic line of prophets whom God would raise up.

It also indicates clearly the nature of the inspiration of Scripture. The words Jeremiah spoke are his own words – hammered out in his own heart (and bones) – and distinct from the words of an Amos or an Ezekiel. But at a deeper level, they are the words of God. That, of course, is the essence of being a spokesperson or herald. The words of the herald are assumed to be the words of his king. That's what he has been sent for.

Jeremiah uses the language of God's sending more than any other prophet, perhaps because the moment of his commissioning is so frighteningly open-ended. God says to him (literally): "To whomever (or wherever) I send you, you shall go; and whatever I command you, you shall speak" (Jer. 1:7). So his mission and his message will alike be unlimited. He will have no free choice of audience and no free choice of message. And as it turns out, God sends him to places in which he faces hostility and danger and gives him words that are interpreted as rank treason by the government and blasphemy by the religious authorities. It was a lonely, dangerous, desolate sending that was Jeremiah's. Sometimes it was the only thing he could appeal to in order to save his own life (Jer. 26:15).

Any missional hermeneutic of the book of Jeremiah needs to pay attention to the missional cost to the messenger.

Jeremiah was surrounded by false prophets. Of course, that is a term we can now apply retrospectively. The reality on the ground must have been confusing. Someone like Hananiah did not wear a lapel-badge reading, *"Hananiah: False Prophet"*. Yet Jeremiah knew, and ruthlessly condemned the fact that many were speaking in the name of YHWH who had never stood in his presence or been sent by YHWH (Jer. 14:15; 23:21; 28:9, 15; 29:9). Such was a serious crime worthy of death according to Deuteronomy 13:1 – 5, which Hananiah's signal death illustrated (Jer. 28:15 – 17).

Even more troubling than the false prophets, unsent by God, to whom the people did listen, was the long line of true prophets, sent by God, to whom the people refused to listen. This bothered Jeremiah greatly (Jer. 7:25–26; 25:4; 26:5; 35:15). It bothered Jesus even more. In fact, Jesus turned it into a parable portraying the whole history of Israel as their rejection of all those servants/prophets whom God had sent—climaxing of course in their anticipated rejection of himself, God's own Son (Mark 12:1–12).

The lesson of Jesus, Jeremiah, and most of the prophets, then, is clearly that the mere fact of being sent by God is no guarantee of popular acceptance or apparent success for the human messenger who gets sent. They can usually expect the opposite (Jer. 1:17–19; Ezek. 2:3–6; 3:4–9). And yet, although there is great grief and anger (human and divine) in response to that, there is no ultimate despair.

For in the end, what God sends will achieve God's purpose. For it is *God, not the messenger*, who is in control of outcomes. That great hope is grounded in two other things that the Old Testament refers to as being sent by God—God's Spirit and God's Word.

Spirit and Word

The Spirit of YHWH has a major role in the Old Testament—much more than many people imagine, especially those whose mental connection between the Holy Spirit and mission is governed entirely by the day of Pentecost and the book of Acts. We have been looking at people whom God sent in relation to his work of salvation and of revelation. The Spirit is explicitly connected to both.[4]

Only once in the Old Testament, however, is God said to "send" his Spirit, and that is in relation to the life-giving power of God within the whole created order (Ps. 104:30). Ezekiel comes close to that language when he is told to prophesy to the breath/spirit of God to bring resurrection life to God's people. It is Jesus, specifically the risen Jesus, who commands the Spirit, breathes the Spirit, and sends the Spirit to empower his disciples for mission (Luke 24:49; John 20:21–22; Acts 1:8).

Missionaries come and missionaries go, and they may or may not achieve what they were sent for. The Word of God, however, which is sent by God through those whom he commissions to speak it, has no such uncertainty.

God's word is the perfect missionary, bearing fruit entirely as God plans. Here is God's purposeful sending, accomplishing God's ultimate desire.

> As the rain and the snow
>   come down from heaven,
> and do not return to it
>   without watering the earth

---

4. For a broad survey of the role of the Spirit of God in the Old Testament, see Wright, *Knowing the Holy Spirit Through the Old Testament*.

and making it bud and flourish,
    so that it yields seed for the sower and bread for the eater,
so is *my word* that goes out from my mouth:
    It will not return to me empty,
but will accomplish what I desire
    and achieve *the purpose for which I sent it* (Isa. 55:10–11; italics added)

So the Old Testament segment of our journey of biblical theology on the theme of "sending" has given us three main things to consider.

Sending for Salvation and Revelation

First, God can send anybody on a mission, but most frequently it is to be an agent of his deliverance, or to be the mouthpiece for his message, or both. God's sending is an integral part of God's saving and God's speaking – of God's salvation and God's revelation.

Now since we know that the mission of God is ultimately the redemption of his whole creation and the extension of the knowledge of his glory to the ends of the earth, the fact that God chooses human agents to send and to use in accomplishing that mission is of great significance. The mission of God's people must include providing a reservoir of those whom God can send in support of that overarching objective. To belong to God's people is, therefore, at the very least to be available to be sent.

Sending with Authority

Second, the person who is sent embodies the presence and authority of the person who sends. This was true even of ordinary human sending. To treat messengers with respect or with humiliation was effectively to honour or shame the person who sent them. The way you responded to messengers was taken as your response to their sender and treated accordingly (1 Sam. 25:39–41; contrast 2 Sam. 10:1–5).

Similarly, then, to reject the authority of Moses (Num. 12:8), or the ministry of Samuel (1 Sam. 8:7), was to reject the Lord himself. Jesus affirmed the same thing about how people responded to himself as the one sent by his Father (John 5:23), and about how people would respond to his disciples as the ones sent by Jesus (Matt. 10:40–41; John 13:16, 20; 15:18–21).

Sending and Suffering

Third, being chosen by God to be sent may seem to carry great honour and responsibility, but the more pressing reality was that it normally also involved suffering, rejection, persecution and sometimes death. God's mission *involved* a host of sent-ones, deliverers and messengers, but ultimately the accomplishment of God's mission did not *depend* on such human agents, but on the sovereign power of God himself, though his Spirit and his Word.

The only exception to that last sentence was the one who actually embodied all three of the above points—the Servant of the Lord. For he certainly is portrayed as the agent of God's salvation and revelation; he embodies the presence and authority of God himself; and he suffers rejection, violence and death. But above all, he *will* accomplish the mission of God and be exalted for so doing (Isa. 42:1, 4; 53:10).

From there, it is but a short step to the New Testament.

THE SENDING GOD

Sending, in fact, is an activity of all three Persons of the Trinity. There is a missional dynamic within God himself in relation to the world. And in line with what we have seen in the Old Testament, it relates primarily to salvation and revelation.

The Father as Sender: Of the Son and the Spirit

Jesus did not just arrive; he was sent. It is one of the most noticeable dimensions of his self-consciousness—the driving awareness that he had been sent by his Father to do his will. It is certainly one of the dominant motifs in John's presentation of Jesus. Approximately forty times in John's gospel we read about Jesus being sent—whether from the evangelist or from Jesus' own lips (e.g., John 3:17, 34: 4:34; chs. 5–8 passim; 11:42; 17:18; cf. also 1 John 4:9, 14). Indeed, coming to believe that Jesus is the one whom God sent is part of John's express purpose for his readers, for in believing that, they will come to salvation and eternal life.

The Synoptics use the word less, but it is not absent (e.g., Matt. 15:24; Luke 4:18, 43 = Mark 1:38; and cf. Acts 3:20 for the expectation that God would send Jesus back as reigning Messiah). Paul joins the chorus of conviction that the coming of the Messiah Jesus was no accident, but the well-timed sending of the Son by the Father (Rom. 8:3; Gal. 4:4). And the writer to the Hebrews could even speak of Jesus as "our apostle" (Heb. 3:1), emphasizing that he was sent and appointed by God like Moses, only greater.

Since God sends his Spirit in the Old Testament, it is not surprising that God the Father is said to do the same in the New (John 14:16, 26; 15:26), or that Jesus will do it according to the Father's promise (Luke 24:49).

The Son as Sender: Of the Spirit and the Apostles

Jesus sends the Spirit with specific missional tasks related to salvation and revelation (John 15:26; 16:7–15; 20:22–23).

And Jesus also, of course, sends his disciples. He sent them twice on missions during his earthly lifetime, and then, after his resurrection, in the various forms of the Great Commission. Noticeably, it is John who records that Jesus models his sending of the disciples on his own sending by the Father – something he has emphasized so repeatedly throughout the gospel (John 20:21).

The Holy Spirit as Sender: Of Jesus and the Apostles

The Holy Spirit is involved in the sending of Jesus. It is never quite expressed in the form that the Spirit "sent" Jesus, but certainly Jesus is sent with, or in the power of, the Spirit. His mission is precisely one that is laid on him by the anointing of the Spirit (Luke 4:18 – 19), and Luke stresses at several points that all Jesus did was by the filling or leading of the Spirit. He further records Peter as telling the same thing to Cornelius (Acts 10:38). Paul sees the instrumentality of the Spirit in the resurrection of Jesus (Rom. 1:4), while Hebrews connects "the eternal Spirit" with Christ's self-offering in sacrificial death (Heb. 5:14).

Moreover, the Holy Spirit, along with Jesus, is the sender of the apostles. It was the Holy Spirit who expressly chose and named the first missionaries from Antioch and sent them on their way (Acts 13:1 – 4). And it was the Holy Spirit who guided their journeys, sometimes by prevention as much as direction (Acts 16:6 – 7).

There is, therefore, a marvelous interlocking network of sending in the New Testament presentation of God's involvement in the mission of Jesus and the church. God the Son is sent by God the Father and God the Spirit. God the Spirit is sent by God the Son and God the Father. The apostles are sent by God the Son and God the Spirit. Only God the Father is the unsent sender. He sends the Son and the Spirit, but he himself is never "sent".

The mission of God's people, then, is not some external structure built by the church itself – a program or a strategy devised by an institution. Sending in mission is a participation in the life of God. The mission of God's people, in this dimension of sending and being sent, is to be caught up within the dynamic sending and being sent that God the Holy Trinity has done and continues to do for the salvation of the world and the revelation of his truth.

APOSTLES

The Twelve

The very word "apostles" means "sent ones". Two Greek words could be used for sending, *pempo*, and *apostello*, and both are found in the New Testament, with little difference. However, when applied to the original twelve disciples whom Jesus called to himself, the noun form, *apostolos*, did acquire special significance in relation to that group (even though, as we will see in a moment, it could be used more loosely as well).

Being sent was of the essence of apostleship, though the sending was conceived more as commissioning or authorizing for a task than as *necessarily* involving geographical travel. The disciples were apostles in Jerusalem itself before some of them engaged in itinerant ministry. And some of those who became itinerant preachers (like Philip) were not necessarily apostles.

The First Disciples

The gospel accounts of the calling of the original twelve are revealing and worth pausing to read in full for what they say about Jesus' intentions in this decisive action (Matt. 10:1–2, 5; Mark 3:13–15; Luke 6:12–13).

Matthew 10 shows clearly that the ministry of the apostles is a continuation of the work of Jesus himself. Their message is an exact repeat of the words of John the Baptist and Jesus—"the kingdom of heaven is near" (7). Their healing ministry is also a continuation of the miraculous healings that Jesus had already performed. They were to heal the sick, raise the dead, cleanse those with leprosy and drive out demons.... Jesus is preparing the ground for the post-ascension period of history when his task of mission will be entrusted to his followers. That mission will be at *his* command, under *his* authority, but he will pass on to his disciples the baton of active responsibility.

Martin Goldsmith[5]

What do we learn? Jesus chose twelve. The number is undoubtedly significant, reflecting the twelve tribes of Israel. These apostles will be the nucleus of Israel in the Messiah, embodying the role and the mission of Israel that we have seen throughout this book.

They were disciples who became apostles, but they remained disciples (as they are still referred to in Matt. 28 at the moment of the Great Commission). That is, it was only as humble followers of, and learners from, Jesus their Lord and Master that they were to function as apostles.

They were chosen and called by Jesus, not self-appointed or elected by the rest of the disciples (of whom, in a general sense, we know there were many). Whatever their authority and function and ministry may be, it derives from Christ alone.

They were to "*be with him*". That is, they would simply spend time with Jesus, learning from him, being trained by him, understanding his identity and mission, bearing the cost of radical discipleship, witnessing his life and teaching, his death and above all his resurrection. This in itself made this group of twelve unique, so much so that when Judas dropped out, the criteria they set for whoever should replace him included the same elements—he had to have been a witness of Jesus from the days of John the Baptist to the resurrection (Acts 1:21–22).

They were authoritatively *to replicate and extend the ministry of Jesus himself.* He sent them out. He gave them authority. And with that authority they were to do as he was doing—preaching the good news of the kingdom of God, driving out demons and healing the sick. What the apostles said and did, Jesus was saying and doing through them.

Matthew prefaces his account of the sending out of the Twelve with a summary account of all that *Jesus* was doing (Matt. 9:35–36), before telling the disciples to

5. Martin Goldsmith, *Matthew and Mission: The Gospel through Jewish Eyes* (Carlisle: Paternoster, 2001), 92–93.

pray that God would send out workers, and then commissioning them to be the answer to their own prayer by doing exactly the same things as Jesus did. That is why Luke can describe his first volume as an account of "all that Jesus began to do and to teach", the implication being that the second volume, what we call the Acts of the Apostles, was what *Jesus* continued to do and to teach through these authorized agents.

The Apostle Paul

With the exception of being a companion of Jesus before the crucifixion, all the above points are highlighted by the calling and sending of Saul of Tarsus as the apostle Paul. He was granted a special encounter with the risen Christ and could describe himself as a witness of the resurrection. He knew that he had been sent by Christ into the mission that occupied the rest of his life. And he claimed, without boasting, that his authority to preach the gospel, confirmed with works of power, healing and driving out demons, came from Christ alone (see Acts 22:14 – 21; 26:15 – 18; Rom. 1:1; Gal. 1:1, 15 – 16 – interestingly, Paul places his calling before his birth, like Jeremiah).

Paul also reflects the other apostles in the early chapters of Acts in his single-minded commitment to preaching the gospel (with accompanying "works and wonders"). He counted his life worth nothing apart from being able to "complete the task the Lord Jesus has given me – the task of testifying to the good news of God's grace" (Acts 20:24). His "priestly duty" was "proclaiming the gospel of God" (Rom. 15:16 – 21).

Paul's whole life, in other words, was dedicated to being a living fulfillment of Isaiah 52:7, in being a messenger of the good news of the kingdom of God to the nations (Acts 20:25). That's what it meant to be an apostle, on a par with Peter and the others (Gal. 2:8 – 10).

Apostolic Priorities

We find the same emphasis on the crucial importance of communicating the message in early Acts. The apostles could not help speaking about what they had seen and heard (Acts 4:20), and their determination to preach the gospel survived prohibitions and threats (4:18, 21), imprisonment (5:17 – 42), martyrdom and persecution (6:8 – 8:4). There is no doubt that the task of proclaiming the message of the gospel of Jesus Christ was the persistently top priority for the apostles, though that did not exclude other key tasks that were integral to the gospel, as we will see in a moment.

This apostolic priority of preaching also survived the growing complexity of the Jesus movement and its need for practical and logistical organization. Acts 6:1 – 7 is well-known as the moment when the apostles preserved their own prime responsibility of bearing witness to Christ through preaching the word from being swallowed up in the tasks of social care and the tensions of ethnic discrimination that were surfacing as the community grew.

The apostles' response shows great wisdom in recognizing the priority of what *they* as apostles had been called and sent by Christ to do, while ensuring that other necessary tasks were entrusted to godly and competent people. The relevance of this passage for mission, however, needs careful handling.

It is surely deliberate that the work of the Twelve and the work of the Seven are alike called *diakonia* (1, 4), "ministry" or "service". The former is "ministry of the word" (4) or pastoral work, the latter "the ministry of tables" (2) or social work. Neither ministry is superior to the other. On the contrary, both are Christian ministries, that is, ways of serving God and his people. Both require spiritual people, "full of the Spirit", to exercise them. And both can be full-time Christian ministries. The only difference between them lies in the form the ministry takes, requiring different gifts and different callings.

John Stott[6]

The words of the apostles in Acts 6:2 can be easily misused. "So the Twelve gathered all the disciples together and said, 'It would not be right for us to neglect [the ministry of] the word of God in order to wait on tables.'" It can be made to sound as if the apostles regarded the task of serving food at tables to widows as something beneath them. The TNIV gives this impression by inserting "the ministry of" (which is not in the Greek) in front of "the word of God", by obscuring the fact that what was happening at the tables was *also* "serving/ministering", and by translating the verb *diakonein* (which is in the Greek) merely as "to wait on". The impression, then, is that it is much more important to be a preacher ("minister") than a waiter.

However, the serving or ministering term (*diakonia, diakonein*) is used *both* for what was being done in the provision of food for the needy (in Acts 6:2) *and* for the preaching of the word ("ministry of the word" in v. 4). They were *both* ministries of the church, and they were *both* important enough to need to be done by people filled with the Holy Spirit (v. 3). The apostles' point was simply that distribution of food to the needy was not what *they, the Twelve,* had been primarily called and sent to do (even if it had been part of their training with Jesus). It must be done, however, and it must be done by people selected and appointed for that ministry.

So it is a distortion of this text to use it to suggest that the preaching of the Word has primacy and priority *for the church as a whole in its mission,* as over against all forms of social or compassionate service for the needy. Luke is careful to distinguish "the Twelve" from "all the disciples" in verse 2, and to record that they said, "it would not be right *for us*", which means that they were talking about the fundamental ministry priority *for themselves as Christ's commissioned apostles,* not what was an overriding priority for the whole body of disciples.

Luke has already made it clear that the social and economic concern of the church for the needy was itself connected to the teaching of the apostles, and that the rapid growth of the church was the result of *both* the teaching and evange-

6. John Stott, *The Message of Acts* (The Bible Speaks Today; Leicester: IVP. and Downers Grove, IL: IVP, 1990), 122. See also John Stott, *The Living Church: Convictions of a Lifelong Pastor* (Nottingham, IVP, and Downers Grove. IL: IVP, 2007), ch. 4, "Ministry: The Twelve and the Seven".

lism of the apostles *and* the quality of love and care within the community of Jesus-followers (Acts 2:42–47; 4:32–35).

Furthermore, while the ministry of the Word continued to be the urgent priority for the apostles, the "ministry at tables" became the priority for those appointed to that task as *their* ministry. However, we can also see that such priorities were not mutually exclusive. Those who ministered at tables could also preach and evangelize (like Stephen and Philip). And those who were apostles could also carry relief to the needy (Acts 11:27–29; cf. Paul's important collection for the poor in Jerusalem, Rom. 15:25–33; 1 Cor. 16:1–4; 2 Cor. 8–9). Indeed, remembering the poor was a criterion of acceptance into the fellowship of the apostles (Gal. 2:9–10).

It is remarkable, actually, how little attention is given to Paul's collection for the poor in Jerusalem in standard works on Paul's theology or his mission. Yet it occupied years of his life, and he refers to it in three of his largest letters, giving two whole chapters to it in 2 Corinthians. Jason Hood, who speaks of "Paul's great passion for the poor", points out that "Paul's collection and other teaching on possessions and generosity occupy more space in his letters than his teaching on justification by faith. Yet Pauline scholars and contemporary church leaders often fail to give the collection the attention it deserves."

> For Paul, care for the poor cannot be pitted against "gospel ministry". The return to Judea to deliver the collection takes priority over Paul's visit to Rome. As he explains to the Romans (Rom. 15), this visit was to be the great launch of gospel ministry in the western half of the Empire all the way to Spain. We do not know if Paul achieved this mission, but we do know that he delivered the collection. *The collection was so vital that its delivery was at that moment a more urgent matter for Paul than his desire to evangelize and plant churches on the missionary frontier.*
>
> Jason Hood[7]

Hood goes on to make a point that should be noted by those who allege that the only legitimate priority for the apostles (and their evangelistic successors) was proclamation and church planting. At the end of Romans, Paul *postpones* his plan to engage in such ministry in the western Mediterranean in order to give priority at that moment to the delivery of the collection to the poor in Jerusalem. Far from regarding this as an interruption or neglect of "gospel ministry", Paul actually saw it as a crucial demonstration of the gospel at work.

Apostles: The Others

So there were twelve apostles. Or were there?

Undoubtedly the original Twelve had a unique status and role within the early church. They were the source of authoritative witness to the life, death and resurrection of Jesus, and so it was vital that their voice, and later the writings of some of them, should be heard and should be decisive. They played a foundational role in the Jerusalem church, being frequently mentioned by Luke as the leaders there, even when persecution scattered many believers elsewhere and even as the mission-

---

7. Jason Hood, "Theology in Action: Paul and Christian Social Care", *Transforming the World: The Gospel and Social Responsibility* (eds. Jamie A. Grant and Dewi A. Hughes, Nottingham: Apollos, 2009), 129–46. Quotation taken from p. 134; italics original.

ary movement got underway from other centres like Antioch (Acts 5:27–32; 8:1, 14; 9:27; 11:1; 15:1–6, 22; 16:4).

But then we hear about quite a number of other people who are also described as "apostles" in the more general sense of people who were sent to do various tasks. Here is a list of places where apostles are mentioned who were not among the original, authoritative Twelve-plus-Paul.

1 Cor. 15:7	Paul says that Jesus appeared to "all the apostles" after his resurrection. But he has just listed Peter and the Twelve in verse 5, so this would seem to refer to a wider group of people with some kind of apostolic ministry.
Acts 14:14	Barnabas is called an apostle along with Paul, probably in the sense of a commissioned "missionary". Barnabas, though an important figure in the early church, was not among the Twelve. But he was appointed, commissioned and sent by the church at Antioch.
2 Cor. 8:23	Paul has been describing the role of Titus as his own trusted representative in the matter of administering the financial gift that the churches in Greece were making to the church in Jerusalem (8:16–24). But there were others who accompanied Titus, whom Paul describes literally as "apostles of the churches", which is usually translated "representatives" or "messengers". They also have Paul's approval as "an honor to Christ".
Phil. 2:25	Paul speaks warmly of Epaphroditus as "my brother, co-worker and fellow soldier, who is also your messenger [lit., *your apostle*], whom you sent to take care of my needs." This is almost identical to the role of Titus. Epaphroditus had been sent by the church at Philippi, as their representative and messenger, with financial support for Paul's missionary work.
Rom. 16:7	Andronicus and Junia, probably a husband and wife, are greeted by Paul as "outstanding among the apostles". This almost certainly means that he saw them as outstanding apostles themselves, rather than that they were regarded as outstanding by the apostles (or merely "well-known to the apostles", ESV). We are not told what their apostleship involved, but they may have had an itinerant evangelistic or church teaching function, similar to Priscilla and Aquila, who had served "all the churches of the Gentiles" (16:3–4). Perhaps Philologus and Julia (v. 15) were another such husband and wife team, but we don't know.
1 Cor. 12:28–29; Eph 4:11	Paul includes apostles along with prophets, pastors, teachers, evangelists, healers, administrators, etc. in the ministry gifts that God has given to his church. Perhaps he is referring to the unique and nonreplaceable status of the Twelve, the foundation pillars of the church. But in view of the breadth and plurality and diversity of the other ministries, he may well be referring to the wider apostolic (missionary) role, especially in planting and nurturing churches in the first place.

MARKS OF MISSION SENDING AND SUPPORTING CHURCHES

The New Testament tells us not only about individuals like those above – individuals who traveled in all directions on various missions. It also gives us several examples of churches that were remarkable in mission. There was of course the "mother church" in *Jerusalem*, where the power of the apostles' preaching combined with the spiritual fellowship, social community and economic compassion of the first believers led to such remarkable growth. But Jerusalem did not remain the only centre for the spread of the church.

Antioch becomes the hub for mission to the north and west. And the foundation for that missionary expansion is equally clear: it was a church that was *well-mixed* ethnically (and so already open to the international vision and power of the gospel), *well-taught* by Paul and Barnabas (and so understanding the "whole counsel of God" such as Paul would later teach the church in Ephesus), and *well-led* by people who were themselves open to the Holy Spirit and exercising gifts of prophecy, teaching and discernment (Acts 11:19 – 26; 13:1 – 3).

Then the church in *Philippi*, the first foothold of the gospel in Europe, becomes the support centre for Paul's missionary work further south. Paul speaks warmly also of the radiating message of the gospel that was going out from the nearby church in Thessalonica (1 Thess. 1:7 – 8), but only the Philippian Christians, he says, had entered into partnership (*koinonia*) in the gospel with him by sending financial support again and again. The letter to the Philippians we have in our Bible is essentially a "thank you" letter and receipt for one such generous gift at the hands of their "apostle", Epaphroditus (Phil. 4:14 – 20).

Third John – Double Faithfulness

There is, however, another rather neglected example of a mission sending and supporting church, tucked in at the end of the Bible – the community to whom the letter of 3 John was addressed.

Most probably this was one of the churches in or near Ephesus, somehow associated with John. "The elder", who writes the letter, may be one of John's disciples, but since his name is attached to the letter, we will simply refer to the author as John. There seem to have been problems and divisions in the church (when were there ever not?). John has sent messengers, "the brothers", but they have met with a mixed reception. Some like Gaius have welcomed and supported them (vv. 1 – 8). Others like Diotrephes had obstructed and evicted them (vv. 9 – 10). What John says to Gaius is informative and sets us a model for what a mission sending and supporting church is like.

John commends Gaius for his faithfulness in two areas: *faithfulness to the truth* (vv. 3 – 4), and *faithfulness to the brothers and sisters* (vv. 5 – 8). Both are essential for churches committed to mission.

Faithfulness to the Truth

Faithfulness to the truth is a shorthand expression (understandable, since the author is apparently short of paper and ink, v. 13), but from the rest of John's writings we know what it would have included:

- the truth of the incarnation (that Jesus was truly God in human flesh)
- the truth of Jesus' messiahship (that he fulfilled the Old Testament story and promise)
- the truth of the cross and Jesus' atoning death for our sins
- the truth of his bodily resurrection
- the truth of his uniqueness as saviour and Lord

All of these are part of the essential truth of the gospel. Gaius believed it, lived it, "walked in it", and supported those who did the same. Naturally, therefore, he and those in the church who thought and lived like him supported the mission of those who came and went in the name of Christ.

For mission is the inevitable overflow of wholehearted commitment to the truth. Just as the church at Antioch supported mission after the faithful teaching of Paul and Barnabas, so the church of 3 John supported mission on the foundation of the faithful "walking in the truth" of Gaius.

Mission-sending churches are truth-walking churches. Sadly, the opposite is also the case.

Faithfulness to the Missionaries

"Dear friend," writes John to Gaius, "you are faithful in what you are doing for the brothers and sisters, even though they are strangers to you" (v. 5). The TNIV is right to add "and sisters", since the Greek *adelphoi* was a generic term that included men and women. Some translations say "the friends" or "our colleagues". But who were they?

Most likely these were the kind of itinerant missionaries we have seen in the table above, people engaged in traveling ministries of evangelism, church planting, and all that followed on from that: liaising between the local churches, teaching, building structures of local leadership, networking, carrying letters and news, sharing resources, bringing questions and taking back answers, correcting false teaching, encouraging perseverance. In the life of Paul we find many such men and women who traveled for such purposes—notably people like Apollos, Phoebe, Priscilla and Aquila, Timothy and Titus (e.g., Rom. 16:1–2; 1 Cor. 3:6; Eph. 6:21–22; 1 Thess. 3:2; Tit. 1:5; 2 Tim. 4:12).

So 3 John is, in our terms, talking about the relationship between a local church and traveling missionaries. Fundamentally, John describes it as a relationship of "love" (v. 6a). But it was a love that took practical form, in three distinct ways: sending, going, and supporting.

Sending (3 John 6)

"You will do well to send them on their way in a manner worthy of God," writes John to Gaius and his church members. It is a challenging responsibility. "Send them on their way" meant more than waving good-bye. The verb *propempo* is almost a technical term elsewhere in the New Testament for making all the necessary arrangements and provision for someone's journey (Acts 15:3; 21:5; Rom. 15:24; 1 Cor. 16:6, 10–11; 2 Cor. 1:16; Titus 3:13). It would include providing food, money for fares or overnight accommodation, perhaps companions for safety, and letters of introduction or commendation for those at the other end.

Moreover, John says, all these things should be done for missionaries "in a manner worthy of God". That means, in such a way that one can look

I once spoke from 3 John 6 to the full staff of All Nations Christian College at our meeting before the start of the academic year. I emphasized that although we were a training and not a sending institution, there was a sense in which the challenge of this verse applied to all our work on behalf of the students while they were with us—whether teaching, cooking, cleaning, handling their money, maintaining the college, printing handouts or whatever. It all needed to be done "in a manner worthy of God" for the sake of those we were sending on.

I was delighted the next day to see that my secretary had printed the text out on a small card and stuck it at the top of her computer screen: "You will do well to send them on their way in a manner worthy of God." The message had got through.

up to God and expect *his* approval. Or, in such a way as we would do it if it were Jesus himself whom we were sending on his way. What would we not do for him? Would such a perspective and such an ideal not transform the way we make provision for the sending out of mission partners, whether as churches or as mission agencies?

Third John 6 should be written as a motto on the walls, desk calendars, or computer screens of all those with responsibility for the sending of people in mission, in churches or mission agencies, or in training institutions.

Going (3 John 7)

John turns from those who send to those who go, and he makes two points about them.

First, they are not tourists. They go out "for the sake of the Name" – by which, of course, he can only mean the name of the Lord Jesus Christ. Just as in the Old Testament the name of YHWH was the power and authority with which victories were won, priests blessed, and prophets spoke, so in the New Testament the name of Jesus means his presence, power and authority.

Missionaries go out into the world for the sake of the name of Christ. That is, with Christ's authority, with Christ's presence, for Christ's glory.

Second, they are not commercial travelers, living by what they can sell, including their own skill as orators. The first-century Mediterranean world was awash with itinerant lecturers—somewhat like the televangelists of their day, competing for the popular ear and purse. Paul had to distinguish himself from such charlatans (2 Cor. 2:17). John reminds the church that these Christian missionaries had no financial support from secular sources. Their going out was an act of faith in God's people as well as loyalty to God's name.

Supporting (3 John 8)

John's conclusion follows emphatically. "We ought therefore to show hospitality to such people so that we may work together for the truth." "We ought" is weak; it would be better translated: "we are obliged to", "we owe it to them".

The grace of giving is a spiritual gift (Rom. 12:8). Many of God's gifts are both generously bestowed in some measure on all believers and given in special measure to some. For example, all Christians are called to share the gospel with others, but some have the gift of an evangelist. All Christians are called to exercise pastoral care for others, but some are called to be pastors. Just so, all Christians are called to be generous, but some are given the particular "gift of giving". Those entrusted with significant financial resources have a special responsibility to be good stewards of those resources.

John Stott[8]

Christian fellowships have a duty to support those who are sent out in the name of Christ. Paul argues this strongly in 1 Corinthians 9, with a range of arguments from common humanity, Old Testament examples and the teaching of Jesus. Churches that do not adequately provide for the needs of mission partners may talk about how wonderfully their missionaries are "living by faith". That is hypocritical if the church itself is living in disobedience to the plain command of the New Testament. For such financial provision is indeed, as Paul expressed it, a matter of "obedience to the gospel of Christ" (2 Cor. 9:12–14).

Supporting includes generosity in giving, and that is undoubtedly a major part of the mission of God's people. It is, as Paul gratefully said to the Christians at Philippi, a matter of "fellowship in the gospel".

Then, finally, John brings his whole tight argument around full circle with the final phrase: "so that we may work together for the truth". It is not that *they* (the missionaries) are working for the truth, while *we* (the supporters) pay the bills. It is that *all of us*, the sent and the senders, are working together for the truth. That is the responsibility and the privilege of Christian mission.

SUMMARY

The mission of God's people, then, calls them to participate in a long and rich tradition of sending and being sent that originates within God the Holy Trinity. The God of the Bible is the sending God—even within the relationships of Father, Son and Holy Spirit.

8. John Stott, *The Living Church: Convictions of a Lifelong Pastor*, 122.

That dynamic sending flows first through many examples of people whom God sent in and to Old Testament Israel, as agents of salvation and messengers of revelation. To be sent by God, for whatever purpose, meant bearing the authority of God (e.g., in achieving deliverance or in speaking in his name), but it also frequently involved suffering and rejection.

The long story of God's sending reaches its climax in the one whom God sent into the world so that the world through him should be saved. Jesus embodies all the dimensions of Old Testament sendings, but with the supreme distinction that he finally and completely accomplished the purpose for which he was sent, as we hear from his prayer in John 17 and his climactic cry, "It is finished!"

From Jesus, then, flows the mission of the church until he comes again. His final words to his disciples and action form a sending, a commission, a mandate. Those who are disciples of Jesus today are to be like the disciples of Jesus in the Gospels—called to be with him and to go in his name to do his work, to the ends of the earth and until the end of the world.

Churches, then, are to be communities around the world, planted, nurtured and connected through ministries of sending, going and supporting—for the sake of the name of Christ and the truth of the gospel.

Where are we sent? Into the world, said Jesus, just as the Father had sent him into the world. So we are to be "in the world", and yet in another sense we do not belong to the world. How are we to carry on our mission within the world's public arena without being swallowed up by the world itself? We turn to that in our next chapter.

RELEVANT QUESTIONS

1. In what senses do you think of yourself as "sent" by God—not necessarily in geographical or physical terms, but as living under his orders and doing his will?

2. How would you distinguish between the Twelve apostles in their unique status and role, and the wider picture of apostles ("sent ones") that the New Testament shows us? Are there apostles today? If so, what should they be, and what should they not be?

3. How does your church measure up to the picture of missional church as portrayed in 3 John? Think particularly of the twin challenge of "faithfulness to the truth" and "faithfulness to the brothers and sisters (in mission)".

4. If your church is involved in sending people out in mission, what difference would it make if you consciously aimed to "send them on their way in a manner worthy of God" (3 John 6)?

CHAPTER 13

PEOPLE WHO LIVE AND WORK IN THE PUBLIC SQUARE

We ended the last chapter thinking about those who are sent and received as itinerant Christian missionaries—those who travel across borders for the sake of the name of Christ and are supported by the giving and hospitality of Christian churches. But the mission of God's people is far too big to be left only to missionaries (just as the ministry of the church is far too big to be left to those we commonly call "ministers").

The great majority of believers do not get sent out as traveling missionaries in the traditional sense, and this seems to have been as true in the New Testament church as today. Most Christians live in the ordinary everyday world, working, making a living, raising families, paying taxes, contributing to society and culture, getting along, doing their bit. In what sense, if any, is the life of believers in that realm—what we will call the public square—part of the mission of God's people? Does such routine ordinary life have any purpose other than to give us opportunities to bear witness to our faith and to earn enough money to have some to spare to give to missionaries and "real mission"?

That is the question we will think about in this chapter—the mission of God's people in the public square. I am using that expression in its broadest sense. Another term might be "the marketplace", again in a wide sense—not just "the market" as a purely economic or financial mechanism, but the whole world of human cooperative effort in productive projects and creative activity: work, trade, professions, law, industry, agriculture, engineering, education, medicine, media, politics and government—even leisure, sport, art and entertainment.

The Old Testament word for all this was "the gate"—the public square in every town or village where people met and did their business together, of whatever kind. This is the world of human social engagement and activity, where most of us spend most of our time.

GOD AND THE PUBLIC SQUARE

Is God interested in the public square? Many Christians seem to operate on the everyday assumption that God is not. Or at least, they assume that God is not interested in the world of everyday work for its own sake, as distinct from being interested in it as a context for evangelism. God, it would seem, cares about the church and its affairs, about missions and missionaries, about getting people to heaven, but not about how society and its public places are conducted on earth.

The result of such dichotomized thinking is an equally dichotomized Christian life. In fact it is a dichotomy that gives many Christians a great deal of inner discomfort caused by the glaring disconnect between what they think God most wants and what they most have to do. Many of us invest most of the available time that matters (our working lives) in a place and a task that we have been led to believe *does not* really matter much to God – the so-called secular world of work – while struggling to find opportunities to give some leftover time to the only thing we are told *does* matter to God – evangelism.[1]

Yet the Bible clearly and comprehensively, in both Testaments, portrays God as intensely interested in the public arena of human social and economic life – interested, involved, in charge, and full of plans for it.

Let's think of some key assertions that the Bible makes about God's involvement with the human marketplace. In each case we will think of some questions that these assertions raise for Christians who live and work there. This will then give us a biblical platform for thinking about the mission of God's people in that context, both in terms of our engagement in the public square and also of our confrontation with the anti-God forces at work within it.

What, then, does the Bible say about God and the public square, the world of all human work in all its amazing diversity?

God Created It

Work is God's idea. Genesis 1 – 2 give us our first picture of the biblical God as a worker – thinking, choosing, planning, executing, evaluating. So when God decided to create humankind in the image and likeness of God, what else could humans be but workers, reflecting in their working lives something of the nature of God?

Specifically, God laid on human beings the task of ruling the earth (Gen. 1), and of serving and keeping it (Gen. 2), which we explored in chapter 3. This enormous task required not only the complementarity and mutual help of our male-female gender identities, but also implies some other fundamental economic and ecological dimensions to human life. God has given us a planet with vast diversity of resources scattered all over its surface. Some places have lots of fertile soil. Other places have vast mineral deposits. There is, therefore, a natural necessity for trade and exchange between groups living in different places in order to meet common needs.

---

1. Darrel Cosden, *The Heavenly Good of Earthly Work* (London: Paternoster, and Peabody, MA: Hendrickson, 2006) provides an excellent critique of this dichotomized and, frankly, unbiblical viewpoint, and a fine theology of work in the process.

That task in turn necessitates economic relationships, and so there is the need for fairness and justice throughout the social and economic realm. There must be justice both in the sharing of the raw resources with which we work, and in the distribution of the products of our work. The biblical witness is that all of this great human economic endeavour is an essential part of God's purpose for human life on earth. Work matters because it was God's intention for us. It was what God had in mind when he made us. It is *our* part in *his* creation. As we saw in chapter 3, it is part of our mission as humans.

The first question we need to ask those who seek to follow Jesus in the marketplace is: Do you see your work as nothing more than a necessary evil, or only as the context for evangelistic opportunities? Or do you see it as a means of glorifying God through participating in his purposes for creation and therefore having *intrinsic* value? How do you relate what you do in your daily work to the Bible's teaching about human responsibility in creation and society?

Work, then, is not the result of "the curse". Of course, all work is now affected in myriad detrimental ways by our fallenness. But work itself is of the essence of our human nature. We were created to be workers, like God, the worker. This has been called the "cultural mandate". All that we are and do in the public sphere of work, whether at the level of individual jobs, or of the family, or of whole communities, right up to whole cultures and civilizations over historical time, is connected to our createdness and is therefore of interest to our Creator. The public square and marketplace are, of course, polluted and distorted by our sinfulness. But then that is true of all spheres of human existence. Our fallenness is not a reason to excuse ourselves from the public arena, any more than the fact that sickness and death are ultimately the results of sin is a reason for Christians not to become doctors or conduct funerals.

God Audits It

We are all familiar with the function of an auditor. The auditor provides independent, impartial and objective scrutiny of a company's activities and claims. The auditor has access to all documents and evidence. To the auditor all books are opened and all decisions made known; from him no secrets are hidden. That, at least, is the theory.

According to the Bible, God is the independent judge of all that goes on in the public square. The Old Testament speaks repeatedly of YHWH as the God who sees and knows and evaluates. This is true in the most universal sense and pertains to every individual (Ps. 33:13–15).

But it is specifically true of the public square. Israel was reminded repeatedly that God calls for justice "in the gate", which is, in contemporary terms, the marketplace, the public arena. Amos probably surprised his listeners by insisting that God was actually more interested in what happened "in the gate" than in the sanctuary (Amos 5:12–15).

Furthermore, God hears the kind of talk that would go on either in the hidden places of the greedy heart, or in the confidence of a business deal. Amos, again, pictures the divine auditor listening to the muttered dark intentions of the corrupt business people of his day (Amos 8:4–7). And to those who think that God is confined to his temple and sees only what goes on in religious observance comes the shock that he has been watching what goes on the rest of the week in public (Jer. 7:9–11).

God is the auditor – the independent inspector of all that happens in the public arena. What God therefore demands, as any auditor should, is complete integrity and transparency. This is the standard that is expected of human judges in their exercise of public office. The case of Samuel is revealing, as he defends his public record and calls God as witness – as his divine auditor (1 Sam. 12:1–5).

The second question we need to ask of all those who seek to follow Jesus in the marketplace is this: Where, in all your activity, is the deliberate acknowledgment of, and submission to, the divine auditor? In what way does accountability to God impinge on your everyday work?

God Governs It

We often speak of "market forces" and of the whole realm of business and politics as if they were all independent, as "a law unto themselves". "The Market" (often with a capital M) is objectified and given a kind of divine, autonomous power. At any rate, at a personal level, we feel we are at the mercy of forces beyond our individual control, forces determined by millions of other people's choices. Or in some cases, as the financial crisis of 2008 – 2009 demonstrated, millions of people seemed to be at the mercy of the wild and irresponsible choices of a few, which equally appeared to throw the whole "Market" out of control and into panic.

The Bible has a more subtle view. Yes, human public life is made up of human choices, for which human beings are responsible. So in that sense, all that happens in the marketplace is a matter of human action, choice and moral responsibility. Yet at the same time, the Bible puts it all under God's sovereign government. By stressing the first (human choices) as well as the second (God's ultimate control), the Bible avoids sliding into fatalism or determinism. It affirms both sides of the paradox: humans are morally responsible for our choices and actions and their public consequences; yet God retains sovereign control over final outcomes and destinies.

Many Bible stories illustrate this. The story of Joseph oscillates between the sphere of the family and the public arena at the highest level of state power. Joseph is involved in political, judicial, agricultural, economic and foreign affairs. All the actors in the stories are responsible for their own motives, words and deeds – whether good or evil. But the perspective of the author of Genesis, through the words of Joseph, is crystal clear (even though it enshrines a tantalizing mystery):

> But Joseph said to them, "Don't be afraid. Am I in the place of God? You intended to harm me, but God intended it for good to accomplish what is now being done, the saving of many lives." (Gen. 50:19–20)

Moving to prophetic texts, it is significant that when prophets turn their attention to the great empires of their day, they affirm YHWH's government as much over *them* as over his covenant people Israel. Furthermore, all their public works are included, the marketplace as much as the military.

The third question we have to ask of those who follow Jesus in the marketplace is: How do you perceive the governance of God in the marketplace (which is another way of seeking the kingdom of God and his justice), and what difference does it make when you do? Is it really the case that "Heaven rules" on Sundays, but The Market rules from Monday to Friday (with Saturdays as a day off for gods and humans)?

Isaiah 19:1–15 puts the whole of Egypt under God's judgment, including its religion, irrigation, agriculture, fisheries, textile industry, politicians and universities.

Ezekiel 26–28 is a sustained lament for the great trading city of Tyre, while chs. 29–32 pour similar doom on the great imperial culture of Egypt. In both cases, the public marketplace of economic and political power is the focus of God's sovereign activity.

Daniel 4 portrays the arrogance of Nebuchadnezzar gloating over his city: "Is not this the great Babylon I have built as the royal residence, by my mighty power and for the glory of my majesty?" (Dan. 4:30). But the verdict of God is that his whole building project has been borne on the backs of the poor and oppressed, as Daniel points out: "Therefore, Your Majesty, be pleased to accept my advice: Renounce your sins by doing what is right, and your wickedness by being kind to the oppressed. It may be that then your prosperity will continue" (Dan. 4:27).

The lesson Nebuchadnezzar had to learn is the one we are pressing here: God governs the public square, along with all else. Or, in Daniel's more graphic words, "Heaven rules … the Most High is sovereign over the kingdoms of men and gives them to anyone he wishes" (Dan. 4:26, 32).

God Redeems It

A common Christian assumption is that all that happens here on earth is nothing more than temporary and transient. Human history is nothing more than the vestibule for eternity, so it doesn't really matter very much. To this negative comparison is added the idea, drawn from a mistaken interpretation of the language of 2 Peter 2, that we are headed for total obliteration of the whole earth and indeed of all the physical creation. With such a prospect, what eternal value can possibly attach to the work we do in the local or globalized public square here and now?[2]

But the Bible presents a different prospect. God plans to redeem all that he has made (because "he has compassion on all he has made", Ps. 145:9), and included within that will be the redemption of all that *we* have made with what *God* first made–that is, our use of creation within the great cultural mandate. Of course, all

---

2. Darrel Cosden, *The Heavenly Good of Earthly Work*, is particularly helpful on this theme of the eternal significance of human work accomplished in time. See also Michael E. Wittmer, *Heaven Is a Place on Earth*; N. T. Wright, *Surprised by Hope: Rethinking Heaven, the Resurrection, and the Mission of the Church* (London: SPCK, 2005).

that we have done has been tainted and twisted by our sinful, fallen human nature. And all that flows from that evil source will have to be purged and purified by God. But that is exactly the picture we have in both Old and New Testaments. It is a vision of redemption, not of obliteration; of the restoration and renewal of creation, not its replacement with something else.

Of course the Bible presents the public square, human life lived in society and the marketplace, as riddled with sin, corruption, greed, injustice and violence. That can be seen at local and global dimensions, from sharp practices at the market stall or corner shop, to the massive distortions and inequities of international trade. As Christians, we need a radical understanding of sin in its public dimensions, and we need to see part of our mission as being called to confront that prophetically in the name of Christ (as we will discuss below). But for God, the corruption of the public square is not a reason to vaporize it, but to purge and redeem it.

Isaiah 65:17 – 25 is a glorious portrayal of the new creation – a new heavens and a new earth. It looks forward to human life that is no longer subject to weariness and decay, in which there will be fulfillment in family and work, in which the curses of frustration and injustice will be gone forever, in which there will be close and joyful fellowship with God, and in which there will be environmental harmony and safety. The whole of life – personal life, family life, public life, animal life – will be redeemed and restored to God-glorifying productiveness and human-fulfilling enjoyment.

The New Testament carries this vision forward in the light of the redemption achieved by Christ through the cross, and especially in the light of the resurrection. Paul comprehensively and repeatedly includes "*all things*" not only in what God *created* through Christ, but what he plans to *redeem* through Christ. It is clear in this text that "all things" means the whole created order in both descriptions of the work of Christ (Col. 1:16 – 20). Because of that plan of cosmic redemption, the whole of creation can look forward to the future as a time of liberation and freedom from frustration (Rom. 8:19 – 21).

Even the text that is often used to speak of the destruction of the cosmos (when in fact, in my view, it is actually portraying redemptive purging),[3] immediately goes on to the expectation of a justice-filled new creation (2 Peter 3:13).

And the final vision of the whole Bible is not of our escaping from the world to some ethereal paradise, but rather of God coming down to live with us once again in a purged and restored creation, in which all the fruit of human civilization will be brought into the city of God (Rev. 21:24 – 27, building on Isa. 60).

The "splendour", "glory" and "honour" of kings and nations is the combined product of generations of human beings whose lives and efforts will have generated

---

3. In 2 Peter 3, the "destruction" referred to in v. 12 must be read in the light of the "destruction" (same word) by the flood in vv. 6 – 7. What was destroyed in the flood was not the planet itself, but the "world" of human wickedness and rebellion. Similarly, the final "destruction" will not be an obliteration of the whole creation, but a purging judgment that removes all wickedness, evil and opposition to God from creation forever.

the vast store of human cultures and civilizations. In other words, what will be brought into the great city of God in the new creation will be the vast accumulated output of human work through the ages. All this will be purged, redeemed and laid at the feet of Christ, for the enhancement of the life of eternity in the new creation.

Does that not transform our perspective on a Monday morning?

Here is what I wrote on this topic elsewhere:

All that has enriched and honoured the life of all nations in all history will be brought in to enrich the new creation. The new creation will not be a blank page, as if God will simply crumple up the whole of human historical life in this creation and toss it in the cosmic bin, and then hand us a new sheet to start all over again. The new creation will *start* with the unimaginable reservoir of all that human civilization has accomplished in the old creation—but purged, cleansed, disinfected, sanctified and blessed. And we shall have eternity to enjoy it and to build upon it in ways we cannot dream of now as we will exercise the powers of creativity of our redeemed humanity.

I don't understand *how* God will enable the wealth of human civilization to be redeemed and brought cleansed into the city of God in the new creation, as the Bible says he will.... But I know I will be there in the glory of a resurrection body, as the person I am and have been—but redeemed, rid of all sin, and raring to go. So I believe there will be some comparable resurrection glory for all that humans have accomplished in fulfilment of the creation mandate—redeemed but real.

Ancient kings served as the primary authorities over the broad patterns of the cultural lives of their nations. And when they stood over against other nations, they were the *bearers*, the *representatives*, of their respective cultures. To assemble kings together, then, was in an important sense to assemble their national cultures together. The king of a given nation could bear, singly, a far-reaching authority that is today divided among many different kinds of leaders: the captains of industry; the molders of public opinion in art, entertainment, and sexuality; educational leaders; representatives of family interests; and so on. That is why Isaiah and John link the entrance of the kings into the City with the gathering-in of the "wealth of nations."

Richard J. Mouw [4]

We lament the "lost civilizations" of past millennia, civilizations we can only partially reconstruct from archaeological remains or in epic movies. But if we take Revelation 21 seriously, they are not "lost" forever. The kings and nations who will bring their glory into the city of God will presumably not be limited only to those who happen to be alive in the generation of Christ's return. Who can tell what nations will have risen or fallen, or what civilizations will have become "lost" by then—like the lost civilizations of previous millennia? No—the promise spans all ages, all continents, and all generations in human history. The prayer of the Psalmist will one day be answered—for all history past, present and future,

May all the kings of the earth praise you, LORD,
when they hear what you have decreed.

4. Richard J. Mouw, *When the Kings Come Marching In: Isaiah and the New Jerusalem* (Grand Rapids: Eerdmans, 1983), 26.

> May they sing of the ways of the LORD,
> for the glory of the LORD is great. (Ps. 138:4–5)

Think of the prospect! All human culture, language, literature, art, music, science, business, sport, technological achievement—actual and potential—all available to us. *All of it with the poison of evil and sin sucked out of it forever.* All of it glorifying God. All of it under his loving and approving smile. All of it for us to enjoy with God and indeed being enjoyed by God. And all eternity for us to explore it, understand it, appreciate it, and expand it.[5]

All human history, which takes place in the public square of human public interaction, will be redeemed and fulfilled in the new creation, not just abandoned or destroyed. All human productive work, then, has its own value and eternal significance, not just because of our understanding of creation and the mandate it laid upon us, but also because of the new creation and the eschatological hope it sets before us. With such a hope, we can heartily follow Paul's exhortation: "Always give yourselves fully to the work of the Lord, because you know that your labor in the Lord is not in vain" (1 Cor. 15:58); we know that "the work of the Lord" does not mean just "religious" work, but any work done "as unto the Lord", including even the manual labour of slaves (Col. 3:22–24).

> So a fourth question arises for the follower of Jesus in the marketplace: In what ways is your daily labour transformed by the knowledge that it is all contributing to that which God will one day redeem and include within his new creation?

If that, then, is God's view of the public life and work of the marketplace, what ought to be the attitude, role and mission of God's people in that sphere?

We have to respond at two levels. On the one hand, we are called to *constructive engagement* in the world—because it is God's world, created, loved, valued and redeemed by him. But on the other hand, we are called to *courageous confrontation* with the world—because it is a world in rebellion against God, the playground of other gods, standing under God's condemnation and ultimate judgment.

The challenge of the mission of God's people is to live with the constant tension of *doing both with equal biblical conviction.* It is essentially the challenge of being "in the world but not of it". Fortunately the Bible, as always, comes to our aid by giving us plenty of examples of what that means.

MISSIONAL ENGAGEMENT IN THE PUBLIC SQUARE

God's people are called to engagement in the created world. The Bible teaches us various ways in which engagement by believers in the "secular" public square is entirely consistent with God's calling and God's mission for his people.

---

5. Wright, *The God I Don't Understand*, 202–3.

Positioned to Serve the State

There are some things that might give a person an advantage for seeking high political office. There are others that we could not possibly recommend. Being trafficked as a slave to a foreign country and reported "missing-presumed-dead" back home? Not a good start. Being taken prisoner by an invader and ending up with other children as part of a despised ethnic minority in an enemy land? Unlikely. And what about joining the abducted sex-slaves of an oriental despot? Hardly.

Just so, however, begin the stories of *Joseph*, *Daniel* and *Esther*, and they all ended up serving at top levels in pagan imperial governments and proving that even in such positions they could serve God and God's people. The contrast between the beginnings of their stories and the positions they later found themselves in points to one common factor – the hand of God. None of them chose the post they occupied, but certainly Joseph and Daniel both acknowledged that it was God who put them there for a purpose. So what do we learn from them?

First, they accepted the realities of the public sphere they became part of, in spite of all its ambiguity. Daniel and his three friends accepted a massive degree of cultural adjustment before they reached a line that they would not cross (Dan. 1). They accepted Babylonian names, Babylonian education in the Babylonian language, and entered Babylonian employment. Joseph obviously learned the language of Egypt so fluently that his own brothers did not know he was not a native (Gen. 42:23). Esther, though she had little choice in the matter other than martyrdom for refusal, accepted a cultural practice that must have been profoundly distasteful, and with Mordecai's help came to see it as an opportunity to save lives.

Secondly, they worked constructively and conscientiously for the government and for social benefit. Even Daniel's political enemies could not fault him on this score:

> ... the administrators and the satraps tried to find grounds for charges against Daniel in his conduct of government affairs, but they were unable to do so. They could find no corruption in him, because he was trustworthy and neither corrupt nor negligent. (Dan. 6:4)

One can imagine that life for ordinary Babylonians was better when Daniel was in charge of civic affairs. In the case of Joseph, we know that many Egyptian lives were saved by his wise administration, before any of his own family were saved from the famine (Gen. 41). Esther's achievements were for her own people, of course, but the principle of using office for good ends is clear.

Third, they preserved their integrity. For Joseph it was his moral integrity, though the trust of his employer was also a key factor (Gen. 39:7 – 10). For Daniel and his friends, it was their loyalty to their covenant God and refusal to cede such total loyalty to the king (such as eating from his table probably signified) that was their sticking point. Later it came to more overt matters of idolatry, but again their integrity stood firm.

In the New Testament, the evidence for believers in political service is thinner, but if one can build an argument by inference, it seems likely that since Paul can speak of the Roman governing authorities as "God's servants", using words otherwise used for Christian ministry (*diakonos* twice in Rom. 13:4 and *leitourgos* in v. 6), he would not have disallowed Christians from serving in political office. Political and judicial service can both be service of God. Erastus is a good example of this, as we will see in a moment.

Commanded to Pray for the Government

In the next chapter we will consider prayer as a dimension of the mission of God's people, but it is fitting at this point to mention that God's people in both Testaments are commanded to pray for the state where they are, not just for other believers, whether Israelites or Christians.

The first example comes from that shocking letter of Jeremiah to the exiles in Babylon.

> Also, seek the peace and prosperity [*šalom*] of the city to which I have carried you into exile. Pray to the LORD for it, because if it prospers, you too will prosper [lit., 'in its *šalom* is *šalom* for you']. (Jer. 29:7)

It was probably hard enough for the exiles to imagine that it was even possible to pray to YHWH *in* Babylon, let alone that they should pray to him *for* Babylon. They knew exactly what they wanted for Babylon (Ps. 137:8–9), and they knew whose *šalom* they should be praying for (Ps. 122:6).

> In writing about the ministry of the state [in Rom. 13:4–6], Paul twice uses the very same word which he has used elsewhere of the ministers of the church.... *Diakonia* is a generic term which can embrace a wide variety of ministries. Those who serve the state as legislators, civil servants, magistrates, police, social workers or tax-collectors are just as much "ministers of God" as those who serve the church as pastors, teachers, evangelists or administrators.
>
> *John Stott*[6]

But "No," says Jeremiah. "Once you've accepted that you are there because God has put you there (and thus stop thinking of yourselves *in transit* and become residents; vv. 4–6), you have an ongoing *mission*–the Abrahamic mission of being a blessing to the nations. And that includes praying for them–as Abraham prayed for Sodom and Gomorrah."

I've no proof at all, but I like to think that Daniel was among those who heard this letter of Jeremiah and did what it said:[7] "Daniel was a man of prayer; daily he prayed three times" (another song remembered from my childhood; cf. Dan. 6:10). Who was at the top of his prayer list? Nebuchadnezzar, would you believe? How else can you explain the fact that when Daniel heard that Nebuchadnezzar (the man who had destroyed his city and slaughtered his countrymen) was for the chop, he did not gloat, but was so upset he struggled even to tell the king the truth. But he did tell him, along with some careful advice as to how he could avoid his fate (Dan.

---

6. John Stott, *The Message of Romans* (The Bible Speaks Today; Leicester: IVP, and Downers Grove, IL: IVP, 1994), 343–44.

7. We do know that he was familiar with the Scriptures of Jeremiah (Dan. 9:2), so he may have got hold of a copy of his letter.

4:19–27). Where did such concern for the archenemy of his people come from, if not from prayer? It's hard to go on hating somebody (let alone praying the ending of Ps. 137), if you're praying for them every day.

The New Testament counterpart to this command specifies prayer for all forms of governing authorities, which in Paul's day would have been almost entirely unbelieving, pagan men and women (with a few exceptions like Erastus, as we will see below).

> I urge, then, first of all, that petitions, prayers, intercession and thanksgiving be made for everyone—for kings and all those in authority, that we may live peaceful and quiet lives in all godliness and holiness. This is good, and pleases God our Savior, who wants all people to be saved and to come to a knowledge of the truth. (1 Tim. 2:1–4)

From a missional point of view, we should notice how seamlessly Paul moves from such prayer for political authorities to the saving power and spread of the gospel.

Commanded to Seek the Welfare of the City

Returning to Jeremiah's letter to the exiles, that first phrase demands a closer look: "Seek the *šalom* of the city to which I have carried you" (Jer. 29:7a). *Šalom*, as is well known, is a wonderfully broad word. It goes beyond peace as the absence of conflict or war, to all-around welfare or well-being. It speaks of wholeness of life and the kind of prospering that the Old Testament included in the blessing of God as the fruit of covenant faithfulness.

It really is remarkable that Jeremiah urges the exiles to seek such blessing for their Babylonian neighbours.

"But they are our enemies!"

"So what? Pray for them. Seek their welfare."

It is a short step from this amazing instruction that Jeremiah gave the exiles to the equally jaw-dropping mission that Jesus lays on his disciples:

While teaching pastors-in-training in India, I took a group to different churches in Pune each Sunday and then asked them to reflect on their observations later, back in class. We compared the prayer times. In one church in the Anglican tradition, the prayers were mainly formal and liturgical, to the point, and not very prolonged. In a charismatic fellowship, the prayers were loud, spontaneous, and very long. However, it was noticeable that in the first case, the prayers covered the world, and named the leaders in state and national governments, whereas in the second, the prayers were almost entirely inward-focused on the church members themselves. I pointed out that in relation to 1 Timothy 2, one church avoided any "lifting up of holy hands" (v. 8), but they did at least obey vv. 1–2, whereas the other church had hands lifted up till our arms ached, but no prayer "for kings and those in authority". Which was being more "biblical"?

"Love your enemies and pray for those who persecute you" (Matt. 5:44).

It must have been such advice that created the freedom that Daniel and his friends felt to settle down in Babylon and accept jobs in its government service. And their position in such office was clearly not "just a job". Nor are we told that it was some form of "tent-making" to help them earn a living while they held Bible studies in the office or evangelistic meetings in their homes. For all I know, they may have done that—they made no secret of their faith, as the rest of the stories show.

But what the text emphasizes is that they were first-class students, model citizens and hard-working civil servants, and they were distinguished for trustworthiness and integrity. Even the king recognized that his own interests were being served by such people. The "welfare of the city" was what they pursued, as Jeremiah said they should. And in doing so for a lifetime, opportunities to bear witness to the God they served, and to his moral demands, judgment and mercy, came along at key points—one in each of the first six chapters in fact.

Coming to the New Testament, there is one person who probably held high civic office and was also a Christian believer—and that is *Erastus*.

Erastus was one of Paul's helpers in his church-planting ministry (Acts 19:22), but when Paul wrote his letter to Rome from Corinth, Erastus is included in the closing greetings, where he describes himself as "the city's director of public works" (Rom. 16:23). The phrase strongly suggests that Erastus held the post of *aedile* in this important Roman city, a political office in the Roman administration that carried major responsibilities, requiring considerable personal wealth and a strong civic generosity.

Paul did not normally mention the present, secular occupations of the other Christians who are mentioned in his letters. In doing so in the case of Erastus, he was able to provide an example for his readers of the role that the well-to-do Christian could undertake in seeking the welfare of the city. The filling of this public office by Erastus was an outworking of the role of the Christian as a civic benefactor referred to in Romans 13:3–4 and 1 Peter 2:14–15. He was engaging in the time-consuming office of *aedile* during the year in which the letter to the Romans was written.... Erastus was a Christian of substantial means, active in two spheres. After he "ministered to Paul" in Ephesus as part of the apostolic team, he was sent into Macedonia to the churches. He subsequently engaged in civic duties in Corinth.... The office undertaken then by Erastus in Corinth for the year demanded commitment and accountability for it was no sinecure as the duties show.

If this is correct, then there was no dichotomy in the thinking of the early church between gospel/church ministry and seeking the welfare of Corinth as benefactors. This conclusion ... appears to find confirmation in the person of Erastus.... Paul wrote in such a way as to imply that the secular and spiritual welfare of the city were two sides of a single coin and not separate spheres. The combination of these activities in this prominent Christian citizen may never have been perceived by him as incompatible or autonomous entities for Christians. Both roles were concerned with the welfare of those who lived in the city. They were what Paul saw as an imitation of the ministry of Christ who, in Acts 10:38, was recorded as "having gone about [undertaking] benefactions or doing good works".

Bruce Winter [8]

Serving God and serving the community in public office were by no means incompatible. In fact, such public service and benefaction were part of what Paul

8. Bruce W. Winter, *Seek the Welfare of the City: Christians as Benefactors and Citizens* (Grand Rapids and Carlisle: Eerdmans and Paternoster, 1994), 195–97.

strongly encouraged Christians to engage in, through his repeated emphasis that they should "do good"—a single verb (*agathopoein*) that had exactly that technical meaning in the Roman empire: public service as a civic benefactor.

Commanded to Earn a Living by Ordinary Work

It seems that some people in the churches Paul planted had come to the view that ordinary work was no longer of any value, and so they became lazy, and then spiritualized their idleness with fervid expectations of Christ's return. Paul shared their convictions about Christ's return, but not their work-shy opting out of normal human responsibilities:

> Make it your ambition to lead a quiet life: You should mind your own business and work with your hands, just as we told you, so that your daily life may win the respect of outsiders and so that you will not be dependent on anybody.... Warn those who are idle. (1 Thess. 4:11–12; 5:14)

Paul had no hesitation in appealing to his own example in this regard, as one who had supported himself from his own labour in the marketplace. Paul's lengthy exhortation in 2 Thessalonians 3:6–13 is worth reading in full—it clearly addresses an issue that Paul felt strongly about. Christians should be diligent workers.

Paul's frequent exhortations to "do good" should not be construed merely as "being nice". As we mentioned above, the term also carried a common social connotation of public service and benefaction.[9] Christians should be among those who bring the greatest public good to the public arena and thereby commend the biblical gospel.

I was leading a Langham Preaching seminar in Argentina. Over breakfast I was chatting with the main organizer of the event—the leader of the national movement. I commended three men in particular who were helping to lead and teach during the seminar—all of them Argentinian Christians in secular professions, but committed to Bible teaching. My friend immediately said, "Yes, they are good preachers, but that's not all. They are good husbands, good fathers, and good citizens." I asked her why she included the last item. "Because," she said, "they are committed to staying here in Argentina, not trying to get to the United States. They are honest, they work hard and they pay their taxes. They are a blessing to our country." That's authentic, biblical, Abrahamic, Pauline, integral mission in the public square. It blessed my heart.

Christians are to be good citizens and good workers, *and thereby* to be good witnesses. Work is still a creational good. It is *good* to work, and it is good to *do good* by working. All this is part of the mission of God's people too.

---

9. Bruce Winter (*Seek the Welfare of the City*) develops this theme in great depth, utilizing wide background supporting evidence from the Greek and Roman world of Paul's day.

And in the letters of Paul, one does not get the impression that new converts were expected to leave the occupations they had in the secular world and go out as missionaries—though obviously a few did. On the contrary, Paul seems to envisage most of them still there, working and earning, paying their taxes (Rom. 13:6–8), and doing good in the community. One imagines the Philippian jailer back at his post, Lydia carrying on her textile business, and Erastus somehow combining his ministry as "mayor of Corinth" with helping Paul's ministry too.

Such people had a missional engagement in the public square, living out the gospel there. Their kind is needed just as much in the twenty-first- as in the first-century world.

MISSIONAL CONFRONTATION IN THE PUBLIC SQUARE

Living out the gospel, however, while it has to be done in engagement with the world, inevitably brings conflict with the world, and the public square is the arena for that confrontation. The mission of God's people involves stepping into that confrontation with our eyes open, our heads engaged, and our spiritual armour in place.

We Are Called to Be Different

So we are to be engaged in the public square, the local and global marketplace. But we are to do so as *saints* in the marketplace. We are those who are called to be holy, which means different or distinctive. In chapter 7 we explored in some depth the theme of distinctiveness in biblical theology, starting out from the initial call to Israel to be different from the cultures of Egypt or Canaan:

> You must not do as they do in Egypt, where you used to live, and you must not do as they do in the land of Canaan, where I am bringing you. Do not follow their practices. You must obey my laws and be careful to follow my decrees. I am the LORD your God. Keep my decrees and laws, for the man who obeys them will live by them. I am the LORD. (Lev. 18:3–5)

And we saw that this essential distinctiveness is what holiness actually meant for Israel. It was grounded in the holiness (i.e., the distinctive otherness) of YHWH, and it was to be worked out ethically in everyday, ordinary, social life—the public square—as much as the private home. Leviticus 19, beginning with the demand that Israel should be holy as the Lord their God is holy, goes on to articulate a whole range of contexts in which that holy difference is to be seen—contexts that include personal, familial, social, judicial, agricultural and commercial realms.

The distinctiveness of God's people in the Bible is not merely religious (we happen to worship a different god from most other people), but ethical (we are called to live by different standards). And this includes public as well as private morality, though they cannot really be separated.

The twin sayings of Jesus about being "salt" and "light" in the world (Matt. 5:13–16) are still crucial insights into what it means to have missional involvement in the world.[10]

A strong contrast is implied. If disciples are to be salt and light, then the world must be corrupt and dark. The whole point of the metaphors depends on this contrast. Jesus compares the world to meat or fish that, left to itself, will very quickly become putrid. The primary use of salt in his day was to preserve meat or fish by soaking it in brine, or rubbing salt thoroughly into it. And Jesus compares the world to a room in a house after the sun goes down. It gets dark. Lamps have to be lit to avoid damage and danger. So, the world in which we live–the public square–is a corrupt and dark place. In this sense salt and light are both *missional* (they are used for a purpose) and *confrontational* (they challenge decay and darkness, and transform both).

If a piece of meat goes rotten, it's no use blaming the meat. That's what happens when meat is left out on its own. The question to ask is, Where is the salt? If a house gets dark at night, it's no use blaming the house. That's what happens when the sun goes down. The question to ask is, Where is the light? If society becomes more corrupt and dark, it's no use blaming society. That's what fallen human nature does, left unchecked and unchallenged. The question to ask is, Where are the Christians? Where are the saints who will actually live as saints–God's different people, God's counterculture–in the public square? Where are those who see their mission as God's people to live and work and witness in the marketplace, and pay the cost of doing so?

Moral integrity is essential to Christian distinctiveness, which in turn is essential to Christian mission in the public arena. Integrity means that there is no dichotomy between our private and public "face"; between the sacred and the secular in our lives; between the person I am at work and the person I am in church; between what we say and what we do; between what we claim to believe and what we actually practice. This is a major challenge to all believers who live and work in the non-Christian world, and it raises endless ethical dilemmas and often wrenching difficulties of conscience. It is indeed a battlefield–internally and externally. But it is a struggle that cannot be avoided if we are to function with any effectiveness at all as salt and light in society.

We Are Called to Resist Idolatry

But why are Christians called to be ethically distinctive in the public square? The answer is that we have a different view of the world itself. We dance to a different

---

10. I owe the points below to having heard John Stott preach from this text on many occasions. His rich exposition can be savoured in John R. W. Stott, *The Message of the Sermon on the Mount* (The Bible Speaks Today; Leicester, IVP, and Downers Grove, IL: IVP, 1978), 57–68. See also John Stott, *The Living Church*, chapter 8, "Impact: Salt and Light", 137–52.

tune, march to a different beat. Or to return to chapter 2, we are living in a different story.

We see the world as the creation of the one single transcendent God of the Bible, and thus we reject the seductive gods who crowd the public arena today as much as they did in the Athenian *agora* in Paul's day. In fact, we see the world from two perspectives, both biblical, but sometimes difficult to hold together (though that is what we are seeking to do in this chapter).

On the one hand, we view the world in the light of Col. 1:15–23. This is the world created by Christ, sustained by Christ, redeemed by Christ. It is God's world, Christ's inheritance, and our home. It is where God has put us to live for his glory, to witness to his identity, to engage in the care of creation and whatever productive work enhances the world and pleases God. And so we live in this world by the biblical story reviewed in chapter 2, which sets the whole of human life, work, ambitions and achievement within the context of God's creation, redemption and future plans. The public square is part of this world, and we engage in it under God and for God.

But on the other hand,

> we know that we are children of God, and that the whole world is under the control of the evil one. We know also that the Son of God has come and has given us understanding, so that we may know him who is true. And we are in him who is true by being in his Son Jesus Christ. He is the true God and eternal life.
>
> Dear children, keep yourselves from idols. (1 John 5:19–21)

This is the world as John commonly sees it – the world of human and satanic rebellion against God, the world that hates God, hates Christ and hates God's people, and would kill all three if it could (and in the case of Jesus, thought that it had). And the public square is part of this world too and displays all its ugliness – the ugliness of human sin and of demonic evil and the unholy combination of both in the gods and idols that usurp the place of the one living God. This is the world we are *not* to love, because its sinful cravings draw us away from our love for God and into fundamental idolatry (1 John 2:15–17).

That is why John, having assured us that in Christ we know the living and true God and that "the reason the Son of God appeared was to destroy the devil's work" (1 John 3:8), concludes with his warning to stay away from idols. For idols are all around us, not least in the public square, the marketplace, the world of work.

Work is a creational good, but the Bible is well aware of the temptation to turn work into an idol – when we live for what we can do and achieve, and then derive our identity and fulfillment from that. This is even more so when work is driven by greed. Paul equates covetousness with idolatry: break the tenth commandment and you break the first (Col. 3:5; cf. Deut. 8, esp. vv. 17–18).

The idolatries of career, status and success are all connected to one of the most dominant gods of the public square (in the West at least, and wherever it extends its cultural tentacles)–consumerism. Other idols abound, of course, which we cannot analyze in depth here–idols of ethnic superiority, national pride and patriotism, individual freedom, military security, health and longevity, beauty, celebrity. Some of these idols inhabit the media or state propaganda, others permeate the world of advertising, many just walk around unnoticed and unchallenged in the assumptions and conversations that fill the public arena 24/7. Their power is all the greater at that level.[11]

To live for God in the world of the gods is inevitably to face conflict. The mission of God's people in the public square is, therefore, a calling to unremitting spiritual warfare. And the first act of that warfare is to recognize the enemy–that there even is an enemy. The trouble is that Christians are children of their culture too–wherever that culture may be–and may be blissfully unaware of the extent to which the public square they inhabit daily is infested with spiritual realities that are opposed to God and the gospel.

Discerning the gods of the public square is a first crucial, missional task. Being equipped to resist them is the next.

It is significant that Paul's classic exposition of spiritual warfare comes immediately after his instructions about Christians living in marriage, family and the workplace. In all these realms, there is a battle to be fought if we are to be able "to stand" (rather than sink or swim with the tide), and to fulfill our role as messengers of the "gospel of peace" (Eph. 6:15, echoing Isa. 52:7). It is in the whole of life, including the public square, that "our struggle [lit., "our wrestling match"] is not against flesh and blood, but against the rulers, against the authorities, against the powers of this dark world and against the spiritual forces of evil in the heavenly realms" (Eph. 6:12).

This is not the place for detailed analysis of "rulers, authorities and powers", and there are plenty of other resources on them.[12] Personally, I reject two opposite extremes: those who "demythologize" them as simply a cipher for human structures, political powers, economic forces, or social conventions; and those who view them as exclusively spiritual, demonic beings, with no connection to the world of political or economic powers and forces. It seems to me that both aspects are biblically valid.

There is a reality of satanic and demonic presence and work within the world, and it operates in and through human agency. This is especially true in collective human arrangements where it seems that some structures or forces take on "a life of their own", greater than the sum of human wills involved.

---

11. I have tried to offer a more extensive biblical analysis of idolatry in relation to mission–its varieties, causes, results, and the ways in which God's people respond to it–in *The Mission of God*, 136–90.

12. The trilogy of Walter Wink is a classic survey, though many criticize him for an over "demythologized" interpretation: *Naming the Powers: The Language of Power in the New Testament* (Philadelphia: Fortress, 1984); *Unmasking the Powers: The Invisible Forces That Determine Human Existence* (Philadelphia: Fortress, 1986); *Engaging the Powers: Discernment and Resistance in a World of Domination* (Minneapolis: Fortress, 1992). A shorter and more biblically conservative approach is Clinton Arnold, *Powers of Darkness: A Thoughtful, Biblical Look at an Urgent Challenge Facing the Church* (Leicester: IVP, and Downers Grove, IL: IVP, 1992). See also Nigel G. Wright, *A Theology of the Dark Side: Putting the Power of Evil in Its Place* (Carlisle: Paternoster, 2003).

It is in the public arena where such combined spiritual and human power is at work that Christians are called to live and work, to recognize and resist the idolatry that surrounds them, and to stand against it, offering a witness and a signpost to the good news of the kingdom of God through which, by the power of the cross (see ch. 6), those idolatrous powers have been defeated.

We Are Called to Suffer

Warfare causes suffering, spiritual warfare being no exception. Those who take up the mission of God's people by simply living, working and witnessing in the public square so dominated by the gods of this world, who choose to live by the distinctive ethical standards that flow from their biblical worldview, who confess Jesus as Lord, and not Caesar or Mammon — such people will suffer in one way or another.

The biblical material relating to the suffering of God's people — individually and collectively — is too vast even to do nothing more than list relevant passages. What is unavoidably clear is that suffering is an integral part of the lives of multitudes in the Bible who were *faithful* to God's calling and their mission. I say this because there is a distorted popular theology that deems suffering to be a sign of lack of faith or the result some disobedience. The friends of Job are alive and well and vocal in some forms of prosperity teaching and evangelical piety. Of course God's people suffered when they sinned, but many suffered for being faithful.

Jesus warned us that it would be so, and, in another of those jaw-dropping pronouncements of his, told his disciples to rejoice about it, since they could look back for good biblical precedents and look forward to the approval of God:

> Blessed are you when people insult you, persecute you and falsely say all kinds of evil against you because of me. Rejoice and be glad, because great is your reward in heaven, for in the same way they persecuted the prophets who were before you. (Matt. 5:11 – 12)

Acts records that suffering reared up quickly among the early believers, but they did exactly what Jesus said by rejoicing in the privilege and continuing to witness (Acts 5:40 – 42). From those early days, the story records that the persecution kept on getting worse, while the church kept on growing — two facts that we are doubtless meant to see as integrally related.

For Paul, the expectation of suffering was built into his commissioning (Acts 9:16), and since he had been one of those inflicting it on the believers, he knew what would be coming his way — as it did. But it was more than just an incidental side-effect of his missional calling in a hostile world. For Paul, it seems, his suffering was actually part of the proof of the validity of his apostleship and of the truth of the gospel he preached. His paradoxical claims in 2 Corinthians 11 – 12 climax in his famous words, "for Christ's sake, I delight in weaknesses, in insults, in hardships, in persecutions, in difficulties. For when I am weak, then I am strong" (12:10). These claims are not masochism or bravado, but authenticating testimony to the power of the gospel.

Peter, who had known a thing or two about suffering for Jesus, writes more about this theme than any other in his letter. The thrust of his words of encouragement in 1 Peter to those who were suffering for their faith can be summed up in three phrases: *no surprise* (4:12), *no retaliation* (2:21–22), and *no giving up* (3:13–17; 4:19). Above all, his readers should be inspired by the example of the Lord Jesus Christ, for whose sake they were suffering.

The kind of suffering that Paul and Peter refer to certainly took place in the public arena, but Revelation makes it even more plain that the global marketplace will be among the prime contexts for the battle between God and the idolatrous, bestial forces that oppose God and God's people. The notorious word about the "number of the beast" in Revelation 13:16–18 is not an apocalyptic nightmare involving tattoos, bar codes or credit card numbers, but a chilling exposure of the kind of exclusion from the marketplace that can be expected for those who refuse to bow down to the idolatry that controls it.

> The glue that united Paul's thought and life with the message he preached and the mission he conducted was his suffering as an apostle of Jesus Christ. Paul's suffering was the vehicle through which the saving power of God, climactically revealed in Christ, was being made known in the world. To reject the suffering Paul was therefore to reject Christ; to identify with Paul in his suffering was a sure sign that one was being saved by the "foolishness" and "stumbling-block" of the cross.
>
> *Scott Hafemann[13]*

> The place of suffering in service and of passion in mission is hardly ever taught today. But the greatest single secret of evangelistic or missionary effectiveness is the willingness to suffer and die. It may be a death to popularity (by faithfully preaching the unpopular biblical gospel), or to pride (by the use of modest methods in reliance on the Holy Spirit), or to racial and national prejudice (by identification with another culture), or to material comfort (by adopting a simpler lifestyle). But the servant must suffer if he is to bring light to the nations, and the seed must die if it is to multiply.
>
> *John Stott[14]*

But there is a dimension to all this that is not usually pointed out. Many books on mission warn about the necessary suffering of God's people that is inevitable for those who are faithful to their confession of Christ. Persecution and martyrdom are the stuff of mission history and mission experience to this day. The neglected element is *the suffering of God.*

The mission of God's people is our participation in the mission of God. So the suffering of God's people in mission is a participation in the suffering of God in mission. And the mission of God is God's determination, through the whole biblical narrative, to bring about the redemption of his whole creation from the ravages of sin and evil. For God, that involved the long trek through the centuries of Israel's faithlessness and rebel-

13. Scott Hafemann, "The Role of Suffering in the Mission of Paul," *The Gospel to the Nations: Perspectives on Paul's Mission,* Peter Bolt and Mark Thompson (Leicester: Apollos, and Downers Grove, IL: IVP, 2000), 131–46 (esp. 140).

14. John Stott, *The Cross of Christ* (Leicester: IVP, and Downers Grove, IL: IVP, 1986), 322.

lion—bearing it, judging it, mending it. Then it led to the ultimate suffering—when God in Christ bore the sin of the world on the cross. Since then, God has suffered

with his people as they have borne the cost of being messengers of his kingdom to the ends of the earth.

Elsewhere I have written the phrase, "the cross was the unavoidable cost of the mission of God." Given, then, that the one who bore the cross told us to take up our own crosses to follow him, there is an unavoidable cost for those who identify themselves with the suffering mission of the suffering God—a cost that will one day be

Finally we note that God, in order to enable a new creation which transcends the present order of suffering and death, engages in such a giving of self that only one of the sharpest of human pains known can adequately portray what is involved for God. But such an event is not thought of solely in terms of the internal life of God. God's suffering is the heavenly counterpart to the suffering of the earthly servant of God. The suffering servant takes upon himself the suffering of God and does what is finally necessary for the forces of evil in this world to be overcome: suffering unto death.

Terence Fretheim[15]

vindicated with the final victory of the one who, "for the joy set before him endured the cross, scorning its shame, and sat down at the right hand of the throne of God. Consider him who endured such opposition from sinners, so that you will not grow weary and lose heart" (Heb. 12:2–3).

CONCLUSION – A PERSONAL MESSAGE TO CHRISTIANS IN THE PUBLIC SQUARE

This has been the hardest chapter in the book to write—especially the last section on suffering. The first two main sections of the chapter seem straightforwardly biblical to me. God created the world of work and social engagement and he remains passionately interested and involved in it. And the Bible describes many people who served God precisely by serving in public offices of all kinds. We can learn much from their examples.

However, when it comes to the warfare and suffering part—it is not easy to write on something one knows nothing about. For the honest reality is that, like many Christians in the relatively friendly West, I cannot speak out of any significant experience of having suffered for my faith. And yet I know that as I sit in privacy and comfort looking out to sea as I write these words, I have sisters and brothers across that sea and all over the world who at this moment are being harassed, beaten, falsely accused, imprisoned and oppressed in every conceivable way because of their faith in Christ. The language of Hebrews 11:35–38 still applies.

---

15. Terence E. Fretheim, *The Suffering of God: An Old Testament Perspective* (Philadelphia: Fortress, 1984), 148. This is a profound and moving book, almost unrivaled in the way it handles this neglected subject, rich in scriptural exposition. Fretheim explores how God suffers *because* of his people (in their rejection of him); suffers *with* his people (in their suffering under God's own judgment); and suffers *for* his people (in achieving their salvation). In all these dimensions, the suffering of the prophets was a mysterious entering into, and sharing, the suffering of God's own self.

I get emails from friends in countries where churches are burned, pastors beheaded, and the lives of ordinary believers turned to destitution and misery. And sometimes I weep about it, and often I pray for them. But I know nothing of what that is like, other than in my imagination.

Some who read this book may well live in such circumstances, and all I can do is hold out a hand through this book to embrace you with love and prayer. May the Lord comfort and strengthen you and keep you faithful to himself.

But then also, I know that in my own country and other parts of the "Christian" West, the tide is turning relentlessly against Christian profession of faith in the public square. People lose their jobs for even offering to pray with a patient or for mentioning God in the workplace. The irony is that they are the ones who get accused of harassment and hatred! Meanwhile, Christians in so many professions are faced with constant ethical dilemmas that have no easy or obvious solutions. Finding "the Christian thing to do" can be deeply disturbing and stressful.

So once again, my heart goes out to believers at the sharp end of living as Christians in the secular world.

I have to say that, on this particular topic, I feel that I speak as a coward, for my own working life is not spent in the secular marketplace. I had a few years as a school teacher before moving into ordained pastoral ministry and then into theological education and Christian organizational leadership for the rest of my life. Who am I to talk about these things?

But I have enormous and sincere admiration and great concern for all you Christians who do engage every day in the workplaces of the world.

- You set forth every morning into that public square that is both the world of God's creation and the world of Satan's usurped (and temporary) dominion—as well as the world of your participation in God's mission.
- You are the Daniels of the present world—or at least, you can and you should be.
- You are the disciples of whom Jesus said that you are "in the world" but not "of the world".
- You live and work in the world's public square, but you take your ultimate goals and values in life from another source—the kingdom of God.
- You are the salt and light of the world.

What would the world be like if all the millions of Christians who do earn their living in the public square were to take seriously what Jesus meant by being salt and light?

Your daily work matters because it matters to God. It has its own intrinsic value and worth. If it contributes in any way to the needs of society, the service of others, the stewardship of the earth's resources, then it has some place in God's plans for this creation and in the new creation. And if you do it conscientiously as a disciple of Jesus, bearing witness to him, being always ready to give an answer to those who enquire about your faith, and being willing to suffer for Christ if called to—then he will enable your life to bear fruit in ways you may never be aware of. You are engaged in the mission of God's people.

May God strengthen you and may your tribe increase.

RELEVANT QUESTIONS

1. Go back to the questions in the sidebars of the first section of this chapter and review how you would now answer them. What difference it will make as you go back to your work next week?

2. In what ways has the range of biblical material we have surveyed in this chapter about believers who served in public office affected your view of Christian life in the secular world?

3. Did you expect a book on mission to have a chapter about ordinary work in the everyday world? Having now read it, do you think it was right to include it? In what ways has it impacted your conception of what the mission of God's people includes?

4. "If everything is mission, then nothing is mission." Having read this chapter, how would you now respond biblically to this "put-down"?

5. How will you seek to be more discerning about the realities of satanic evil and spiritual warfare in the public arena where you spend your working life?

6. What could your church be doing to address such issues more biblically and to support those who struggle and suffer in the public arena because of their faith or their ethical stance?

PEOPLE WHO PRAISE AND PRAY

"Missions exists because worship doesn't." These striking words in the opening paragraph of John Piper's book *Let the Nations be Glad* lead us dramatically into the final chapter of our survey of biblical themes. Quite rightly Piper points out that the ultimate reason for the church's existence is to glorify God by worshiping and enjoying him for all eternity. And because the world is still full of people who are *not* worshiping and enjoying the living God, the mission of the church is to bring them into the fold of those who do. There is a self-evident truth about this, and it needs to be endorsed here before we go any further.

WORSHIP AS THE GOAL OF MISSION

The goal of all our mission is the worship and glory of the one true living God. That's because the goal of *all* human life is to love, worship, glorify and enjoy God.

> Missions is not the ultimate goal of the church. Worship is. Missions exists because worship doesn't. Worship is ultimate, not missions, because God is ultimate, not man. When this age is over, and the countless millions of the redeemed fall on their faces before the throne of God, missions will be no more. It is a temporary necessity. But worship abides forever. Worship is, therefore, the fuel and the goal of missions.
>
> *John Piper[1]*

That is where our own deepest fulfillment and flourishing lie. The satisfaction of our ultimate human potential as creatures made in the image of God is completely at one with the worship and glory of God.

To put it another way, we are most fully ourselves as human beings when we are in a relationship with God in which God is glorified in and through our enjoyment of that relationship. That is why the biblical pictures of life in the new creation can combine so seamlessly descriptions of human life in its richest perfection and the worship of God in all his splendour, for each will be part of the substance of the other (Isa. 65:17–25; Rev. 21–22).

The *mission of God*, therefore, is that dynamic divine love that drives God to seek the ultimate well-being and blessing of human beings by bringing them into

---

1. John Piper, *Let the Nations Be Glad: The Supremacy of God in Missions* (rev. ed.; Grand Rapids: Baker, and Leicester: IVP, 2003), 17.

a relationship with himself in which they love, worship, and glorify him, and find their greatest joy in doing so. So also the *mission of God's people* is to be agents of that redemptive love of God. We live to bring others to worship and glorify the living God, for that is where they will find their greatest and eternal fulfillment and joy. For that reason, we should see evangelism not as something we are imposing on others but as the best thing we could ever do for them in the long run.

That is how Paul saw the ultimate goal of his own mission – and not only his own, but indeed, the mission of Jesus Christ. At the end of his letter to the Romans, Paul sums up his whole argument in the book and relates it to his own life's work. God's great mission, as he had said in the opening verses of the letter, is to bring all nations to faith's obedience (Rom. 1:5). That is, in fulfillment of his promise to Abraham and through the work of the Lord Jesus Christ, God is bringing people of *all nations* into that place of redemptive blessing that is constituted (as it was for Abraham) by trusting in God and demonstrating that trust through obedient living. The gospel is the message that makes that possible and the power that accomplishes it.

Having stated this at the outset of the letter, Paul returns to it at the end (Rom. 16:26),[2] but with amplified emphasis on how this work of the gospel in bringing all nations to the obedience of faith is ultimately for the glory of God *and* a matter of joy for the nations. It is worth hearing Paul's own excitement in piling up Old Testament Scriptures in support of this great prospect, and in seeing how he links the self-sacrificing servanthood of the Messiah Jesus and his own missionary apostleship in accomplishing it. Bear in mind as you read this passage that "the Gentiles" are "the nations" – it is the same word in Greek – *ta ethne*. The variation in translation in most English versions can obscure this important point in Paul's theology and practice of mission. Paul saw his mission in thoroughly Abrahamic terms: blessing to all nations on earth. What could be more joy-generating than that?

> For I tell you that Christ has become a servant of the Jews on behalf of God's truth, so that the promises made to the patriarchs might be confirmed and, moreover, that the Gentiles [*nations*] might glorify God for his mercy. As it is written:

> "Therefore I will praise you among the Gentiles [*nations*];
> I will sing the praises of your name."[3]

> Again, it says,

> "Rejoice, you Gentiles [*nations*], with his people."[4]

> And again,

> "Praise the Lord, all you Gentiles [*nations*];
> let all the peoples extol him."[5]

---

2. Notice how Rom. 1:1–5 and 16:25–27 use matching phrases in a way that must be deliberate.

3. 2 Sam. 22:50.

4. Ps. 18:49.

5. Deut. 32:43.

And again, Isaiah says,

> "The Root of Jesse will spring up,
>   one who will arise to rule over the nations;
>   in him the Gentiles [*nations*] will hope."[6]

. . . I have written you quite boldly on some points to remind you of them again, because of the grace God gave me to be a minister of Christ Jesus to the Gentiles [*nations*]. He gave me the priestly duty of proclaiming the gospel of God, so that the Gentiles [*nations*] might become an offering acceptable to God, sanctified by the Holy Spirit.

If God desires every knee to bow to Jesus and every tongue to confess him, so should we. We should be "jealous" (as Scripture sometimes puts it) for the honour of his name—troubled when it remains unknown, hurt when it is ignored, indignant when it is blasphemed, and all the time anxious and determined that it shall be given the honour and glory which are due to it. The highest of all missionary motives is neither obedience to the Great Commission (important as that is), nor love for sinners who are alienated and perishing (strong as that incentive is, especially when we contemplate the wrath of God) but rather zeal—burning and passionate zeal—for the glory of Jesus Christ. . . . Before this supreme goal of the Christian mission, all unworthy motives wither and die.

John Stott[7]

Therefore I glory in Christ Jesus in my service to God. I will not venture to speak of anything except what Christ has accomplished through me in leading the Gentiles [*nations*] to obey God by what I have said and done—by the power of signs and wonders, through the power of the Spirit of God. (Rom. 15:8–12, 15–19; my insertions in italics)

• • •

Now to him who is able to establish you in accordance with my gospel, the message I proclaim about Jesus Christ, in keeping with the revelation of the mystery hidden for long ages past, but now revealed and made known through the prophetic writings by the command of the eternal God, so that all the Gentiles [*nations*] might come to faith and obedience—to the only wise God be glory forever through Jesus Christ! Amen. (Rom. 16:25–27; my insertions in italics)

The great final vision of the Bible in Revelation goes further still, in seeing not only all the nations of humanity united in praising God, but every creature in the whole creation bringing glory to God.

Then I heard every creature in heaven and on earth and under the earth and on the sea, and all that is in them, saying:

> "To him who sits on the throne and to the Lamb
>   be praise and honor and glory and power,
>   for ever and ever!" (Rev. 5:13)

It is not enough, however, to recognize that worship is the ultimate *goal of mission*, in the sense of bringing all nations to glorify God by worshiping, trusting and

---

6. Isa. 11:10.   7. Stott, *The Message of Romans*, 53.

obeying him through the gospel of Jesus Christ. We also need to see how worship is part of the *means of mission.*

Now there is an obvious pragmatic reason for this that we can mention first. Those whose reason for existence on earth is to bring others to praise the living God and pray to him need to be doing so themselves or their whole mission is a hypocritical impossibility. However, a more profound reason is that, since glorifying God and enjoying him forever will be the joyful privilege of the redeemed humanity in the new creation for all eternity, to engage in such praise and prayer here and now is

> The very nature of God, God's majesty and goodness, evoke adoration and gratitude. Such a response serves to honour God *while proclaiming to all who hear that this YHWH God is worthy of one's love and fidelity.* Hence praise is not only devotion but also testimony, both an exalting of God and *a proclamation that seeks to draw others into the worship of God.* (italics added)
>
> *Samuel E. Balentine* [8]

an act of anticipation, a signpost toward the future. And when we do it boldly and affirmatively, we invite others not only into the present experience of worship, but also into the future glory of a redeemed eternity.

So let us trace just a few themes in our biblical theology where praise and prayer can be seen to have missional dimensions.

MISSIONAL PRAISE

Created for Praise

Throughout this book we have been finding answers to the question, "For what do God's people exist?" Thinking of God's people in Old Testament terms, we have seen the crucial importance of God's promise to Abraham that, through him and his descendants, all nations on earth would find blessing. Old Testament Israel, then, was created for the sake of the blessing of all nations of humanity. Israel was the nation that existed for the sake of other nations.

Other texts, however, present a different divine purpose in the creation of Israel:

> ... everyone who is called by my name,
>> whom I created *for my glory,*
>> whom I formed and made. (Isa. 43:7; italics added)

> ... my people, my chosen,
>> the people I formed *for myself*
>> that they may proclaim *my praise.* (Isa. 43:20b – 21; italics added)

•   •   •

---

8. Samuel E. Balentine, *Prayer in the Hebrew Bible: The Drama of Divine-Human Dialogue* (Minneapolis: Augsburg Fortress, 1993), 199.

"For as a belt is bound around the waist, so I bound the whole house of Israel and the whole house of Judah to me," declares the LORD, "to be my people for *my renown and praise and honor.*" (Jer. 13:11; italics added)

These texts affirm that God created Israel for the sake of his own glory, to bring him praise. So is there a contradiction here? Was Israel created for the sake of the nations or for the sake of God's glory and praise?

The answer, of course, is – both. For as we have seen, God's ultimate purpose for the blessing of the nations is that they should come to know and glorify him as their greatest good. Thus Israel's existence for that global purpose is bound up with the requirement that they themselves should be a people who embody that knowledge and worship.

This is most succinctly seen in Psalm 100, which puts the fact that Israel is a people created by and belonging to God (v. 3) right in the middle of the summons to worship and praise him that is found on either side (vv. 2 and 4). This is, indeed, universalized horizontally to "all the earth" (v. 1) and vertically to "all generations" (v. 5). In other words, Israel's existence as a people created for the praise of God (vv. 2 – 4) is bound up with the glory of God that fills all space and all history (vv. 1 and 5).

The mission of God's people, then, is derived from the fact that they were created to bring praise and glory to God *and* to bring the nations of the world into the same orchestra of doxology.

Redeemed for Praise

The language of creation and redemption blends together rather seamlessly, of course – especially in Isaiah, where Israel is both created and redeemed by God. When we come to the New Testament, the redeeming work of God is linked to the responsibility of bringing praise and glory to God in two key texts from Paul and Peter.

Ephesians 1:3 – 14

In this most amazing passage (which is incredibly one whole sentence in Greek), Paul uses the phrase *"the praise of his glory"* three times, in verses 6 (with the addition of "of his grace"), 12 and 14.

In verse 6, Paul is speaking of the love of God that chose us from all eternity to belong to him "for the praise of the glory of His grace" (NASB).

In verse 12 he is almost certainly speaking about Old Testament Israel – the nation from whom came the first people to know about and put their faith in the Messiah Jesus. They had been called "to be for the praise of his glory" (echoing Old Testament texts such as those referred to above).

And then in verse 14 he summarizes the whole work of salvation, which now includes Gentiles as well as Jews ("you also"; v. 13), as being "to the praise of his glory".

This triple emphasis shows how deeply Paul had drunk from the well of Old Testament ecclesiology – Israel's self-understanding of their identity and role as the people of God. Israel had been created and redeemed to bring praise and glory to the living God, and whatever was true of *them* was inevitably true for *Christians* – those from all nations who were now being brought into the covenant people of God through Jesus Christ.

In this way, the *worshiping* life of God's people and their *missional* function of extending that worship among the nations (such as the cosmopolitan, multiethnic communities of Ephesus) were integral to each other.

> The glory of God is the revelation of God, and the glory of his grace is his self-disclosure as a gracious God. To live to the praise of the glory of his grace is both to worship him ourselves by our words and deeds as the gracious God he is, *and to cause others to see and praise him too*. This was God's will for Israel in Old Testament days (Isa. 43:21; Jer. 13:11), and it is also his purpose for his people today. (italics added)
>
> John Stott[9]

1 Peter 2:9 – 12

Peter makes the same point by a different route and with even more echoes of the Old Testament. Earlier in the chapter he had compared the people of God in Christ both to the Old Testament temple (as "living stones", just as Paul had done in Eph. 2:21 – 22), and also to the priests who offered sacrifices there (1 Peter 2:5). But what are those "spiritual sacrifices" that Christian believers, God's "royal priesthood" (v. 9), now to offer? They are the worship and praise that they "declare" as part of the "good lives" that they live in the midst of the nations. We need to put the two side by side to see how integral they are (sadly many Bible translations put a paragraph division or new heading before verse 11, obscuring the urgent flow of Peter's point).

> But you are a chosen people, a royal priesthood, a holy nation, God's special possession, that you may declare the praises of him who called you out of darkness into his wonderful light....
>
> ... Live such good lives among the pagans [*the nations*] that, though they accuse you of doing wrong, they may see your good deeds and glorify God on the day he visits us. (1 Peter 2:9, 12; my insertion in italics)

Peter's thought is so saturated with the Scriptures that almost every phrase he writes has one or more echoes of Old Testament texts. The purpose of being God's people expressed in v. 9 – "that you may declare the praises of him who called you out of darkness into his wonderful light" – clearly has an exodus allusion in the second half. Christians too have had their taste of God's redemption ("out of ... into").

But the first half of the phrase, "that you may declare the praises", probably has two specific Old Testament texts in mind (this is Biblical Theology for Life in action!).

---

9. John Stott, *The Message of Ephesians: God's New Society* (The Bible Speaks Today; Leicester: IVP, and Downers Grove, IL: IVP, 1979), 50.

Isaiah 43:21 (quoted above). The word Peter uses, translated "praises" (*aretas*), is the same as the LXX version of Isaiah 43:21 – "that they may proclaim my praise". It is not the commonest word for "praise" in either Testament, and in fact it occurs in the plural like this only four times in the Old Testament – all of them in Isaiah (Isa. 42:8, 12; 43:21; 63:7). It is clear that it refers to praise, not as general affirmations of nice things about God, but specifically as celebrating his great acts of salvation and mercy. And Isaiah, like Peter, envisages such praise as the responsibility of God's people *with the clear intention of drawing other people to do the same* (in Isa. 42:12, "Let *them* ... proclaim his praise" refers to foreign nations). This is missional praise.

Psalm 9:14. The word Peter uses, translated "declare" (*exangello*), is the same as the LXX version of Psalm 9:14, "that I may declare your praises ..." (v. 15 in LXX). This term refers to the declaration of mighty acts of God (whether his historic acts of redemption for Israel as a whole, or personal acts on behalf of the worshiper), in the context of public worship. Wherever this word is used in the Psalms, it has this sense of public declaration of what God has done, as an act of praise and rejoicing (Pss. 71:15; 73:28; 79:13; 107:22).

So it seems certain then that Peter is making a double point here.

First, he insists that just as Christians inherit the identity and titles of Old Testament Israel (a chosen, priestly, holy people belonging to God), so also they inherit the purpose of Israel's creation and redemption (to declare the praise of God and bring glory to him).

But second, he insists that the purpose of such declarative praise is not a private affair between God and the worshipers, but it spills out into the public arena as one of the means by which God draws the nations to himself. It is in, other words, part of what it means to fulfill the Abrahamic commission of being God's people for the sake of the rest of the nations coming to enjoy God's blessing.

The praise of God's people is missional. The mission of God's people includes doxology.

There is an evangelistic power in public worship that declares the praise of God, which cannot merely be equated with personal evangelism, but certainly complements it. John Dickson makes the point very effectively:

> The theme of promoting the gospel looms large in the middle chapters of 1 Peter. In 2:12 the apostle urges believers to live such good lives that their pagan neighbours would end up giving glory to God (compare Matthew 5:14 – 16). In 3:1 Peter drives this point home by urging wives to win their unbelieving husbands to faith through godly conduct. Then, just a few paragraphs later in 3:15, he calls on us "to give an answer to everyone who asks you to give the reason for the hope that you have" (a statement we'll explore in the next chapter). Given the missionary thrust of these chapters it seems likely that Peter is thinking of some kind of evangelism in the words of 1 Peter 2:9: "declare the praises of him who called you out of darkness."

But what type of evangelism is Peter talking about? I once assumed (and taught) that the apostle was talking about *personal* evangelism. I interpreted the phrase "declare the praises" to mean something like tell the gospel to your friends and family. I now think that was probably a bit hasty. The expression "declare the praises" ... comes straight out of the Old Testament's description of Israel's public praise, with its creeds, prayers and ever-present psalm-singing.

When we remember that the biblical Judaism of Peter's day already thought of its public praise as beneficial to outsiders, it seems far more likely that the apostle is talking in 1 Peter 2:9 not so much about conversational evangelism but about the evangelism that goes on when God's people gather to celebrate in word and song the saving wonders of the Lord..... Peter's words are strongly evangelistic without actually having anything to do with what we call personal evangelism....

Worship involves witness. The factor which unites them is the name of God. For what is worship but to "glory in His holy name", to "praise", "bless", or "stand in awe of" it? And what is witness but to "proclaim the name of the Lord" to others? These expressions are found in the Psalter, and it is in the Psalms that the proper combination of worship and witness is most clearly and commonly found.... Worship is "worth-ship", an acknowledgement of the worth of Almighty God.... It is therefore impossible for me to worship God and yet not care two cents whether anybody else worships Him too.... Worship which does not beget witness is hypocrisy. We cannot acclaim the worth of God if we have no desire to proclaim it.

John Stott[10]

Declaring God's praises together—in our readings, creeds, preaching, psalms, hymns and spiritual songs—is one of our central acts of worship as the people of God.... One reason for the central importance of praise is God's sheer worthiness; we need no other reason for viewing praise as a high and holy activity. But, given the strong mission theme in 1 Peter, combined with the equally strong Jewish biblical tradition of doxological evangelism, we are probably right to detect a secondary reason for the great importance of public praise. Through it, we announce God's mercy and power to those who overhear us, who have not yet been called out of darkness into his wonderful light.[11]

Witnessing through Praise

So we were *created* to bring glory to God our creator. We are *redeemed* to declare the praises of God our redeemer. And what makes both missional is that we are to do all this in the midst of the nations who do *not* yet know God as creator and redeemer. Worship and witness are closely intertwined.

That is exactly the thrust of Psalm 96—which I regard as one of the most richly missional songs in the whole Bible. Its opening three verses are a remarkable call to praise, addressed to "all the earth", but clearly intended to be sung (initially at least) by those who have experienced the great realities of which it speaks:

10. Stott, *Our Guilty Silence*, 27–28.   11. Dickson, *Best Kept Secret*, 160–61, 163.

> Sing to the LORD a new song;
>> sing to the LORD, all the earth.
> Sing to the LORD, praise his name;
>> proclaim his salvation day after day.
> Declare his glory among the nations,
>> his marvelous deeds among all peoples. (Ps. 96:1 – 3)

"Let's sing a new song!" cries the songwriter.

"Sure, what are the lyrics?" we respond.

"Let's sing about the *name* of YHWH, the *salvation* of YHWH, the *glory* of YHWH and the *marvelous deeds* of YHWH."

"But those are the old songs!" we protest. "Those are the words of all our great songs since Israel was redeemed from Egypt, learned the name of YHWH at Sinai, saw his glory in the tabernacle, and experienced repeated acts of salvation at his hand. What makes this a new song?"

"It may be an old song for us," our psalmist replies, undeterred, "but it will be a new song 'among the nations', 'among all peoples'."

That seems to be the thrust of this great summons. The celebratory worship of Israel will constitute a witness to the nations. The old songs of Israel become the new song of the nations.

But how were the nations to hear, we might wonder? We do not usually think of the Israelites of the Old Testament engaged in cross-cultural missionary evangelism. No, indeed. Even Jonah only fits that description in a reluctant way. But there were at least two ways in which the nations were exposed to the witnessing worship of Israelites.

First, Jerusalem itself was a cosmopolitan city from the days of Solomon on, with people from many of the surrounding nations coming and going–in trading, cultural and political activities. Many of them would have visited the temple and experienced the worship of YHWH, the God of Israelites. Solomon envisaged precisely that in his prayer of dedication of the temple (1 Kings 8:41 – 43). The Queen of Sheba, the mother of all tourists, is the most illustrious example (1 Kings 10).

Second, from the exile on, there were substantial numbers of Jews living in the communities of the diaspora, throughout Mesopotamia and the eastern Mediterranean lands.[12] And we know that the faith, worship and Scriptures of the Jews were a talking point among other peoples, many of whom were attracted and became what the New Testament describes as "God-fearers".

---

12. In fact the extent of the Jewish diaspora was far wider than that. There is evidence for settlements of Jews, and the acceptance of Jewish faith among indigenous peoples, in China, India, Arabia and Yemen, through northeastern Africa, right across North Africa, and the furthest extent of Europe under the Roman empire. There is equally no doubt that in many of these places, the prior existence of significant Jewish communities provided a platform for the earliest arrival of Christianity (as we see in the work of Paul in the New Testament). A detailed survey of this can be read in De Ridder, *Discipling the Nations*, 58 – 87. For a thorough survey of the impact of the Jewish diaspora, and especially of their synagogue worship, in bringing Gentiles to conversion and faith in the God of Israel, see John P. Dickson, *Mission-Commitment in Ancient Judaism and in the Pauline Communities*, 74 – 85, and for the influence of this on Paul's mission practice and expectation, ibid., 293 – 302.

John Dickson, again, who has thoroughly researched Jewish practice during those centuries, points out how the worship of Israel had a missional dimension, long before the New Testament church embarked on the task of itinerant evangelistic mission. Indeed, it is clear that Paul made effective use of this periphery of God-fearing Gentiles in the synagogues he routinely visited in the course of his missionary work:

> It may surprise you to know that many Jews in the period between the Old and New Testaments took seriously the idea of public worship as an act of mission. They knew full well that the collective praise of God in the synagogue or the temple was one of God's ways of convincing Gentiles to bow their knee to the Lord. In some cases the Jews had great success. We know that numerous synagogues in the first century attracted great crowds of pagans wanting to know more about the God of the Jews....
>
> From the psalm singing of ancient Israel to the synagogue services of Jesus' day, public praise of the true God was believed to serve a missionary function. This was not the purpose of the gatherings—I am not suggesting these were Jewish "seeker services"—but it was considered an important by-product of the corporate praise of God.[14]

> One can hardly conceive of more providentially supplied means for the Christian mission to reach the Gentile community [than the Jewish diaspora]. Wherever the community of Christ went it found at hand the tools needed to reach the nations: a people living under covenant promise and responsible election, and the Scriptures, God's revelation to all men.... What Old Testament Israel and the nations could not know, until someone would tell them, was the exceedingly good news of the fulfillment of God's covenant in Christ.
>
> *Richard R. De Ridder*[13]

Perhaps this gives us some insight into why it was that the conversion of the continent of Europe began in a prison when two Jews (who had been "severely flogged") "were praying and singing hymns to God and the other prisoners were listening to them" (Acts 16:25); and why the same apostle Paul was sure that if the church in Corinth would worship God aright, any unbeliever who came into their meeting would "fall down and worship God, exclaiming, 'God is really among you'" (1 Cor. 14:25).

That's missional praise.

MISSIONAL PRAYER
Prayer as a Mark of Distinction from the Nations

Israel was intended to be a visible model to the nations. As we saw in chapter 8, this was a significant motivating factor for keeping God's law and living in the way he

---

13. De Ridder, *Discipling the Nations*, 87.   14. Dickson, *Best Kept Secret*, 158–59.

provided for them. In Deuteronomy 4:6–8, Moses puts the worship of Israel alongside the social justice of their society as distinguishing markers that should arouse the curiosity and admiration of the nations:

This crucial place of prayer reaffirms the great goal of God to uphold and display his glory for the enjoyment of the redeemed from all the nations.... The missionary purpose of God is as invincible as the fact that he is God. He will achieve his purpose by creating white-hot worshipers from every people, tongue, tribe and nation (Rev. 5:9; 7:9). And he will be engaged to do it through prayer. Therefore, it is almost impossible to overemphasize the awesome place of prayer in the purposes of God for the world.

John Piper[15]

Observe them [*God's laws*] carefully, for this will show your wisdom and understanding to the nations, who will hear about all these decrees and say, "Surely this great nation is a wise and understanding people." What other nation is so great as to have their gods near them the way the Lord our God is near us whenever we pray to him? And what other nation is so great as to have such righteous decrees and laws as this body of laws I am setting before you today? (Deut. 4:6–8)

So the prayer life of Israel was intended to be missional. It was a demonstration of the nearness of God. Moses is not suggesting that Israel should pray *in order to* be seen and admired by others (in conflict with the instructions of Jesus to the contrary), but that the normal exercise of their relationship with God in prayer should form one part of that witness to the reality of the living God for which they were created.

Prayer for the Blessing of the Nations

It seems a long time since we were having lunch with Abraham and his three guests in Genesis 18 (see ch. 5). We paid close attention to verse 19, where God links his missional purpose for blessing all nations to his election of Abraham and the ethical contrast between Abraham's future community and the world characterized by Sodom. Abraham was told to teach his own household, but the first thing he did in the wake of God's revelation of his plans to him was to pray for the city.

Abraham's intercession for Sodom is a remarkable passage (Gen. 18:22–33). It provides yet another way in which Abraham was a model for his descendants— physical and spiritual. Knowing that Sodom stood in the blast path of God's judgment did not make him turn away, but made him turn to prayer. Moses and Daniel were among those who followed his example on behalf of Israel in similar plight (Ex. 32–34; Dan. 9). Intercessory prayer for the nations is an essential part of mission to the nations.

The Israelites knew they could pray anywhere, for God was everywhere, as David knew to his comfort (Ps. 139), and Jonah proved in possibly the strangest place

15. Piper, *Let the Nations Be Glad*, 63.

prayer has ever been offered (Jonah 2:1). But above all they prayed in the temple because it was, by God's intention, "a house of prayer". We know it also, of course, as the place of sacrifice. But it is a remarkable fact that on the great occasion of its dedication by Solomon, not a word is said about sacrifices in Solomon's speeches on that day (though sacrifices were offered), but a great deal is said about prayer.

In fact, Solomon's prayer at the dedication of the temple is a prayer about prayer! He envisages a variety of situations in which Israel would particularly pray to God in the temple, or "toward" it—situations in which Solomon then asks God to hear and answer their prayers (1 Kings 8:22–53).

But then, as we saw in chapter 8, Solomon extends the focus of his prayer to the people of other nations, who will also turn up at the temple to pray. As we said above, Jerusalem was a cosmopolitan city, full of foreigners for all kinds of reasons. What if they decide to bring their requests to YHWH the God of Israel?

"Do whatever the foreigners ask of you," prays Solomon—asking God to do for foreigners what God had never promised in such terms to do for Israel. It is a remarkable prayer for God to hear and answer the prayers of the nations, and the reason Solomon suggests to support the request goes right to God's missional heart, "so that all the peoples of the earth may know your name and fear you, as do your own people Israel" (1 Kings 8:43). Here is the Abrahamic commission translated into missional prayer. Solomon prays *for* the nations, that they will pray *to* YHWH God, and prays *to* God that he will answer them, for his own name's sake. This is surely one of the most missional moments in the Old Testament—at least until we come to this next one.

In Jeremiah 29, Jeremiah is not praying but writing a letter in which he urges other people to pray. In fact, he is writing to Israelites who are in one of the situations described by Solomon in his prayer—"When they sin against you—for there is no one who does not sin—and you become angry with them and give them over to their enemies, who take them captive to their own lands, far away or near" (1 Kings 8:46). Yes, Israel is in exile in Babylon. And they doubtless are praying to God in desperation for themselves and for some hope of future return. But that is not what Jeremiah tells them to pray for. Amazingly he instructs them to pray *for Babylon*! Pray for their enemies! Seek their *šalom*.

Jeremiah 29:7 provides chapter and verse (except they didn't have them at the time!) for the teaching of Jesus: "Love your enemies, do good to those who hate you, bless those who curse you, *pray for those who mistreat you*" (Luke 6:27–28; italics added).

As we saw in chapter 13, this instruction of Jeremiah is part of a strong biblical tradition that the people of God exist in the world to bring the blessing of God, the presence of God, the power of God, into the public arena—even in the heart of enemy territory. Prayer is one powerful means of doing that.

Solomon, then, prays that foreigners will pray to God for themselves while Jeremiah asks Israel to pray to God for foreigners. Both believed that God would answer such prayer for the glory of his name and for the *šalom* of both those who pray and those who are prayed for.

That's missional prayer.

Prayer as Subversion of the Idolatry of the Nations

I like to think, as I said before, that Daniel heard that letter from Jeremiah when it was read to the first wave of exiles (for he and his young friends were among that first group of exiles). And I like to think that he took it seriously and included prayer for Babylon in his habit of thrice-daily prayer. I find such a conjecture as at least a reasonable explanation for his apparent affection for Nebuchadnezzar and desire to help him avoid God's judgment (Dan. 4; see ch. 13).

However, there is an even stronger element to the prayer of Daniel in Daniel 6. It circumvents the idolatrous *hubris* of the king. You recall that Darius, giving in to the flattery of those in his government who simply wanted to get Daniel out of the way so that his diligence and integrity would not block their own corrupt ambitions, passed a decree that for a month everybody in his kingdom should pray to no god other than himself. It was an absurd decree, when you think about it. First, it claimed deity for the king himself – always a dangerous project as we have known since Pharaoh tried it in Egypt.

But second, it is symptomatic of a diluted view of what it means to be "god" – as if any other gods that happened to be around in the multiethnic religious plurality of the Persian empire would politely have a moratorium on their own prayer-answering credentials for a few weeks and allow all requests to be diverted to this upstart human king and wannabe god. Yet, for all its absurdity, it is typical of the arrogance of state power. States like to posture as the sole source of all benefit to their citizens and to demand in return ultimate loyalty. We may not quite deify our kings or presidents, but we easily turn patriotism into a creed and alleged lack of it into a heresy.

But what did Daniel do, faced with this demand to acknowledge no god but the king he was otherwise serving so efficiently? He subverted it. He went on praying to the one whom he knew to be the only living God. Whether he knew it would get him into trouble or not, he made no effort to conceal it (Dan. 6:10; all he had to do, after all, was close his windows!).

For Darius was not God. The Persian empire was not God. Only YHWH was God, and the act of prayer was an act that relativized and subverted all human political authority.

Prayer is to say, "There is a higher throne." Prayer appeals to a higher authority. Prayer is, in short, a political act. It affirms that all human political power is subordinate not ultimate, relative not absolute – to be obeyed so long as it is consistent with obedience to the living God (as it had clearly been so far for Daniel), but to be disobeyed whenever it presumes to command what God prohibits or to prohibit what God commands.

The response of Daniel is mirrored in the response of the earliest followers of Jesus (not yet even called "Christians") when faced with the explicit command of the authorities to stop speaking about Jesus. They turn to prayer. And in their prayer they robustly affirm the sovereignty of God over heaven and earth *and over all nations and their rulers*, and they pray for boldness to disobey the state in order to obey Jesus (Acts 4:23–31).

That's missional prayer too.

Prayer and the Work of Mission

When we turn to the New Testament, we find prayer as the saturating medium of the mission of Jesus, of the church in Acts, and of Paul's instructions to the churches in relation to his own missionary work.

Jesus

Few things confirm and illustrate the incarnate humanity of the Son of God in the person of Jesus of Nazareth than his life of prayer. "I and the Father are one," he could say, and yet that did not dissolve the reality of his human dependence on his Father and the need for prayer.

His earthly mission began at his baptism, and it was while he was praying that the wonderfully Trinitarian moment of affirmation of his identity occurred (Luke 3:21). If he was fasting in the wilderness at the time of his struggle and testing there, it is certain that he was also praying. The pressure of his healing ministry did not drive out his times of prayer (Mark 1:35). The choice of twelve disciples for their mission was made after a night of prayer (Luke 6:12–14). Their early missionary training was carried out with Jesus engaged in spiritual warfare on their behalf (Luke 10:17–21). Peter's faith survived the collapse of his courage because Jesus prayed for him so that his mission could continue beyond his repentance (Luke 22:31–32). His last evening with the disciples before his death included prayer for them and for the church's ongoing mission to the world (John 17). Gethsemane was above all else an agony of prayer. Not even the cruelty of crucifixion could stop him praying.

And of course, Jesus taught his disciples to pray. But although it would be instructive to work through the Lord's Prayer as a fundamentally missional prayer, we can take note here of what my colleague Hugh Palmer[17] calls, "The other Lord's

> Why is prayer so critical for mission? [Colossians 4:2–4] provides the answer. In prayer we lift the work of the gospel above mere circumstances and into the hands of the One who governs everything . . . [the One who can provide] an "open door", even though the current messenger is locked up "in chains".
>
> John Dickson[16]

16. Dickson, *The Best Kept Secret*, 73.   17. Rector of All Souls Church, Langham Place, London,

Prayer". In fact, as he points out, it is the only other time in the Gospels when Jesus explicitly tells the disciples *what* to pray. And it is unmistakably missional—in context and content.

> When he saw the crowds, he had compassion on them, because they were harassed and helpless, like sheep without a shepherd. Then he said to his disciples, "The harvest is plentiful but the workers are few. Ask the Lord of the harvest, therefore, to send out workers into his harvest field." (Matt. 9:36–38)

Why, asks Hugh Palmer, do we use the "Our Father" prayer so regularly in Christian liturgy, and this "other Lord's Prayer" so spasmodically? What might have been the story of Christian mission if *this* prayer had become the one we had memorized and repeated (and meant) down through the centuries? Of course, it's a dangerous prayer to pray. It tends to become self-answering, as the disciples found. For if they did do as Jesus told them, the very next thing that happens is that they become the answer to their own prayer as Jesus sends them out (Matt. 10).

Acts

It would consume more space than we can afford to list all the instances of prayer in the book of Acts, but it would make an instructive personal study to go through the book taking note of every occasion—noting especially how closely prayer is bound up with the mission of the church. A few examples give the flavour.

Even before Pentecost, having been told by the risen Christ that they were to be his witnesses to the ends of the earth, the first response of the disciples was to gather for prayer (Acts 1:12–14). Prayer was a fundamental ingredient of the growing number of believers (2:42). It was their response to opposition and persecution (4:23–31; 12:12), their first act in situations of new evangelism (8:14–15). It was in the context of worship, prayer and fasting that the church at Antioch was led by the Holy Spirit to initiate the first intentionally centrifugal Gentile mission (13:1–3). Prayer was the first evangelistic action on the soil of Europe (16:13), and a miraculously effective one when combined with late night singing (13:25).

Paul

Paul had unbounded faith in the power of God and in the power of the gospel. But he also knew the power of prayer. And he knew that all three mysteriously worked together in the accomplishment of God's mission. His own personal survival depended on God's deliverance—"helped", as he put it, by the prayers of others. We all know what it is to ask others to pray for us in times of trouble or danger, but for Paul it was particularly focused on his desire to be delivered in order that he could carry on his missionary task of proclaiming the gospel (2 Cor. 1:9–11; Phil. 1:19–26).

Even his prayers for deliverance were connected to asking the churches to pray for his boldness in evangelistic proclamation. Again, a moment to read the following three prayers would be a moment well spent (2 Thess. 3:1–2; Col. 4:2–3; Eph. 6:18–20).

There has been some debate as to why Paul's instructions about prayer do not specifically call for prayer for *evangelistic* mission more frequently than this. Was it because Paul did not expect his churches to be engaged in evangelistic witness? That has been argued, but decisively refuted in my view.[18] More likely is the view of D. A. Carson that, for Paul, mission and prayer were both alike comprehensive realities. There should be all kinds of prayer for all kinds of mission.

Our tendency is to compartmentalize the various tasks entrusted by God to the church as a whole, and to label some of them as "mission" and give other names to other things, and then to assign special prayer to one or the other. But this does not reflect New Testament realities:

> We have tended to think of mission as a discrete project (or as discrete projects), often of a cross-cultural kind, with the result that special prayer for this isolable function is called for. But apart from the special calling on his own life as an apostle (indeed as the apostle to the Gentiles), Paul sees mission in holistic, even cosmic terms. The glory of God, the reign of Christ, the declaration of the mystery of the gospel, the conversion of men and women, the growth and edification of the church, the defeat of cosmic powers, the pursuit of holiness, the passion for godly fellowship and unity in the church, the unification of Jews and Gentiles, doing good to all, but especially to fellow believers – these are all woven into a seamless garment. All the elements are held together by a vision in which God is at the centre and Jesus Christ effects the changes for his glory and his people's good. This means that thanksgiving and intercessory prayer, though sweeping in the range of topics touched, are held together by a unified, God-centred, vision. Our more piecemeal approach looks for certain kinds of links which for the apostle are embedded in a comprehensive vision.[19]

That is a fine statement of some key elements of the holistic mission of God's people that I have been arguing for throughout this book, following the contours of the Bible's story line. Prayer accompanies the whole Bible story – from the prayer of Abraham for Sodom in Genesis to the prayers of the saints and martyrs in Revelation.

Prayer as Spiritual Warfare
Prayer accompanies the Bible story precisely because it is the story of war – the great battle throughout history in which God relentlessly drives back the forces of evil and darkness, decisively defeated them at the cross of Christ, and will utterly elimi-

18. A finely argued refutation of the view that Paul did not particularly expect his churches to engage in evangelism (from the shortage of explicit instructions to do so) is provided by Peter T. O'Brien, *Gospel and Mission in the Writings of Paul* (Grand Rapids: Baker, 1993; Carlisle: Paternoster, 1995).

19. D. A. Carson, "Paul's Mission and Prayer," in *The Gospel to the Nations: Perspectives on Paul's Mission,* Peter Bold and Mark Thompson, eds. (Downers Grove: IVP, and Leicester: Apollos, 2000), 175–84 (esp. 182).

nate them at the climactic end of the story. This is a war whose outcome is assured, guaranteed by the very "Godness" of God. God will have the victory.

God has ordained prayer to have a crucial place in the mission of the church. The purpose of prayer is to make clear to all the participants in this war that the victory belongs to the Lord. Prayer is God's appointed means of bringing grace to us and glory to himself.... That is why the missionary enterprise advances by prayer. The chief end of God is to glorify God. He will do this in the sovereign triumph of his missionary purpose that the nations worship him. He will secure this triumph by entering into the warfare and becoming the main combatant. And he will make that engagement plain to all the participants *through prayer,* because prayer shows that the power is from the Lord....

Prayer is the walkie-talkie of the church on the battlefield of the world in the service of the Word. It is not a domestic intercom to increase the temporal comforts of the saints.... It is for those on active duty. And in their hands it proves the supremacy of God in the pursuit of the nations. When mission moves forward by prayer, it magnifies the power of God. When it moves by human management, it magnifies man.

John Piper[20]

Spiritual warfare is not about naming territorial spirits, claiming the ground or binding demons. It is all about the gospel. It is to live a gospel life, to preserve gospel unity and to proclaim gospel truth. It is to do this in the face of a hostile world, a deceptive enemy and our own sinful natures. And it is to pray to a sovereign God for gospel opportunities. Advance comes through godliness, unity, proclamation and prayer.

Timothy Chester, on Ephesians 6[21]

Prayer is participation in that ultimate victory and in the struggle that leads to it. For this is the mission of God, and the mission of God's people is to be coworkers with God in the field that is God's world. If the battle is the Lord's, then those who are involved in the battle need to stay in constant intimate communication with their commander. This is clear even in the ministry of Jesus, which from beginning to end involved combat with the evil one and his demonic minions. And prayer was his most effective weapon – ours, too.

So it is not surprising then that Paul follows his instructions about putting on the armour of the Lord for spiritual warfare in Ephesians 6 with immediate reference to prayer. In fact, Ephesians 6:10 – 20 is one of those amazing single sentences of Paul, which begins with the reminder that "our struggle is not against flesh and blood, but against the rulers, against the authorities, against the powers of this dark world and against the spiritual forces of evil in the heavenly realms", but then does not stop its list of instructions for combat readiness until we are told to "pray in the Spirit on all occasions with all kinds of prayers and requests. With this in mind, be alert and always keep on praying for all the Lord's people."

Prayer is as much part of our armour and weaponry as truth, righteousness, faith and salvation. And such prayer is essentially missional, for it accompanies the battle for the gospel. Peter O'Brien, indeed, refers to this great climax of Ephesians as "The Pauline Great Commission":

---

20. Piper, *Let the Nations Be Glad,* 57, 59, 67 (his italics).
21. Timothy Chester, *The Message of Prayer* (The Bible Speaks Today; Leicester, IVP, and Downers Grove, IL: IVP, 2003), 231.

Our circumstances may be vastly different from Paul's; our spiritual gifts and opportunities may vary significantly from his. But we are involved in the same spiritual warfare as the apostle, we have the same injunction laid upon us to stand firm, the same divine weapons available for us to use (especially the essential spiritual weapon of prayer), and the same defensive and offensive postures to adopt. We are to resist temptation and to devote our lives energetically to spreading the gospel. These are not optional extras. They are musts and this is why the apostle's words about sharing the gospel effectively in the power of the Spirit wherever we find ourselves may be styled "The Pauline Great Commission".[22]

SUMMARY

Praise and prayer—two of the most fundamental activities of the people of God, two things by which they are most identified, and two things through which they engage in their mission as God's people—whatever other activities such mission may also include, as we have seen all through this book. In this chapter we have observed as a theme of biblical theology that praise is what we were created for and redeemed for, and it is our missional task to share in God's will that all peoples and all creation should come to praise and worship him, to find their greatest joy in glorifying him. And we have seen that prayer weaves its way through the whole Bible as a mark of God's people, undergirding their mission, and in some circumstances even constituting a dimension of their mission.

Samuel Balentine has a fine conclusion to his survey of the biblical theology of prayer in the Old Testament. He argues that the role of the church, as a "house of prayer" that has inherited one of the prime functions of the temple, is "to keep the community and the world in God" and "to keep God in the community and the world". If our mission is indeed to share in the mission of the God who so loved the world that he gave his own Son to save it and ultimately to dwell again within it, then this is a challenging way to express the purpose of prayer. Balentine's closing words to the church are a fitting challenge with which to finish this chapter too:

> What if we do not exercise our God-given responsibility as a community of faith? What if we do not pray to keep ourselves and our world in God? What if we do not pray and fight to keep God in the world? I submit that if we do not, either the church will become a den of robbers where thieves congregate to count their loot and hide out from God, or it will become a shining, splendid edifice, pointing to the heavens but counting for nothing on earth. In either case, God is anguished and the world is impoverished.
>
> I was ready to respond, but no one asked,
> ready to be found, but no one sought me.

---

22. O'Brien, *Gospel and Mission*, 125.

23. Balentine, *Prayer in the Hebrew Bible*, 295.

I said, "Here I am, here I am,"
to a nation that did not call on my name. (Isa. 65:1)[23]

RELEVANT QUESTIONS

1. What changes (of understanding and of practice) might reading this chapter make in your personal prayer life?

2. How has your understanding of "missional prayer" expanded beyond regarding it as "praying for missionaries" (vital though that is)?

3. Are churches making a false dichotomy when they think of "doing worship" and "doing mission"? Without transforming all our public worship into "seeker-sensitive" mode, how should we strengthen the missional dimension of our church's public worship (again, both in the way we understand it and the way we do it)?

PART THREE

REFLECTING ON RELEVANCE

CHAPTER 15

THE JOURNEY SO FAR AND THE JOURNEY AHEAD

So what?
At the end of any journey through biblical texts we have to ask that question—especially when we are engaged in biblical theology for life (though one wonders what other kind of biblical theology is worth engaging in). So in this final chapter we try to gather up some of the threads of part 2.

We have been asking throughout this book, "What are God's people on earth for? What does the Bible tell us about what God expects from his people? For what purpose or mission do they exist?" What have we discovered in answer to those questions?

OUR JOURNEY THROUGH THE BIBLE

We have seen that we have a mission that is as broad as the earth, for which we are commanded to care (ch. 3), and as extensive as all the nations, for whom we are to be the agents of God's blessing (ch. 4). We have seen that God's longing to fulfill his promise to Abraham that all nations should indeed be blessed is bound up with the people of Abraham (which now includes all those in Christ) living in God's way in righteousness and justice (ch. 5). We are redeemed and called to live redemptively in the world in ways that mirror the comprehensiveness of God's own act of redemption (ch. 6). We represent God to the world and are intended to be those who attract the world to God by the quality of transformed lives (chs. 7–8). For all these dimensions of our calling there is a radically ethical dimension to our mission. We are to *live* our mission. As I say so often, there is no biblical mission without biblical ethics.

We then went on to see that our mission demands a fundamental loyalty to the truth of the one living God, whom we have come to know through his great historical acts of revelation and salvation, climactically in Christ (ch. 9). We are to know and tell what we have seen and heard of what God has done. Therefore the heart of our message, the word that we are to declare alongside the way that we live, is fundamentally a matter of bearing witness to the living God in Christ (ch. 10). We have incredibly good news to share when we survey the breadth of the biblical gospel and go out to tell the world that God was in Christ reconciling the world to himself, that through the cross and resurrection of Jesus of Nazareth God's kingdom has come and Jesus is Lord (ch. 11).

Thus, in our mission we join the ranks of those all down through history whom God has sent to accomplish many different aspects of God's own mission in the world. Sending and being sent are fundamental dimensions of the church's life and mission (ch. 12). But the church that is sent into the world is, in another sense, already in the world, for all believers live within the public arena of the society in which God has placed them, and the vast majority of them work and earn their living in the great marketplace of human social and economic interaction. And so we must see our mission as something that happens *in and for* that public world, for it is the place of God's creation (though desperately fallen) and of God's ultimate redemption in the new creation (ch. 13).

Finally, we saw that the church has a more fundamental reason for existence, a reason that will last into all eternity beyond the redemption of our fallen world — and that is to live for the worship and praise and glory of God and to bring people from all nations to the same goal. For our greatest human fulfillment is found in God's being glorified in and through our enjoyment of him. Praise and prayer, therefore are not merely surrounding background music for the real missional work. Praise and prayer are themselves missional actions and must be integral to all else that God's mission requires of us (ch. 14).

All of these aspects of our answer to the fundamental question about the mission of God's people drove us backward and forward within the Bible, seeing again and again the strong connections between Old and New Testament texts and themes. Therefore, right at the outset we emphasized how important it is for God's people to know their own story, or rather to know God's story in which they are called to participate — the great biblical narrative from creation to new creation (ch. 2).

So perhaps the first "reflection on relevance" that is called for is to say that if, as we suggested in chapter 1, mission has to do with the whole church taking the whole gospel to the whole world, that means using the whole Bible. It simply will not do to quote a verse or two from favourite "missionary" bits of the Bible and call that a "biblical theology of mission".

I am sure that there is a lot more that could have been included in this book by way of exploration of biblical texts and themes relevant to the mission of God's people. We have not, for example, been able to include discussion of the relevance of the Wisdom Literature, though it has much to teach us about living in God's world. We have had to be selective.

But at least we began in Genesis with God's purpose for us as the inhabitants of his creation, and we ended in Revelation with the vision of God's redeemed people joining in the praise and worship of every creature in God's new creation. We have taken a glimpse at most of the spectacular scenery of the Bible on the way—Abraham; Moses, the exodus and Sinai; the kings, prophets and psalmists of Israel; the life, death and resurrection of Jesus; the church in Acts; the letters of Paul and of Peter, James and John; and the book of Revelation. And in all of it we found rich nourishment for a biblical theology for life in relation to the mission of God's people.

If the basic argument of my earlier book, *The Mission of God*, was that we need to read the whole Bible in all its parts comprehensively to discern and describe *God's* great mission of cosmic redemption, then the argument of this book, *The Mission of God's People*, is that we likewise need to read the whole Bible comprehensively to discern and describe what the implications are for us, the *people* whom God has loved, chosen, called, redeemed, shaped and sent into the world in the name of Christ.

Every chapter could carry its own freight of reflections on the relevance of the biblical texts studied in it. But I will gather our final reflections around the same triple framework as in chapter 1. For the mission of God's people is carried on in and for the *world*; it centres on the *gospel* of God; and it lays a demanding privilege on the *church*.

THE WORLD

At numerous places in our survey we have considered the world in which our mission takes place. Two areas call for more determined application from us.

Serving Creation

In chapter 3 we laid the foundation for a biblical theology of creation and our responsibility within in it. But does that amount to a biblical theology of *mission* in relation to creation? I believe it does. Let's first recall the distinction we made in chapter 1 between mission and missions. I would certainly argue that, for all Christians, ecologically responsible behaviour is right and good as part of Christian discipleship to the Lord of the earth. In that sense it is part of our "mission" in the widest sense.

But I would go further and argue that God calls some Christians to ecological "missions" as their primary field of ministry in God's world. Just as medicine, education, community development, and many other forms of service are viewed as God's calling on different people, which they can put at his disposal as intentionally missional, so there are many ecological functions that Christians can take up as their specific missional calling—scientific research, habitat conservation, political advocacy, etc. The work of A Rocha International has been a pioneering and prophetic initiative in this.[1]

---

1. See www.arocha.org.

In *The Mission of God* I set out some reasons why I believe that Christians should regard such callings to specific tasks of creation care as among legitimate missional vocations. In order to press the case for the relevance of this dimension of the mission of God's people, I quote selectively from that book here.

Creation Care Is an Urgent Issue in Today's World

Does this need to be repeated? Only a willful blindness worse than any proverbial ostrich's head in the sand can ignore the facts of environmental destruction and its accelerating pace. The list is depressingly long:

- the pollution of the air, the sea, rivers, lakes and great aquifers
- the destruction of rainforests and many other habitats, with the terrible effect on dependent life forms
- desertification and soil loss
- the loss of species—of animals, plants, birds and insects—and the huge reduction of essential biodiversity on a planet that depends on it
- the hunting of some species to extinction
- the depletion of the ozone layer
- the increase of "greenhouse gases" and consequent global warming

All this is a vast and interrelated impending catastrophe of loss and destruction, affecting the whole planet and all its human and nonhuman inhabitants. To be unconcerned about it is to be either desperately ignorant or irresponsibly callous.

In the past, Christians have instinctively been concerned about great and urgent issues in every generation, and they rightly included them in their overall concept of mission calling and practice. These have included the evils of disease, ignorance, slavery and many other forms of brutality and exploitation. Christians have taken up the cause of widows, orphans, refugees, prisoners, the insane, the hungry—and, most recently, have swelled the numbers of those committed to "making poverty history".

Faced now with the horrific facts of the suffering of the earth itself, we must surely ask how God himself responds to such abuse of his creation and seek to align our mission objectives to include what matters to him. If, as Jesus tells us, God cares about his creation to the level of knowing when a sparrow falls to earth, what kind of care is required of us by the level of our own knowledge? Granted Jesus made that point in order to compare it with the even greater care God has for his own children. But it would be an utter distortion of Scripture to argue that because God cares for us *more than* for the sparrows, we need not care for sparrows *at all*, or that because we are of greater value than they are, they have no value at all.

However, our care for creation should not be merely a negative, prudential or preventive reaction to a growing problem. There is a much more positive reason for it.

Creation Care Flows from Love for the Creator and Obedience to His Command

"Love the LORD your God" is the first and greatest commandment. Now in human experience, to love someone means that you care for what belongs to them. To trash someone else's property is incompatible with any claim to love that other person. We have seen how emphatically the Bible affirms that the earth is God's property, and more specifically, that it belongs to Christ, who made it, redeemed it and is heir to it. To take good care of the earth, for Christ's sake, is surely a fundamental dimension of the calling on all God's people to love him. It seems inexplicable to me that there are some Christians who claim to love and worship God, to be disciples of Jesus, and yet have no concern for the earth that bears his stamp of ownership. They do not care about the abuse of the earth and indeed, by their wasteful and overconsumptive lifestyles, they contribute to it.

"If you love me, keep my commandments" (John 14:15), said Jesus, echoing as he so often did the practical ethical devotion of Deuteronomy. And the Lord's commandments begin with the fundamental creation mandate to care for the earth. Obedience to that command is as much part of our human mission and duty as any of the other duties and responsibilities built into creation—such as the task of filling the earth, engaging in the rhythm of productive work and rest, and marriage.

Being Christian does not release us from being human. Nor does a distinctively Christian mission negate our human mission, for God holds us accountable as much for our humanity as for our Christianity. As *Christian* human beings, therefore, we are doubly bound to see active care for creation as a fundamental part of what it means to love and obey God.

Creation Care Tests Our Motivation for Mission

Our ultimate starting point and finishing point in our biblical theology of mission must be the mission of God himself. What is "the whole counsel of God"? What is the overarching mission to which God has committed himself and the whole outworking of history? It is not only the salvation of human beings, but also the redemption of the whole creation. God is in the business of establishing a new creation through the transformation and renewal of creation in a manner analogous to the resurrection of his Son, and as a habitation for the resurrection bodies of his redeemed people.

Holistic mission, then, is not truly holistic if it includes only human beings (even if it includes them holistically!) and excludes the rest of the creation for whose reconciliation Christ shed his blood (Col. 1:20). Those Christians who have responded to God's call to serve him through serving his nonhuman creatures in ecological projects are engaged in a specialized form of mission that has its rightful place within the broad framework of all that God's mission has as its goal. Their motivation flows from an awareness of God's own heart for his creation and a desire to respond to that. It is certainly not the case that Christians involved in creation care have no corresponding care for human needs. On the contrary, it often seems to my observation that Christian tenderness toward the nonhuman creation amplifies itself in concern for human needs.

Creation Care Embodies a Biblical Balance of Compassion and Justice

We must exercise compassion, because to care for God's creation is essentially an unselfish form of love, exercised for the sake of creatures that cannot thank or repay you. It is a form of truly biblical and godly altruism. In this respect, it reflects the same quality in the love of God – not only in the sense that God loves human beings in spite of our unlovable enmity toward him, but also in the wider sense that "the LORD has compassion / is loving toward *all that he has made*" (Ps. 145:9, 13, 17; my translation and italics).

Again, Jesus used God's loving care for birds and adornment of grasses and flowers as a model for his even greater love for his human children. If God cares with such minute compassion for his nonhuman creation, how much more should those who wish to emulate him? I have been particularly moved in witnessing the compassionate care that is unselfconsciously practised by A Rocha staff as they handle every bird in their ringing programme. It is a warm, caring, and in my opinion genuinely Christlike attitude towards these tiny specimens of God's creation.

We must exercise justice, because environmental action is a form of defending the weak against the strong, the defenceless against the powerful, the violated against the attacker, the voiceless against the stridency of the greedy. These too are features of the character of God as expressed in his exercise of justice. Psalm 145 includes God's provision for all his creatures in its definition of his *righteousness* as well as his love (Ps. 145:13 – 17). In fact, it places God's care for creation in precise parallel with his liberating and vindicating acts of justice for his people – thus bringing the creational and redemptive traditions of the Old Testament together in beautiful harmony.

So it is not surprising, then, that when the Old Testament comes to define the marks of a righteous *person*, it does not stop at a practical concern for poor and needy *humans* (though that is, of course, the dominant note). It is true that "the righteous care about justice for the poor" (Prov. 29:7). But the sage also makes the warmhearted observation that "the righteous care for the needs of their *animals*" (12:10). Biblical mission is as holistic as biblical righteousness.[2]

Serving Society

We have seen the strong biblical evidence for God's interest in human society at every level – political, economic, legal, familial, and the like. In chapter 4 we noted

---

2. Wright, *The Mission of God*, selections from 412 – 20.

that the concept of "blessing the nations" is broad, since the biblical understanding of blessing is rich and diverse.

Who can count the number of ways that Christians can be a blessing to the nations? And what difference would it make to every Christian's sense of intimate personal involvement in the mission of God's people if they could see every day of ordinary work and involvement in society as an opportunity to "be a blessing", to "seek the welfare of the city" where God has placed them? What damage have we done to the mission of God by restricting mission to paid professional ministers and missionaries? It seems to me that the gospel that should be shared on our lips will be more abundant and more effective if it flows from a life that is resonating with gospel blessing in all the ordinariness of everyday Christian living in the midst of the world.

And in chapter 13 especially we saw that God clearly expects his people to be engaged in the public arena, the marketplace of the world. If this too is part of our biblical mission as God's people, the church needs to take it more seriously, in at least two practical and relevant ways.

The Prophetic Task

We are called to the role of the prophet, not just of the chaplain. That is, the church's role is not simply to put a veneer of uncritical blessing on whatever social or economic (or military) enterprises take place in the public arena. That was one of the massive distortions that Christendom generated.

The people of God are called to maintain a critical distance and to speak on behalf of the independent Divine Auditor. This does not mean we adopt a posture of elevated superiority, for we know our own sinfulness. But it does mean we must offer the voice of evaluation, of critique or approval, according to the standards we learn in God's own revelation. We are to renounce evil and hold fast to what is good; that calls for minds and hearts attuned to recognize the difference.

The church collectively can still perform this prophetic function in the public square, though it will also always suffer for doing so – sometimes from the coopted chaplains of the marketplace themselves. We need to recover the voice of biblical engagement with all that goes on around us and the courage needed to go with it. Wherever Christians enter professions that do give them public voice – in politics, journalism, broadcasting and other media – they need to be supported and encouraged by the church to understand the front-line missional nature of their calling.

The Pastoral Task

It is also the function of the church to support those who live their lives daily as saints in the marketplace. Paul tells us that God has given to his church pastors and teachers "to equip the saints for works of service" (Eph. 4:12). I believe that "works of service" here does not just mean Christian activity (i.e., church-based ministry or evangelism), but all and any form of service within society as a whole, including the church.

This turns right upside down one of the commonest misconceptions that sadly still permeates the church and cripples its effectiveness. Believe it or not, God did not invent the church to support the clergy. Rather, God gave pastors and teachers to the church in order to equip the saints.

People don't go to church on Sundays to support their pastors in their ministry. The pastor goes to church on Sunday to support the people in *their* ministry. And *their* ministry, the ministry that really counts as mission, is *outside* the walls of the church, in the world, being salt and light in the marketplace.

> This church sends out 1,500 missionaries every week. Some of them are even serving overseas.
>
> *Hugh Palmer,*
> *Rector of All Souls Church,*
> *Langham Place, London*

Every church should have a prominent notice over the inside of the door that people use to leave the church, "You are now entering the mission field."

The challenge to those of us who are pastors (and those who train pastors), therefore, is:

- Are we mobilizing, training and supporting our people for mission—not (only) by sending some overseas as "missionaries", but seeing the whole church as engaged in mission in the world every working day of their lives?
- Are we helping ordinary working Christians to understand the world they live and work in, or just dangling before them the prospect of a better world when they die?
- Are we teaching our people what the Bible teaches about responsible citizenship?
- Are we encouraging believers to "seek the welfare of the city" where God has put them?
- Are we building a biblical worldview for sustaining Christian ethical witness?
- Are we helping working Christians to wrestle with the ethical issues they face in the workplace, encouraging faithfulness, integrity, courage and perseverance?
- Are we caring sympathetically for those who get bruised and crushed in their daily conflict with a hostile world, if that is what they face in their work?

In order to exercise such supportive ministry, we ourselves, who are pastors and teachers in the church, need to know the problems and temptations our people face in the world. We need to keep up-to-date with the realities of the marketplace and not live in an isolated spiritual bubble of only religious activity.

We also need to keep abreast of developments in missional understanding and practice such as is represented by the growing movement that goes under the general phrase, "Business as Mission". This is the recognition that "tent-making" need not be only a means of self-support for the "real" job of doing evangelism, nor

a somewhat phony cover for getting access to countries otherwise closed to Christian witness. Rather, it is the conviction that engaging in legitimate business is intrinsically valuable for the sake of society, for human welfare, for positive social and spiritual ends. There is a missional dimension to conducting sound business in God's world for God's sake.[3]

I remember with sadness the time I spoke to a conference of graduate Christians in India—all of them professional "lay" people. In the context of teaching about Old Testament ethics, we were discussing the multiple complex problems of ethics and conscience that face Indian Christians daily—from bribery and corruption to exploitation and violence. I asked if they were able to talk such things over with their pastors. There was hollow laughter. "Our pastors never talk, or think, or preach about such things," they said. "Some of them are involved in that kind of thing themselves anyway."

THE GOSPEL
Recovering the Wholeness of the Gospel

I hope that one of the effects of this book will have been to lift up our eyes to see the glorious richness of the gospel of God. The Bible brings us the most amazing good news that speaks to and can transform every area of human life that is touched by sin (which means, every area of human life there is). The trouble is that we have tended to concentrate on one or another aspect of the biblical good news, to the detriment of others. What God has joined together, we have put asunder. Then we struggle to articulate how they are "related" when we should never have separated them in the first place.

Let's remind ourselves of some of the great "wholes" that we have noted in our survey. The gospel integrates the following, though sadly we so often tend to polarize them.

Individual and Cosmic

We have tended to separate the individual from the cosmic and corporate dimensions of the gospel, and then we tend to prioritize the first. That is, we put individual salvation and personal evangelism at the centre of all our efforts (and, of course, personal evangelism *is* an essential part of our commitment). But Paul's order of the gospel message in Ephesians and in Colossians 1:15–26 is *creation* (all things in heaven and earth, created by Christ, sustained by Christ and redeemed by Christ); then, *church* (with Christ as head); and then individual Gentile *believers*—"and you also".

---

3. See the excellent book by Mark Russell, *The Missional Entrepreneur: Principles and Practices for Business as Mission* (Birmingham, AL: New Hope, 2010). See also the "Business as Mission Manifesto" from the Lausanne Movement, available at www.lausanne.org/all-documents/manifesto.html, and the Lausanne Occasional Paper No. 40, *Marketplace Ministry*, which can be downloaded at www.lausanne.org/2004forum/documents.html.

All of this, says Paul, has been "reconciled through the blood of Christ shed on the cross". So we are not saved *out of* creation, but *as part of creation* that God has redeemed through Christ. The church is not just a container for souls until they get to heaven, but the living demonstration of the unity that is God's intention for the whole creation.

The bad result of breaking up this "whole" is that Christians who are evangelized by truncated versions of the biblical gospel have little interest in the world, the public square, God's plan for society and the nations, and even less understanding of God's intention for creation itself. The scale of our mission efforts, therefore, is in danger of being a lot smaller than the scope of the mission of God.

Believing and Living

We have tended to separate believing the gospel from living out the gospel. And then we tend to prioritize the first. That is, we seem to think that there can be a *belief* of faith separate from the *life* of faith; that people can be saved by something that goes on in their heads without worrying too much about what happens in their lives. So long as they have prayed the right prayer and believed the right doctrine, nothing else ultimately matters, or at least, whatever happens next is secondary and distinct.

Yet in the Bible, as we have seen repeatedly in this book, faith and obedience are inseparable. Now of course, it is important to stress that we are saved only by the work of Christ and through our faith in him, and not by or because of our good works. But the faith by which we are savingly united to Christ inevitably demonstrates its existence and authenticity in obedience. Paul actually defines his missionary life's work as bringing about "*the obedience of faith* ... among all the nations" (Rom. 1:5; 15:18; 16:26 ESV). That is a doublet that echoes Abraham, Jesus, Paul and James. You can't obey God's Word unless you believe it. But you can't claim to believe God's Word unless you are obeying it. Faith without works is dead.

The bad result of breaking up this "whole" is that all over the world there are people who call themselves believers and evangelicals, but whose actual lives are indistinguishable from the culture around them—whether in terms of moral standards, social and political prejudices and actual behaviour. They are, in the biblical sense, a "scandal"—a stumbling block that hinders others from considering the claims of Christ.

Proclamation and Demonstration

The gospel is good news that needs to be heard *and* to be seen. It needs words and deeds. Message and proof. We have tended to separate these and to prioritize the first. We speak most easily of mission as "*preaching* the gospel". But though that is absolutely vital (for good news simply *has to be* communicated with words), it is not the whole biblical picture of how the gospel is communicated.

Peter summarizes the ministry of Jesus as *both* telling the message that God sent to Israel—the good news of peace—*and* that, anointed and empowered by the Holy Spirit, "he went around doing good" (Acts 10:36–38).

The same combination is found in Paul's own practice: in Romans 15 he reflects on his whole missionary work and speaks of "what Christ has accomplished through me in leading the nations to *obey* God by what I have *said* and *done*—by the power of signs and wonders, through the *power of the Spirit of God*" (Rom. 15:18–19, italics added). Words, works, and wonders, as some have said.

The bad result of breaking up this "whole" is that our evangelistic efforts are sometimes derided by the world because people discern the hypocrisy of those who talk a lot but whose lives don't support what they say. Lack of integrity in this area has been identified by various researches as the major obstacle to the acceptance of the message of the gospel.

The Amity Foundation is a Chinese Christian development organization. Along with many other Christians they have been active in relief and reconstruction after the devastating earthquake in Sichuan province. Pastor Gu Yumei and her husband were among the first to help in their town.

"Many people didn't know the church before the earthquake," says Pastor Gu. When members of the congregation took part in the relief efforts wherever they were able to help, distributing candles, lighters or mosquito repellants, the church became better known among people in Mianzhu. "Social work and God's love made people realise that there is a church," says Pastor Gu.

The congregation has grown at least fivefold since that time. Now, the church conducts special leadership courses for staff at the thirteen new preaching points of the congregation.[4]

I have been saying above that many of us tend to prioritize the first of the two poles of each pair. But of course, there are those who prioritize at the opposite pole. They stress the importance of the social dimension of the church, the need for radical social ethics and for a form of Christian presence in society that should be a force for justice, even if the name of Christ is not evangelistically proclaimed; moreover, they are passionately concerned for the relief of poverty and suffering among the neediest of the world, but they are markedly less interested in people coming to faith in the Lord Jesus Christ and being added to his church.

Whatever else might be said about such thinking or practice, it certainly is not "holistic (or wholistic) mission"—even though that term is sometimes inappropriately applied to concepts of mission that stress social and economic action. Social action with no evangelistic interest is as nonholistic as is evangelism with no social concern. To be concerned for the poor and hungry but not concerned for people hearing the good news of Jesus is not even to follow the example of Jesus, let alone "holistic mission".

---

4. *Amity Newsletter* (April–June, 2009), 7.

But why do we have to go on polarizing around this artificially created dichotomy when the Bible gives us abundant warrant for holding the two together in integrated unity?

"Primacy?"

This issue was a source of some division in the Lausanne movement in the decade after the first Lausanne Congress of 1974. John Stott convened a consultation to think it through theologically—the Consultation on the Relationship between Evangelism and Social Responsibility (CRESR)—in Grand Rapids in 1982. There were, and still are, those who insist that within our commitment to holistic mission, evangelism needs to be seen as having primacy. I think that the way the CRESR report responded to this and articulated what is meant by such primacy with careful qualifications is still most helpful, even if, as I would argue, it was attempting to "reconcile" two things which should never have been separated in the first place. The whole document is worth studying carefully, but the following extract addresses the nub of this issue.[5]

The concluding sentences of this extract show that the drafters were aware that, *in missional practice*, the distinction is hardly, if ever, a real one:

> To proclaim Jesus as Lord and Saviour (evangelism) has social implications, since it summons people to repent of social as well as personal sins, and to live a new life of righteousness and peace in the new society which challenges the old.
>
> To give food to the hungry (social responsibility) has evangelistic implications, since good works of love, if done in the name of Christ, are a demonstration and commendation of the gospel.
>
> It has been said, therefore, that evangelism, even when it does not have a primarily social intention, nevertheless has a social dimension, while social responsibility, even when it does not have a primarily evangelistic intention, nevertheless has an evangelistic dimension.
>
> Thus, evangelism and social responsibility, while distinct from one another, are integrally related in our proclamation of and obedience to the gospel. The partnership is, in reality, a marriage.
>
> This brings us to the question whether the partnership between evangelism and social responsibility is equal or unequal; that is, whether they are of identical importance or whether one takes precedence over the other. The Lausanne Covenant affirms that "in the church's mission of sacrificial service evangelism is primary" (Paragraph 6). Although some of us have felt uncomfortable about this phrase, lest by it we should be breaking the partnership, yet we are able to endorse and explain it in two ways, in addition to the particular situations and callings already mentioned.
>
> First, evangelism has a certain priority. We are not referring to an invariable temporal priority, because in some situations a social ministry will take precedence,

5. *Evangelism and Social Responsibility: An Evangelical Commitment.* It can be downloaded as Lausanne Occasional Paper No. 21, at: www.lausanne.org/all-documents/lop–21.html.

but to a logical one. The very fact of Christian social responsibility presupposes socially responsible Christians, and it can only be by evangelism and discipling that they have become such. If social activity is a consequence and aim of evangelism (as we have asserted), then evangelism must precede it. In addition, social progress is being hindered in some countries by the prevailing religious culture; only evangelism can change this.

Secondly, evangelism relates to people's eternal destiny, and in bringing them Good News of salvation, Christians are doing what nobody else can do. Seldom if ever should we have to choose between satisfying physical hunger and spiritual hunger, or between healing bodies and saving souls, since an authentic love for our neighbour will lead us to serve him or her as a whole person. Nevertheless, if we must choose, then we have to say that the supreme and ultimate[6] need of all humankind is the saving grace of Jesus Christ, and that therefore a person's eternal, spiritual salvation is of greater importance than his or her temporal and material well-being (cf. 2 Cor. 4:16–18). As the Thailand Statement expressed it, "of all the tragic needs of human beings none is greater than their alienation from their Creator and the terrible reality of eternal death for those who refuse to repent and believe." Yet this fact must not make us indifferent to the degradations of human poverty and oppression.

The choice, we believe, is largely conceptual. In practice, as in the public ministry of Jesus, the two are inseparable, at least in open societies. Rather than competing with each other, they mutually support and strengthen each other in an upward spiral of increased concern for both.[7]

Evangelical Christians like to stress the importance of a life of daily devotion to God, in which Bible reading and prayer are fundamental. Now, reading the Bible and praying are distinct activities. But have you ever heard evangelicals arguing, conferencing, dividing, publishing and campaigning in support of one or the other having "primacy" in the life of Christian discipleship? The very question: "Bible reading or prayer – which has primacy?" makes little sense in real life. Both are vital. Both are biblical. Both are integral to a living relationship with God. Why cannot we adopt the same integrated understanding of mission?

"Integral mission" is the currently preferred term for this understanding, and I find myself biblically persuaded of its truth and validity. If mission is a living, dynamic reality, we need organic analogies for all that it encompasses. Perhaps breathing and drinking provide such an analogy. Again – they are different activities, but they are both utterly necessary for an integrated living human body. It makes no sense in practice to talk of either one as having "primacy", for if you neglect either, you will die.

---

6. This truth led me to say, in *The Mission of God*, that I prefer to speak of "the ultimacy of evangelism" rather than its primacy – not because it is the last thing we should do, but because it is the one thing, of all the things that we rightly and biblically do, that addresses the "last enemy" – death. See *Mission of God*, 439–41.

7. *Evangelism and Social Responsibility* (my italics at the end).

Some suggest that "centrality" rather than "primacy" might be a better word for evangelism within mission. This applies the model of a wheel. A wheel is an integrated object that necessarily must have both a hub at the centre (connected to an axle and an engine), and a rim (connected to the road). Without a rim, a hub is just a rotating axle end. Without a hub, a rim is just a hoop, spinning anywhere and soon falling over. A hub and a rim are distinct things, but unless they are integrally working together, neither constitutes a wheel. If evangelism is like the hub, connected to the engine of the gospel power of God, then it also takes the living demonstration of the gospel in Christians' engagement with the world to give the hub connection and traction with the context – the road.

> Integral mission is the proclamation and demonstration of the gospel. It is not simply that evangelism and social involvement are to be done alongside each other. Rather, in integral mission our proclamation has social consequences as we call people to love and repentance in all areas of life. And our social involvement has evangelistic consequences as we bear witness to the transforming grace of Jesus Christ. If we ignore the world we betray the word of God that sends us out to serve the world. If we ignore the word of God we have nothing to bring to the world. Justice and justification by faith, worship and political action, the spiritual and the material, personal change and structural change belong together. As in the life of Jesus, being, doing and saying are at the heart of our integral task.
>
> *The Micah Declaration on Integral Mission*[8]

Recovering Our Humility as Servants of the Gospel

The mission of God's people is to be gospel people – understanding the word gospel in all its wholeness as we have just outlined. But gospel people are, by definition, humble people. It is the gospel that is great and glorious. We are simply its obedient servants. Or, to use some of the other metaphors that we find in the Bible, we are stewards of the gospel (we do not own it); we are witnesses to the gospel (we did not invent it).

Or as Paul more vividly put it, the gospel is the treasure, and we are nothing more than the clay pots in which it is kept (2 Cor. 4:7). Clay pots were the commonest form of carrying anything in the biblical world. They were the supermarket carrier bags of their day. That's a humble enough description for our missional role, perhaps: carrier bags for the gospel.

Now of course I have not forgotten what I said in chapter 1 about the danger of imagining the church as only a delivery mechanism, with no concern for the quality of life of the messenger. My point is simply this: gospel ministry has to be done in self-effacing humility or it is a denial of the gospel itself.

Two ways in which this suggests relevant application come to mind – one relatively minor, the other deadly serious.

---

8. The whole document can be read at: www.micahnetwork.org/en/integral-mission/micah-declaration.

Whose Testimony and to Whom?

In chapter 10 we explored the biblical theme of witness. We marveled at the fact that God called Israel, even in their state of apparent paralysis and failure (deaf and blind), to be witnesses to himself as the living God. Their witness was certainly not to themselves, but to him. Likewise, in the New Testament, Jesus tells the disciples, "You will be *my* witnesses." The whole point of testimony in the Bible is not so much the person who does the testifying (however interesting their story), but the person to whom, or on whose behalf, the testimony is borne, or the events about which testimony is being given.

So what then should it mean when we "give our testimony"? A tradition has grown up in evangelical circles that "testimony" is all about what I have experienced. Evangelism training includes "preparing your testimony" – which is telling your own story of how you became a Christian.

Now I do not for a moment want to belittle this practice. There is plenty of biblical support (especially in the Psalms) for public declaration of the good things God has done for me (though even there the stress is on "God has done" than on "me"). But our reflection on the texts we studied in chapter 10 would encourage us to make sure that our "testimony" has a more objective element, of bearing witness to God, to the Lord Jesus Christ, to the truth of the biblical story of redemption, with its warning of judgment and its hope of glory. Otherwise "testimony time" can degenerate into a subtle form of self-advertisement, into something that is the antithesis of the gospel that is supposedly being commended. Gospel humility should dictate otherwise.

When people hear our "testimony", do they go away thinking, "What a wonderful story that person has! What incredible experiences!"? Or do they gasp in amazement at the wonder of God, the beauty of Jesus and the glory of the gospel?

Prostituted Gospel

Paul sharply distinguished himself from those who would "peddle the word of God for profit" (2 Cor. 2:17) – that is, those who used the preaching or evangelizing ministry as a means of making money for themselves. The ancient Greek world was awash with traveling lecturers who competed in selling their philosophies to crowds for entertainment, and some of whom became famous and rich. They were the televangelists of their day. Paul refused to be like them.

Sadly, they have their counterparts today in some of the purveyors of "prosperity gospel" teachings. For such people the gospel has become a manipulated product, packaged and marketed to appeal to the consumer's needs and wants, and pumped out through highly charged media of communication, to the enormous enrichment of the salesmen.

Now, I am well aware that there is a valid reality of biblical prosperity that includes material blessing. I know that "prosperity" teachers take seriously the promises of the Bible and the power of God to overcome all that is evil in the spiritual realms. I know that God is still the miracle-working God of the Bible. I know that, in their writings, some of these teachers emphasize hard work and the need to overcome the challenges of poverty and lack of opportunity. I know that the teaching thrives in places where such poverty is endemic and offers some form of hope of a way out of a situation that in itself is grievous to God and a shame on the human community, including the church.

Welcome every apostle on arriving, as if he were the Lord. But he must not stay beyond one day. In case of necessity, however, the next day too. If he stays three days, he is a false prophet. On departing, an apostle must not accept anything save sufficient food to carry him till his next lodging. *If he asks for money, he is a false prophet . . . .*

Everyone who comes to you in the name of the Lord must be welcomed. Afterward, when you have tested him, you will find out about him, for you have insight into right and wrong. If he is a traveler who arrives, help him all you can. But he must not stay with you more than two days, or, if necessary, three. If he wants to settle with you and is an artisan, he must work for his living. If, however, he has no trade, use your judgment in taking steps for him to live with you as a Christian without being idle. *If he refuses to do this, he is trading on Christ. You must be on your guard against such people.*
The Didache 11:4–6 and 12:1–5 (italics added)[9]

But still.

There is no doubt that what fuels a great deal of prosperity teaching is greed. A lot of the preaching and writing appeals to that inordinate desire for material wealth that the Bible constantly warns us against – from the tenth commandment, to the warning of Jesus and the condemnation of Paul. And the most blatantly obvious result of the teaching is that those who engage in it are the ones who end up with most of the prosperity.

But can a "gospel" that asks for (often aggressively demands) money be remotely consistent with the gospel of the New Testament, where such practice is uncompromisingly condemned? And can a lifestyle of affluence, gluttony, extravagant expenditure on cars and private jet planes reflect in any way at all the face of the Son of Man, the suffering Servant, the crucified Christ?

A "gospel" that sells its blessings is no different from the scandal of indulgences in the pre-Reformation church, by which people were told they could buy themselves early release from the pains of purgatory. Now people are deceived into buying themselves hoped-for release from obstacles in this life.

Indeed, a "gospel" that sells *anything* is a prostituted gospel, a denial of the suffering grace of the cross.

My "reflection on relevance" at this point is really a passionate longing that the church of the twenty-first century would name this heresy for what it is and reject it as having any part in the mission of God's people.[10]

---

9. *The Didache* was a second-century manual of church teaching and discipline. In *The Library of Christian Classics*, Vol. 1, *Early Christian Fathers* (trans. and ed. Cyril C. Richardson; London: SCM, 1953), 176–77.

10. A concise and powerful critique of Prosperity teaching has recently been produced by a group of African theologians, convened by the Lausanne Theology Working Group. It can be read at: www.christianitytoday.com/ct/2009/decemberweb-only/gc-prosperitystatement.html

Recovering Our Confidence in the Gospel

Being humble about oneself as a servant of the gospel does not imply being uncertain or diffident about the gospel itself. On the contrary, the greatest joy of the servant is to point to the splendour of his or her master. Likewise the greatest privilege of the servant of the gospel is to exalt the glorious gospel of God for all its worth, in all the rich wholeness of its breadth and height and depth.

Few things are more essential to the mission of God's people than that we recover our confidence in the gospel.

The Truth of the Gospel

We need to reaffirm our conviction of the *truth* of the gospel and build our whole lives upon it. This has always been a battle in a world of competing truth claims—religious or antireligious. It is even more of a battle in a world of postmodern denial of the very possibility of truth. Postmodernism is essentially a stance of disbelief in any grand narrative. It is a great believer in *stories*—the multiplicity of stories with which every historical culture decorates its float in the great carnival of human plurality and relativity. But no Story claiming universal truth will be allowed to wander unchallenged around the festivities.

In such a world, we still go out on our mission of declaring that the Bible tells *the Story*, the grand narrative that makes sense of life, the universe, and everything. And that story ultimately is good news—it is gospel—for it tells the bad news as it really is, and it declares what God and God alone has done for the redemption of all our bad stories and their one terrifyingly bad ending. It tells us that God so loved the world that he gave his only Son, that God was in Christ reconciling the world to himself, that the cross and resurrection of Jesus of Nazareth have inaugurated a new creation, and that the kingdoms of this world will become the kingdom of our God and of his Christ.

The Uniqueness of the Gospel

We need to reaffirm our conviction of the *uniqueness* of the gospel, for it is the message of the one unique living God, and the one unique human person in whom that God has lived and died and risen again. This was scandalous when it was first proclaimed in the religious pluralism of the first-century world, and it is no less scandalous in the pluralism of the twenty-first century.

But the relevance of our biblical theology, especially in chapter 9, is that we must affirm the uniqueness of Christ and the salvation that is in him alone on the broad, firm foundation of the whole Bible and the story it tells of the one God and his plan, since Abraham, to bring blessing to all nations and redemption to creation.

Provided it is *this* Jesus, fulfilling *this* story, achieving the redemption of *this* God, our affirmation of the uniqueness of Jesus will stand firm. Christ is not unique because we say so or merely because he is better than the religious competition. He is unique because in him alone the biblical God accomplished his biblically revealed plan for the biblically defined redemption of our biblically diagnosed world within his biblically valued creation.

The Power of the Gospel

Furthermore, we need to reaffirm our conviction of the *power* of the gospel. This was Paul's great boast. He was nothing in himself, but he could *see* and *prove* that the gospel was the power of God, for he could point to the *transformed* lives of people from every racial, social and religious background. And so can we.

Sadly, however, we can also point to lives that claim the benefits of the gospel but give no evidence of its transforming power – and that leads to our final area of reflection.

THE CHURCH

What reflections can we offer from our biblical theology of the mission of God's people in relation to those people themselves? It is all too easy to talk about mission as a task, as a project, as an ideal, as a strategy, as a whole range of accomplishments. But if our journey in the central chapters of this book has taught us anything it is that the people whom God has called into partnership with himself in his great redemptive mission need to take a look at themselves. They need the constant challenge that comes from the enormous privilege it is to be called by God's name and entrusted with God's mission.

Repent and Return

The first recorded command of Jesus was not "Go", but "Repent". In this respect, he joined the ranks of the great Old Testament prophets, for that was their unanimous message to God's people across all the centuries of their existence. We have seen how some of the most profound missional passages in the Old Testament come in contexts of the exposure of Israel's failure and the call for radical repentance.

So it must be for the church. We cannot go forth in mission to the world without attending to ourselves. This is not to suggest that we have to wait until we are perfect before we engage in mission. There never would have been any mission – Old or New Testament – if that had been the case. It means that part of our missional responsibility has to include facing up to the failings and shortcomings of the church itself – precisely because they are such a damning hindrance to God's mission through us.

To start analysing the contemporary failings of the church would be to start a whole new book, and there are plenty that do it well enough. But surely they must include at least the following shameful realities that ruin our witness to the world, deface the likeness of Christ and deny the gospel of his transforming grace:

- the scandal of a tiny fraction of the global body of Christ living in a level of affluence that is unimaginable to the vast majority of believers who experience the daily grinding struggle of poverty
- the scandal of multiple fractures within the church, along the same lines that divide the rest of fallen humanity – divisions of ethnicity, tribe, colour and caste; the violence, injustice, oppression and cruelty that go on *within and between* Christian communities in some parts of the world
- the scandal of obsession with status, greed and power – which can be seen in every corner of the global church. The teaching of Jesus on servanthood, on first and last, on the least and the greatest in the kingdom of God, is routinely ignored by those who most loudly claim to lead God's flock
- the scandal of ideological captivity, through which churches simply absorb the dominating cultural and national worldview, and then decorate it with a veneer of piety and advocate it with as much passion and prejudice as any pagan patriot
- the scandal of false teaching, both in relation to the most central truths of God's revelation in Scripture, and in relation to ethical issues in which some portions of the church seem more determined to reflect the world than to be governed by the Bible

All these and many more deface the image of Christ and deny the purging and transforming power of the gospel of God's grace. All of them mirror the same scandals in principle that we find condemned in the Bible. There can be no response to such things other than repentance. And there can be no effective mission that does not include such repentance as a constant state of mind and heart, for the old idols and scandals quickly slip back into place even after they have been driven out once.

And then we need to return to the way of the Lord, for as we have seen strongly in chapters 5, 7 and 8 that unless God's people walk in God's way, there is no visible mission to the nations. The need for the church to be a "contrast society", a community that attracts the world to God by the sheer, surprising power of missional holiness, remains one of the greatest challenges that a biblical theology of the mission of God's people lays before the church.

Go and Make Disciples

As we repent and return to the way of the Lord, we hear again the enduring words of his Great Commission that direct us on that way. It is not, as I have tried to show, the *first* great commission; I put God's call and promise to Abraham in that box. But as the final words of the risen Lord to his disciples, it exercises enormous leverage in the task of world mission.

The version of the Great Commission at the end of Matthew's gospel tends to have pride of place. It has certainly functioned as a driving text in the modern missionary movement. Unfortunately it has not always been read for all its content.

The idea of church as contrast-society does not mean contradiction of the rest of society *for the sake of contradiction*. Still less does the church as contrast-society mean despising the rest of society due to elitist thought. The only thing meant is contrast *on behalf of others* and *for the sake of the others*, the contrast function that is unsurpassably expressed in the images of "salt of the earth", "light of the world", and "city on a hill" (Matt. 5:13–14). *Precisely because the church does not exist for itself, but completely and exclusively for the world, it is necessary that the church not become the world, that it retain its own countenance.* If the church loses its own contours, if it lets its light be extinguished and its salt become tasteless, then it can no longer transform the rest of society. Neither missionary activity nor social engagement, no matter how strenuous, helps anymore....

What makes the church the divine contrast-society is not self-acquired holiness, nor cramped efforts and moral achievements, but the saving deed of God, who justifies the godless, accepts failures and reconciles himself with the guilty. Only in this gift of reconciliation ... does what is here termed contrast-society flourish.

Gerhard Lohfink[11]

In another of those sad dichotomies to add to the list above, the Great Commission has sometimes been portrayed exclusively as an evangelistic mandate to go and preach the gospel everywhere, when actually the single and central imperative verb in the text is "make disciples". Now of course, making disciples requires evangelism, and the first added instruction, or step in the process of making disciples, is "baptizing them". Baptism presupposes the preaching of the gospel and a response to it of repentance and faith in the Lord Jesus Christ. But the second added instruction – Great Commission Line Three, as we might call it – is "teaching them to obey all that I have commanded you". And such teaching is of the essence of discipling.

Basically, the New Testament was written by disciples, for disciples, to make disciples. Yet our emphasis has often been on getting decisions, claiming converts, making Christians. Actually the word Christian occurs three times in the New Testament, whereas the word "disciple" occurs 269 times.

The Great Commission, along with all the practice of the New Testament church, tells us that there is *mission beyond evangelism*. Paul clearly believed this. Had he stopped being a "missionary" when he spent three years teaching the church in Ephesus the whole counsel of God? He affirmed the mission of Apollos (a cross-cultural missionary if ever there was: converted in Africa, instructed in Asia, and sent to Europe), which was a teaching mission (Acts 18:24–27), and Paul refused to allow that either was more important than the other – the one who planted or the one who watered (1 Cor. 3:5–9).

Evangelism and teaching/discipling are *together* integral and essential parts of our mission. Paul told Timothy to "do the work of an evangelist", and also to teach

11. Gerhard Lohfink, *Jesus and Community: The Social Dimension of Christian Faith* (London: SPCK, 1985), 146–47; as quoted in Eckhard Schnabel, *Early Christian Mission*, Vol. 2, *Paul and the Early Church* (Downers Grove, IL: IVP, and Leicester: IVP and Apollos, 2004), 1577–78.

sound doctrine, and to mentor others to teach others also. And he did not imply that one was more important than the other: they were all essential parts of the mission entrusted to Timothy. For Paul, mission included church nurture as much as church planting.

The bad result of separating evangelism from discipleship and prioritizing the first is shallowness, immaturity and vulnerability to false teaching, church growth without depth and rapid withering away (as Jesus warned in the parable of the sower; Matt. 13:20–22).

We should not treat the Great Commission as a ticking clock, just waiting for the last people group to "hear" the gospel before the Lord is, as it were, permitted to return. That kind of thinking

> From his *practice* of residential missions (at Corinth and Ephesus) and nurture of churches (1 Thess. 2:10–12), from his *priorities* (1 Thess. 2:17–3:13; 2 Cor. 2:12–13; 10:13–16), and from his *description of his assignment* (Col. 1:24–2:7; Rom. 1:1–15; 15:14–16), in relation to admonition and teaching believers to bring them to full maturity in Christ, it is clear that *the nurture of emerging churches* is understood by Paul to be an integral feature of his missionary task.... Proclaiming the gospel meant for Paul not simply an initial preaching or with it the reaping of converts; it included also a whole range of nurture and strengthening activities which led to the firm establishment of congregations.
>
> *Peter T. O'Brien*[12]

has transformed it into a "job to complete", "an unfinished task". But with its command to disciples to make disciples, it is a self-replicating mandate that we will never "complete" – not in the sense that we can never reach all the nations (we can and we should), but in the sense that the making of disciples, and the rediscipling of those who have formerly been evangelized, are tasks that go on through multiple lives and generations.

To the Ends of the Earth

The Great Commission is not a timetable for the end of the world. But it is certainly a trajectory to the ends of the earth. "Make disciples of all the nations," said Jesus. As Lord of heaven and earth, Jesus was more aware of the sheer scale of that concept – "all the nations" – than any of his disciples could have been. From Old and New Testament texts we know that God will not be satisfied until the ends of the earth have heard the good news of his great work of redemption and Jesus has disciples among all peoples.

So our (almost) final reflection on relevance has to be the continued importance and urgency of the task of making it possible for that to be the case – that men and women in all peoples around the world should have the opportunity to hear the gospel of our Lord Jesus Christ in a way they can understand, and to respond to it in repentance, faith and obedience.

For a book that is published in 2010, it is surely another scandal to add to the list above that the proportion of the human race that would call themselves Christians by any meaning of that word is hardly changed from what it was in 1910 (approximately

---

12. O'Brien, *Gospel and Mission*, 42–43.

one-third). This means that although the church has grown phenomenally in the past century and taken root in more nations than even existed in 1910, there are still millions of individuals and thousands of peoples who have never yet even heard the name of the Lord Jesus Christ and the good news of what God has done through his cross and resurrection for the salvation of the world. Millions still wait for any portion of the Word of God to exist in their mother tongue.

So the challenge remains of peoples as yet unreached by any form of gospel message, of languages with no portion of the Bible in them yet, of millions of oral communicators who need to hear the Word in a form that does not rely on the written Word, of peoples whose only exposure to the Christian message has come along with horrendous violence done to them by nations they have been told are "Christian", or with a lurid immorality that they cannot help but associate with the same Western cultures.

"Ye shall receive power, when the Holy Spirit is come upon you: and ye shall be my witnesses." Although the final victory is not yet revealed, the gift of the Spirit is the sign of its coming, or our sharing in Him is a foretaste of the powers of the age to come. The Spirit is given us in order that we may be witnesses, for He is the primary witness to Christ, bringing the world now under the judgment which is the final judgment, granting signs of the hidden victory, and giving to the human words of Christ's messengers the power of God Himself. By the Spirit, men of all nations and tongues are brought to acknowledge the mighty works of God in Christ.

... it is the Spirit who gives Christ's people the word to speak when they are brought before kings and governors for His sake. It is the Spirit who grants signs and wonders to accompany the ministry of the apostles, as that of Jesus Himself. It is by the Spirit that the words of the Gospel preaching come with power to the hearers—power to be the actual instrument of God's election (1 Thess. 1:4–5). The gift of the Spirit, itself the sign and foretaste of the age to come, is the means by which the Church is enabled to lead this present age to its consummation, by bringing the Gospel to all nations.

Lesslie Newbigin[13]

The missional challenge of reaching the ends of the earth with the gospel, so that the whole earth may be filled with the knowledge of the glory of God, faces us still with all its diversity and complexity. The evangelization of the world, in the fullest sense of both the words in that phrase, remains as urgent a priority for the church as it was when Jesus laid it as a mandate on his disciples before his ascension.

The earth, of course, is a globe that has no "ends". From a missional perspective, the "ends of the earth" are as likely to be found in your own street as far across the sea. The missional task of the church, in sending and being sent, in fulfilling the three functions of 3 John 6–8—sending, going and supporting—is as necessary for local as for international mission.

For the Glory of God

It is striking that three of the accounts of the Great Commission are framed in worship (Matt. 28:17; Luke 24:52; John 20:28). And that is where we must draw this

---

13. Newbigin, *Household of God*, 138.

book to a close, just as we finished part 2 by seeing praise and prayer as integral to the mission of God's people.

A missional people must be a worshiping people, or what is their mission for? Mission is, in the words of Psalm 96, a matter of singing the new song of the Lord – the new song that celebrates the Lord's name, salvation, glory and mighty deeds – and then inviting the nations to join in.

But worship does one other thing. It reminds us constantly of our dependence on the God whose mission we serve. And that means that the mission of God's people must be carried on in the power of God's Spirit.

And so we finish with a note of worship – in the form of a hymn that does not so much address God as address the church of God, reminding us of the many-faceted mission that God has entrusted to us.

It would be a fascinating exercise to work slowly through this wonderful hymn, written by a British missionary, and to make a note of all the echoes and allusions to specific biblical texts that it contains. Though clearly triggered by 1 Peter 2:9 – 12, it follows Peter in drawing its themes and challenges from all over the Bible – which makes it a fitting end to this book, which has sought to do the same.

Here is the mission of God's people – in song.

Church of God, elect and glorious, holy nation, chosen race;
Called as God's own special people, royal priests and heirs of grace,
Know the purpose of your calling, show to all his mighty deeds;
Tell of love which knows no limits, grace which meets all human needs.

God has called you out of darkness into his most marvellous light;
Brought his truth to life within you, turned your blindness into sight.
Let your light so shine around you that God's name is glorified;
And all find fresh hope and purpose in Christ Jesus crucified.

Once you were an alien people, strangers to God's heart of love;
But he brought you home in mercy, citizens of heaven above.
Let his love flow out to others, let them feel a Father's care;
That they too may know his welcome and his countless blessings share.

Church of God, elect and holy, be the people he intends;
Strong in faith and swift to answer each command your master sends;
Royal priests fulfil your calling through your sacrifice and prayer;
Give your lives in joyful service – sing his praise, his love declare.

© James E. Seddon (1915 – 1983?). To be sung to the tune *Lux Eoi*[14]

---

14. Words: James E. Seddon; © 1982 The Jubilee Group (Admin. Hope Publishing Company, Carol Stream, IL 60188). All rights reserved. Used by permission.

SCRIPTURE INDEX

SUBJECT INDEX

Share Your Thoughts

With the Author: Your comments will be forwarded to the author when you send them to *zauthor@zondervan.com*.

With Zondervan: Submit your review of this book by writing to *zreview@zondervan.com*.

Free Online Resources at

www.zondervan.com

Zondervan AuthorTracker: Be notified whenever your favorite authors publish new books, go on tour, or post an update about what's happening in their lives at www.zondervan.com/authortracker.

Daily Bible Verses and Devotions: Enrich your life with daily Bible verses or devotions that help you start every morning focused on God. Visit www.zondervan.com/newsletters.

Free Email Publications: Sign up for newsletters on Christian living, academic resources, church ministry, fiction, children's resources, and more. Visit www.zondervan.com/newsletters.

Zondervan Bible Search: Find and compare Bible passages in a variety of translations at www.zondervanbiblesearch.com.

Other Benefits: Register yourself to receive online benefits like coupons and special offers, or to participate in research.